German Aircraft Cockpits

German Aircraft Cockpits
1911-1970

Peter W. Cohausz

Schiffer Military History
Atglen, PA

Translated from the German by David Johnston
Book Design by Ian Robertson.

Library of Congress Catalog Number: 2003103119

Printed in China.
ISBN: 0-7643-1873-X

This book was originally printed under the title,
Cockpits deutscher Flugzeuge by Aviatic Verlag

We are interested in hearing from authors with book ideas on related topics.

Published by Schiffer Publishing Ltd.
4880 Lower Valley Road
Atglen, PA 19310
Phone: (610) 593-1777
FAX: (610) 593-2002
E-mail: info@schifferbooks.com.
Visit our web site at: www.schifferbooks.com
Please write for a free catalog.
This book may be purchased from the publisher.
Please include $3.95 postage.
Try your bookstore first.

In Europe, Schiffer books are distributed by:
Bushwood Books
6 Marksbury Avenue
Kew Gardens
Surrey TW9 4JF
England
Phone: 44 (0) 20 8392-8585
FAX: 44 (0) 20 8392-9876
E-mail: Bushwd@aol.com.
Free postage in the UK. Europe: air mail at cost.
Try your bookstore first.

Contents

Foreword

As the interface between man and machine, the cockpit is one of the most interesting areas of an aircraft. It is surprising, therefore, that this theme has received little attention in the aviation literature. As a result, the desired information must be gleaned from a variety of sources.

This was the motivation for producing this book, which describes the instrumentations of historical German aircraft of various periods from 1911 to approximately 1970 and follows the development of aircraft instruments in Germany during this time.

As one of the great aircraft-producing nations, Germany possessed a capable and innovative aviation industry until 1918 and, in particular, from the 1930s until 1945. This industry produced many inventions, developments and standards which achieved national and international success.

After the end of the Second World War in 1945 there was a halt in development caused by the Allied ban on aviation in Germany. By the time aviation-related activities resumed in 1955, international standards had largely been accepted. By the late 1960s at the latest, this globalization had left little of German developments and standards.

Overall, the period described in this book was the era of precision- and electro-mechanics in instrument construction. The subsequent introduction of the computer, microelectronics and displays is another story.

A comparison of the simply-equipped aircraft of earlier years with modern aircraft reveals the tremendous technical development that has taken place. Anyone who has grown up with head-up displays and fly-by-wire technology can scarcely imagine flying an aircraft equipped with a few mechanical instruments and control cables.

This book is based largely on photographs of museum aircraft and vintage aircraft still flying. Whenever possible these are supplemented by historical photographs and other illustrations from handbooks and replacement part lists.

Approximately sixty aircraft types are covered in this book, with selections limited to aircraft of which examples have survived, making color illustrations possible. There are of course gaps, as there are no surviving examples of some technically-significant aircraft.

As numerous standards and norms were adopted in the course of German aviation development, the types described here make it possible to draw many conclusions about comparable aircraft types which are not described.

Some of the descriptions here are reconstructions and there are, of course, many gaps and contradictions in this documentation. The author and publishers would therefore be grateful for any corrections and additional information provided by readers.

Introduction into the Science of Instruments

General

Instruments make it possible for a pilot to safely carrying out flights in virtually any weather at any time of day. They are the link between the aircraft's systems and the pilot's senses, enabling the latter to determine the aircraft's attitude and monitor its systems. Instrument flight makes it possible to control an aircraft regardless of weather and without relying on the pilot's senses.

In the early years of flight it was believed that it was possible to do without instruments. The pilot made control inputs and monitored the engine using his senses. Altitude was estimated by looking downwards. The whistle of the bracing wires gave an indication of airspeed. The position of the horizon and feel informed the pilot of the aircraft's attitude, while hearing allowed him to assess the status of the engine and its speed.

Typical instrument panel of a large multi-engine aircraft, in this case a Focke Wulf Fw 200. Note the clear separation of flight and engine instruments. (Soppa Collection)

The use of the senses for controlling flight soon proved unreliable and in some cases unsafe, and it was not long before equipment and instruments were introduced. In the beginning these were adapted from equipment used in balloons, automobiles, meteorology or ships. Many instruments had to be specifically developed or redesigned for aeronautical applications, as the size and weight of many instruments did not lend themselves well to light aircraft structures.

Glider pilots, too, soon recognized the necessity of instruments. Record-setting flights, in particular, were impossible without precise data.

The Instrument Panel

As new aircraft were developed, it became apparent that the instruments should be grouped in a panel in front of the pilot, so as to allow him to read these quickly and accurately and thus determine the aircraft's attitude, navigate, and monitor the functioning of the engine. Basic principles were developed which applied to all aircraft—from small sporting machines to multi-engine commercial transports.

The instrument panels of larger aircraft could contain as many as forty instruments. In an effort to conserve space and display even more information on the instrument panel, multiple indicators and combined instruments were developed, for example the turn and bank indicator, combined RPM indicator and boost pressure gauge, undercarriage and landing flap position indicator, and combined trim indicator. In addition, some aircraft, such as the Bf 110 and Ju 88, were equipped with small instrument panels in the engine nacelles.

As time went on, crew size was increased to avoid excessive workload, with the tasks of flight monitoring, navigation and engine monitoring shared by several people. The crews of large aircraft operating over long distances, such as commercial transports and reconnaissance aircraft, usually consisted of a pilot, co-pilot, flight engineer, radio operator and navigator. Consequently the instruments were grouped in several instrument panels. In the present day, when personnel costs have skyrocketed, computers have taken over many of these tasks and the crews of most commercial aircraft consist of just a pilot and co-pilot.

Instruments are divided into categories determined by their function:

- flight instruments
- navigational equipment
- autopilot systems
- engine monitoring equipment
- airframe monitoring equipment

The flight instruments are placed directly in front of the pilot. They are grouped in such a way that he can obtain several types of information with one look. The so-called "T Arrangement" has been adopted as the international standard, especially in larger aircraft, with the airspeed indicator, artificial horizon or turn and bank indicator or vertical speed indicator in a row. Centered beneath these is the directional gyro or distant-reading compass.

The upper row of instruments may also contained specialized devices such as an airspeed indicator with a rotating scale. The pilot sets the desired cruising speed, and once this speed is achieved the pointer moves to the horizontal position. When the aircraft is in level flight, the pointers of the airspeed and vertical speed indicators and the horizon bar are in a line. The remaining flight and navigation instruments, such as altimeter, course indicator and clock, are placed nearby according to their importance.

In aircraft with dual controls there are usually two instrument panels with duplicated flight and navigation equipment. In such cases the engine instruments, which are usually on the right, are grouped in the center together with the throttle levers, so that they may be viewed and reached from either seat.

The selection of instruments and equipment is based on the intended role of the aircraft. The operating range of the instruments is determined by the type of power plants installed and the designed performance range of the aircraft.

In the development of a new aircraft, instrumentation is conceived during the planning stage and evaluated through the use of a cockpit mock-up or, more recently, a computer simulation. The result is included in the building specification.

Testing usually begins with several prototypes plus airframes which are tested to destruction. This is followed by a small preproduction series before the aircraft enters production. Information gained through testing and operational experience constantly flows into the development process, and this is also reflected in the instrumentation. As well, combat aircraft are often modified in the field in response to changing operational profiles, the desires of individual pilots and the spares situation.

All of this means that the instrumentation and equipment installed in an aircraft constantly changes throughout its development. For this reason, the instrumentations presented here are often representative of a certain variant and in some cases a single aircraft.

Operating Conditions and Stresses

Instruments installed in an aircraft are often subjected to greater physical and chemical influences than those employed on the ground. Consequently, they must be more resistant to many influences:

- **Vibration, acceleration and shocks**

Vibration caused by the motor, accelerations during flight, and stresses during takeoff and landing are addressed by light construction and the counter-balancing of moving components.

- **Changes of attitude**

Flight is movement, not always symmetrical, in a three-dimensional space, resulting in constantly changing gravitational forces.

- **Temperature and humidity**

Temperature differences in an aircraft can be as great as 130° C. An aircraft parked in the sun can reach temperatures as high as 70° C, while at altitude temperatures may be as low as minus 60° C. These effects are countered by the use of suitable construction materials and compensating elements.

- **Changes in air pressure**

Air pressure decreases as altitude increases.

Other demands on aircraft instruments are:

- **Minimal weight and size**

Reducing weight and conserving space are fundamentals of aircraft design and of course also apply to aircraft instruments. For this reason multiple or combined indicators are often used.

- **Reliability and accuracy**

The pilot must be able to depend on the functioning of the equipment and the information it provides.

- **Corrosion resistance**

Moisture, and salt-laden sea air in particular, can affect the operation of instruments and cause permanent damage.

- **Readability and illumination**

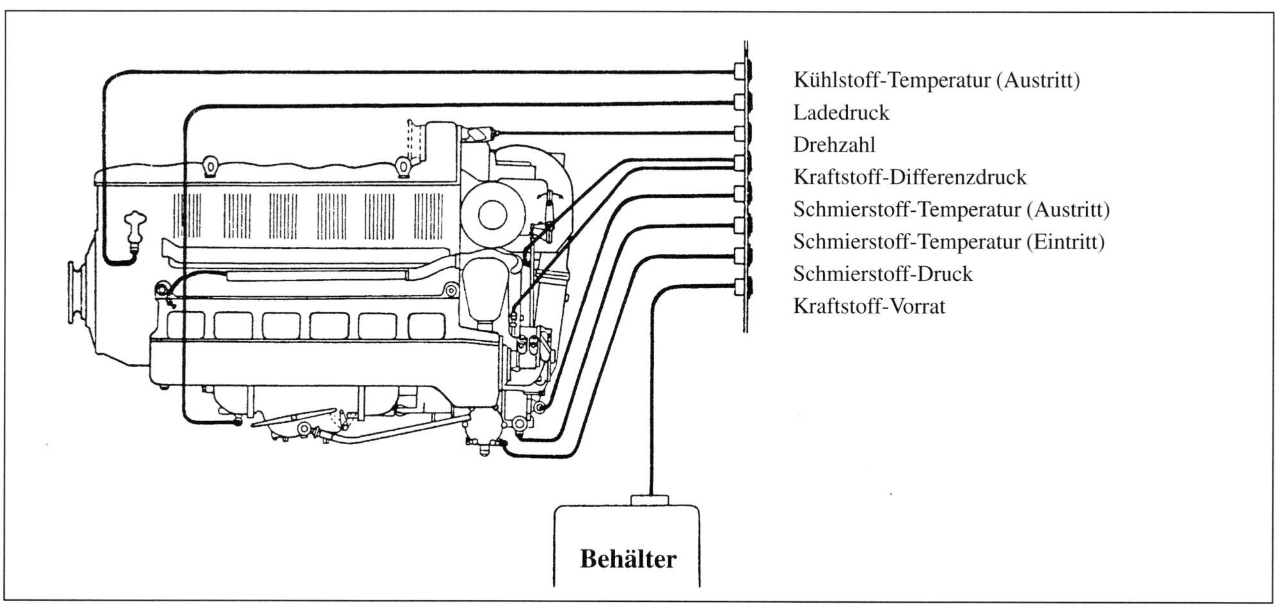

Check points for monitoring engine operation: coolant temperature (outlet), boost pressure, revolutions, fuel pressure differential, oil temperature (outlet), oil temperature (inlet), oil pressure, fuel contents.

The faces must be designed in such a way as to avoid causing fatigue and the instruments arranged to prevent reflection of sunlight. The instruments are to be illuminated for night use with luminescent numbers and pointers.

• Elimination of compass interference

The installation of numerous pieces of equipment in a confined space may cause problems, as some electrical instruments produce magnetic fields. This may be countered through compensation or the use of demagnetized construction materials.

• Adherence to standards and technical specifications

This applies principally to the size and shape of instruments and the nature of the instrument face and connections, so as to enable the necessary spares to be kept on hand for repairs or modernization.

Direct-reading RPM indicator based on the eddy current principle, 0 to 1,600 rpm (Deuta, 1918).

Direct-reading RPM indicator based on the centrifugal pendulum principle, 600 to 2,400 rpm (Deuta, 1934), Fl 20206.

Remote-reading RPM indicator 500 to 3,600 rpm (Deuta, 1934), Fl 20286.

Combined RPM indicator and boost pressure gauge, 500 to 3,600 rpm and 0.6 to 1.8 atm (Horn, 1944), Fl 20569.

Engine Instruments

• RPM Indicator

Revolutions are an indication of the demand being placed on the engine. This is especially important in aircraft equipped with variable-pitch propellers. In machines so equipped a desired engine speed can be achieved by setting the throttle or by adjusting propeller pitch. An indication of engine speed is also important in detecting engine problems, as such problems are usually associated with a change in revolutions.

The RPM indicator indicates the number of crankshaft revolutions per minute. The instrument face usually consists of a linear scale with numbers in hundreds, which makes for easier reading. The necessary range of measurement is determined by the type of engine installed. The use of direct- or distant-reading RPM indicators is determined by the distance between the indicator and the engine(s).

• Direct-Reading RPM Indicator

This instrument is used when the distance between the indicator and engine is three meters or less. It is thus employed mainly in single-engine aircraft or for the central engine of aircraft with three power plants.

The engine speed (revolutions) is transmitted by a mechanical connection, usually a straight shaft. To limit stress on the system, the transmission shaft is attached to the camshaft instead of the crankshaft, as the former rotates at half the speed of the latter. To achieve the correct indication, a translating gear (1 : 2) is built into the instrument. The design of direct-reading RPM indicators is usually based on one of two operating principles:

• Centrifugal Pendulum Principle

Based on steam engine technology. Two fly masses are arranged around a movable axis and the degree to which they are forced outward is directly proportionate to the revolutions. This deflection is then transmitted to the indicator. The accuracy of this type of indicator decreases at low revolutions.

• Eddy Current Principle

The eddy current RPM indicator had its origins in locomotive design. A ring-shaped magnet spins in a light-metal housing. This results in eddy currents, which produce a magnetic field and cause the housing to spin. These revolutions are then transmitted to the indicator. When installing this type of instrument in an instrument panel, consideration must be given to the magnetic effects on the compass.

Distant-Reading RPM Indicators

In multi-engine aircraft the distance from the engines to the instrument panel is too great for direct mechanical transmission. In such cases the revolutions are read by a device on the engine and transmitted to the indicator. Multiple indicators may be connected to a distant-reading system.

In the early days of aviation, transmission was usually pneumatic or hydraulic. A ring pendulum was installed in the transmitter and, when spun, this produced centrifugal force. The centrifugal force was transmitted by a pressure line to a diaphragm in the indicator, which produced a reading.

In the course of development, the purely electrical transmission of engine RPM came to be favored. The RPM transmitter became an alternating current generator. Because of the heat produced by the engine it was not attached directly to the engine, but was instead linked to it by a short shaft. The principle of operation is essentially similar to that of a bicycle headlight generator. The indicator is nothing more than a voltmeter calibrated in revolutions per minute. This type of instrument also produces magnetic fields which can influence a compass.

The design principle makes possible the installation of multiple RPM indicators, a practice which was begun as early as 1918, when the indicators for two engines were combined in a single instrument.

The **RPM Indicator-Boost Pressure Gauge** is a specialized design. When, during the course of the Second World War, instrument panels became increasingly crowded, combination instruments were designed in an effort to conserve space. This resulted in the combination of an electric RPM indicator and boost pressure gauge. Such instruments were installed in the Do 335, Ju 388 and Ta 152 in 1944-45.

Two fuel pressure gauges 0 to 0.5 kg/cm2 (Maximall, circa 1918) and 0 to 0.3 kg/cm2 (Schäffer & Buddenberg, circa 1916) in the Dornier Museum. These devices were built in large numbers and continued in use into the 1920s.

Oxygen pressure gauge 0 to 250 kg/cm2 (S&B, 1943), Fl 30496.

Pressure Gauges

The operation of aircraft requires the measurement of several types of pressure:

- **Atmospheric pressure** (air pressure) for the determination of altitude.
- **Technical pressure** on a medium: this pressure is produced by pumps and compressors (fuel pressure, boost pressure, etc.)
- **Differential pressure**: the pressure to be measured is compared to another pressure which differs from that of the atmosphere.

Several units of measurement are employed in pressure readings:

- kg/cm²: one kg/cm² is the pressure of a column of water 10 000 mm tall on a surface area of one square centimeter. This value is also equivalent to one technical atmosphere (1 atm).
- mm WS: small pressure values are indicated by a column of water one millimeter tall on a surface area of one square centimeter
- atm: stands for absolute atmosphere. The zero value is the total absence of pressure (vacuum). Calibration is in atmospheres whenever the same pressure-compression ratio must be maintained independent of changing air pressure, for example the boost pressure of an engine.

Depending on the equipment installed in an aircraft, the following pressures may be measured using the corresponding units of measurement:

- Fuel pressure (between 0.5 and 3 kg/cm² depending on engine)
- Pressure of special fluids, such as methanol-water (up to 3 kg/cm²)
- Oil pressure (between 10 and 15 kg/cm² depending on engine)
- Shock absorber (undercarriage) pressure (in kg/cm²)
- Boost pressure (1.2 to 2.5 atm depending on engine)
- Compressed air pressure (150 to 250 kg/cm² depending on system)
- Suction pressure for equipment powered by negative pressure (measured in mm WS or kg/cm²)
- Oxygen pressure for the high-altitude breathing system (up to 250 kg/cm²)

Reliable operating ranges were depicted on the instrument faces in colored markings or as operating range marks.

Double pressure gauge for fuel and oil 0 to 0.5 and 0 to 10 kg/cm2 (Gradenwitz, circa 1938), Fl 20512.

Electric quad-indicator for fuel and oil pressure 0 to 1 and 0 to 10 kg/cm² and oil inlet and outlet temperature 2 x 0 to 130° C (Siemens LGW, 1944), Fl 20682.

Boost pressure gauge 0.6 to 1.8 atm (Fuess, 1944), Fl 20555

Bellows Pressure Gauge

This is the most commonly used type of pressure gauge for pressure values of more than 0.5 kg/cm². The measuring element consists of a circular section of oval tube (Bourdon Tube) made of a flexible metal. The liquid to be measured flows on one side, while the other side is sealed and free to move.

As the pressure increases, the tube flexes because of the pressure differential. The deflection is displayed by a pointer. Because the liquid to be measured flows directly into the instrument, this method is called direct pressure measurement.

Relay Pressure Gauge

A small relay is situated at the pressure measuring point. Inside is a system of membranes which is linked to the indicator by a transfer fluid.

The advantage of this method of measurement is that while a break in the measuring line makes a reading impossible, no oil or fuel is lost as occurs with the direct pressure measurement.

Electric Distant Pressure Indicator

Electric transmission is used to eliminate the danger of broken tubes or blockages. A pressure transmitter with a diaphragm or bellows as measuring instrument is positioned on the pressure line. The deflection of the bellows or the hub of the diaphragm is determined by an ohmmeter, which controls the indicator as resistance changes. The indicator itself is a cross-coil gauge independent of the aircraft's electrical system, which eliminates variations in resistance caused by the operation of other electrical components.

Boost Pressure Gauge

This device indicates the pressure of the fuel-air mixture in carburettor engines or the pressure of the supercharger air in fuel-injected engines prior to entry into the cylinder. The supercharger increases inlet pressure to boost the performance of aircraft engines. Maintaining engine performance is especially important at high altitude, where outside air pressure decreases. The role of the supercharger is to maintain pressure and compression conditions near those at the surface.

On the ground with the engine off, the instrument displays the prevailing air pressure of approximately 1 atm.

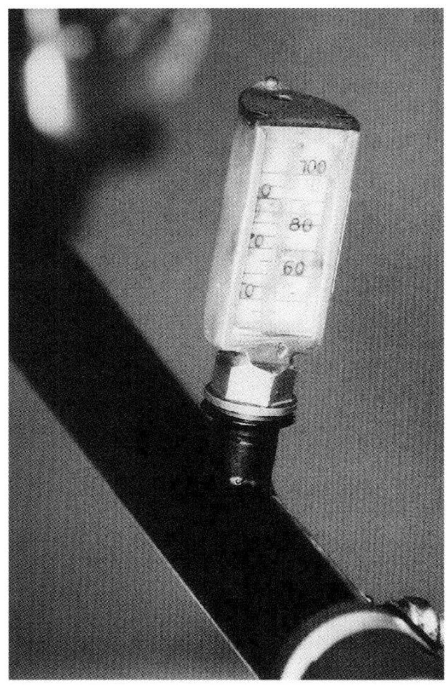

Direct-reading thermometer for coolant 0 to 100° C (Schlegelmilch, circa 1917).

The boost pressure gauge is a diaphragm instrument. The air mixture to be measured is fed into the device, where it presses on the diaphragm, which consists of soldered-together circular plates of phosphor bronze. The changing thickness of the membrane is transmitted to the indicator.

Temperature Gauges

These instruments are used mainly to monitor the engine, indicating for example the coolant, oil or cylinder head temperature.

An important special function is performed by the outside air temperature gauge, which alerts the pilot to the possibility of icing.

Direct Thermometer

This is the best known type of temperature gauge as it is used in the home. A liquid, usually mercury or colored alcohol, is contained in a small reservoir at the base of a glass tube. The level of the fluid in the tube, which is marked with a scale, indicates the temperature.

Vapor pressure temperature gauge 0 to 160° C (I.C. Eckardt, 1940), Fl 20308-06.

Electric temperature gauge 0 to 140° C (Hartmann & Braun, 1938).

Electric temperature gauge, switchable, 0 to 160° C (Siemens LGW, 1940), Fl 20343.

This device was standard until the end of the First World War and was located at the measuring point in the line. As a rule it was only used to measure coolant and was placed directly in front of the radiator where the highest temperatures occurred. Colored alcohol was generally used for better readability. The disadvantage of this type of temperature gauge was that it could only be used at measuring points near the cockpit.

Vapor Pressure Thermometer

This device is a sealed system consisting of a sensing element and an indicator with a capillary tube linkage. Inside the sensing element is a liquid with a low boiling point, such as ethyl-ether, which becomes gaseous as temperature increases, producing vapor pressure.

The indicator is a bellows pressure gauge calibrated in degrees Centigrade. One limitation of this type of temperature gauge is caused by the physical characteristics of the fluid, which make it impossible to indicate temperatures below 40° C.

There are various versions of this device—single or multiple—with varying capillary tube lengths.

Variations of the device with similar designs are the liquid pressure thermometer and the gas pressure thermometer, in which the systems are filled with mercury and nitrogen, respectively.

Electric Distant Thermometer

The operating principle used here is that the electrical resistance of a metal increases as temperature rises. The indicator is a cross-coil instrument calibrated in degrees Centigrade. Because of its design, with a cable connection, there is no limitation in the distance between measuring point and indicator. As well the instrument is more accurate than a vapor pressure thermometer and can also be used at low temperatures. This design permits multiple indicator systems with up to four indicators.

Fuel Contents Gauge

Information on the amount of fuel remaining is important in flight planning. As a rule this is achieved by means of a float in the fuel tank. Transmission of the float's position to the indicator is achieved mechanically or electrically.

Fuel contents gauge for wing tank of Ju 52/3m to 1260 liters with scales for level flight and on the ground (tail-down) (Maximall, 1936), Fl 20709.

In most cases the float is located in the center of the fluid tank, because there it is less affected by the gravitational forces produced when the aircraft turns. Nevertheless, only in certain situations does the float accurately measure the amount of fluid in the tank. False indications are regularly caused by nose up or down attitudes, centrifugal forces in turns, and in the tail-down position on the ground.

In the case of the Ju 52 an effort was made to counter this by fitting the indicators for the wing tanks with two scales—one for level flight attitude and one for the tail-down position on the ground. In large aircraft there are also contents gauges for oil and coolant.

There are numerous types of contents gauges, some of which are described here.

Level Indicator

This simple system consists of a glass tube mounted outside the fuel tank, with the level in the tube indicating the level in the tank. Its disadvantages are false indications in some flight attitudes and discoloration caused by fuel. This type of gauge was used only in

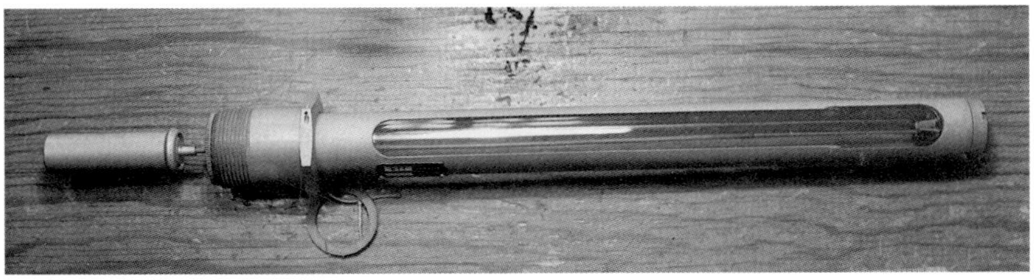

Floating-reed fuel contents gauge as used in the Ju 52 (DEMA, 1943).

the early days of aviation.

Spinning Float Contents Gauge

A cork float moves in guide rails. As the amount of fuel decreases, the float sinks, turning a spindle connected to the indicator. Movement of the spindle between the top and bottom of the tank is 360 degrees. This design is only useful when the top of the tank is visible.

Magnetic Fuel Contents Gauge

This type of fuel gauge was used in tanks mounted in the upper wing of biplanes. Once again a cork float is attached to a spindle, in this case inside the tank. At its end is a magnet, which affects another magnet on the outside of the tank. The latter is connected to the instrument's pointer on the underside of the tank. The advantage of this type of gauge is that it is no need for holes in the tank and possible fuel leaks.

Floating Pointer Fuel Gauge

Attached to the float is an indicator rod, the top of which projects from the tank into a vertical sight-glass with graduations. This system was used mainly in fuel tanks located in the wings or the forward fuselage, for example in the Bü 131, Fe 44, Fi 156 and Ju 52.

String Float Fuel Gauge

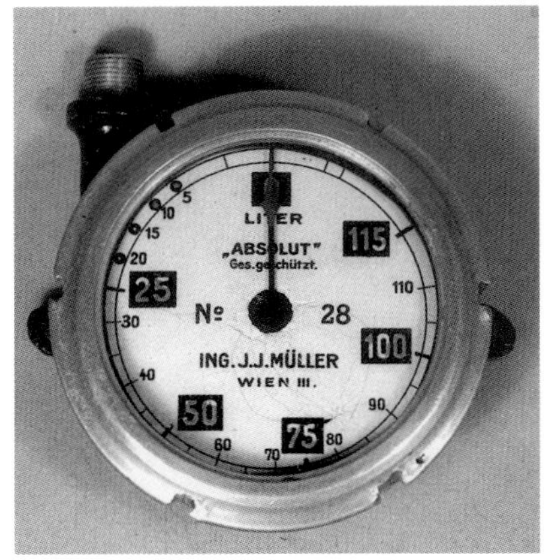

Float fuel gauge to 115 liters (Müller/Vienna, 1918), similar in design to a Maximall fuel gauge.

This was the most commonly-used type of fuel contents gauge in the 1920s. Movement of the float was transmitted to the indicator by means of a string on a sprung roller. For protection, the string moved over return pulleys inside and inside an aluminium tube.

Pneumatic Measuring System

This system requires no float. Just above the base of the tank is a submerged tube. The measurement process begins with the pilot operating a hand pump on the instrument panel, forcing air into the tube and slowly expelling the liquid. The liquid lever in the tank requires a certain amount of pressure to force the liquid from the tube.

The indicator is a diaphragm pressure gauge calibrated in liters. It displays the pressure and thus the level of fuel in the tank. For safety a non-return valve is installed in the system to prevent any fuel from reaching the pump or the instrument. If there is more than one tank a selector switch is required. This system was very common until the end of the 1930s.

Electric Remote Metering

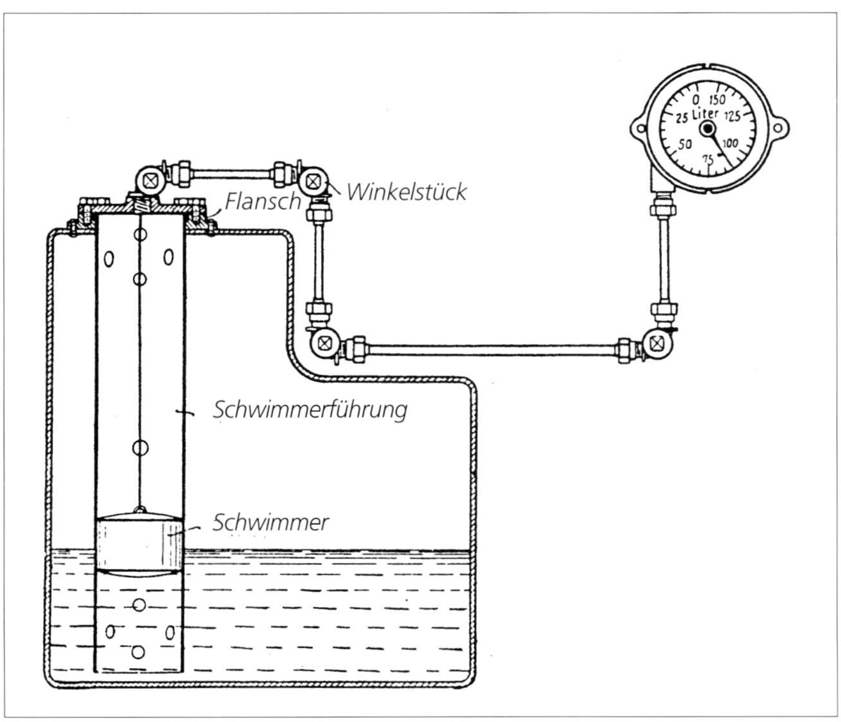

Diagram illustrating the method of operation of a float fuel gauge.

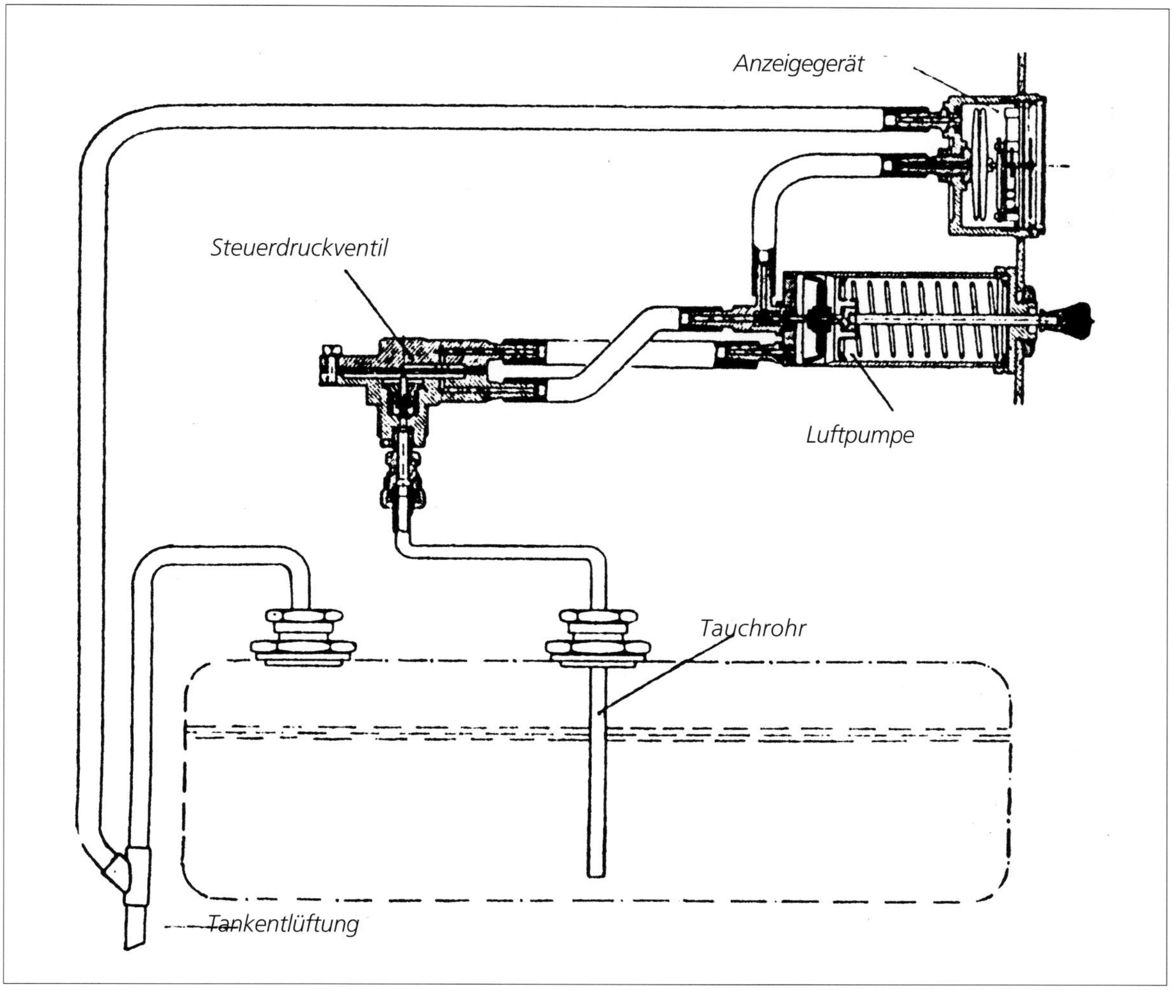

Design of a pneumatic fuel contents measuring system.

The pneumatic system was replaced by the electric. Movement of the float causes a change in resistance on a circular resistor attached to the tank. As the fuel level decreases, the float turns up to 360 degrees in an helically fluted tube. Each position equates to a certain resistance, which is displayed on an indicator graduated in liters.

Whenever possible the scales on the instrument face are linear to simplify the process of determining fuel remaining. For design reasons tanks are often irregular in shape. Fuel contents gauges often have two scales for several tanks. Prior to reading, a tank selector switch is used to select the desired tank for measurement.

Pneumatic fuel gauge to 40 liters from the Klemm L 25c (Maximall, 1934).

Fuel contents gauge to 380 and 270 liters for the Bf 110 C (Norma, 1041), Fl 20723.

Electric fuel consumption gauge to 500 l/h (Siemens LGW, 1944), 9-2182 B-1.

Trim indicator for the Ju 188 (I.C. Eckardt, 1944), Fl 22810.

Radiator flap position indicator to 60°, (Siemens LGW, circa 1940), Fl 20853-2.

Fuel Consumption Gauge

This instrument indicates the amount of fuel being fed to the engine at a given moment, measured in liters per hour. This is especially important on long flights when fuel consumption is a factor. Engine speed, airspeed and fuel consumption all depend on one another, and the pilot of a long-range commercial aircraft, transport or reconnaissance aircraft must select the correct throttle setting to achieve the highest possible speed with the most favorable fuel consumption.

Pioneer System

Measurement takes place by the determination of a differential pressure of changing amounts of fuel flowing through a venturi tube inserted into a fuel line.

Elliott System

The fuel flows through a conical tube containing a baffle. The flow speed of the fuel moves the baffle and the distance is measured.

Electric Remote-Sensing Systems for Continuous Indication

This measuring technique operates differently in carburettor and fuel-injected engines.

In a carburettor engine a baffle plate is placed between the fuel pump and carburettor. The strength of the flow influences the position of the plate, which is then transmitted to an electric instrument—usually a cross-coil gauge.

In a fuel-injected engine a control rod is attached to the throttle rod. The position of the rod relative to a fixed point provides a scale for the amount of fuel being injected and thus the consumption rate. The control rod guides an alternating current generator, whose current is measured by a moving coil amp meter calibrated in liters per hour.

Flight Instruments

Mechanical Position Indicators

There are many systems and control surfaces in an aircraft whose position must be known to the pilot in order to assure safe operation of the machine. Examples of these are landing flaps, trim tabs, variable-pitch propellers, undercarriage and radiator flaps. The measurement and indication of their position can be electrical or mechanical.

Mechanical propeller position indicator (VDO, 1939), 9-9500.31.

Landing Flap Position Indicator

Mechanical indication shows the position of the hand wheel in the cockpit or of the landing flap via a direct connection.

In the first case the indicator is connected to the hand wheel by means of a drive and spindle and shows the degree of the selected setting but not the actual position of the flap. A direct connection with the flap by means of a chain is somewhat more reliable.

Electrical indication depicts the actual position of the landing flap. Measurement is based on the principle of the electrical bridge, with a cross-current gauge as indicator. The sensor is located near the flap and is mechanically connected to it. A slider in the resistance sensor moves with the flap and changes the bridge state of balance. The indicator is thus independent of the electrical system.

Trim Indicator

Its function is similar to that of the flap position indicator. In mechanical indicators the position of the tab is transmitted by chains similar to small bicycle chains. In the case of electric indicators, multiple indicators are often used, depicting the position of the tabs in degrees or visually using aircraft symbols.

Undercarriage and landing flap position indicator for the Ju 88 (Siemens LGW, 1941), Fl 22854.

Undercarriage position indicator, "Four-Lamp System" (SAM, 1943), Fl 32526.

Voltmeter to 15 V (PGCD, circa 1938).

Radiator Flap Position Indicator

This position indicator operates in a similar manner to the two previous systems. Indication is often in degrees or simply by depiction of the final positions OPEN and CLOSED.

Position Indicators for Variable Pitch Propellers

In Germany in the 1930s and 40s the standard propeller pitch indicator resembled a clock with large and small pointers. Ten minutes was equivalent to one degree of propeller pitch.

The 12 o'clock position was selected for takeoff. To control propeller pitch the pilot simply had to master a relatively small number of "clock" positions. Here, too, indication could be mechanical or electrical. In mechanical systems a shaft ran from the pitch control motor to the instrument, which had to be located near the engine. In some twin-engined machines, such as the Ju 88 and Bf 110, the indicators were located in the engine nacelles. The advantage of mechanical indication is its continuous connection.

In contrast, electrical transmission takes place at intervals of 2.5 minutes, with the pitch control motor on the engine driving a pulse generator.

Undercarriage Indicator

Most aircraft equipped with a retractable undercarriage have a mechanical or electrical indicator. Among the aircraft which employed mechanical indication were the Fw 190 and Bf 109. In the case of the former, red metal rods projected from the wing surface when the undercarriage was down, while the latter employed a simple indicator in the cockpit operated by Bowden cables.

Electrical indication usually employed a number of colored lamps or visual indicators showing the final positions UP or DOWN.

The most familiar is the "Four Lamp System" with two red (UP) and two green (DOWN) lamps which illuminated only after the undercarriage locked into position. There were also combined indicators which depicted the position of the undercarriage and landing flaps. These included multiple visual indicators, nine-lamp systems, eleven-lamp systems for double undercarriages (He 177), and twelve-lamp systems.

Some indicators with pointers (early Ju 88s) also showed the interim position of the undercarriage, which required resistance sensors on the undercarriage legs.

Voltmeters and Amp meters

The use of volt and amp meters became more important as aircraft electrical systems became more extensive with a large number of electrically-driven systems. In the early days of aviation only a few machines were equipped with such indicators, aircraft with radios or multi-engine types.

Knowledge of the performance of electrical systems is important for the safe operation of an aircraft. This function is performed by the amp meter and voltmeter. These designs are usually moving coil instruments with a shielding iron case to prevent affecting the compass.

Twelve-lamp indicator for undercarriage and landing flap position (List, 1944), Fl 32532.

Most common in the 1930s and 40s were combined voltmeters-voltmeters with different instrument ranges. These indicators normally depicted current rate, with a push button switch to engage voltage indication.

Flight Instruments

Altimeter

In flight a knowledge of the aircraft's height is vitally important. Two types of indication are absolute and relative height.

Absolute height is defined as the height above a measuring plane, which internationally is based on the Amsterdam Level. Knowledge of absolute height is particularly important in overland, acceptance and record-setting flights, as well as in topographical flights.

Volt- and ammeter to 30 V or A (Siemens, 1940), Fl 32502-4.

Altimeter to 8000 m (Morell, circa 1920).

Relative height is defined as the height above ground, or the surface of the earth. Knowledge of relative height is important in instrument landings, overland flights, especially in mountainous regions, and in military low-level flights.

The measurement of absolute height is based on decreasing air pressure as height increases and therefore employs an aneroid or diaphragm barometer. The latter is a metal vacuum chamber with great elasticity, which is compressed by the pressure of the outside air and connected to an indicator. The barometric altimeter is calibrated in a laboratory using a pre-defined standard atmosphere, as air pressure varies with weather.

In an aircraft, air pressure measurement is achieved by the pitot tube airspeed measuring system with static pressure balance. Direct measurement using an opening in the fuselage is not possible, because the influence of the slipstream produces false indications. The instrument housing of the altimeter is sealed, as there can be pressure variations in the cockpit as well.

To compensate for variations in air pressure, the altimeter usually has a setting button for the zero position and a millibars scale. Before flight the pilot sets the device to zero, which means the surface air pressure or altimeter setting at the departure airfield, and the instrument shows the height of the airfield. Prior to landing, the pilot obtains the altimeter setting for the destination airfield.

By the middle of the 1930s most Luftwaffe aircraft were equipped with fine and coarse altimeters. To mark the air pressure at departure and destination, it became standard practise to include on the instrument two slides with the letters "E" and "F". E stood for QFE, or surface air pressure at destination, while F stood for QFF, or the air pressure of a station relative to height above sea level. The so-called "Q-Codes" were used to abbreviate information in radio transmissions.

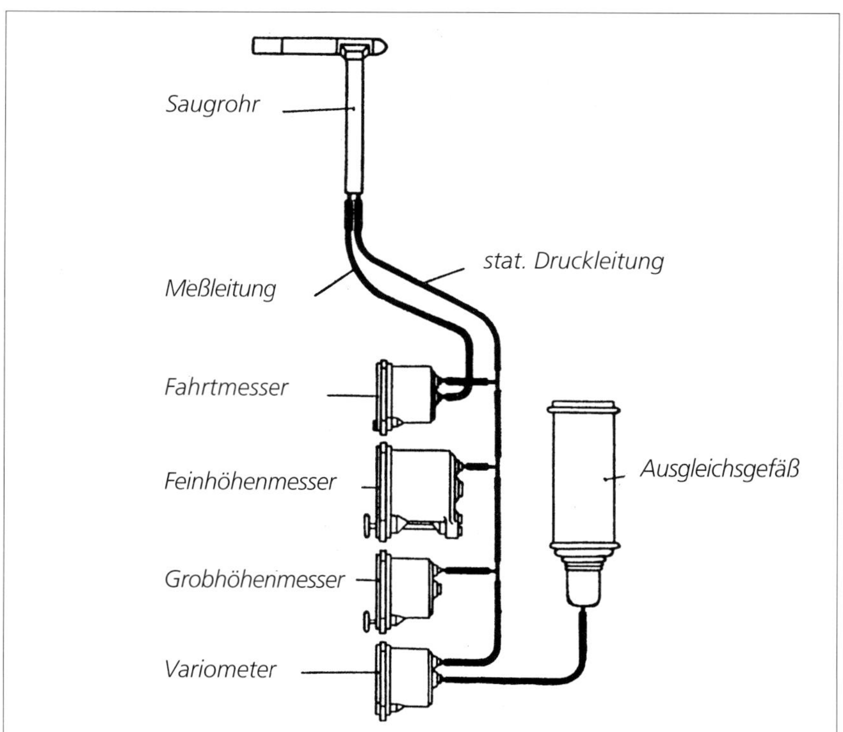

Layout of instruments with static pressure balance.

Fine altimeter to 1000 m (Fuess, 1938), Fl 22316-1.

Coarse altimeter to 6000 m (Lufft, 1936), Fl 22310.

Contact altimeter to 6000 m (Kroneis, circa 1940), Fl 22317.

Fine and coarse altimeter to 16000 m, double indicator instrument (Scholz, 1945), Fl 22326.

Fine and coarse altimeter to 13000 m, single indicator instrument (Fuess, 1944), Fl 22322.

Measurement of relative height cannot be accomplished by barometric devices, as deviations in air pressure can result in errors of +/- 30 meters. Instead landing probes or sound-ranging systems are used for this purpose. Electric altimeters remain in use to the present day, with a radio wave measuring the height above ground.

In the early days of aviation and until 1918, in Germany most altimeters consisted of a barometric device in a leather housing suspended on a spring or cord between struts and bracing wires. At the time it was feared that mounting the instrument in the fuselage would result in errors caused by air turbulence. There were various sizes of altimeter, ranging from pocket or wrist devices for the crew, through medium to large instruments with diameters of up to 15 cm. Beginning in the 1920s the altimeter was mounted in the instrument panel, although the barometric devices sampled air pressure by way of a small hole in the housing. Connection to the airspeed measuring system did not begin until the end of the 1920s. The following types of barometric altimeter are used:

Fine Altimeter

A precise instrument which is calibrated up to 1000 meters and is especially important in instrument approaches. Its use is usually combined with the coarse altimeter.

Coarse Altimeter

Depending on its use, it has instrument ranges of 3000, 6000, 8000 or 10000 meters. This is the only type of altimeter in many training and sporting aircraft.

Fine and Coarse Altimeter

A space-saving combined instrument, usually calibrated up to 10 000 meters, equipped with two diaphragms. By 1945 some fighter aircraft were equipped with altimeters with an instrument range of up to 16 000 meters.

There were two basic types of fine and coarse altimeters:

Double Indicator Instrument: design similar to that of a clock with the large pointer indicating hundreds of meters and the small one thousands. One revolution of the large pointer was equivalent to 1 000 meters. In England and the USA, where altimeters are calibrated in feet, there are even instruments with three pointers, the smallest indicating tens of thousands.

Single Pointer Instrument: includes a window with a number plate which shows kilometers and a pointer for hundreds. This was standard *Luftwaffe* equipment until 1945.

Glider Altimeter

As a rule these were coarse altimeters with a range of 3 000 or 6 000 meters. Many types lacked the barometric correction plate as there was no requirement for instrument approaches.

Contact Altimeter

This instrument was also based on the coarse altimeter, usually with an instrument range of 6 000 or 10 000 meters. The design also includes an electric switch which closes a contact on reaching a selected altitude. This altimeter was used in dive bombers to activate the automatic pull-out mechanism. The altitude could be selected with a second setting button and was indicated by a second pointer, usually painted red.

Statoscope

The determination of aircraft performance figures often requires the maintaining of a precise altitude. The usual barometric altimeters are too imprecise for this. The statoscope is a highly sensitive diaphragm altimeter with a tension spring against which the air pressure acts.

On reaching the desired altitude an adjusting screw is used to set the pointer to zero, at which point the spring and diaphragm tension are in balance. Any deviation from the desired altitude results in movement of the pointer. The instrument is capable of displaying deviations of from plus to minus two meters.

Recording Altimeter

Certain record-setting and training aircraft require a precise record of altitude so that the altitude achieved can be documented after the flight. A barograph or recording altimeter is used for this purpose.

A diaphragm system moves a pen arm, which writes on a strip of paper which is slowly rolled onto a revolving drum. The drum is driven by a clockwork mechanism.

The recording altimeter is suspended from elastic cords to eliminate vibration. Connection to the pitot tube's static pressure compensator is necessary, as otherwise errors of up to 100 meters are possible.

Various means are used to measure an aircraft's **height above ground**:

Acoustic Altitude Measurement

This system was based on the principle of sonar. A pulse was transmitted to the ground and the interval until reception timed. This system was particularly useful in conditions of poor visibility and major changes in air pressure.

The system consisted of a pulse transmitter, a start and echo microphone, a control box and an indicator. Up to 25 to 30 cartridges were carried on each flight. The range of the system depended on engine noise. Best results were achieved over water or solid ground.

Landing Device or Landing Probe

This method was employed mainly by seaplanes. A cable approximately 40 meters in length was fed from a shaft inclined thirty degrees to the rear. The end of the cable was weighted with a chain. When the aircraft descended below a certain altitude the chain touched the surface of the water, changing the angle of the cable. This activated a contact switch which caused a warning light to illuminate.

Radio Altimeter

Variations in air pressure may result in errors of plus-minus 30 meters in heights determined barometrically. This is too great for instrument landings or low-level flight. The best known device for measuring height above ground was the FuG 101 radio altimeter, which was installed in many *Luftwaffe* aircraft in the 1940s.

A radio wave was transmitted from the aircraft and reflected by the ground. Measuring the frequency shift between the transmitted and return waves revealed the height above ground. Depending on the version, the instrument could be used to heights of 750 or 1500 meters and had two sensitivity ranges. In the lower range altitude variations of plus-minus three meters could be read.

Indicator for the FuG 101a radio altimeter to 750 m, switchable to 150 m (Siemens LGW, circa 1944), Ln 28330-1.

Variometer (Vertical Speed Indicator)

This device indicates an aircraft's rate of climb or descent. This is especially important in glider flying when the pilot is seeking thermals to keep him aloft.

The method of operation is simple: the increase or decrease in air pressure is measured over an interval, as a rule in meters per second. These instruments differ in design, with the most important types being:

Bestelmeier Variometer

This design was adopted from balloons and was used until about 1918. The decrease in air density was compared with the pressure balance between a measuring body (a balloon) and the outside air by means of a capillary. The pressure was measured by a liquid pressure gauge calibrated in meters per second.

Diaphragm Variometer

This system consists of an indicator and a compensator, which is constructed as a thermos bottle to make it temperature resistant. The external static pressure is fed into the housing to which the diaphragm is connected by a capillary tube. When an altitude is maintained, the pressure in the diaphragm and the housing is in balance and the indicator shows zero.

When altitude changes, the static pressure in the housing changes, which is followed by a slow pressure compensation through the capillary. The difference in pressure between the diaphragm and housing in directly proportional to the speed of the pressure change and thus the rate of climb or descent. The indicator stops as long as pressure compensation is taking place, meaning as long as the aircraft is climbing or descending.

Baffle Plate Variometer

These instruments are much more sensitive than the diaphragm types and soon came to replace them. A ring-shaped chamber was divided in two halves by a movable baffle plate which left only a small area for air to pass through. The pointer was connected to the baffle plate and a spring held it in the zero position when the pressure was equal in both chambers.

On one side of the chamber was the static pressure, while the compensator was attached to the other. Pressure was equal in both parts of the chamber when the aircraft was in level flight. A change in altitude produced a pressure differential on the baffle plate, which

Diaphragm vertical speed indicator to 5 m/s (Askania, circa 1938). This was standard equipment in gliders.

Baffle-plate vertical speed indicator -25 to +150 m/s for the Me 163 (Horn, 1945), Fl 22385.

Statoscope-vertical speed indicator to 10 m/s (Askania, 1942), Fl 22381-10. Knob at bottom switched instrument to statoscope function.

Altimeter to 8000 m (Goerz, circa 1917), Bestelmeier vertical speed indicator to 3 m/s (circa 1916) and cup anemometer 50 to 250 km/h (Morell, circa 1918) in the Transportation Museum in Dresden.

in turn moved the pointer. The greater the pressure difference, the greater the deflection. When the pressure change ceased, the pressure in the two sides of the chamber once again balanced and the pointer returned to zero.

Statoscope-Variometer

This instrument is a combination of a vertical speed indicator and a fine altimeter. The capillaries of this diaphragm device can be closed, preventing pressure compensation. Every deviation from a selected altitude then produces a pointer deflection of TOO HIGH or TOO LOW.

Airspeed Indicator

For aerodynamic reasons, airspeed is of vital importance to the pilot. It is not for nothing that pilots claim that speed is half the battle. Two types of airspeed are measured:

- **Absolute Speed:** the horizontal speed relative to the earth.
- **Relative Speed:** horizontal speed relative to the surrounding air.

Relative speed is vital in monitoring the state of the aircraft. Flying too slow will result in a loss of lift, while exceeding the maximum allowable speed can result in the airframe becoming overstressed.

For these reasons the precise measurement of an aircraft's speed is vital. For technical reasons, only the relative speed is measured, although this is of limited use in navigation. The absolute speed is needed for navigation, however this can only be calculated with knowledge of wind speed and direction.

The following devices have been used to measure airspeed:

Pressure Plate

This primitive device was used in the early days of aviation. A metal pressure plate with a return spring and an indicator scale was attached to a wing strut. The slipstream forced the pressure plate backwards, the distance depending on airspeed, allowing the pilot to read the speed off the scale.

Cup Anemometer

This device, whose operating principle is similar to that of the centrifugal RPM indicator, has its origins in meteorology where it was used to measure wind speed. The cup anemometer was a standard type airspeed indicator in Germany into the 1920s.

The cups turn in the slipstream and the greater the number of revolutions the higher the airspeed. The centrifugal force generated by the movement of the shaft forces a double torsion pendulum outwards, moving the airspeed indicator.

Airspeed indicator 80 to 400 km/h, linear type (Askania, circa 1929).

Airspeed indicator with nozzle for installation on wing struts, 50 to 250 km/h (Bruhn, circa 1918).

Airspeed indicator for pitot tube 80 to 750 km/h (Bruhn, circa 1940), Fl 22231.

To avoid false indications produced by the airflow from the propeller, the anemometer had to be placed outboard, for example on a wing strut. Air density and pressure have little effect on the instrument, however it reacts slowly to sudden changes in speed. The distance from the cockpit made it difficult for the pilot to read the instrument in some conditions, especially in bad weather and at night. For this reason an electric remote transmission system was developed with an indicator in the cockpit. The cups drove an alternating current generator and the indicator was a voltmeter calibrated for speed.

Pressure-Head Airspeed Indicator

When air flows against an object the result is dynamic pressure which varies according to air speed and density. Dynamic pressure increases as the square of speed. Pressure is measured at a point on the aircraft where there is no interference from the propeller, usually at one of the wingtips.

The measuring system consists of a pitot tube, a diaphragm pressure gauge as indicator and the necessary lines. The pitot tube is a hollow shaft open at one end with two fittings for dynamic pressure and static pressure. Both static and dynamic pressure are present inside the instrument, while only dynamic pressure exists outside the diaphragm. Measurement of the pressure difference reveals the airspeed.

The pitot tube is designed to prevent rain water from entering and most are equipped with pitot heat to prevent icing.

With the decrease in air density as height increases, dynamic pressure drops even though airspeed remains the same. Correction is required for accurate navigation.

At speeds under 200 km/h the pressure differences to be measured are very small and consequently indications become imprecise. Sensitivity of the indicator can only be increased so far for reasons of reliability and life of the equipment.

Negative Pressure or Venturi Tube Airspeed Indicator

This design is used in aircraft with low airspeeds. The measuring system consists of a horn-shaped tube. The reduction in cross-section accelerates the incoming air. At the narrowest point is located the line attachment point and there the flowing air produces negative pressure.

The indicator is a diaphragm pressure gauge. Inside is the pressure to be measured, while outside static pressure prevails.

For measurement of airspeeds not exceeding 180 km/h, two venturi tubes (one inside the other) are used. This arrangement produces large negative pressure values even at low speeds.

Gliders often employ a combination of pitot and venturi tubes to measure airspeed, thus eliminating the need for static pressure.

Liquid bank indicator, capsule style (Petravic/Vienna, circa 1918). Goerz built similar instruments in Germany into the 1930s.

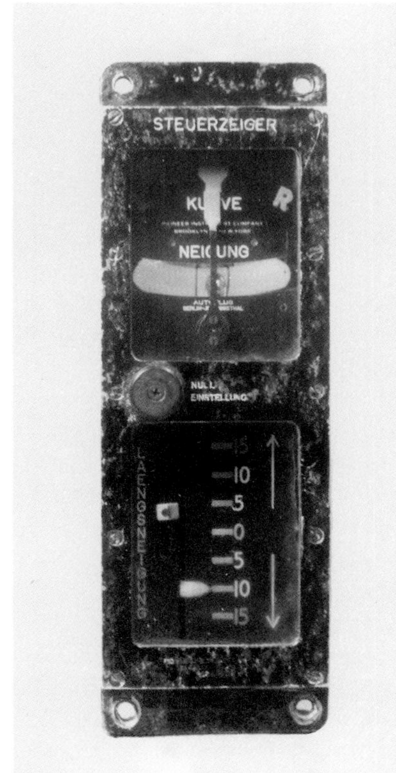

Course indicator (Autoflug, circa 1925), a double-gyro system consisting of turn-and-bank indicator and pitch indicator.

U-tube type liquid pitch indicator by a Czech manufacturer. In Germany Askania built various versions of such instruments.

Flight Attitude Indicators

Awareness of an aircraft's attitude is important for navigation and flight monitoring. In clear visibility a pilot can align himself with the horizon, however this becomes problematical at night or in cloud during instrument flight.

Turbulence can also hamper navigation by causing the aircraft to yaw or turn. Gravity and centrifugal force can also deceive the pilot's senses, resulting in a false assessment of the aircraft's attitude.

Early designers sought aids which could provide the pilot with an indication of the horizon even when the ground could not be seen, however few of them were successful. Flight inclinometers, mainly liquid-based, were widely used well into the 1930s, when they were replaced by gyroscopic instruments.

Spirit Level Inclinometer

Here a steel ball moves in a glass tube filled with a damping fluid. This device is mainly used to display bank angle and is still used today as a supplementary aid in turn and bank indicators. The greatest drawback of the spirit level inclinometer is the effect of centrifugal force in turns, which makes an accurate reading of attitude impossible.

Fluid Inclinometer

The simplest design is a flat, vertical fluid gauge chamber with a glass front. The chamber is filled to the halfway point with a viscous, colored liquid. The surface of the liquid remains parallel to the earth's surface under the effect of gravity and tilts under the combined effects of gravity and centrifugal force.

Another inclinometer design consists of a U-shaped tube arranged along the aircraft's longitudinal axis. Its fluid columns rise or fall as the aircraft's pitch angle changes. This device was often found in seaplanes and high-performance gliders.

Gyro Pitch Indicator

This device is usually seen in combination with a turn and bank indicator. Its function is similar to that of the rate-of-turn gyroscope, except that the gyro reacts to movements about the pitch axis.

Dynamic Pressure Turn and Bank Indicator

A very rare instrument. A venturi tube is installed in each wingtip and the differential pressure produced in a turn is translated into a reading.

Pneumatic turn-and-bank indicator (Askania, 1940), Fl 22402.

Pneumatic turn-and-bank indicator for gliders (Askania, circa 1938).

Electric backup indicator with battery (Askania, circa 1942), Fl 22414-1.

Gyroscopic Devices

Gyroscopic instruments have long been standard items of blind-flying equipment. The pointer of the turn and bank indicator displays yaw rotation, while the spirit level displays centrifugal forces acting upon the vertical axis. The artificial horizon displays deflections about the longitudinal and lateral axes. The operating principle of both devices is the gyroscope, a body rotating at high speed about an axis, which is in balance in all attitudes. Gimbal-mounted, it is free to move about all axes.

The gyroscope's mass moment of inertia allows it to retain its position in space when no forces are acting upon its axis of rotation. When force is applied to its axis of rotation, the gyroscope moves in response. This movement is also referred to as precession.

The **turn and bank indicator** consists of a gyroscope, driven by negative pressure or electrically, with a horizontal axis in the direction of flight. In negative pressure devices equipped with a venturi tube or suction pump, air is sucked out of a housing. The inrushing air drives the gyroscope, which spins at approximately 6,000 to 7,000 rpm.

If the aircraft turns to the left about its vertical axis, the gyroscope makes a precession which is transmitted to an upwards-pointing needle, as a result of which the needle is deflected to the left. The degree of deflection indicates the rate of turn.

The other component of the turn and bank indicator is the spirit level, which is arranged beneath the indicator needle. The spirit level displays deflections about the longitudinal axis. When the aircraft turns, centrifugal forces act upon the ball, while in straight and level flight the ball remains centered.

The first turn and bank indicators made by Askania in the 1920s had the spirit level on top with the indicator needle beneath.

The **turn and bank indicator for gliders** has a similar design but is less sensitive, as gliders generally turn more sharply than powered aircraft. The gyroscope is powered by a feed nozzle. The sensitivity of the indicator varies, as it is dependent on negative pressure and therefore airspeed, which can be relatively low.

To overcome this disadvantage, designers turned to electrically-powered turn and bank indicators. Energy is provided by a 4-Volt flashlight battery which permits up to eight hours running time with constant sensitivity. In larger aircraft such devices are used as **backup turn and bank indicators**.

Gyroscopic instruments for displaying the horizon were already in development during the First World War. Their size and weight limited their usefulness, however, and they were only used in larger aircraft.

Aviator's Horizon by Anschütz

This consisted of a vertically placed rotary current gyroscope with a pendulum for aligning the gyroscope in the perpendicular. Indication was by means of a movable horizon disc, the lower half of which was dark. The device in fact only displayed bank angle.

A further development in 1918 was the attitude gyro, which had all the features of the later Sperry gyro-horizon. Production was limited to a single example, and in 1932 Askania was forced to pay substantial fees to produce the Sperry design under license.

Drexler Flight Indicator

Developed in 1917, this device had a gimbal-mounted three-phase gyroscope and was in most respects equivalent to a turn and bank indicator. A pointer with an aircraft symbol indicated a turn to the left or right. There was also a spirit level to display bank angle. The gyro spun at 18,000 to 20,000 rpm and was glycerine damped. A subsequent development was the Universal Flight Indicator, which also incorporated an airspeed indicator and altimeter.

Gyroscopic Flight Direction, Rosenbaum System

This artificial horizon was developed in 1910 and was built until 1923. The heart of the system was a gimbal-mounted gyroscope, which was suspended like a pendulum and spun at 18,000 rpm. The pendulum was connected to a disc which displayed the horizon. Two spirit levels displayed pitch and dynamic vertical. Power was provided by an airstream-driven generator. The gyroscope was dampened by a backup engine, which counteracted disturbing accelerations.

Artificial horizon, Sperry type (Askania, 1938), Fl 22426.

Combined turn-and-bank indicator and artificial horizon (Feinapparatebau, 1944), Fl 22415-1 with locking mechanism.

No aerobatics were permitted when the system was switched on, in order to avoid damage. Later versions had a locking device operated by a rotating ring on the front of the instrument.

The Combined Turn and Bank Indicator and Artificial Horizon was a combined instrument designed to save space on the instrument panel. The electrically-powered device had two gyroscopes.

The directional gyro will be described in the following section.

Navigational Equipment

Until the 1970s, in the days before the Global Positioning System (GPS) and other satellite navigation systems, aviators relied on compass and radio navigation .

Artificial Horizon, Sperry Type

This design, which was built under license by Askania beginning in 1932, replaced all others. It consisted of a fully gimbal-mounted pendulum gyroscope which held the horizon bar in the horizontal. In response to deviation of the gyro, a return body restored it to its original position. Sensitivity was greatest in horizontal flight.

As in the case of the turn and bank indicator, the gyroscope was powered by suction. The necessary feed nozzle was located near the exhaust to provide some measure of heating. Operating negative pressure was 1000 mm WS and approximately 40 liters of air were sucked through the device per minute. Speed of the gyro was 12,000 rpm.

Compass

The magnetic compass has been used in marine navigation for centuries. Its operating principle is based on magnetic rods aligned in the earth's magnetic field. To improve directional performance, a magnetic field system of several magnets connected to a compass rose is used. The system is liquid damped (compass fluid), to prevent vibrations from causing swing. Compensation is necessary to prevent deviations caused by the many metal parts such as the engine or electrical magnetic fields in the aircraft. This is achieved by placing small bar magnets in specific chambers in the housing. As a rule, compensation is not required in gliders as the devices are smaller and there is little metal in the aircraft structure.

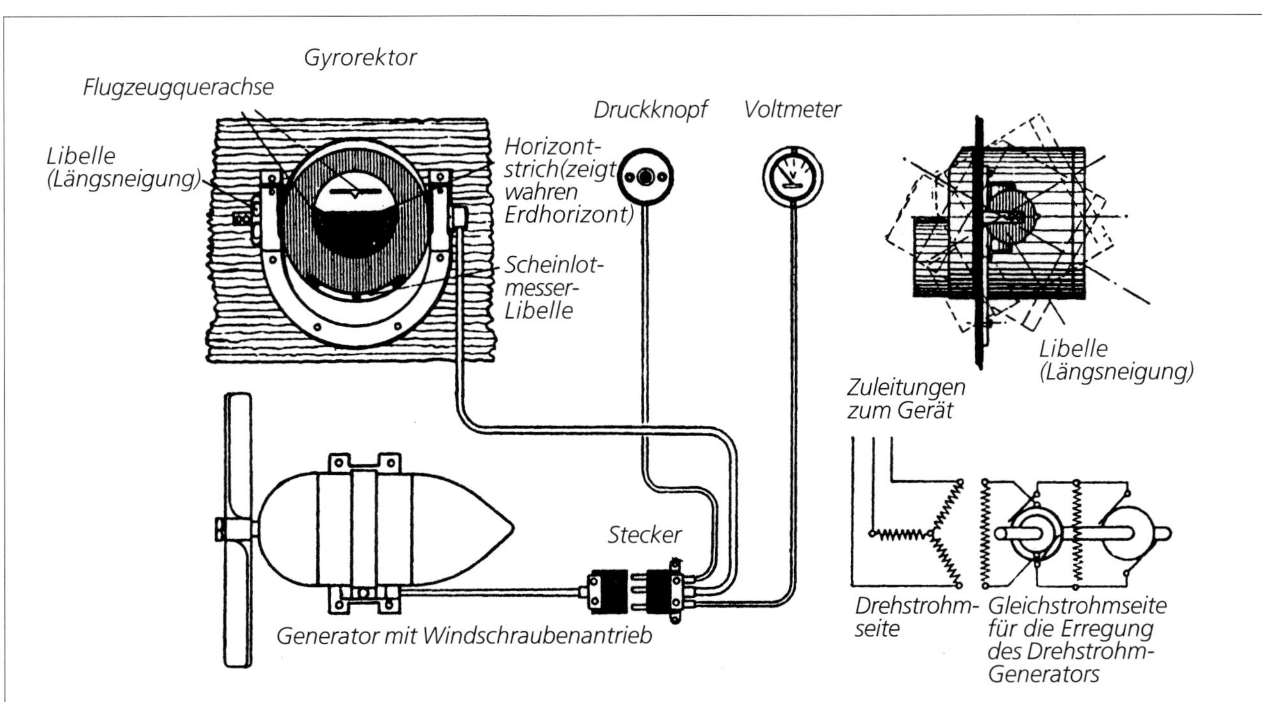

Layout of the Gyrorektor.

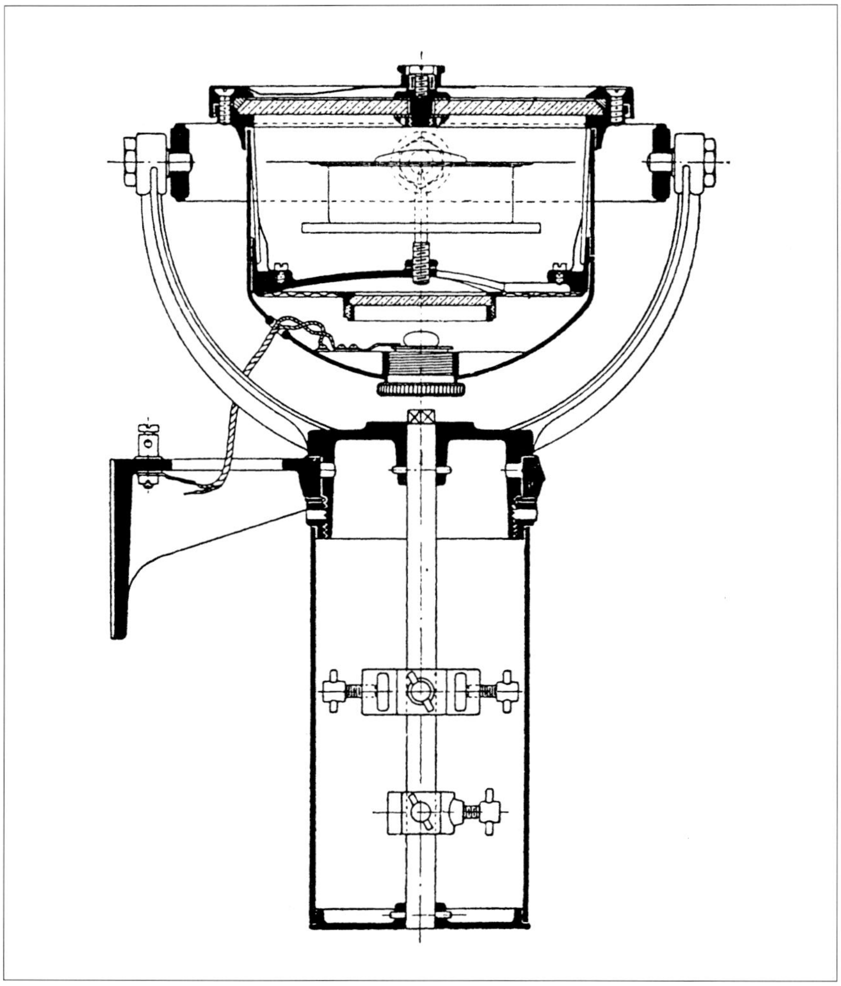

Layout of a magnetic compass circa 1918.

FK 5 master compass (Ludolph, circa 1936), Fl 23211.

OK 42 navigator's compass (Kadlec, circa 1944), Fl 23238.

Most types of aviation compass in use until 1918 were derived from ship's compasses. They were horizontal-face instruments with compensation and an adjustable course indicator. Compasses were mounted in the fuselage in front of the pilot or in the lower wing abeam the cockpit.

The Inspectorate of Aviation Forces developed standards for even these relatively simple compass types, specifying the style of the instrument face, design of the mounting and compensation.

Vertical-face compass types which could be mounted in the instrument panel did not appear until the 1920s. With the numerous standards introduced in the 1930s, the following types of compass or compass systems were identified:

Direct-Reading Compass

This device was a magnetic compass which was installed where required. Two variations were the master compass in the instrument panel in front of the pilot, which was used to maintain course, and the observer's or navigator's compass, which was used by the observer for navigation. As a rule the master compass was a vertical-face instrument while the observer's compass was a horizontal-face device.

Askania designated its compasses based on the German nicknames for the pilot and observer (Emil and Franz): master compass Emil and Little Emil, and observer's compass Franz and Little Franz, depending on the size of the instrument.

Distant-Reading Compass

The actual compass was placed in a magnetically favorable location in the aircraft, usually in the aft fuselage, as far away from the engine(s) as possible. This largely eliminated deviations and improved accuracy of readings. Indications were transmitted to the instrument panel by pneumatic or electrical impulses.

The two most widely-used distant-reading compasses in Germany until 1945 were the Askania pneumatic system and the Patin electric system, which became standard equipment in the *Luftwaffe*.

Magnetic compass (Bamberg, 1918), viewed from above.

Zürn Z7, Type DLV master compass (1934).

Askania Pneumatic Distant-reading Compass System

The system consisted of a master compass in the aft fuselage and a course selector and course indicator in the instrument panel.

The pilot set the desired course using the course selector. If he maintained this course the course indicator remained centered. If, for example, the aircraft deviated to the left of the desired course, the indicator would also move to the left. Course was maintained by observing the course indicator and making any necessary corrections.

The system was powered by a feed nozzle or suction pump, which sucked air through the master compass. Deviation from the selected course caused the inflowing air to produce a pressure differential in a jet chamber at two nozzles connected to the course indicator.

The position of the jet chamber was determined by the course selector. The course indicator was essentially a pressure differential gauge which centered when the pressure differential reading was zero.

The Askania system was developed in the 1920s and was the first practical distant-reading compass.

Patin Distant-Reading Compass

This system used a direct current transmission system between the master and slave compasses. The master compass had a compensation scale and floated in a cold-resistant liquid to reduce bearing friction. The compass kettle was gimbal-mounted and housed in a casing with numerous coil springs.

The indicator device was the slave compass in the instrument panel. It had a course ring for course and neutral indications. When in use, the aircraft symbol always pointed upward, where the course being flown could be read from the compass rose.

The Patin distant-reading compass became standard *Luftwaffe* equipment in 1938 and was used as a component of the Siemens and Patin autopilot systems.

PFK-f2 master compass indicator, small version for fighter aircraft (Patin, circa 1944), Fl 23334.

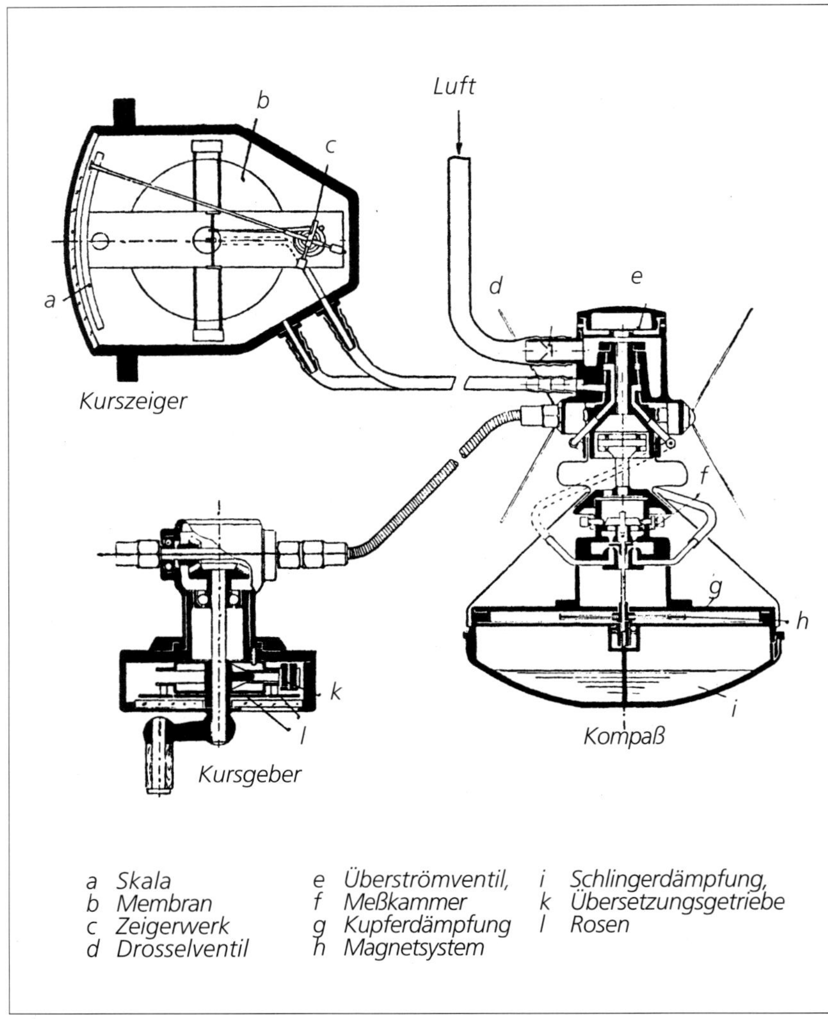

Cross-section of the Askania distant-reading compass system.

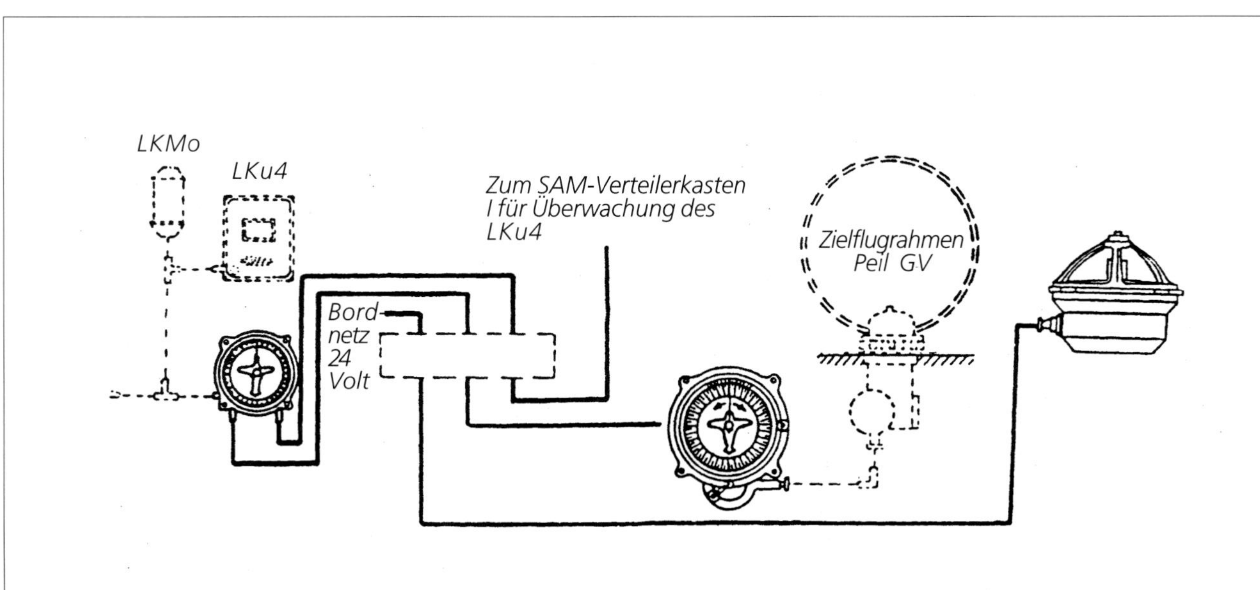

Overview of the Patin distant-reading compass system.

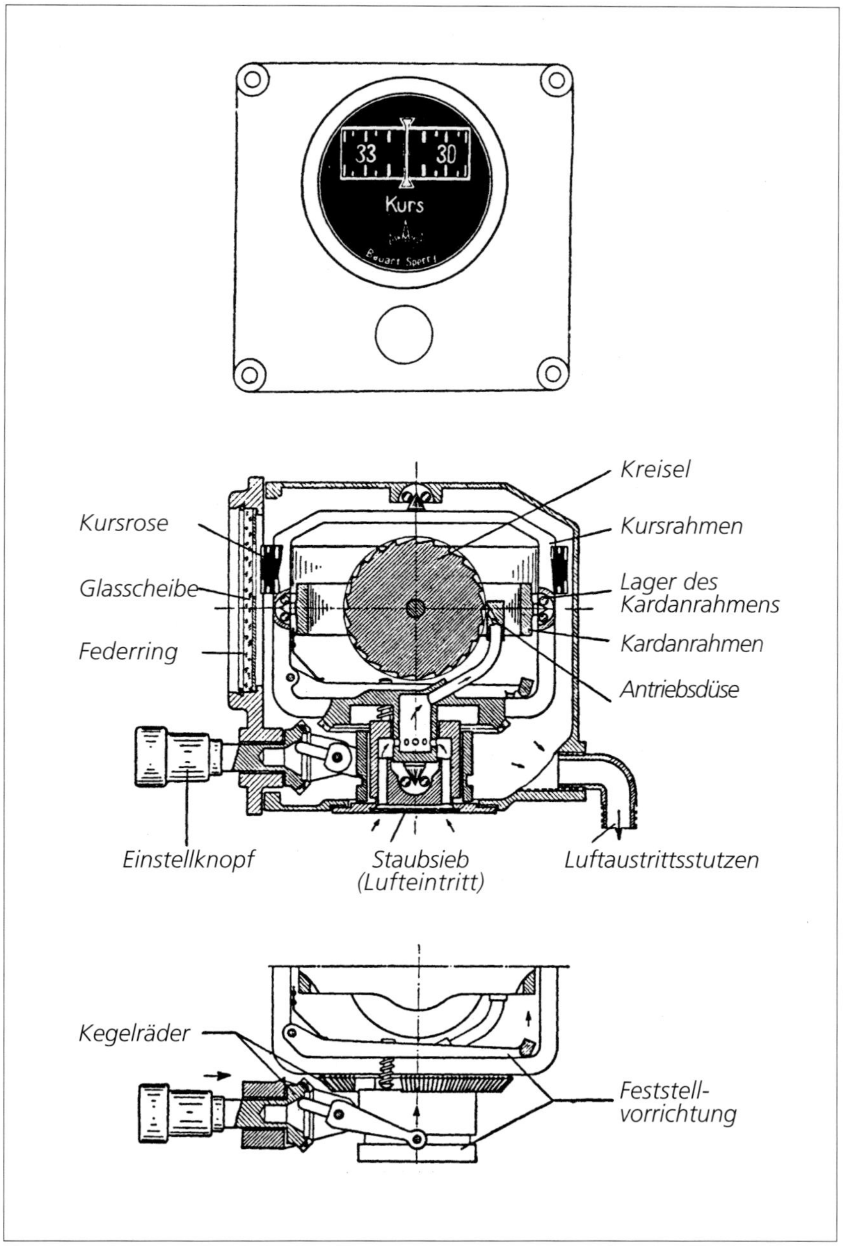

Askania Lgc 3 gyro-compass, Sperry type (1938-39), Fl 22428.

Siemens Lku 4 gyro-compass (circa 1942), Fl 22561.

Gyro Compass

In larger aircraft the gyro compass was used for navigation and was an important blind-flying aid. In contrast to the magnetic compass, the gyro compass provided indications which were not influenced by the effects of acceleration and which were vibration-proof.

All the pilot had to do was switch on the gyro compass and set the desired course. The mechanical design did produce friction forces, however, which caused the gyro compass to deviate over time. For this reason it had to be reset approximately every 15 minutes. Instrument readings were taken from a drum-shaped compass rose.

In the 1930s Askania built the Sperry system under license. Like the artificial horizon, the device was pneumatically driven. The gimbal-mounted gyroscope spun at 7,000 to 8,000 rpm. The subsequent model was the gyro compass for the Askania autopilot system.

The Askania device was replaced by the electrically-powered Lku4 gyro compass by Siemens, which could also be operated independent of the Siemens autopilot. As a result of its high rotation speed of approximately 30,000 rpm, this gyro compass provided reliable and steady readings even in turbulence. As it was electrically powered, the system was also largely immune to the influences of temperature and pressure.

Radio Navigation Equipment

Radio navigation using radio ranges was introduced in the 1930s, for the first time offering reliable navigation even in bad weather. The first attempts to produce directional radio beams had taken place at the turn of the century, however.

Toward the end of the First World War German R-aircraft were equipped with the first direction-finders, however it would not be until 1927 that the first successful tests of a DF receiver were carried out, in a Junkers F 13. Beginning in 1931 Peil G I DF receivers were installed in a few aircraft operated by *Lufthansa* and the *Reichswehr*. Later designs became standard equipment, beginning in 1934.

In 1936-37 the airline *Lufthansa* introduced the 118N DF and homing system, which had a very large indicator. Remote operation was by means of towed aerial and radio waves. Available modes were receive, DF bearing, homing by indication and homing by tone. The indicator was a simple device (KJ 130 N and others) which indicated whether the pilot was on a direct course to the transmitter or to the left or right.

Homing indicator for the KJ 130 N radio navigation aid (AEG-Telefunken, circa 1938).

Homing indicator for the AFN 2 radio navigation aid (AEG, circa 1943), Ln 27002.

KT-p2 DF repeater compass (Patin 1944), Fl 23474 for Peil G 6.

Homing indicator for AFN 1 radio navigation aid (AEG, 1939), Ln 27000.

PFA/R DF repeater compass (Patin, circa 1942), Fl 23470 for Peil G V.

Beginning in 1937, the Peil G V was introduced as standard equipment in commercial aircraft and larger types used by the *Luftwaffe*. Remote control was mechanical and for indications and navigations there was the AFN 1 homing indicator for radio navigation and the Patin DF repeater compass.

The AFN 1 had two needles and one lamp. One needle pointed downward and indicated deviations to the left and right of course to the transmitter. When flying directly towards the transmitter the needle pointed vertically downwards. The horizontal needle gave an approximate distance from the radio range and the lamp illuminated when the aircraft overflew the transmitter. The DF repeater compass was a combination of slave compass and direction finding corrector.

In 1942-43 the Peil G 6 replaced the older systems. Available modes were homing, DF bearing and reception. A new Patin DF repeater compass was installed as indicator.

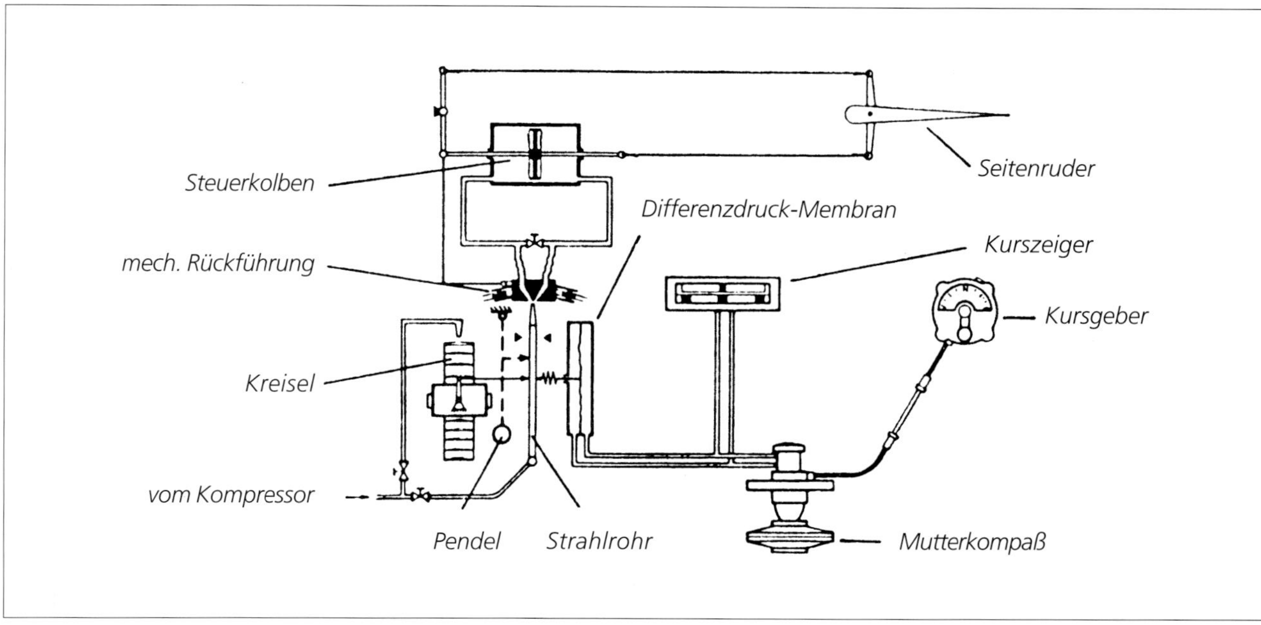

Overview of the Askania autopilot.

Space limitations meant that a radio navigation system was not installed in fighter aircraft until early 1942, and then as a supplementary system to the standard FuG 16 and FuG 17 radio systems which made it possible to home onto a selected transmitter.

The system (FuG 16 Z) consisted of a homing adapter for the FuG 16, a fixed DF loop on the fuselage spine, and the AFN 2 homing indicator, a miniaturized development of the AFN 1.

The most widely used system was the FuG 16 ZY, of which more than 120,000 examples were produced from the summer of 1943 until the end of the war. The system's operating modes were voice communication, telegraphy, homing and range measurement.

Autopilot Systems

The autopilot holds an aircraft on a selected course and is thus an important instrument for navigation. The two basic types of autopilot are the stabilizing autopilot, which maintains a course being flown, and the navigating autopilot, which automatically finds a selected course.

Mode of operation is similar to manual instrument flight based on indications from the gyro compass and turn and bank indicator, however in the case of the autopilot the source of power for control inputs is a servo. Overall, the use of an autopilot provides greater course stability than manual control. The autopilot serves the following purposes:

- automatic control of aircraft movements about the vertical axis or all three axes, depending on the system
- more accurate approach to the target on military missions
- simplified navigation using radio beacons
- reduction of crew workload on long flights

In order to fulfill these tasks, an autopilot must have the following capabilities:

- deviation from course must result in appropriate control surface movements
- additional control movements must counteract oscillations
- effect control movements to counteract effects of engine failure or out of trim situation
- the autopilot's natural frequency must be different than that of the airframe
- system weight and size must be kept to a minimum

The most important German autopilot systems were developed by Askania, Siemens and Patin and will be described in detail. One must differentiate between full control systems and those which controlled the rudder only.

Pneumatic System

In the years up to 1939 Askania developed a number of systems based on this principle for stabilization about the vertical axis. These systems were used mainly in Do 18 and Ha 139 aircraft of *Lufthansa*'s North Atlantic service and in early Do 17s and He 111s of the *Luftwaffe*. A total of about 2,000 Askania autopilots was built, some of which remained in use until 1945.

The pneumatic autopilot, of which the **Askania Lz 11a** was one, was powered by compressed air produced by an air compressor on the engine.

The central element of the system was the course control device, which consisted of a turn and bank indicator gyroscope, a jet tube, a pressure junction block and a differential pressure chamber. Powered by compressed air and rotating at 16,000 rpm, the gyroscope also served as a damping element which limited the aircraft's rotational speed about the vertical axis and stabilized the aircraft on course.

The direction-setting element of the system was the gyro compass, which was electromagnetically supported by the master compass. The gyro compass delivered the impulse to hold and change course in the form of pressure differences to the pressure chamber in the course control device. The pressure chamber and gyroscope in the control device affected the jet tube, into which was fed compressed air (1.5 atm). In the center position the air from the jet tube blew with equal force against two jets on the pressure junction block. When the jet tube was deflected by a course deviation, the jets were subjected to different pressures. The pressure difference moved the actuator piston and thus the control surface.

Operation of the pneumatic autopilot was relatively simple, with the pilot taking the following steps:

1. Set the course to be flown on the distant-reading compass system's course selector.
2. Manually place the aircraft on course. When the desired course was achieved the course indicator is centered.
3. Set the gyro compass' course rose to the value on the course selector.
4. Switch on the autopilot system, after which the aircraft maintained the selected course.

To make a course change, the desired course was set on the course selector, after which the aircraft turned itself onto the new course with the pilot assisting with aileron inputs.

Pneumatic-Hydraulic System

In design terms this was largely similar to the pneumatic system, however amplification of the control impulse was achieved by means of an hydraulically-operated valve rather than a jet tube. Control surface movements were not as smooth as those of the purely pneumatic system.

Electric-Hydraulic System

The best known system based on this operating principle was the **K4ü by Siemens**. Approximately 50,000 examples were built and it was one of the most widely used systems in the *Luftwaffe* until 1945, primarily in types such as the He 111, Ju 52, Ju 88 and Bf 110.

There were several variants, differing mainly in the arrangement of one or more course selectors, depending on whether the course would be set by the pilot only from other locations in the aircraft as well.

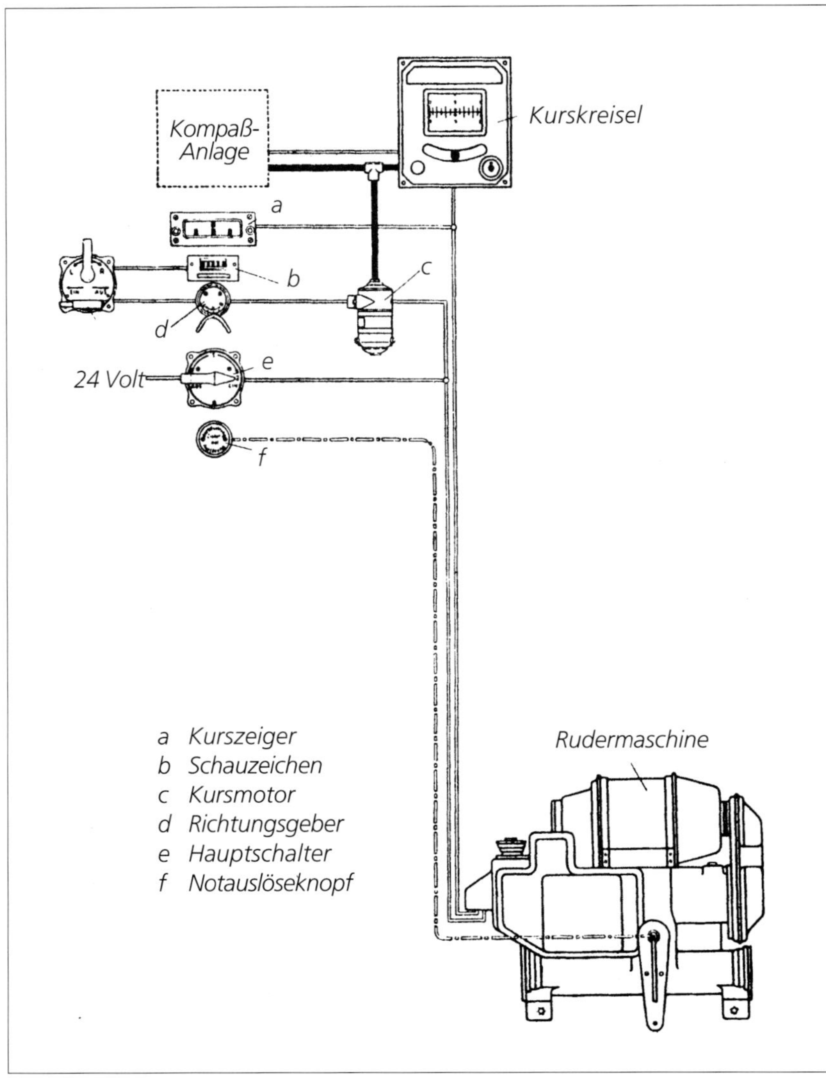

Overview of the Siemens K4ü autopilot.

In contrast to the pneumatic system, control impulses were transmitted to the servos electrically. The necessary energy came from the aircraft's electrical system and the sealed unit construction of the servos resulted in a high degree of reliability.

The K4ü system consisted of the following elements:

- Gyro Compass: The lower rose of the gyro compass showed the course being flown, while the course to be flown was set on the upper rose. It delivered the electrical control impulse to the servo. The gyro compass was monitored by the Patin distant-reading compass system, which reported any deviations caused by friction.
- Course Indicator: Fine indicator displaying deviations from course.
- Course Selectors: One or more for setting the gyro compass rose for course changes. When multiple course selectors were installed, the bomb aimer, for example, could override the pilot's course selector to make course changes during the bomb run.
- Master Switch: The system master switch had three positions:
  1 = Off
  1 = Vibration-free course indications by the gyro compass (manual control)
  1 = Autopilot switched on
- A visual indicator to show when the system was switched on.
- Emergency disengage button, which disengaged the system from the controls in an emergency.
- The servo with a damping gyroscope to reduce rotational sped about the vertical axis.
- Other accessories such as course motor, resistance box and distributor.

Functioning of the system was relatively simple. If the aircraft turned off course, for example because of wind, the control force

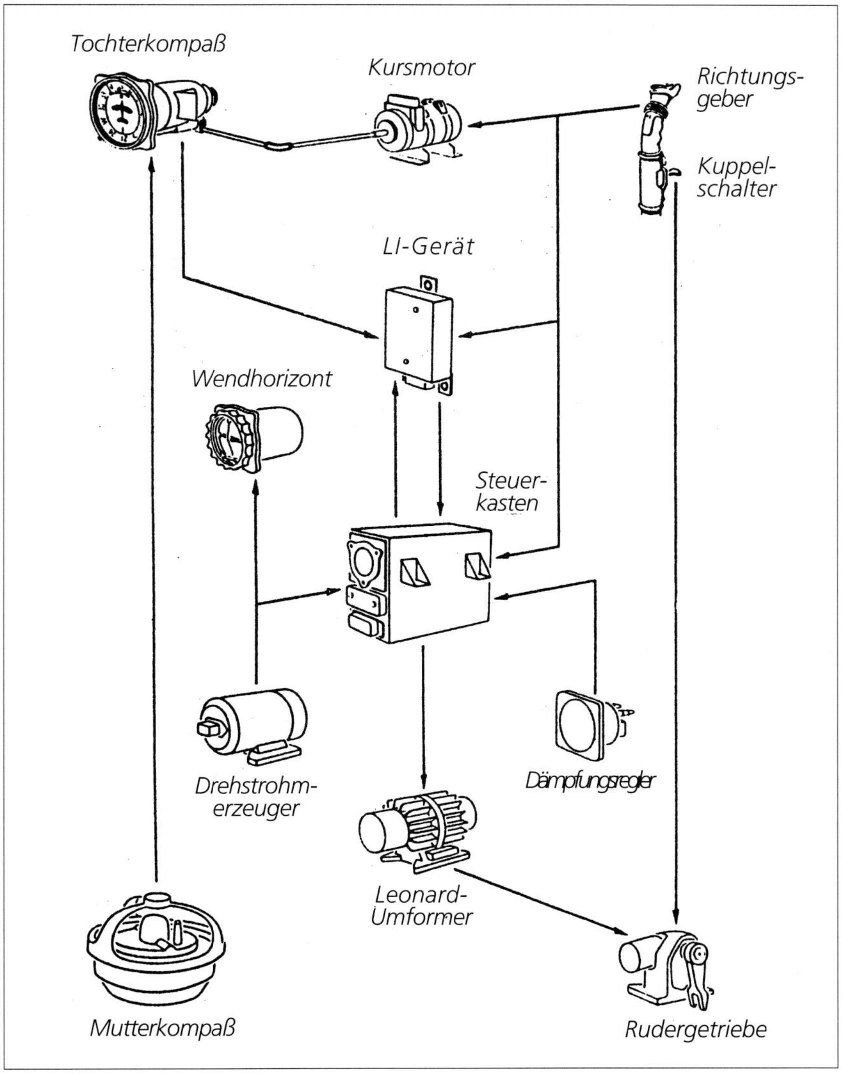

Overview of the Patin KS 12b-1 fighter autopilot.

on the servo generated a correcting rudder movement. Holding course precisely was only possible with the damping gyroscope and the gyro compass operating in unison. Siemens combined three K4ü systems to produce the DK4 three-axis autopilot, however it progressed no further than the experimental stage and development was abandoned in favor of the Patin three-axis autopilot.

The **Patin KS 12b-1 Fighter Autopilot** was designed to assist the pilots of fighter aircraft in bad weather and, in particular, in penetrating solid cloud layers. Beginning in 1944 it was installed mainly in fighter aircraft such as the Fw 190, Ta 152, Bf 109 and Me 262.

The KS 12b-1 was a simplified single-axis autopilot based on the Patin distant-reading compass system. The heart of the system consisted of a control box and the LI device, which replaced the gyro compass. Other components were the course motor, transformer, damping control and servo. The course selector and coupling switch were located on the control stick. Readings were taken from the repeater compass and the combined turn and bank indicator-artificial horizon.

Three-Axis Autopilots

All of the autopilots described so far were single-axis systems controlling the rudder only. From an early date, the manufacturers of autopilot systems and aircraft instruments were thinking about an autopilot for all three axes. Physically and technically complex, at that time these systems were relatively large and could therefore only be installed in larger aircraft.

In 1932 the American Sperry company produced the **Sperry Gyropilot Model A2**, which was tested in a Ju 52 operated by Lufthansa. This system was a basic autopilot without an oscillation-damping rate of turn gyroscope and was limited to a narrow speed range near cruising speed.

The **Askania Autopilot I and II** were developments of the Sperry system. These systems provided full control about all three axes by way of the rudder, ailerons and elevators, making possible level flight, turns, and climb and descent.

If an aircraft was blown off the set course by wind gusts, for example, then the resulting movements (precession) of the gyroscopes were transmitted by connected pneumatic membranes to the control pistons. These controlled the hydraulic lines for the actuator rods, which were connected to the control surfaces by cables. A feedback system prevented over control.

Sperry autopilots were widely used in the USA, where more than 11,000 examples were installed, mainly in DC 2 and DC 3 aircraft. The system was also built under license in Japan and the USSR.

The **Patin PDS Three-Axis Autopilot** was based on a development by the Rechlin Test Station which was dubbed the "Rechliner Emil". It was fully electric system with dynamic feedback and dynamic control monitoring.

The most important elements of the system were:

- Gyro compass by Siemens or Anschütz. It was monitored and corrected by the Patin distant-reading compass.
- An airspeed indicator which could be set to a desired speed.

Arbeitsweise der Askania-Flugzeug-Vollsteuerung, Bauart Sperry

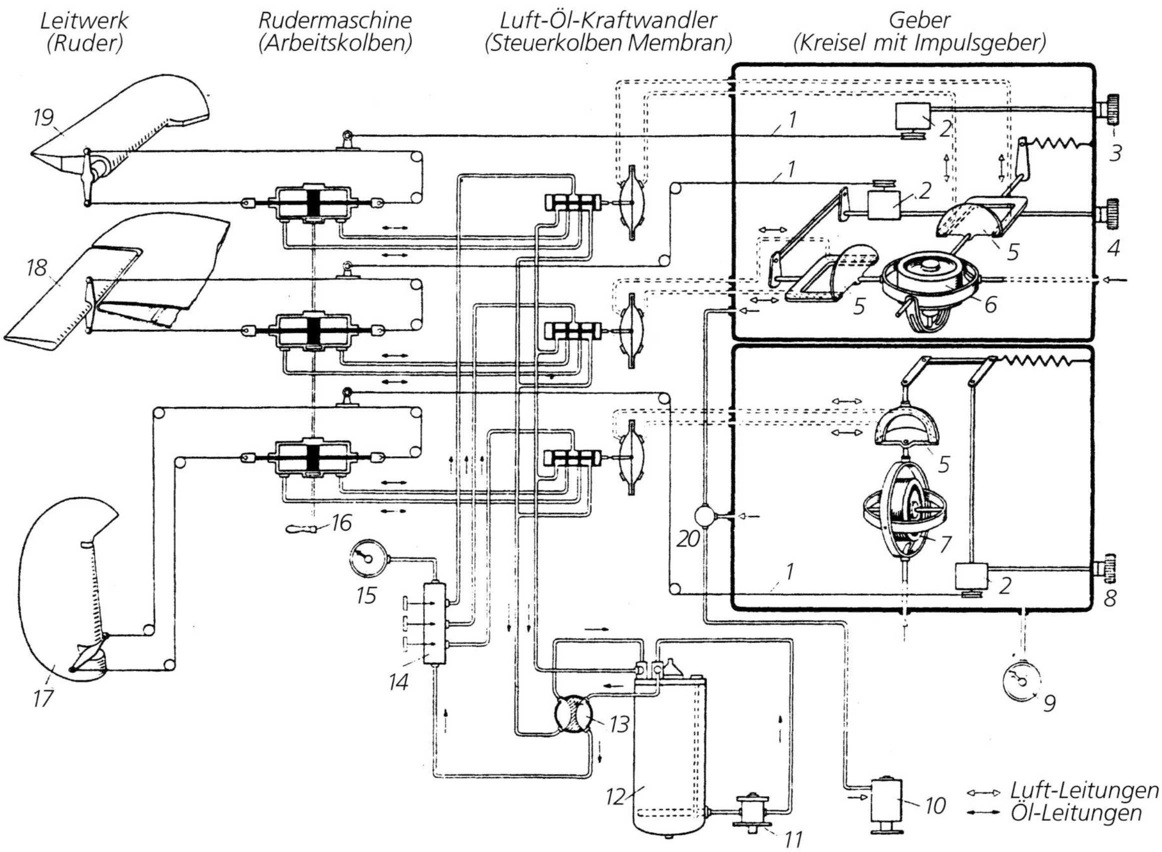

Geber
1 Rückführseil
2 Rückführgetriebe
3 Höhenrudereinstellung
4 Querrudereinstellung
5 Impulsgeber
6 Horizontkreisel
7 Kurskreisel
8 Seitenruder-Einstellung (Kurs)
9 Sogmesser
10 Sogpumpe

Luft-Ol-Kraftwandler
11 Ölpumpe
12 Ölbehälter
13 Abschalthahn
14 Steuergeschwindigkeit
15 Öldruckmesser

Rudermaschine
16 Kurzschlußhahn

Leitwerk
17 Seitenruder
18 Querruder
19 Höhenruder
20 Sogregler

System diagram of the Askania three-axis autopilot, Sperry-type.

- A gyro-horizon for indicating aircraft attitude (repeater horizon).
- The "Rechliner Emil" control system with gyro-computer for rudder, aileron and elevator signals.
- The guidance center with vertical gyro for forming and transmitting control signals (master horizon).
- The turn selector calculated commands for the ailerons. A rate of turn gyro measured the rotational speed of the aircraft about the vertical axis.

Testing of the Patin Three-Axis Autopilot began in 1939. Initially only the rudder control function was realized, as the Patin PKS 11 autopilot, which was built in large numbers beginning in 1940. It was installed in the Do 217, Do 335, Ju 188, Ju 290, Ju 388, Me 410 and Si 204. The system consisted of a Patin distant-reading compass system, a Siemens gyro compass, a course indicator, a turn control, a course motor, the control device, a transformer and a servo.

The system was later developed into the Patin PDS 5 Three-Axis Autopilot, testing of which began in January 1941 in a Do 217. It was later installed in the Ar 234, Bv 138, Bv 222, Do 217 and Fw 200.

Aircraft clock (Zenith, circa 1918), a Swiss product using a pocket watch mechanism.

Aircraft clock with eight-day mechanism (Kienzle, circa 1925).

Bo-UK 1 clock (Junghans, circa 1944), Fl 23885, the standard aircraft clock of the Luftwaffe.

Aircraft Clocks

Clocks used in aircraft must be capable of withstanding much greater forces than conventional clocks as the crew must be able to rely on them for accurate readings for navigation and flight monitoring.

In the early days of aviation pilots used pocket watches carried on their person or mounted on makeshift mountings on the instrument panel. Later specialized clocks were developed for use in aircraft. Most commercial aircraft of the 1920s and 30s were equipped with accurate eight-day clocks.

With the build-up of the *Luftwaffe* from 1933 on, a number of specialized clocks were developed for a variety of purposes:

- Blind flying clocks with stop feature and revolving time markings
- Observer's watches (special accurate watches worn by the crew)
- Elapsed time clocks
- Aerial photography clocks
- Operating clocks for radio positions

As a rule clocks were installed in prominent positions in the instrument panel or directly in the control wheel or horn. Additional clocks were installed in the radio operator's and navigator's stations and in passenger cabins.

Because of their high quality and usefulness for a variety of purposes, aircraft clocks remain one of the most popular and most used souvenirs.

Aircraft Instrumentation The Early Years Until 1914

In the beginning, flying was strictly a matter of feel, with the pilot using his senses for navigation and engine and flight monitoring. He navigated by using his eyes to observe the terrain below, estimated his height, and made visual observations of the weather. The pilot listened to the engine to ensure that it was running smoothly and estimated his speed by the sound of the wind rushing past the bracing wires. His sense of balance informed him of the aircraft's attitude, and his sense of feel alerted him to unusual vibrations which might suggest a mechanical problem.

Technical developments soon led to increases in aircraft performance, longer flights and more powerful engines. It soon became apparent that the senses no longer sufficed for flight and engine monitoring and that reliable technical aids such as aircraft instruments were required. At first pilots objected to this "unnecessary ballast", but they soon came to realize that they enhanced their safety.

There was, however, a certain period—until approximately 1911—before the industry could offer equipment developed specially for use in aircraft. During this time instruments were used which had their origins in the machine, locomotive, automobile and ship-building industries or in meteorology. In some cases these instruments were large and heavy and had to be subjected to a weight and size reduction process before they could be used in aircraft. Prior to this, however, pilots had to use primitive makeshift aids:

• **Pocket or Marine Compass as Orientation Aid**

An incomplete navigation aid as it lacked the compensation feature made necessary by the many metal parts present in aircraft.

• **Drag Plate:** a pendulum on a return spring acting as an airspeed indicator.

• **Barometer** serving as altimeter.

• **Pilot's Pocket watch or Wristwatch**

An unreliable aid as vibration produced by the motor hampered its operation.

• **Sight Glass**

A fuel contents gauge based on the principle of the corresponding tube. Because of the forces to which it was subjected in flight, it was too inaccurate and insensitive.

By 1914 certain items of equipment had become more or less standard equipment:

• **RPM Indicator**

Provided information on the operation of the engine.

• **Fuel Pressure Gauge**

Important, as lack of fuel pressure would cause the engine to quit.

• **Fuel Contents Gauge**

Depending on design, either a float in the main tank or a sight glass for the header tank.

• **Fuel System Air Pump**

As the tank was usually lower in the fuselage than the engine, the gasoline had to be forced by pressure to the carburettor. A hand pump was used to create this pressure before the engine was started. During flight a fuel pump on the engine maintained pressure.

• **Grease gun**

For lubrication of the water pump, part of the cooling system.

• **Control Wheel**

Control stick grips were not common. The large wooden wheel taken from automobile design was better suited for dealing with the sometimes heavy control forces. In some types, such as the Taube, it controlled wing twist by means of a gear wheel and bicycle chain.

• **Throttle Lever**

Usually latching or locking, to give relief to the pilot.

• **Ignition Timing Adjustment Lever**

• **Fuel System Control Lever**

The fuel system usually consisted of a main and a header tank. The header tank was located above the engine and relied on gravity feed. The header tank was located in the bracing wires above the fuselage and was limited in size for aerodynamic reasons and when increased range became a factor additional tanks were located in the fuselage. These in turn required a hand pump to allow the pilot to transfer the fuel to the header tank. The hand pump was later replaced by engine-driven pumps and the header tank, which tended to restrict the pilot's view, was abandoned.

• **Starting magneto**

Produced electrical current needed for engine start.

• **Ignition Switch**

Other equipment was installed at the request of the pilot or for experimental purposes:

• **Oil Pressure Gauge**

• **Coolant Thermometer**

• **Altimeter or Altitude Recorder**

An aneroid barometer with zero setting, usually suspended on springs or elastic cord from the bracing wire tower above the fuselage.

• **Compass**

A gimbal-mounted liquid compass with compensation, usually installed near the pilot seat or in the bottom wing, as far away as possible from the starting magneto.

- **Pitch Indicator**
- **Usually a glass design filled with a colored liquid.**
- **Anemometer**

An airspeed indicator, usually mounted on a wind strut beyond the airstream produced by the propeller.

- **Clock**
- **Communications Equipment for Pilot and Observer**

For example a mirror on the bracing tower or a speaking and listening tube.

There were no rules for the arrangement and affixing of the instruments in the aircraft. Suitable attachment points were sought around the pilot on struts, steel tubes, bracing wires or fairings. For technical reasons, many instruments had to be located directly on the engine, fuel tank or radiator. Others had to be located outside the propeller airstream.

The result of all this was instruments scattered about the pilot seat in every possible location at varying distances. To take readings the pilot had to constantly turn his head and focus on differing ranges. When moving to another type of aircraft, a pilot had to first conduct a sort of "Easter Egg Hunt" to locate the various items of equipment, for detailed aircraft handbooks and operating manuals did not as yet exist. Poor lighting conditions and twilight caused further problems, for as a rule there was no cockpit lighting. Other complications included hard-to-read white dial faces with black numbers, differing units of measurement, poorly-located instruments—usually with excessive lettering, and non-standard indicators.

The first instrument panels soon appeared, in which most of the instruments were concentrated in a more or less logical arrangement. Development of the first standards for instrument types and the design of instrument faces began prior to the First World War.

Etrich, Jeannin, Rumpler and other Taube

On the Malaysian Archipelago grows the gourd plant *Zanonia macroparca*. Its hemispherically-shaped fruit grows up to 30 cm in length and develops numerous winged seeds spanning up to 16 cm. These display astonishingly good and stable gliding characteristics. In 1897 Professor Ahlborn of Hamburg published the results of his research into the flight characteristics of these seeds in a paper titled "On the Stability of Flying Machines".

Aviation pioneer Igo Etrich and his friend Franz Wels subsequently developed a wing based on the shape of the Zanonia seed. It was initially tested on a glider and was patented in Austria.

By 1910 flight characteristics had become so good that the pair designed a powered aircraft with the wing. Porsche provided a 60-H.P. engine for the monoplane, which was to become famous as the *Taube* (Dove).

The *Taube* was a monoplane with braced wings and wing twisting for lateral control. Depending on the type, the wingtips extended some distance aft (patterned after the Zanonia seed). The tail surfaces were usually cruciform style, with a split rudder above and below the elevator. The fuselage was usually a steel tube structure with fabric covering and the wing was fabric over a wooden structure. Flying the *Taube*, which was probably the most elegant air-

The Jeannin Stahltaube *in the German Technical Museum.*

Etrich Taube of the Instruction and Research Institute for Military Aviation in the summer of 1910. The aircraft's meager instrumentation consisted of a fuel pressure gauge (left), an altimeter or recording altimeter in the bracing wire tower, and an RPM indicator. Note the position of the throttle lever on the pilot's right and the transparent panels in the wing covering. (F. Selinger Collection)

craft of its day, Etrich's foreman Illner won almost every prize at the International Flying Week in Wiener-Neustadt. This was the foundation of the *Taube*'s outstanding reputation.

In Germany Edmund Rumpler obtain rights to produce the aircraft, and his "Etrich-Rumpler Taube" became a sales success. In the beginning Rumpler paid license fees, but when he discovered that Etrich would probably not be able to obtain a patent in Germany, he stopped making payments and sold the aircraft as the "Rumpler Taube".

Etrich subsequently released the design and eventually more than 50 manufacturers offered versions of the *Taube* for sale. As a result, the type became one of the most successful and popular aircraft of its time in the German-speaking world. More than 500 were built in a variety of versions prior to the First World War. The *Taube* was usually a two-seater with the pilot in the rear and the observer or passenger in front. The best-known Taube pilots were Hellmuth Hirth, Alfred Friedrich, Hans Vollmoeller, Günther Plüschow and Melli Beese. They won many prizes and set a number of notable records while flying the *Taube*.

In the First World War the Taube initially served as a training and reconnaissance aircraft (A-Category). In spite of its lack of speed the aircraft achieved a number of notable successes, such as in August 1914 when reconnaissance missions flown by officers Canter and Mertens made a significant contribution to German victory in the Battle of Tannenberg.

Emil Jeannin, who earned his pilot's license in 1910, opened a flying school and a small aircraft factory in 1912. His best-known type was the *Stahltaube* (Steel Taube), of which 37 were built, most powered by a 100-H.P. Argus or Daimler engine. When the First

Pilot's cockpit of a later Taube. Visible are (from left to right): throttle lever, fuel cock, air pump (below), fuel gauge, ignition lock, fuel pressure gauge, control wheel, RPM indicator, starter magneto, ignition timing control lever. The elastic cords hanging down on the right side of the cockpit suggest that an altimeter may also have been installed.

Switchboard of the Jeannin Stahltaube *in the German Technical Museum. Some instruments are missing as suitable equipment could not be found. Visible from the left are: throttle lever mount, grease gun, two levers for the fuel system, control wheel, starter magneto and air pump. (DTM)*

Cockpit of the Rumpler Taube *replica in the* Luftwaffe *Museum in Berlin-Gatow. Much effort was expended to ensure accurate equipment. Visible are (from left): ignition timing lever, throttle lever, grease gun, control wheel, fuel-oil pressure gauge and two levers for the fuel system (behind the control wheel), clock, ignition lock, RPM indicator, starter magneto, air pump. Not visible behind the control wheel is a St. Christopher Medal carried as a good luck charm.*

World War broke out most Steel *Taube* were assigned to the air corps.

Five original *Taube* built by Etrich, Hübner, Jeannin and Rumpler (2) survive in museums in Austria, Germany and Norway. As well there exist six reconstructions of Etrich and Rumpler *Taube* in Germany, Austria and the USA.

The interior photographs presented here depict the Jeannin Steel *Taube* in the German Museum of Technology in Berlin and a reconstructed Rumpler *Taube* of 1913 in the *Luftwaffe* Museum in Gatow. The Jeannin *Taube* was used as a model for this reconstruction.

The equipment of the Taube was typical for an aircraft of the pioneering period of aviation. Its development continued into a period when aviation made dramatic advances. As a result its instrumentation changed from a few simple instruments in the early days to a degree of standardization at the beginning of the First World War.

The German air corps issued a technical description in which it specified the following equipment for the 1914 Jeannin Steel *Taube*:

1 RPM indicator
2 Fuel pressure gauge
3 Fuel contents gauge
4 Ignition switch
5 Starting magneto
6 Grease gun
7 Fuel system air pump
8 Control wheel
9 Throttle lever, latching
10 Ignition timing control lever
11 Two fuel cocks

Given the number of *Taube* built, the variations in equipment described here can only be seen as examples.

In the first *Taube* the instruments were placed wherever there was a suitable location, such as the steel framework of the fuselage around the pilot's seat. Later aircraft were provided with a rudimentary instrument panel in which the most important instruments were placed in view of the pilot.

The First World War, 1914 to 1918

As so often in history, war acted as a motor to accelerate the development of aviation technology. The military soon recognized the potential of the aircraft and both sides strove to achieve superiority over the other in the field of aviation. The military use of aircraft in ever growing numbers produced a demand for simplified production, increased performance and standardized equipment. The aviation industry and the aviation ministry in Berlin began developing and testing equipment designed specifically for aviation purposes. The larger aircraft in particular became gathering places for every possible invention, from gyroscopic devices to communications systems. During the course of the First World War standardized equipment was developed for most German aircraft, which as a rule were single-engined with a crew of one or two. This standard equipment was depicted in Erblich's *Fliegerschule* in 1918. It can only serve as an example, however, as equipment and its location varied a great deal for technical reasons.

In the placing of instruments a differentiation was made between so-called "Frontal" and "Auxiliary" equipment. The most important devices were placed in front of the pilot, while secondary systems were placed wherever there was space, according to importance.

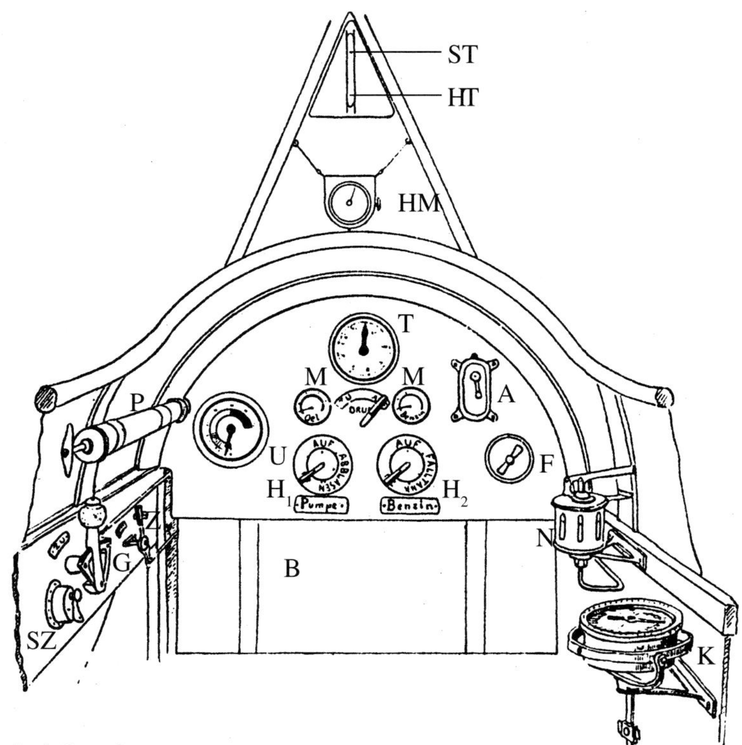

Cockpit Interior

G = throttle lever; Z = ignition timing control; SZ = cutout switch; P = hand pump for pressure; U = fuel gauge; T = RPM indicator; A = starter; H and H = cocks for pressure and fuel lines; M = manometer for oil and fuel pressure; F = grease gun for lubricating the water pump; N = oil pump for lubrication of the camshaft; B = fuel tank; HT = auxiliary tank; ST = sight glass; HM = altimeter; K = compass.

Diese Zeichnung aus dem Buch »Fliegerschule« von Erblich von 1918 zeigt die typische Ausstattung eines einmotorigen deutschen Flugzeugs aus dieser Zeit. Im Detail konnte sie jedoch von Typ zu Typ und aus technischen Gründen variieren.

Frontal Equipment:

- **RPM indicator**
- **Pitch indicator, later also artificial horizon**

Usually installed in larger aircraft, placed at eye level next to the RPM indicator.

- **Airspeed indicator**

Particularly important for landing. In Germany most airspeed indicator's were cup anemometers, Equipment with jets or pitot tubes came later and the indicators themselves were attached directly to the wing struts. Airspeed indicators placed in the instrument panel did not appear in Germany until the 1920s. It is likely that the long pressure lines from the jets or pitot tubes to the indicator caused technical problems in the beginning.

- **Vertical speed indicator and accelerometer**

Installed in a few aircraft toward the end of the war.

- **Clock**

Found mainly in larger aircraft, otherwise the pilot used a pocket watch or wristwatch.

- **Command transmitter, optical indicator systems and warning lights**

Used mainly in larger aircraft with the necessary electrical system.

Historical photograph of an early AEG G IV. Visible beneath the fuselage are the bomb racks.

Auxiliary Equipment:
- **Oil and fuel pressure gauge**
- **Thermometer**
- **Fuel contents gauge**
- **Voltmeter:** usually associated with a radio system

Special places were occupied by:
- **Compass:** located as far away as possible from the starting magneto, usually to the left or right of the pilot's seat or in a cut-out in the bottom wing beside the fuselage.
- **Altimeter:** This instrument was usually suspended from springs or elastic cord to reduce the effects of vibration, either in the cockpit cut-out or on the bracing struts above the cockpit.

In some cases the instruments were also grouped according to function: flight monitoring, navigation and engine monitoring. The standard installation in maritime aircraft saw the engine instruments grouped on the left and the flight monitoring instruments on the right. Most of the giant aircraft had separate engine control stations.

It was soon recognized that there advantages to placing as much equipment as possible in a special instrument panel. This made it possible to obtain all important information with one look. As well, it freed up much space around the pilot's seat and meant that he no longer had to constantly turn his head to view the instruments arranged around his seat. With standardization it also became easier for a pilot to convert from one aircraft to another.

For many instrument types, such as pressure gauges or fuel gauges, there were several manufacturers, all of whom initially had their own housing types. As a result of mass production and the need to maintain a stock of spare parts, during the course of the war the Inspectorate of Aviation Forces developed norms and standards for aircraft equipment.

While instrument housings were not standardized as they were in later years, within the various categories of instrument rules were laid down for:
- **Dial faces:** specified the arrangement of dials, numbers, the zero position (bottom left), indicator direction (clockwise) and the color of markings. For optical reasons, black dial faces with white script became increasingly common toward the end of the war.
- **Housing shapes and colors:** various types of instrument, such as RPM indicators, pressure gauges, thermometers, compasses and altimeters, often had different forms dictated by their design, but within these groups an effort was made for standardization.
- **Fittings:** defined flange shape or screw threads, for example.

A general standardization of instrument housings such as took place in the 1930s was still far off, as the technology of the day sometimes required very large and differing construction forms. The introduction of standards met with some resistance, for many manufacturers of instruments, who had amassed specialized experience in their field, saw standardization as a step backwards rather than an advantage.

AEG G IV

In addition to building a number of biplane trainers, the *Allgemeine Elektrizitäts Gesellschaft, Abteilung Flugzeugbau* (General Electric Corporation, Aircraft Construction Division) based in Berlin-Henningsdorf also produced large aircraft. The most successful type was the AEG G IV, a twin-engined biplane with a crew of four. As a result of its steel tube construction, this relatively small machine—compared to the giants produced by Gotha and Friedrichshafen—was somewhat overweight and as a result its payload was rather small.

Cockpit of the only surviving AEG G IV in Rockcliffe, Canada. The aircraft was equipped with cockpit lighting for night operations.

The following instrumentation for the AEG G IV is based on two surviving illustrations:

No.	Equipment	Instrument Range	Manufacturer/ Remarks
1	Turn and bank indicator?		Goerz
2	2 RPM indicators	300 – 1,600 rpm	Morell
3	2 fuel pressure gauges	0 – 0.5 kg/cm^2	Maximall
4	Electric distant-reading coolant temperature gauge* (switchable, for 2 engines)	0 - 100° C	Hartmann & Braun
5	Engine and fuel system control levers		
6	Fuel contents gauge	0 - ? l	Maximall
7	Throttle levers		
8	Selector switch for Magneto 1 and 2 (double ignition)		Bosch ?
9	Ignition locks		Bosch
10	Electrical system switches (position lights, landing light, etc.)		

The following were also probably present, although they are not visible in the photographs:

No.	Equipment	Instrument Range	Manufacturer/ Remarks
11	Starting magneto		Bosch
12	Fuel system air pump		
13	Magnetic compass		Bamberg
14	Altimeter	0 – 8000 m	Goerz
15	Cup anemometer or airspeed indicator with nozzle	50 – 250 km/h 50 – 250 km/h	Morell Bruhn
16	Bomb release mechanism		

* = absent from museum aircraft.

The aircraft's handling characteristics were good, although longitudinal stability was marginal. As a result, the nose position was rarely occupied and the aircraft was usually flown by a crew of three.

In 1918 AEG modified a G IV in attempt to use ram air to improve engine performance at higher altitudes. Horns were mounted in the nose which sucked in air and fed it to the carburettors. The experiment was a failure, however. Subsequent efforts at improving high altitude performance were more successful. On 30 July 1919 a G IV with supercharged engines reached a height of 6 100 meters with eight persons on board. A total of 216 machines was built, and Fokker built 100 fuselages to speed production.

Only one AEG G IV has survived. Aircraft G. 574/18 was built in 1918 and is currently on display in the Canadian National Aviation Museum in Rockcliffe, Ontario.

Compared to contemporary single-seaters, the AEG G IV had a relatively large amount of room for the crew. The pilot's seat was on the left and most of the instruments and controls were grouped there. Some machines were fitted with dual controls.

Equipment was largely similar to that of single-engined machines, but with the addition of equipment required by two engines. Some aircraft were also equipped with cockpit lighting for night missions.

Albatros D V

Mid-1916 saw a restructuring of the German fighter arm. At the urging of fighter ace Oswald Boelcke, the Inspectorate of Aviation Forces (*IdFlieg*) accelerated the formation of fighter squadrons (*Jastas*), units equipped solely with fighter aircraft. The move proved an immediate success, and April 1917 came to be known to the Allied air forces as "Bloody April".

The story of the Albatros fighter aircraft is linked to this upswing in the fortunes of the German fighter arm. Located in Johannisthal, Albatros had a number of gifted designers who were not satisfied to merely copy captured Nieuports.

Heavily retouched photograph of the cockpit of another AEG G IV. A Bruhn airspeed indicator has been installed at the top left and visible to the right of the control wheel is the indicator for the switchable distant-reading thermometer.

They developed a small, sleek biplane with a clean semi-monocoque plywood fuselage and a number of advanced design features. The first Albatros fighters, the D I and D II, soon proved superior to all enemy machines and Allied air superiority was ended within a matter of a few weeks.

The improved D III powered by a 160-H.P. Mercedes engine appeared by the end of 1916 and more than 1,300 examples were built. The chord of the bottom wing had been reduced considerably to improve the pilot's downward view. Reducing the strength of the bottom wing soon proved to be a mistake, however, as the number of aircraft lost from wing failures began to climb.

In May 1917 Albatros introduced the improved D V with a 180-H.P. Mercedes engine. It differed from its predecessors mainly in having a fuselage of oval cross-section.

The D V and the slightly improved D Va were built in large numbers, however only a few saw front-line service as the problem of the weak bottom wing had never been solved. Of all the Albatros D types only two original D Va have survived. As well, a number of replicas have been built.

The interior photographs depict Albatros D Va 5390/17 of the Australian War Memorial in Canberra. This aircraft force-landed in English-held territory following air combat on 17 December 1917. It was restored to near original condition in 1966. The aircraft's equipment is no longer complete, however it does give a good impression of the equipment installed in a German fighter aircraft of 1917.

The type did not have a complete instrument panel, instead instruments were grouped in small panels, which were then called

Albatros D Va 5390/17 of the Australian War Memorial in Canberra. (E.A. Watson via Merrick)

Left side of the cockpit of D Va 5390/17. The machine is largely in original condition apart from a few missing items such as the starter magneto and RPM indicator.

Right side of the cockpit. The fuel gauge and grease gun are clearly visible. The fuel pressure gauge and compass are hidden. (K.A. Merrick)

Equipment of the Albatros D Va:

No.	Equipment	Instrument Range	Manufacturer/Remarks
1	Ignition lock		Bosch
2	Ignition timing control lever		
3	Starting magneto *		Bosch
4	Auxiliary throttle lever *		
5	Throttle lever (on the control stick)		
6	RPM indicator	200 – 1,600 rpm	Morell
7	Fuel pressure gauge (obscured by cross-member in photograph)	0 – 0.5 kg/cm²	Maximall
8	Fuel pressure gauge control lever		
9	Main tank / reserve tank selector lever		
10	Engine pump / hand pump selector lever		
11	Reserve fuel / pressurized fuel selector lever		
12	Lever for fuel air purge (bottom of switchboard)		
13	Fuel contents gauge		Maximall
14	Fuel system air pump		
15	Water pump grease gun		Stauffer
16	Magnetic compass (right, next to the pilot's seat)		Bamberg, Pfadfinder
17	Cup anemometer (on starboard wing strut)	50 – 250 km/h	Morell
18	Ammunition magazine		
19	Radiator flap position lever (on upper wing)		
20	Pressure release lever (on engine)		

The items marked with an asterisk are absent from the Australian museum aircraft. An altimeter or clock were rarely installed in a D Va and then only at the request of the pilot.

"Switchboards". Items of equipment were arranged about the pilot's seat wherever a suitable location presented itself. Nevertheless, some standards were already apparent.

To the pilot's left were the ignition and starter equipment. Situated in front of the pilot, the RPM indicator was the most important engine instrument. Other engine instruments and controls plus the fuel system levers were located on the right. The operating lever placard was made of pressed zinc sheet.

On the right side of the cockpit floor next to the pilot's seat was the compass, as far away from the starting magneto as possible. The cup anemometer which served as airspeed indicator was affixed to the starboard wing strut outside the propeller thrust area.

A squadron of Fokker E IIIs in front of the then standard hangar tents on a front-line airfield.

The right side of the cockpit of the replica in the Luftwaffe *Museum. Some lines remain to be added.*

Instruments from a Fokker E III. From left: the altimeter (to 5000 m, Bohne) with elastic cords and clips for mounting; the magnetic compass (Plath) and rearview mirror. Beneath the compass is the manufacturer's plate, which was usually affixed to the engine cowling: Type M 14, serial number 488, year built 1916. (SHAA via Couderchon)

Fokker E III

This famous monoplane had its origins in a French Morane-Saulnier H acquired by Anthony Fokker in 1913. From it, Fokker's designer Kreutzer developed the M 5 monoplane powered by a rotary engine. Following the outbreak of war, the type was produced as an artillery spotter.

On 18 April 1915 the French ace Garros was forced down on the German side of the lines. His Morane was found to be equipped with an unsynchronized machine gun firing through the propeller disc. Bullet deflectors protected the propeller blades from errant rounds.

Fokker examined the aircraft and his engineers subsequently developed a synchronization system which prevented the gun from firing whenever a propeller blade was in front of the muzzle. Initial trials were carried out with an M 5 monoplane. This was followed by the E III monoplane, which appeared in August 1915. It was with this type that Boelcke and Immelmann developed their successful tactics. Thus aerial warfare had its true beginnings at the end of 1915.

The Fokker monoplanes were so successful that the Allies came to speak of a "Fokker Scourge". They assured German superiority in the air until the spring of 1916. Then an E III was forced down in Allied territory and it was not long before English and French machines were equipped "à la Fokker". The E III monoplanes period of dominance was over.

Of the 258 machines built, only one original survives, in the Science Museum in London.

The aircraft's legendary reputation and its relatively simple construction have led a number of museums and enthusiasts to construct replicas of the Fokker E III, about 15 all told. Some of the interior photographs presented here depict a replica in the *Luftwaffe* Museum in Berlin-Gatow. A comparison with historical photographs confirms the accuracy of the replica.

Cockpit of a Fokker E III captured by the Allies, probably serial number 488 built in 1916. Note the pattern on the aluminum sheet applied with a wire brush and the leather pads on the stick grip. (SHAA via Couderchon)

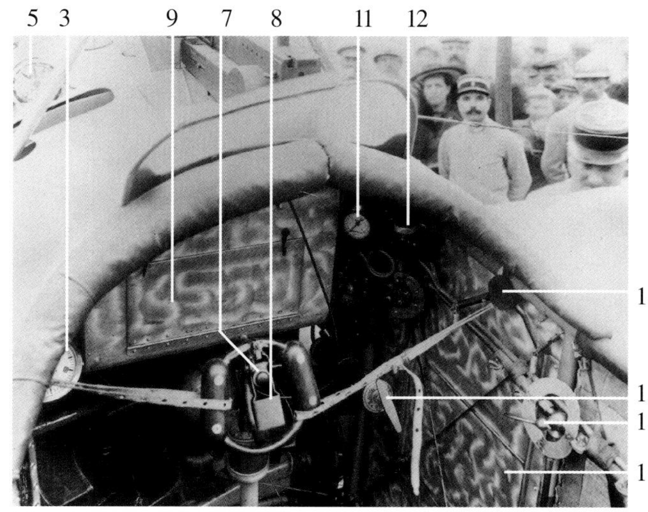

The right side of the cockpit with the oil system controls. The altimeter is missing, however its mount may be seen on the right. Visible on the engine cowling forward of the windscreen are the fuel gauge (left) and machine-gun (right). (SHAA via Couderchon)

Equipment of a Fokker E III:

No.	Equipment	Instrument Range	Manufacturer/Remarks
1	Throttle lever		
2	Fuel cock		
3	RPM indicator	300 – 1,600 rpm	Morell
4	Ignition lock for rotary engines		Bosch
5	Fuel contents gauge	0 – 160 l ?	Maximall
6	Control stick		
7	Pushbutton for ignition cut-off		
8	Machine-gun firing lever		
9	Magazine		
10	Machine-gun synchronization control lever		
11	Oil pressure gauge	0 – 6 meters of water	
12	Pulsometer (sight glass which indicated pulsing of oil pressure with oil pump operating)		
13	Oil system control lever		
14	Altimeter (*)	0 – 5000 m	Bohne
15	Fuel system air pump		
16	"Pfadfinder" compass		Plath
17	Map case (bottom left, next to the control stick)		
18	Sliding covers over windows on floor and fuselage sides		
19	Rear-view mirror (*)		

(*) Not in all machines

The Fokker E III was a pioneer in terms of equipment and instrumentation. A small panel housed some instruments and the oil system control lever. All other control levers and the remaining instruments were distributed about the pilot's seat and were attached to the tubular framework of the fuselage. More sensitive instruments such as the altimeter were suspended on elastic cords or springs or, like the compass, were gimbal-mounted.

The area around the pilot's seat was dominated by aluminum, wood, leather, fabric and steel tube. The steel tube was painted an olive green color, while the remaining materials were unpainted or coated with a clear protectant. The aluminum panels had a finish applied with a wire brush.

Compared with those of modern aircraft, the cockpit of the E III was an uncomfortable, cold, drafty and loud workplace for its pilots. The small windscreen and leather upholstery of the fuselage cut-out provided little protection.

In historical photos only the mountings for the altimeter and map case may be seen. The compass sat in a cut-out in the wing and the fuel contents gauge directly above the fuel tank on the engine cowling. A few aircraft were equipped with an anemometer (airspeed indicator) mounted on the wing outside the propeller thrust area. During the course of production the location and mounting of some instruments was changed based on operational experience.

Following: *The cockpit of the Fokker E III replica in the* Luftwaffe *Museum in Berlin. Even if some details are not historically correct, much care and effort was taken to return the few available original instruments to their original condition.*

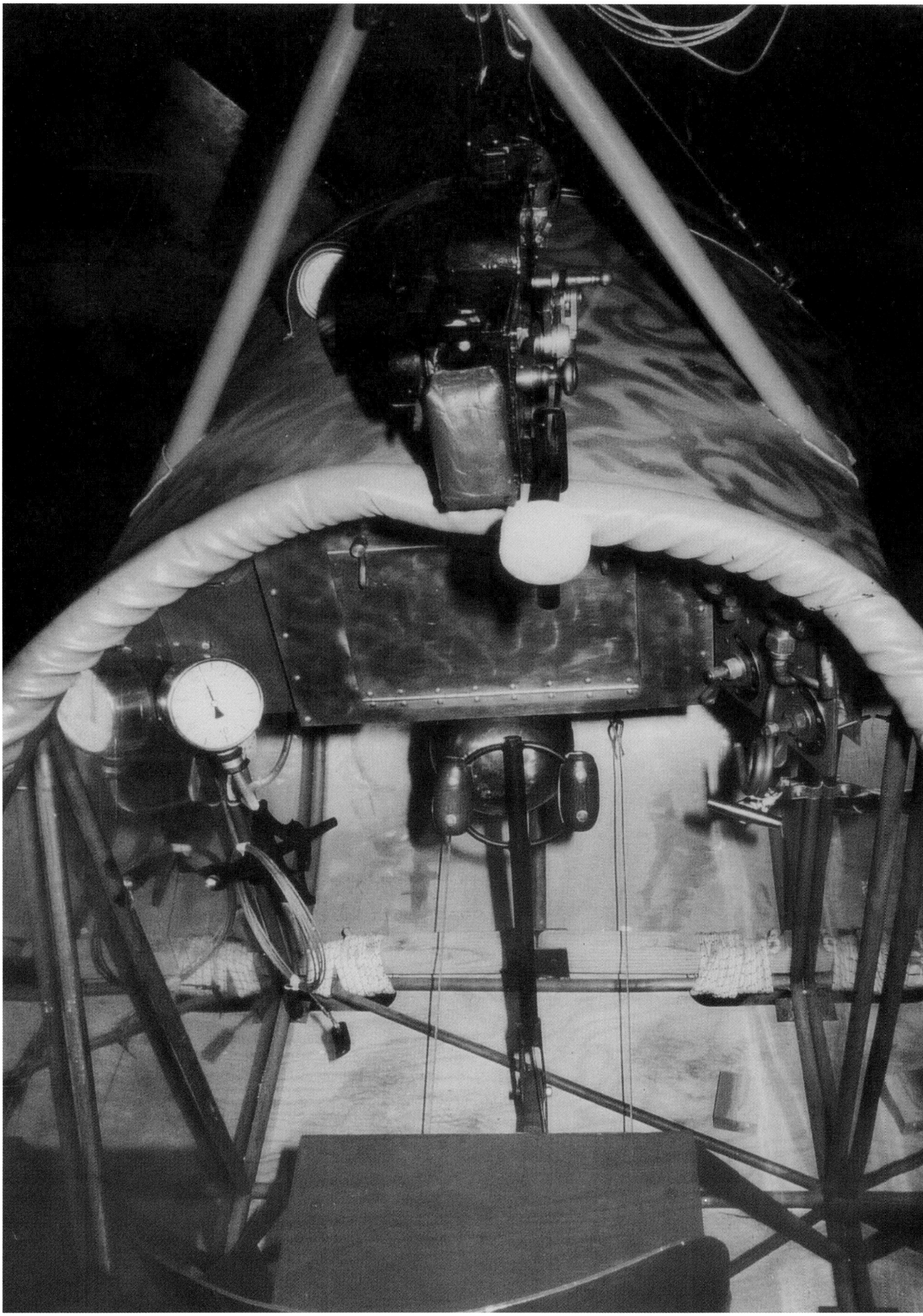

Fokker D VII in the Luftwaffe *Museum.*

Fokker D VII

The demand which the Allies presented to the German Reich in 1919 was clear: "Aircraft are to be surrendered, in particular all Fokker D VIIs." In this way they hoped to acquire more than 2,000 examples of what they considered to be the best fighter aircraft of the First World War. In reality, however, scarcely more than 1,000 D VIIs had been built, and some of these had been secretly moved to Holland by Fokker, while others were hidden in Germany. While the Dutch machines served as far afield as East Asia, some of the German aircraft turned up at a secret *Reichswehr* airfield in Russia where German pilots were being trained.

The D VII was flown by French, English, Polish, Swiss and American pilots. Some appeared in films in the USA, while others were obtained by museums and private collectors.

The Fokker D VII had its origins in a specification issued in 1917. Fokker's design, which featured thick wings and no bracing wires, ran into trouble early in the competition. Its directional stability was insufficient and the machine was nose-heavy, tending to spin with little provocation. As no modifications were permitted, changes were made secretly during the night.

The results were so impressive that Fokker won the competition outright and the D VII was placed into production. Surprisingly, the first machines were built under license by Albatros,

The cockpit of the Fokker D VII (Albatros) in Kamp van Zeist in Holland. Note the air pump on the right. Some items of equipment are reproductions. (Militaire Luchtvaart Museum)

The cockpit of the D VII in the Luftwaffe *Museum. Apart from a few changes such as an additional pressure gauge, French altimeter and the position of the compass and RPM indicator, equipment is typical of a Fokker-built D VII.*

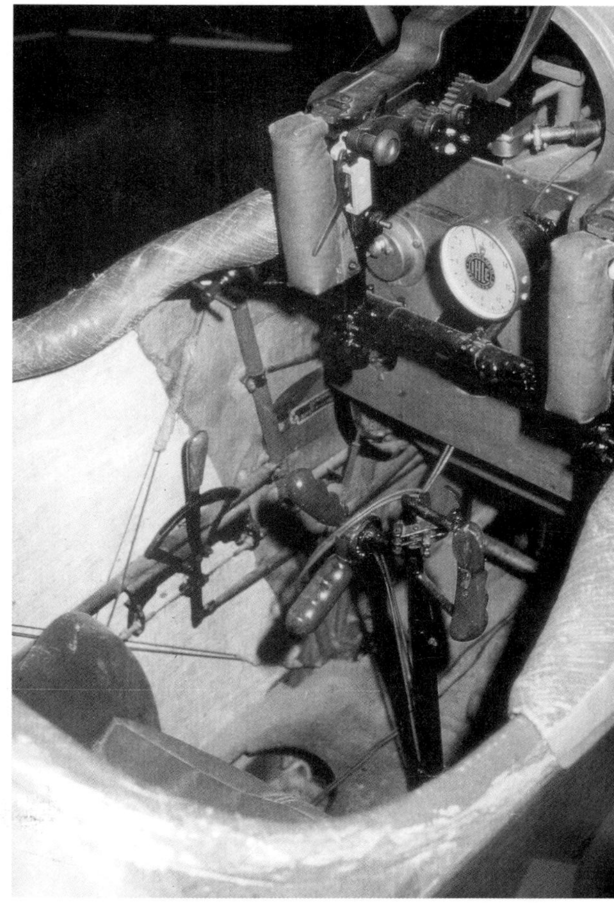

This view of the cockpit of the Fokker D VII (OAW) in Knowlton reveals many original details. An Ihle RPM indicator has been installed in this machine. The starter magneto is missing. The hole in the center of the instrument panel was put there by the Allies, probably for an altimeter. (Ed Stevens)

Fokker's main competitor, as Fokker was already operating at full capacity producing AEG aircraft under license.

The first D VIIs reached the front in April 1918 and the machine soon demonstrated its potential. While not particularly fast, the D VII was extremely maneuverable and had an excellent rate of climb. The D VII's greatest asset in combat, however, was its resistance to spinning. It could continue to climb and turn steeply long after other types would have spun away.

There are many legends surrounding the D VII, but it is a fact that it was one of the few aircraft of its day whose docile handling characteristics could be compared with a modern light aircraft.

Historical photograph of a Swiss D VII, probably an aircraft in the serial range 616 to 622, showing the instrument panel. This machine was based on an Albatros-built Fokker D VII. (Fliegermuseum)

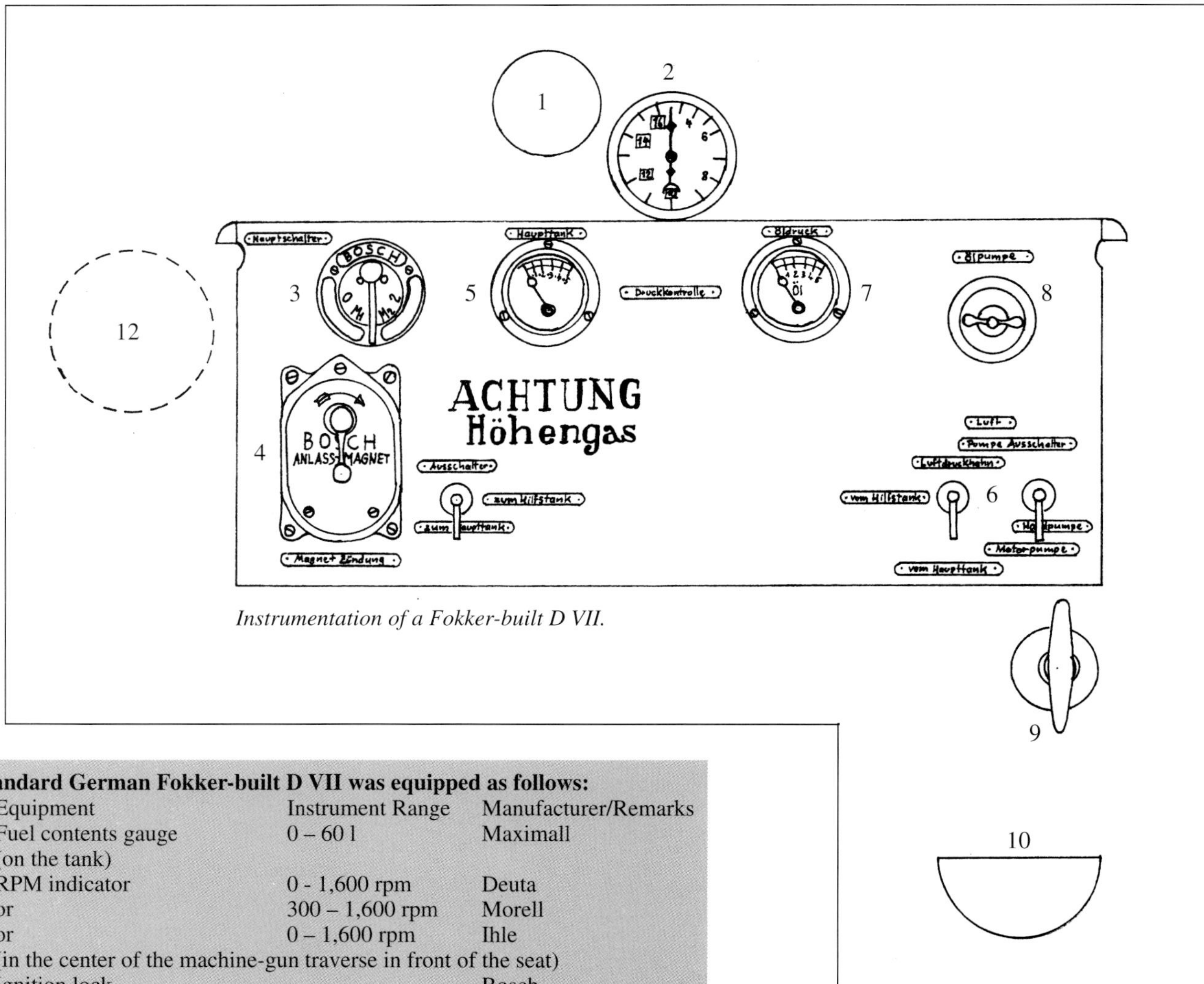

Instrumentation of a Fokker-built D VII.

The standard German Fokker-built D VII was equipped as follows:

No.	Equipment	Instrument Range	Manufacturer/Remarks
1	Fuel contents gauge (on the tank)	0 – 60 l	Maximall
2	RPM indicator	0 - 1,600 rpm	Deuta
	or	300 – 1,600 rpm	Morell
	or	0 – 1,600 rpm	Ihle
	(in the center of the machine-gun traverse in front of the seat)		
3	Ignition lock		Bosch
4	Starter magneto		Bosch
5	Fuel pressure gauge	0 – 0.5 kg/cm²	Maximall
6	Fuel system control lever		
7	Oil pressure gauge *	0 – 5 kg/cm²	Maximall
	or	0 – 6 meters of water	
	(not in all Albatros-built aircraft)		
8	Grease gun for the water or oil pump (on the left of the machine-gun traverse or in instrument panel *)		
9	Fuel system air pump		
10	Magnetic compass (to the right of the pilot's seat. Part of the compensating mechanism projected through the floorboards.)		Bamberg
11	Cup anemometer (on the left or right wing strut)	50 – 250 km/h	Morell
12	Altimeter (on the right or left* side of the fuselage, suspended from springs or elastic cords. Not in all aircraft.)	0 – 8000 m	Goerz

* Variants of Fokker-built machines (see drawings above left and right).

Seven original aircraft and a reconstruction with an original fuselage survive worldwide. A number of replicas have also been built.

Some of the photographs presented here depict the following aircraft:

• Fokker D VII (436/18) on display in the Militaire Luchtvaart Museum in Holland in Dutch markings (Number 266).

• Fokker D VII (4404/18) in the Deutsches Museum in Munich. Many features of this machine suggest that it served after 1918, probably in Holland.

• Fokker D VII (Alb) 6810/18 in the Brome County Historical Museum in Canada. Built under license by Albatros, this machine is closer to original condition than any of the other survivors, although a number of panels and control surfaces come from four other D VIIs.

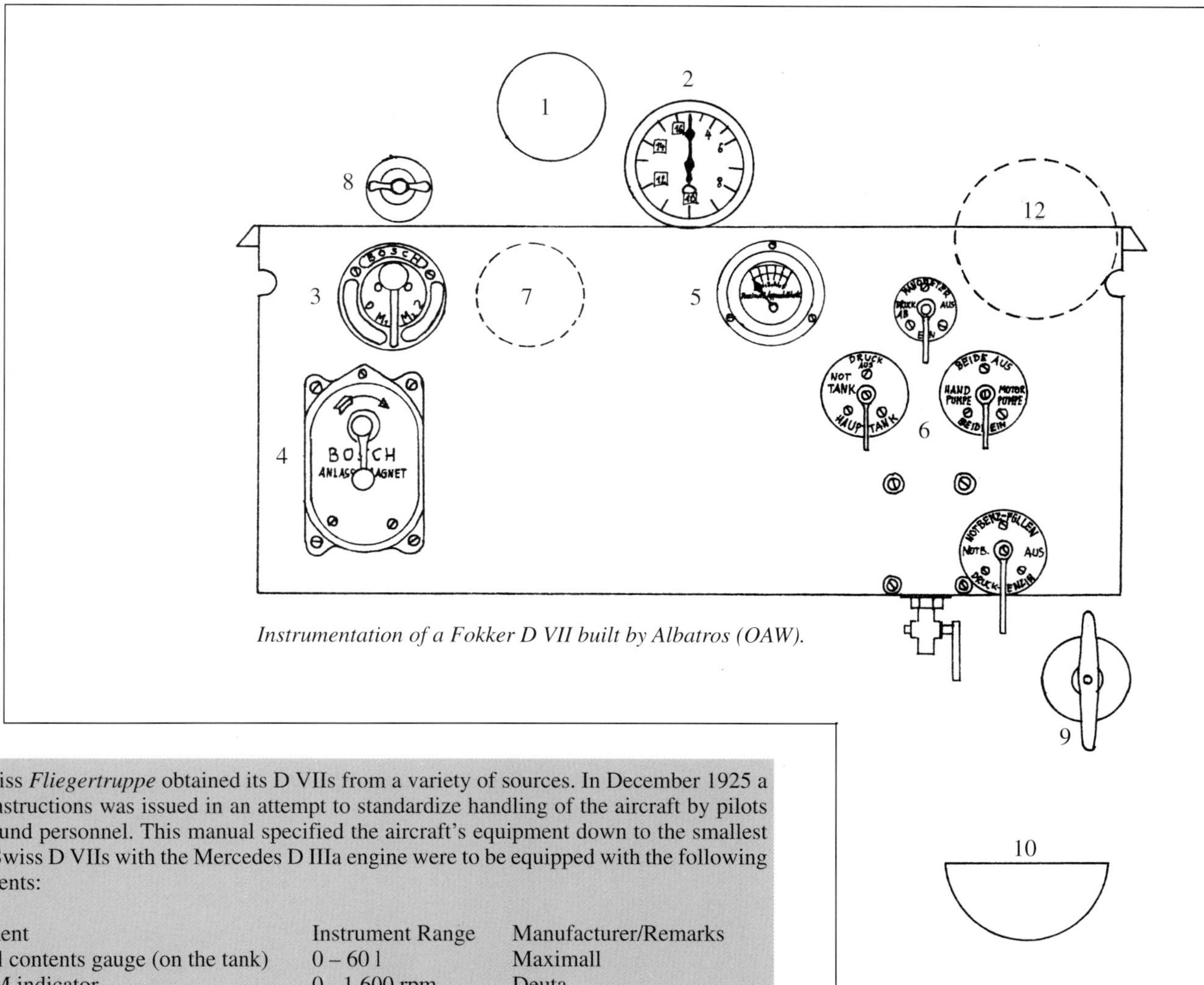

Instrumentation of a Fokker D VII built by Albatros (OAW).

The Swiss *Fliegertruppe* obtained its D VIIs from a variety of sources. In December 1925 a set of instructions was issued in an attempt to standardize handling of the aircraft by pilots and ground personnel. This manual specified the aircraft's equipment down to the smallest detail. Swiss D VIIs with the Mercedes D IIIa engine were to be equipped with the following instruments:

Equipment	Instrument Range	Manufacturer/Remarks
• Fuel contents gauge (on the tank)	0 – 60 l	Maximall
• RPM indicator (in the center of the machine-gun traverse in front of the seat)	0 - 1,600 rpm	Deuta
• Ignition lock		Bosch
• Starter magneto		Bosch
• Fuel pressure gauge	0 – 0.5 kg/cm_2	Maximall
• Fuel system control lever		
• Oil pressure gauge deleted		
• Grease gun for the water or oil pump (on the left of the machine-gun traverse or in instrument panel *)		
• Fuel system air pump		
• Magnetic compass (in floorboards)		Bamberg
• Airspeed indicator (in the instrument panel, the associated nozzle was at the top of the left wing strut)	50 – 250 km/h	Bruhn
• Altimeter (in the instrument panel)	0 – 6000 m	Zenith
• Distant-reading thermometer (in or on the instrument panel)	30 – 100° C	Stoppani
• Clock with eight-day mechanism (in instrument panel)		Zenith

Photographs show that there were also many deviations.

The D VII was one of the few Fokker types with a true instrument panel. The shape of the panel and arrangement of instruments differed between Fokker- and Albatros-built machines. For simplicity's sake, the latter incorporated some features of the Albatros D Va, in particular in the area of the fuel system.

Halberstadt CL IV (Rol) 8103/18 in the Flugwerft Schleissheim. The upper and lower surfaces of the wings are covered in different camouflage pattern fabric. The anemometer is missing from the starboard wing strut.

Halberstadt CL IV

At the beginning of 1918 the Halberstädter Flugzeugwerke brought out the CL IV, a light reconnaissance and bomber aircraft. Apart from a number of design improvements, such as a fully enclosed engine, the aircraft was largely similar to its predecessor, the CL II.

The CL IV earned a bad reputation early in its career after several aircraft were lost, allegedly as a result of wing failures. It was discovered that poorly spliced bracing wires had been at fault. Once this problem had been eliminated, the CL IV served for the rest of the war, by which time 380 had been produced.

Pilots of the CL IV praised its handling qualities. Although it was used mainly in close-support missions, it possessed a number of qualities more typical of a fighter aircraft and was respected by its opponents.

The interior photographs presented here depict two Halberstadt CL IVs with which ace pilot Paul Strähle (1893-1983) operated a civil air service from 1919 until 1923. After the war he obtained

The left side of the cockpit of D-71, a Halberstadt CL IV converted for commercial use. The altimeter was a special installation by operator Paul Strähle. The openings for the fixed weapons have been covered over.

Equipment List for the Halberstadt CL IV:

Equipment	Instrument Range	Manufacturer/Remarks
Ignition lock (WZ 14018)	0, M1, M2, 2	Bosch
Altimeter	0 – 6000 m	Bohne
RPM indicator	0 – 1,600 rpm	Deuta
Fuel pressure gauge	0 – 0.5 kg/cm^2	Maximall
Coolant thermometer	0 – 100° C	Schlegelmilch
Starter magneto		Bosch
Grease gun		
Fuel contents gauge	0 – 400 l	Mars
Compass		Bamberg
Cup anemometer	50 – 250 km/h	Morell

Cockpit of the Halberstadt CL IV in the Flugwerft. The two large openings in the instrument panel were intended to accommodate fixed machine-guns. The following items of equipment are visible (from left): fuel system control lever, fuel pressure gauge, RPM indicator (in front of windscreen), temperature gauge (top right), starter magneto, grease gun (bottom right) and fuel gauge.

three demilitarized aircraft from government surplus. When the Halberstädter Flugzeugwerke was shut down he purchased wings, fuselages and spare parts.

Halberstadt CL IV (Rol) 8103/18 was restored for the National Air and Space Museum in Washington D.C. It is presently on load to the Flugwerft Schleissheim. It was reconstructed from a fuselage which Strähle had used as a spare and represents a military aircraft with standard equipment.

The second CL IV with the registration D-71 (Serial No. 1447) was converted into a commercial aircraft with augmented instrumentation. It is the oldest surviving German commercial aircraft and is presently in the Automuseum in Langenburg.

During the First World War the Inspectorate of Aviation Forces laid down numerous standards for aircraft equipment. These specified both the shape and arrangement of instruments. These standards were not always maintained, however, for example because of the position of fittings and control levers on the various items of equipment.

Several remarks concerning the instrumentation of the Halberstadt CL IV:

- The RPM indicator was located on top of the fuselage in front of the windscreen. This slanted position made it difficult to read the instrument.
- There was no oil pressure gauge.
- The coolant thermometer was attached directly to a line from the radiator in front of the cockpit and was suspended vertically.
- The compass was located in a cut-out in the left lower wing outside the fuselage.
- An altimeter was not standard equipment, however Paul Strähle installed them in his commercial aircraft as they were very important for flights over the Swabian Alps.
- The placard for the fuel system control lever was made of pressed zinc.

Rumpler C IV

During the First World War the Rumpler Flugzeug-Werke, which had become well-known for producing the Taube monoplane, concentrated almost exclusively on building aircraft of the C-class, meaning aircraft for the reconnaissance and artillery spotting roles. Most were biplanes.

The best-known type was the C IV, of which approximately 2,000 were built, making it the most numerous of all the Rumpler types. Compared to its predecessors, the C IV had slightly swept-back wings and a fuselage with cleaner lines.

The C IV was very popular with its crews, for its ability to reach heights of 7000 meters and remain there for four hours placed it almost out of reach of enemy fighters. It was used mainly for long-range photo-reconnaissance behind the enemy lines. After the war the C IV continued flying in a commercial guise, forming the initial equipment of numerous small aviation companies.

A single complete C IV built in 1917 has survived and is on display in the Deutsches Museum in Munich. It is probably serial

Rumpler C IV in the Deutsches Museum.

number 310, which was built by Rumpler's Bavarian factory in Augsburg and which spent World War Two in the Berlin Technical University. All that survived the war was a damaged fuselage and parts of the wings.

In the years from 1974 to 1978 the aircraft was fully restored by MBB in Ottobrunn. To better illustrate the nature of its construction the left side of the fuselage was left uncovered. Two of the photographs presented here depict this aircraft.

The C IV was a classic two-seater, with the pilot in the front cockpit and the observer in the rear. The aircraft's equipment differed little from that of other German C-types. A large "switchboard" in front of the pilot contained most of the instruments and controls.

The cockpit of the Rumpler C IV in the Deutsches Museum. The top part of the instrument panel was apparently added during restoration. Arrangement of the equipment is different than that shown in historical photographs. The RPM indicator is just visible at the top left. Note the clock on the bottom right, a feature which was not standard in 1917-18.

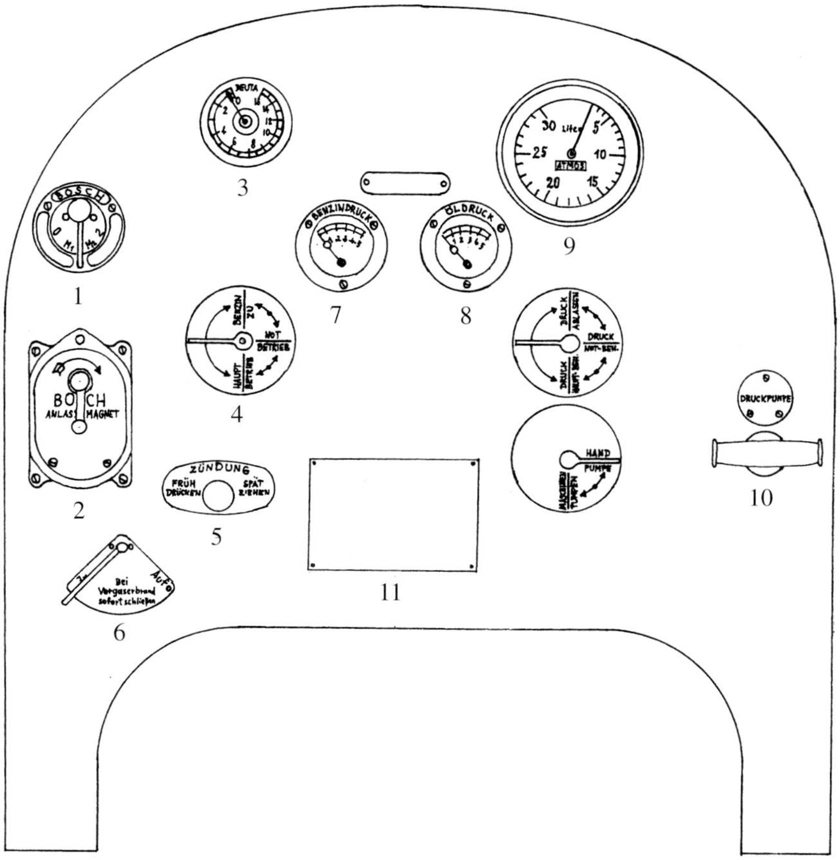

Historische Aufnahme eines Schaltbretts einer Rumpler C-Type, vermutlich einer C IV. Trotz eingeschränkter Bildqualität sind viele Details zu erkennen. Zwecks besserer Übersicht ist das Steuerrad abmontiert worden.

Reconstruction of the Equipment of a Rumpler C IV:

No.	Equipment	Instrument Range	Manufacturer/Remarks
1	Ignition lock		Bosch
2	Starter magneto		Bosch
3	RPM indicator	0 – 1,600 rpm	Deuta
	or	300 – 1,600 rpm	Morell
4	Fuel system control lever		
5	Selector switch for advanced or retarded ignition		
6	Fuel cock		
7	Fuel pressure gauge	0 – 0.5 kg/cm^2	Gradenwitz
8	Oil pressure gauge	0 – 5 kg/cm^2	
9	Fuel contents gauge (?) (This device cannot be identified with certainty in the historical photo.)	0 – 30 l	Atmos
10	Fuel system air pump		
11	Fuel system placard		
12	Water pump grease gun (Not on switchboard)		
13	Coolant thermometer (In line to the radiator in front of pilot's seat)	0 – 100° C	Schlegelmilch
14	Cup anemometer (On the wing strut)	50 – 250 km/h	Morell
15	Magnetic compass (In cut-out in lower right wing.)		Pfadfinder
16	Altimeter (Suspended on elastic cords from the wing struts in front of the pilot's seat.)	0 – 8000 m	Goerz

Unlike fighter aircraft, the C IV had a large wooden control wheel reminiscent of the pioneer period prior to 1914. Presumably this was better suited to long reconnaissance missions.

It has been possible to reconstruct the instrumentation of a Rumpler C IV by referring to the restored aircraft in the Deutsches Museum and an illustration in a book on instrumentation published in 1919. The illustration in the book merely refers to a "Rumpler aircraft", but a comparison of the details suggests that it depicts a C IV.

As may be seen in the aircraft on display in the Deutsches Museum, some Rumpler C IVs had a cut-out at the top right of the switchboard for a fixed forward-firing machine-gun.

The 1920s

The restrictions imposed on Germany by the Treaty of Versailles meant that new developments in the field of aircraft instruments were very slow in coming, and users instead relied on modified wartime equipment. Another limitation was the technology of the day, which in some cases resulted in rather large instruments. As a result of this, the small instrument panels of single-seat aircraft could only accommodate a few instruments.

It was not until *Lufthansa* began its pioneering flights and scheduled operations with newer high-performance aircraft that a requirement was created for more reliable and accurate navigation, engine and flight instruments.

Crossing the Alps at high altitude and flights at night and in bad weather became commonplace. The use of the required blind-flying instruments such as the artificial horizon and course indicator required thorough training and practise, because indications from these instruments did not always agree with the senses and pilots had to learn to trust the new devices.

Gyroscopically-controlled instruments had been used in maritime aircraft and heavy bombers during the First World War, however development of these was temporarily abandoned at war's end. It was some time before the surviving manufacturers resumed development work, but by then they had been technically surpassed by foreign developments, such as Sperry's artificial horizon, and were forced to purchase expensive production licenses.

A gyro-horizon used quite commonly in larger German commercial aircraft was the "*Gyrorektor*" by System Rosenbaum. Development had begun in 1910 and the device was built until 1923. It consisted of a gimbal-mounted, electrically-driven gyroscope powered by a propeller-driven generator. The gyro motor could be switched on by means of a push-button, which made it possible to obtain a horizon indication even after a steep turn. To assist in interpreting readings, there was a spirit level in the housing of the *Gyrorektor* with a ball for bank indication.

Another navigation aid which became available in 1927 was the Askania distant-reading compass system, which was operated by ram-air from a pitot tube. The system consisted of a master compass in the fuselage of the aircraft and a course selector and course indicator in the instrument panel.

The pilot set the desired course using the course selector and this was transmitted to the compass by means of a shaft. The airstreams was directed onto a system of two jets, and any deviation from course produced a pressure differential which was displayed by the needle of the course indicator. The pilot then made course corrections until the pressure differential returned to zero, which returned the indicator needle to the central position.

This distant-reading compass was developed into an autopilot which could be found in many German commercial aircraft until 1939.

In the second half of the 1920s an instrument design standard was adopted in Germany which remained in use until acceptance of the international round instrument standards in 1932. These so-called linear instruments featured vertical linear scales and for quite some time there was doubt as to whether they or the classic round instruments would prevail.

The first of these devices was the control indicator, a double-gyroscope system produced by Autoflug of Berlin (later Askania). It consisted of a turn-and-bank indicator and a pitch indicator. Compared to the large round instruments then standard, this system, originally developed in the USA by Pioneer, saved a considerable amount of space in instrument panels.

Askania later developed a whole series of linear instruments such as altimeters, airspeed indicators, RPM indicators, temperature gauges, pressure gauges and fuel gauges. These instruments had black faces with white characters covered with luminous material. The pointer was red with the zero position at the bottom.

There were two standard housing sizes, with two of the smaller version equal to one of the larger. The small linear instrument standard (approx. 10.5 x 4 cm) was used for temperature gauges, pressure gauges and fuel contents gauges, the large (21 x 4 cm) for flight instruments and RPM indicators. The front of the instrument was covered with flat glass, which was later replaced by curved glass for better readability.

In 1929 Askania offered a complete instrument panel with linear instruments, including airspeed indicator, altimeter, turn-and-bank indicator, course indicator and RPM indicator.

While it was possible to place more linear instruments in an instrument panel than round ones, the former were more difficult to read. Pilot's never really became accustomed to the linear instruments and in ultimately the round form became accepted as standard. The reasons for this are obvious:

- Because of their design, most of the linear instruments had pointers up to 15 cm in length, which made them more susceptible to vibration.
- Linear instruments required more space behind the instrument panel because of vertical housing lengths of up to 17 cm.
- The scale of a round instrument had a greater usable indication area than a comparable linear instrument. For example, the face of a large standard (80 mm) round airspeed indicator was approximately 25 cm, while the comparable linear-scale instrument had a usable length of 17 cm.
- The pointer position in a round instrument made it possible for a pilot to spot deviations with a quick glance.

The Arado V 1, a modern airliner for its day. (F. Selinger Collection)

There were virtually no federal standards at that time, and so each manufacturer of aircraft and equipment developed its own standards. Moreover, aircraft were equipped and painted to meet the wishes of the customer, resulting in countless variations.

Nevertheless, in the 1920s certain standards were developed based on the experiences of pilots and manufacturers:

- Instrument panels were usually painted dark, matte colors to prevent reflections.
- Instruments had black faces with white characters, because for optical reasons this was easier to read than earlier instruments with white faces.
- The zero position of instrument scales was generally at the bottom or bottom left of instrument faces. This made it possible to spot deviations with a quick glance.
- Needles moved clockwise as values increased and most instruments had linear scales to make it possible to read information even with a quick glance. Exceptions were fuel contents gauges, which depended on the type of fuel tank installed.
- The suspension of instruments on elastic cords or springs was replaced by fixed installations in instrument panels. Some instruments were cushioned with foam rubber to dampen vibrations.

The painting of aircraft cockpits was done to the standards of the various manufacturers or wishes of the customers. No federal standards existed.

The most common colors were gray tones to silver. Instrument panels were generally painted dark gray or black to reduce reflections.

The following descriptions concern aircraft with instrumentation typical for the 1920s and early 1930s. With the exception of the Junkers F 13 and Junkers A 50, no examples of these aircraft have survived to the present day.

Arado VI

This mail aircraft of 1928 was a single-engined high-wing monoplane powered by a 500-H.P. Pratt & Whitney Hornet engine. The two pilots and four passengers sat in a fully enclosed cabin.

The aircraft was designed for night and bad weather operations and was equipped with a "*Gyrorektor*" gyro-horizon (an Askania twin-gyroscope device), an Askania distant-reading compass, an outside air temperature gauge, dual controls, a special extinguisher for carburettor fires, landing lights and position lights.

Unfortunately the machine crashed near Berlin on 19 December 1929 after a successful trans-European flight to Spain, the Canary Islands, France and Turkey.

Instrumentation was typical for the 1920s with large, non-standardized round instruments, some of which had their origins in the First World War, however all had black faces with white characters. Two interesting features were the foam-rubber padding to reduce the effects of vibration and lighting for some instruments. The instrument panel was painted matte black.

The list of equipment is derived from a factory photograph. Not all of the instruments could be identified, however, as some are obscured or difficult to see.

Focke Wulf A 32 Bussard (Buzzard)

The Focke Wulf A 32 was a single-engined, high-wing monoplane capable of carrying 6 or 7 passengers and powered by a 310-H.P.

With its large round instruments, the cockpit of the Arado VI is reminiscent of a locomotive. Note the bicycle chains used to transmit control movements to the ailerons, a method used in the pioneering days of aviation. (Arado)

Junkers L 5 engine. Production, which began in 1932, totalled just five aircraft. The handling characteristics of the A 32 were investigated extensively by the DVL, and the aircraft was found to have excellent spin characteristics.

The list of equipment was compiled from a photograph. All of the flight instruments were linear devices. The instrument panel placards were made of polished brass with engraved characters, which stood out well against the black instrument panel. Not visible is the magnetic compass, which was probably suspended from the cockpit roof. Once again it has not been possible to positively identify all of the instruments.

Equipment of the Arado VI

No.	Equipment	Instrument Range	Manufacturer/Remarks
1	Carburettor fire extinguisher handle		
2	Course selector ?		Askania
3	Voltmeter for the Gyrorektor		
4	Altimeter	0 – 3000 m	Goerz
5	Pushbutton for the Gyrorektor (gyroscope motor shut-off)		
6	Course indicator (turn-and-bank indicator and pitch indicator)	+ / - 15°	Autoflug
7	Airspeed indicator	50 – 250 km/h	Bruhn
8	Course indicator for distant-reading compass		Askania
9	FK 6 magnetic compass		Ludolph
10	Gyrorektor artificial horizon with spirit level		
11	Fuel contents gauge with air pump	0 – 300 l (?)	Maximall
12	Unidentified handle		
13	Switch for port and starboard landing lights		
14	Fuel tank switch		
15	Starter pull-handle		
16	RPM indicator	0 – 2,400 rpm	Morell
17	Throttle lever and fuel cocks		
18	Ignition lock		Bosch
19	Starter magneto		Bosch
20	Oil temperature gauge	0 – 115° C	Baecker
21	Unidentified temperature gauge	0 – 115° C	
22	Fuel pressure gauge	0 – 0.5 kg/cm²	Maximall
23	Outside air temperature gauge ?		
24	Gyrorektor master switch		
25	Electrical system cut-out switch		
26	Clock ?		

Cockpit of the A 32. (Focke Wulf)

Focke Wulf A 32 Bussard. (F. Selinger Collection)

Equipment of the Focke Wulf A 32 Bussard

No.	Equipment	Instrument Range	Manufacturer/Remarks
1	Starter injection pump ?		
2	Course selector for distant-reading compass		Askania
3	Altimeter	0 – 3000 m	Askania
4	Pitch indicator	+4 /-4 °	Askania
5	Clock		Junghans ?
6	Turn-and-bank indicator		Askania
7	Course indicator for distant-reading compass		Askania
8	Airspeed indicator	0 – 250 km/h	Askania
9	RPM indicator	0 – 1,800 rpm	Askania
10	Fuel pressure gauge	0 – 5 kg/cm²	
11	Coolant temperature gauge	0 – 115° C	Baecker
12	Oil temperature gauge	0 – 115° C	Baecker
13	Electrical system cut-out switch		
14	Voltmeter		
15	Voltmeter switch		
16	Generator switch		
17	Switch for port and starboard landing lights		
18	Searchlight switch		
19	Fuel tank lighting switch		
20	Compass lighting switch		
21	Lighting dimmer switch		
22	Perspex switch (towed banner ?)		
23	Cockpit lighting switch		
24	Position light switch		
25	Throttle and correction levers		
26	Fuel cock		
27	Ignition timing control lever		
28	Radiator flap control lever		
29	Thermometer	0 – 140° C	BMW
30	Oil pressure gauge ?	0 – 30 kg/cm²	BMW
31	Starter pull-handle		
32	Fire extinguisher		
33	Grease gun		

An He 59 begins its takeoff run. The aircraft has no markings.

The Junkers F 13 in the Deutsches Museum. The aircraft returned from Afghanistan on 1968 and was restored by MBB.

Heinkel He 59

The He 59 was a large, twin-engined fabric-covered biplane with floats which was developed in 1930-32 for the *Reichsmarine*. Powered by two 660-H.P. BMW VI engines, the He 59 was used as a maritime reconnaissance aircraft and until early 1940 as an air-sea rescue machine. Later it was used as a makeshift transport and even a minelayer. Production totalled approximately 150.

The first aircraft were equipped almost exclusively with linear instruments, plus a few conventional round instruments. It is for this reason that the aircraft is included in this chapter.

Beneath the instrument panel were the fire extinguisher, the course selector and the starter magneto, while the electrical system switches were located on the starboard side wall. The arrangement of the instruments was standardized, with the flight and navigation instruments on the left and center of the panel and the engine instruments on the right.

Junkers F 13

The F 13 was the world's first true commercial aircraft to be designed as such. This cantilever monoplane represented a tremendous advance over the open-cockpit, fabric-covered biplanes then in use, most of them former military aircraft. Among its most significant features were:

• An enclosed cabin with four seats, heater and good visibility through large windows. Only the pilots were partially exposed to the elements.

• The fuselage and wings were constructed using Junkers' proven corrugated skin method.

• The aircraft was designed for simplicity and ease of maintenance, which made it suitable for use in remote areas.

• A robust wheeled undercarriage which could easily be exchanged for floats or skis.

These and many other features made the F 13 a success all over the world and assured it a prominent place in aviation history. Developed in the astonishingly short period of six months,

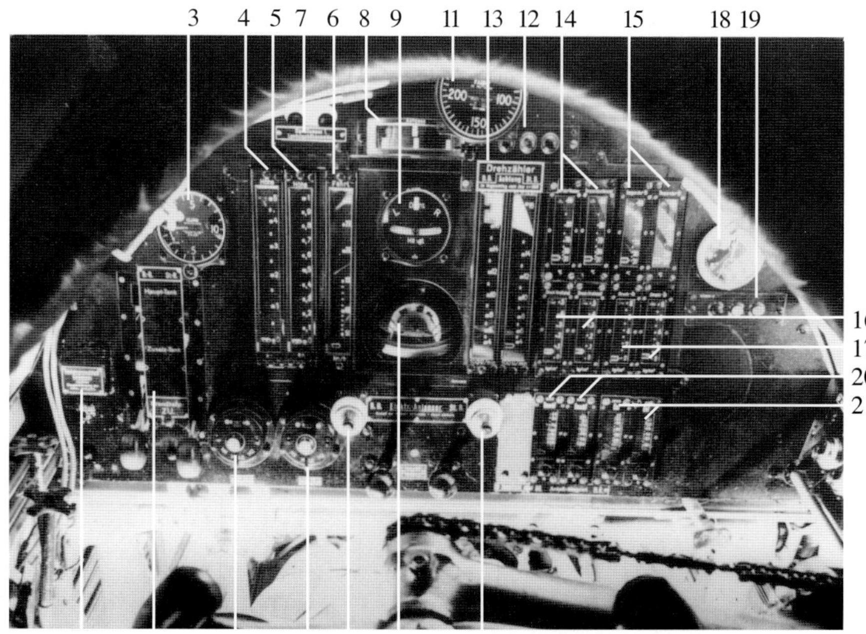

Instrument panel of an He 59 with linear instruments. (B. Lange Collection)
Instrumentierung einer frühen He 59 mit Längsgeräten (Sammlung B. Lange)

No.	Equipment	Instrument Range	Manufacturer/Remarks
1	Electrical system cut-out switch		
2	Tank selector switch and fuel cock for port and starboard tanks		
3	Vertical speed indicator	-10 / +10 m/s	Askania ?
4	Coarse altimeter	0 – 5000 m	Askania
5	Fine altimeter	0 – 1000 m	Askania
6	Airspeed indicator	0 – 300 km/h	Askania
7	Landing light indicator lamps		
8	Course indicator for distant-reading compass		Askania
9	Turn-and-bank indicator		Askania
10	Magnetic compass		Askania ?
11	Airspeed indicator	0 – 250 km/h	Askania ?
12	Intercom indicator lamps		Askania
13	RPM indicators port and starboard	0 – 1,800 rpm	Askania
14	Coolant temperature gauge	0 – 110° C	Askania
15	Oil temperature gauge	0 – 110° C	Askania
16	Fuel pressure gauge	0 – 0.5 kg/cm²	Askania
17	Oil pressure gauge	0 – 8 kg/cm²	Askania
18	Clock		
19	Intercom pushbutton		Askania
20	Fuel contents gauge		Askania
21	Oil contents gauge		Askania
22	ZVZ 12/122 ignition switch		Bosch
23	Starter pushbuttons		

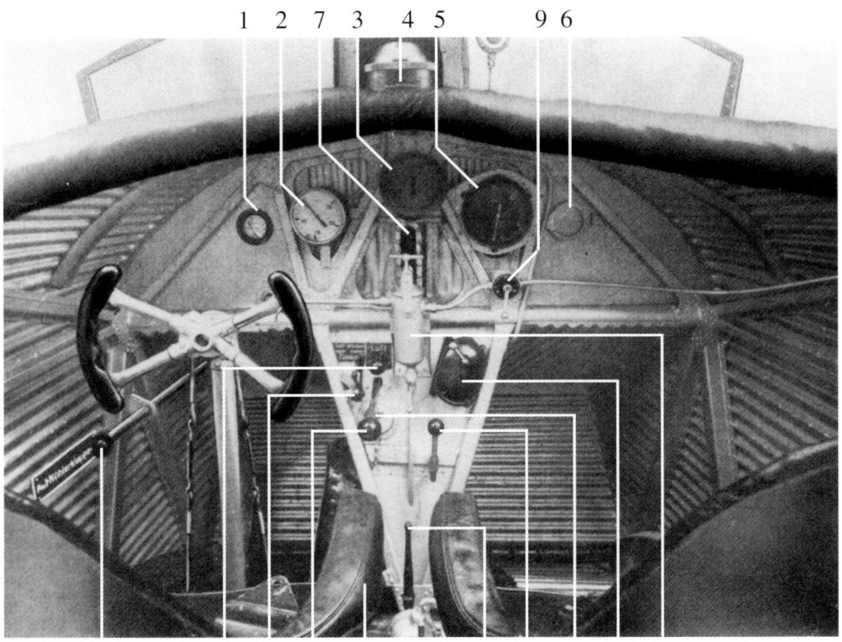

Illustration of the cockpit of the Junkers F 13 from the company brochure. The leather-upholstered seats offered the pilots a degree of comfort.

No.	Equipment	Instrument Range	Manufacturer/Remarks
1	Oil pressure gauge or fuel pressure gauge	0 – 5 kg/cm² 0 – 0.5 kg/cm²	Maximall Maximall
2	Airspeed indicator	50 – 250 km/h	Bruhn
3	RPM indicator	300 – 1,600 rpm	Morell
4	Magnetic compass		Bamberg
5	Altimeter	0 – 8000 m	Morell
6	Clock ?		
7	Sight glass for visual check of fuel pump operation		
8	Fuel filter		
9	Fuel cock		
10	Radiator flap lever		
11	Ignition timing control lever		
12	Mixture control lever		
13	Throttle lever		
14	Ignition lock		Bosch
15	Starter magneto		Bosch
16	Fuel cock (stopped flow of fuel to carburettor in event of fire)		
17	Hand pump for wing tanks in event of engine pump failure		
18	Grease gun (concealed)		
19	Tank selector switch (right/left)		
20	Selector switch (hand pump/engine pump)		
21	Two fuel gauges for wing tanks		Maximall
22	Sight glass on header tank		

the first aircraft was constructed by a team of eight engineers in approximately 9,000 working hours. This haste paid off, for the Treaty of Versailles could well have seriously hindered work on the project or ended it altogether. Initial versions of the F 13 equipped with the BMW IIIa engine producing 185 H.P. were relatively underpowered, however later versions were powered by engines of up to 570 H.P. The F 13 proved to be a robust machine with twice the service life of contemporary types. It was used worldwide to carry mail, freight and passengers.

The F 13 underwent countless modifications and improvements and more than 60 variants were produced. Production totalled 322 by 1932 and *Lufthansa* alone operated fifty of the type, some remaining in service until 1939. The F 13 also set a number of records: a height of 6750 meters with eight passengers in September 1919, an endurance record of 26 hours and 19 minutes in the USA, and in Columbia one F 13 logged more than 400 000 flight kilometers in eight years.

Only four complete F 13s have survived worldwide. The photographs shown here depict D-366, an F 13 fe in the Deutsches Museum, and the F 13 in the Musée de l'Air in Paris. Some are also taken from a Junkers brochure dated 1924.

While the F 13's design incorporated Junkers' experience in the field of metal construction, the initial versions were equipped with instruments from the First World War, which became available in large numbers after the war.

The instrumentation described in the company brochure from 1924 is only an example, as aircraft were often equipped to meet the wishes of the purchaser and were subsequently modified to keep pace with the latest developments in instrumentation.

The fuel gauge was situated on the floor in the center of the cockpit. The gravity-feed tank was located beneath the roof of the cockpit behind the pilot's seats. Cockpit lighting could be installed if desired. Dual controls were also an option.

The Junkers F 13 in Paris is believed to be an aircraft built under licence in the USA by Junkers-Larsen, as the placards in the cockpit are in English. The arrangement of the remaining instruments also differs from that in the brochure. In spite of the missing instruments, the museum aircraft gives a good impression of the pilot's work station in an F 13.

The cockpit of the Junkers F 13 in the Musée de l'Air in Paris. Most of the instruments and the starter magneto are missing. At the bottom are the two fuel gauges and in the center a fuel pressure gauge (Maximall). The type and position of the missing instruments is not known with certainty.

The Junkers A 50 from above. Note the arrangement of the two cockpits.

Junkers A 50 Junior

The Junior was the world's first all-metal sporting aircraft to be built in numbers. The price of the aircraft in 1929 was 16,200 *Reichsmark*. In fact it was this relatively high price and the economic crisis of the day which prevented this technically-superior aircraft from achieving even greater sales success.

Just 80 examples were sold all over the world and the type saw service as an aerobatics trainer, mail carrier, reconnaissance aircraft, courier and sporting machine. Most were powered by an 88-H.P. Armstrong-Siddeley Genet engine. Features included folding wings and the aircraft could easily be converted to a ski or float undercarriage. The A 50 set a number of records and made several long-distance flights, including Berlin to Tokyo and Johannesburg to England. Three Juniors have survived worldwide, and one is still flying in Australia.

No.	Equipment	Instrument Range	Manufacturer/Remarks
1	Throttle lever		
2	Ignition lock	Bosch	
3	Clock	8 day	Kienzle
4	Oil pressure gauge	0 – 8 kg/cm²	Maximall
5	RPM indicator	0 – 2,500 rpm	Horn
6	Altimeter	0 – 5000 m	Goerz
7	Turn-and-bank indicator		Askania
8	Magnetic compass		Plath ?
9	Airspeed indicator	50 – 250 km/h	Bruhn
10	Fuel pressure gauge	0 – 2 kg/cm²	Maximall
11	Unidentified pull handle		
12	Oil temperature gauge	0 – 115° C	Baecker
13	Fuel cock		
14	Header tank hand pump		
15	Starter magneto		Bosch
16	Tank selector switch		

The fuel and oil contents gauges consisted of float indicators over each tank.

Pilot's cockpit in the Junior.

Messerschmitt M 23c (F. Selinger Collection)

The interior photographs shown here depict Junkers A 50 ci, serial number 3575, D-2054, of the Deutsches Museum in Munich. The aircraft was initially delivered to Deutsche Verkehrsflug AG in Fürth with the registration D-2054. From 1931 to 1966 it was registered in Switzerland as HB-UXI. The aircraft subsequently went to the Ulmer Collection in Göppingen. Before it went on display in the new aviation section of the Deutsches Museum, the aircraft was restored as close as possible to delivery standard in 1931. The A 50 design dates to 1929 and it provides an excellent example of German instrumentation in the 1920s with non-standardized round instruments.

The relatively large round instruments are reminiscent of the First World War, although in some cases they reflect developments which took place in the 1920s.

Another variant of the M 23c. Note the magnetic compass suspended from the cockpit framing, which must have hampered the forward view. The front cockpit was somewhat less well equipped. (F. Selinger Collection)

Several remarks concerning the equipment in the Junkers A 50 in the Deutsches Museum:

• The clock is a later model from the 1930s, as it has an Fl number. The type is also known as a "Ju 52 clock" as it was mainly used in that type.

• The RPM indicator is a slightly modified instrument from the First World War, which is evidenced by the location of the zero position at the top of the instrument face.

• The turn-and-bank indicator is an electric instrument from the Second World War (Fl 22407 or 22412).

• The airspeed indicator has an adjustment button on the back for setting the needle to zero.

These later instruments were installed due to non-availability of original equipment. Instruments from the 1920s are especially rare, because production numbers were relatively low and most aircraft of that vintage were scrapped when they were retired from service

Messerschmitt M 23

This single-engine, two-seat sporting aircraft was designed in 1927-28 for the East Prussian Rundflug of 1929. Built entirely of wood, the low-wing monoplane was powered by radial or inline engines producing from 20 to 115 H.P. The initial version had an open cockpit, however the M 23 c, which was built for the Europa Rundflug of 1930 had a new fuselage with metal forward section and an enclosed cockpit.

Most of the main instruments in the cockpit of the M 23 c were linear types. For better readability these instruments had bulged faces with curved glass. The instrument panel was made of wood and was covered with a clear protectant. The following equipment list refers to the rear cockpit, which was occupied by the pilot.

The compass in the instrument panel could be replaced with an FK 6 magnetic compass suspended from the cockpit roof.

Instrument panel in the rear cockpit of the M 23c. (F. Selinger Collection)
Hinteres Instrumentenbrett der M 23c (Sammlung F. Selinger)

Equipment List for the Rear Cockpit of the Messerschmitt M 23 c

No.	Equipment	Instrument Range	Manufacturer/Remarks
1	ZVZ 12/122 ignition lock		Bosch
2	Clock		Junghans
3	Altimeter	0 – 3000 m	Askania
4	Airspeed indicator	0 – 200 km/h	Askania
5	Turn-and-bank indicator	Askania	
6	LKf 7 magnetic compass	Askania	
7	Pitch indicator	-15 / +15°	Askania
8	RPM indicator	0 – 2,400 rpm	Askania
9	Oil temperature gauge	0 – 110° C	
10	Oil pressure gauge	0 – 8 kg/cm²	
11	Fuel contents gauge	0 – 100 l	Maximall
12	Fuel gauge air pump		

The 1930s

The standardization of equipment became increasingly important in the 1930s as the production and export of aircraft grew in scope. This standardization was accelerated by the founding of the State Aviation Ministry (RLM) in 1933 and the secret expansion of the *Luftwaffe*. Already by 1932 the German Committee of Experts for Aviation Standards (FALU) had accepted the international standards for aircraft instruments. The RLM's quality control section monitored these standards and ensured that they were adhered to.

The standards relating to aircraft instruments were developed in the USA in the 1920s and in some cases are still valid today. They laid down guidelines for practically all technical and formal aspects of an instrument. It was desired to limit the physical forms to the minimum possible number, resulting in:

- **Large Standard:** 80 mm installed diameter for flight instruments and some engine instruments (altimeter, airspeed indicator, turn and bank indicator, master compass, rpm indicator, boost pressure gauge, etc.).
- **Small Standard:** 57 mm installed diameter for most engine instruments such as temperature and pressure gauges.
- **Horizon Standard:** 107 mm installed diameter for artificial horizon, as at that time it was impossible to construct a smaller instrument.
- There were **additional directives** for autopilots, radio equipment, indicators and switches. They also regulated fittings, construction materials, threaded connections, methods of installation, colors, the arrangement of dial faces, and even the design of type placards.

The advantages of these standards were:

- Better readability and standardization as a result of uniform appearance.
- Improved interchangeability of equipment, as previously each manufacturer had its own standard sizes. Since the standards were valid internationally, products were more easily exported.
- Simplification and reduction in cost of production.

In addition to these standards, at the end of the 1930s Askania introduced a series of small instruments with an installed diameter of 66.7 mm for small powered aircraft and gliders.

The arrangement of instruments in instrument panels was also standardized. Flight and navigation instruments had to be in the direct view of the pilot sitting on the left. In two-seat cockpits with double instrumentation, these instruments were arranged to the left and right of the engine instruments, which were located in the center of the instrument panel.

The turn and bank indicator and course indicator were directly in front of the pilot behind the control column. The airspeed indicator, which was especially important for landing, was located to the left of the turn and bank indicator, and the vertical speed indicator, when present, to the right.

The artificial horizon and course indicator were also supposed to be arranged on the centerline, however for space reasons these were often positioned to the side. Fine and coarse altimeters were located beneath the airspeed indicator and vertical speed indicator. The magnetic compass had to be clearly visible from both sides of the cockpit. In most cases, therefore, it was located in the center of the cockpit beneath the instrument panel or was duplicated. The clock was installed next to the other instruments or directly on the control column.

The engine instruments, such as pressure gauges, temperature gauges and rpm indicators, were located to the right of the flight instruments or, in the case of double instrumentation, in the center of the cockpit. In the case of multi-engine aircraft, as a rule the instruments were arranged in groups corresponding to the engine layout.

For the electrical system's switchboxes and radio equipment there were special locations and in some cases separate compartments.

The instruments were usually installed in the instrument panel from the front in order to simplify the task of replacement. If the instruments were installed from the rear, as was standard in England and the USA, replacing an instrument required the removal of the complete instrument panel.

In the case of some commercial aircraft, such as the Ju 86 and He116, a shroud was mounted in front of the instrument panel. This housed the lighting system and prevented the lamps from blinding the pilot.

Instruments were usually attached to the instrument panel by bolts and nuts. Occasionally, in the case of wooden instrument panels, wood screws were used.

All items of equipment used in aviation were subject to a certification process which culminated in the issuing of a certificate of airworthiness by an official body. As a rule, this was the *Deutsche Versuchsanstalt für Luftfahrt* (DVL, or German Research Institute for Aviation). Certification included the allocation of a *Flieg-Nummer* (Fl, or aviation number) for aircraft components and a *Luftnachrichtennummer* (Ln, or aviation signals number) for elements of the radio system.

The numbers consisted of the two letters, a five-digit number and, in some cases, an additional number after a dash.

Aviation and Aviation Signals Numbers

An example:

Fl 20222-3	= direct-reading RPM indicator, 600 – 3,600 rpm
Breakdown:	
Fl	= aircraft equipment
20	= engine instrument equipment group
222	= one in a sequence of numbers issued by the DVL
-3	= code for design type, for example gear ratio, type of attachment

The following were the most significant equipment groups:

Fl 18000 – Fl 18999	auxiliary systems (also switches, monitoring devices)
Fl 20000 – Fl 20999	engine instruments
Fl 21000 – Fl 21999	engine accessories (starters, etc.)
Fl 22000 – Fl 22999	flight instruments
Fl 23000 – Fl 23999	navigational equipment
Fl 24000 – Fl 24999	intercom systems
Fl 25000 – Fl 25999	signals equipment
Fl 29600 – Fl 30699	safety and rescue equipment
Fl 32000 – Fl 32999	electrical equipment
Fl 34000 – Fl 34999	auxiliary systems, electrical equipment
Fl 38000 – Fl 38999	photographic equipment, cameras
Fl 47000 – Fl 47999	weapons-related equipment, round counters etc.
Fl 50000 – Fl 50999	weapons-related equipment, bomb release switchboxes, etc.
Fl 52000 – Fl 52999	observation and ranging equipment (reflector gunfights)
Fl 56000 – Fl 56999	lighting equipment
Ln 24000 – Ln 24999	intercom systems
Ln 25000 – Ln 38999	signals equipment, radio systems

The testing station (*E-Stelle*) at Rechlin was responsible for evaluating and accepting equipment and instruments which originated from *Luftwaffe* contracts and were developed according to its guidelines. In such cases another system was used with a category or equipment number.

An example:

9-9548 B	= position indicator for variable-pitch propellers
Breakdown:	
9-	= category engine equipment
9548	= running number assigned by the *Luftwaffe*
procurement office	
B	= design designator

The following is a selection of category numbers applicable to equipment and instrumentation:

8-	= powered aircraft (airframes) and their equipment
9-	= engine equipment
10-	= safety and rescue equipment
18-	= (bomb) release mechanisms
19-500 – 19-2999	= hydraulic equipment
19-5000 – 19-8999	= electrical equipment
108-	= gliders (airframes) and their equipment
109-	= jet engine equipment
124-	= signals equipment
127-	= flight instruments

For special pieces of equipment or airframe components produced for a specific type of aircraft, the equipment number also incorporated part of the RLM type number (8-190, R8-335, etc.).

Otherwise instruments were standard equipment and were used in multiple aircraft types depending on their purpose and operating range. The only devices in which the aircraft type was denoted directly were the Fl 20723 fuel gauges, because of the different tank shapes, and the various bomb release switchboxes such as the ASK 190 and ASK 234.

Both numbering systems were mandatory for the entire German aviation industry as well as for civil and military aviation. Aviation and aviation signals numbers, as well as equipment numbers, were used as requisition numbers for production, logistics and the procurement of spare parts. Some items of equipment had both an aviation or aviation signals number and an equipment number.

In some cases the code Fl E plus the running equipment number was used as a requisition number for electrical components.

(Example: 19-6313-01 = Fl E 6313-01)

The number system was used until the end of the Second World War. In countries where the production and use of German aircraft continued after 1945, such as the CSSR and France, the numbers continued to be used in the replacement part lists.

Overall the Allies respected this system, as it proved to be one of the best nomenclature systems before the introduction of computers.

An Important Note:

In the following descriptions of instrumentation, an attempt has been made to include the requisition and equipment numbers associated with the instruments and equipment. Since, however, replacement part lists are only available for some of the aircraft described, some numbers have had to be reconstructed from photographs or reference to similar aircraft types. Documentation is particularly scarce for aircraft built prior to 1939. For this reason there can be no guarantee that the numbers provided are 100% accurate. Any corrections or additions would be welcomed by the author.

In the 1930s aircraft electrical systems became increasingly complex, requiring a new identification system. A system of letters and numbers was adopted around 1936-37 and it broke down the electrical system and associated equipment into various categories:

A-Equipment
Power supply, wiring system, generator, batteries
B-Equipment
Starter and ignition system, external connection
C-Equipment
Lighting
D-Equipment
Heating, for example for pitot and windscreen
E-Equipment
All electrical drives and monitors for engines and airframe
F-Equipment
Radio equipment
H-Equipment
Electric intercom
K-Equipment
Autopilots
L-Equipment
Navigation and flight instruments
M-Equipment
Engine instruments, fuel gauges
N-Equipment
Photographic systems (aerial cameras)
P-Equipment
Fixed weapons
R-Equipment
Bomb release mechanism and indicators
S-Equipment
Bomb fusing system
T-Equipment
Takeoff-assist rockets, self-destruct systems (for the FuG 25, for example)
V-Equipment
Various, distributors, multipurpose equipment, circuits

Each part of the electrical system, including all instruments, indicators, plugs, transformers, etc., were assigned a designation indicating to which group they belonged (A4, 1D2, F207, L12, 1M4, M17, etc.). In all equipment designators the letter came first, while for circuits the number was first.

Each aircraft type had its own list which was published in the Aircraft Handbook, Part 9 (Electrical System). These designators were used in all construction and servicing manuals.

In the beginning the designators were attached directly to or next to the associated equipment by means of placards riveted in place or decals. Later the information was hand-painted on or beside the piece of equipment, usually in white, but sometimes in red.

On instrument panels manufactured by Messerschmitt or Heinkel, it was common practice to place the information on the side facing the pilot. Others, Junkers for example, placed the information on the back side of the panel.

Until 1936 there were no directives governing the painting of aircraft interiors and instrument panels. Each manufacturer had its own standards or followed the wishes of its customers. *Lufthansa*, for example, had its own regulations for finishes.

Interior surfaces were usually painted pale gray or silver. To reduce reflections, instrument panels were mainly painted dark gray or black. In 1936 the RLM issued instructions for painting the interior and exterior of aircraft. All internal surfaces had to be painted RLM Gray 02, a rather greenish gray. Instrument panels were supposed to be painted Black-Gray 66. Photographs reveal, however, that prior to 1939 some aircraft types had their instrument panels painted in RLM 02 or some other lighter color.

Civil and export aircraft continued to be painted according to the wishes of the purchaser. As well, some *Luftwaffe* camouflage colors were not approved for export.

1936 also saw the appearance of new directives for the marking of various systems. Instruments, controls, switches, equipment and circuits. The following colors (with RLM numbers) were used:

White 21
Instruments, operating ranges
Black 22
Exhaust
Red 23
Fire extinguishers, emergency controls, warning placards and borders
Blue 24
Air
Blue 24/White 21/Blue 24
Oxygen
Blue 24/Red 23/Blue 24
Compressed air
Blue 24/Green 25/Blue 24
Coolant ventilation
Blue 24/Yellow 27/Blue 24
Fuel ventilation
Blue 24/Brown 26/Blue 24
Lubricant ventilation
Green 25
Coolant
Green 25/White 21/Green 25
Glycol coolant
Brown 26
Lubricant, oil
Brown 26/Red 23/Brown 26
Pressure oil
Brown/Red/Brown/Red/Brown
Special pressure oil (brake fluid)
Yellow 27 (or 04)
Fuel (benzene, benzol)

Lines and circuits were marked with bands in the appropriate color. As well, a red arrow was often applied, pointing in the direction of flow. The threaded ring for the glass and the associated housing ring of instruments were usually marked on the front side. In many cases the entire front side surrounding the glass was painted.

In the case of multiple indicators the connectors on the rear also received a color marking. For many instruments there was also a color mask which was applied when the instrument was installed. The divider markings were either painted directly on the face, on the housing or on the instrument glass.

A civil-registered Ar 66 with dual controls for training purposes. Some military versions of the Ar 66 had a radio operator's position in the rear cockpit and a mount for a defensive machine-gun.

The pilot's cockpit of the Ar 66 d in the Deutsches Museum. Although the aircraft has yet to be restored, it does give a good impression of the instrumentation. Missing is the auxiliary panel, which was located beneath the instrument panel and housed the starter injection pump.

Arado Ar 66

Designed as a training aircraft in 1932, this single-bay biplane served well into the Second World War as a training aircraft and, from 1943, was also used as a night harassment aircraft in Russia.

A number of versions appeared over time, these differing mainly in equipment. The principal variants were the Ar 66 C and the Ar 66 D, which were delivered in large numbers to the *Luftwaffe*. The Ar 66 B and E were float-equipped versions built in small numbers. A total of 3,000 Ar 66s were built, however no complete example has survived to the present day.

The Deutsche Museum has an unrestored fuselage of an Ar 66 D built in 1936. The wreck was recovered from Starnberger Lake on 13 November 1983. While searching for a sunken sailboat, the recovery vessel hooked the training aircraft, which had crashed into the lake on 9 April 1945. The remains of six other Arado Ar 66 C aircraft are located in museums in Finland and Norway.

Two examples of standard equipment for an Ar 66 are provided by an illustration from the aircraft handbook and the fuselage in the Deutsches Museum. It is certain that there were other variations depending on the aircraft's mission profile and replacement parts situation.

The arrangement of instruments and controls follows the usual German standards of the 1930s. On the left side of the fuselage are the engine controls, such as the throttle lever and fuel cock. Flight instruments were arranged in the center and left side of the instrument panel, with engine instruments on the right. Equipment associated with the fuel system was located beneath the instrument panel.

Illustration from the Ar 66 c handbook explaining the aircraft's instrumentation.

No.	Equipment	Instrument Range	Requisition/Equipment Number
1	Coarse altimeter	0 – 6000 m	Fl 22307 or 22316-6
2	FK 5 magnetic compass		Fl 23211
3	RPM indicator	500 – 2,400 rpm	Fl 20212 or 20218
4	Connecting hose for the oxygen system		
5	Clock mount	Fl 22600	
6	Fine altimeter	0 – 1000 m	Fl 22316-1
	or vertical speed indicator	+10/-10 m/sec	Fl 22381
7	Turn and bank indicator	Fl 22402	
8	Airspeed indicator	50 – 350 km/h	Fl 22228
9	Ignition lock (Bosch)	Fl 21109 (?)	
10	Electrical system cutout switch		Fl 32301
11	Fuel pressure gauge	0 – 0.5 kg/cm²	Fl 20504 or Fl 20505
12	Sensitivity control for turn and bank indicator		Fl 22405
13	Oil temperature gauge	0 – 120° C	Fl 20335 (?)
14	Oil pressure gauge	0 – 10 kg/cm²	Fl 20606
15	Selector switch for main and auxiliary fuel tanks		
16	Fuel cock		
17	SUM AP 8 starter injection pump		8-4505 A

Beneath the instrument panel on the right are:

Fuel gauge for Ar 66	Fl 20704
Air pump for fuel gauge	Fl 20742-1

The interior was painted according to the RLM directive and the instruments and control levers were painted in the prescribed colors.

A placard beneath the tachometer indicated that the maximum allowable engine speed was 2,000 revolutions per minute.

There was also a switch for an illumination system, navigation lights or landing light, provided these were installed for night operations.

The arrangement of the instruments in the Ar 66 D held by the Deutsches Museum differs little from this. The aircraft does have a deviation table next to the compass and an illumination system for the instrument panel.

Arado Ar 79

When it first appeared in 1937, the Ar 79 was one of the most advanced touring aircraft extant. Its outstanding aerodynamic form and retractable undercarriage resulted in an excellent performance, and the aircraft set a number of speed and range records in Germany and abroad. The Ar 79 thus set the standards for its class, some of which have yet to be improved on by production aircraft. Production of the Arado Ar 79 totaled just 42, of which only one has survived to the present day.

In 1941 Arado delivered the aircraft, which was one of the last Ar 79 Bs built, to the *Luftwaffe*. *Werknummer* 0047 was probably made available to aircraft manufacturer Erich Bachem for use as a communications machine. Its manufacturer's code was VA+HP.

After the war the aircraft was initially used to fly the French high commissioner, then in 1956 it went to the Saarland as SL-AAP. The Arado took part in three Deutschlandflüge before it was sold to collector Fritz Ullmer of Göppingen in 1962. After a complete overhaul the machine flew as D-ECUV until 1969.

In 1993 the Ar 79 was acquired by the German Technical Museum (DTM) in Berlin. As a result of an agreement with the museum, the Deutsche-Lufthansa Berlin Foundation acquired the aircraft for use in its fleet of flying vintage aircraft until 1999. The aircraft was restored and took to the air again for the first time in 1996, now registered as D-EMVT. Later the machine is to be displayed in Berlin as it was flown by Fritz Ullmer in the 1960s, with his color scheme and instrumentation.

Some of the photographs displayed here are of that aircraft. The remaining illustrations are from a company brochure and from a *Luftwaffe* Ar 79 which was flown in Hungary until 1953 with the registration HA-ARA.

The Arado Ar 79 had a glazed canopy with two side-by-side seats and dual controls. The original Arado instrumentation may be determined from the company brochure and photographs of two civil and one military aircraft. The DTM Ar 79 probably also had military equipment.

The surviving machine underwent two further variations in instrumentation after 1945, reflecting the requirements of its owners.

During the last major overhaul while in the hands of Fritz Ullmer, he installed his own instrument panel with former *Luftwaffe* instruments. Some of these may still be installed in the aircraft.

For safety reasons, Lufthansa installed modern instrumentation. Only the ignition switch and RPM indicator were vintage German equipment. When the Arado was returned to the German Technical Museum Fritz Ullmer's instruments were reinstalled.

Arado Ar 79 D-EMVT seen here on one of its final flights in 1999. The aircraft was subsequently handed over to the German Technical Museum.

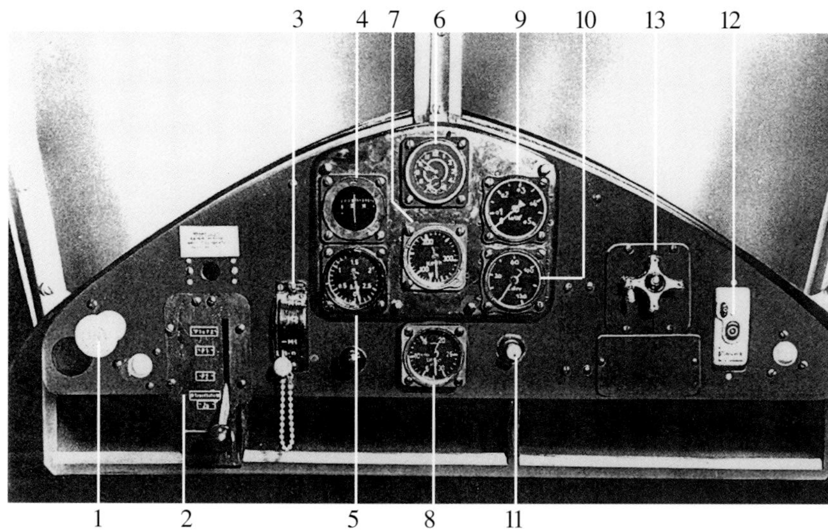

Standard civilian instrumentation with Askania small instruments.

Most of the instruments in the civil version were small Askania ones with a diameter of 66.7 mm. These had actually been developed for use in the small instrument panels of gliders. Beneath the panel were pockets for aeronautical maps.

Like many civil training and touring aircraft, following the outbreak of war the Arado Ar 79 was used as a communications aircraft. The instrumentation of Ar 79s built after 1939 consisted of standard equipment to facilitate the acquisition of spare parts. The instruments installed were therefore both in the large and small standard sizes.

The statoscope-vertical speed indicator could also be used as a fine altimeter. When switched to "*Statoskop*" it indicated even the most minor deviation from the selected altitude.

The Hungarians replaced some of the German placards with Hungarian ones for flight operations in the Ar 79 HA-ARA. The turn and bank indicator was probably a Polish or Czech model. It is likely that the turn and bank indicator and vertical speed indicator were replaced.

It also appears that the fuel gauge was moved to the right, for the fuel pressure gauge was moved down and its original opening covered over. This may have been done by the manufacturer or the *Luftwaffe*, however.

Following a general overhaul in 1962, Fritz Ullmer installed a custom-made panel, mainly with former *Luftwaffe* instruments. He also installed numerous black and red engraved placards.

The cockpit was finished with red artificial leather seats, dark gray carpets and metallic-blue paint, reflecting the owner's tastes. It was rather like the interior of a contemporary luxury automobile. The instrument panel was finished in a blue scale finish and the lower section with the radio was chromed. The interior finish also included ladybugs for luck and Barbie Dolls on the dashing—fitting the aircraft's name: "Miss Evergreen".

For safety reasons Lufthansa equipped the aircraft with modern instruments, mainly American types in the standard sizes.

Civil Ar 79 Based on the Company Brochure

No.	Equipment	Instrument Range	Requisition/Equipment Number
1	SUM AP 8 starter injection pump		8-4505 A
2	Tank selector switch and fuel cock		
3	Ignition switch		Fl 21118
4	Magnetic compass		Lke 1K
5	Altimeter	0 – 3000 m	Lh 1K
6	Clock		Lu 1K
7	Airspeed indicator	0 – 350 km/h	Lr 1K
8	RPM indicator	0 – 3,000 rpm	Ln 1K (?)
9	Fuel pressure gauge	0 – 0.5 kg/cm^2	Fl 20504 or 20505
10	Fuel gauge	0 – 120 l	Fl 20704
11	Air pump for fuel gauge		Fl 20742-1
12	Electrical system automatic switch		Fl 32408 (?)
13	Fire extinguisher valve		

The instrument panel was painted matte black and most of the instruments were installed from the back, as is standard today, even though replacing an instrument requires removing the entire panel.

Compared to the original instrumentation, this is extremely lavish, however the growing number or rules and regulations would scarcely allow any less.

Another variant with civil instrumentation.

Civil Equipment with Modifications

No.	Equipment	Instrument Range	Requisition/Equipment Number
1	SUM AP 8 starter injection pump		8-4505 A
2	Throttle lever, tank selector switch and fuel cock		
3	Clock		Lu 1K
4	Ignition switch		Fl 21118
5	Altimeter	0 – 3000 m	Lh 1K
6	Airspeed indicator	0 – 350 km/h	Fl 22230
7	Electrical system automatic switch		Fl 32408 (?)
8	Magnetic compass		Lke 1K
9	Turn and bank indicator		Fl 22402
10	RPM indicator	0 – 3,000 rpm	Ln 1K (?)
11	Fuel pressure gauge	0 – 0.5 kg/cm²	Fl 20504 or 20505
12	Fuel gauge	0 – 120 l	Fl 20704
13	Air pump for fuel gauge		Fl 20742-1
14	Mount for ?		

The instrument panel of HA-ARA, an Ar 79 B which flew in Hungary until 1953. This photograph was taken in flight: heading 250 degrees, altitude 930 meters, speed 200 km/h and slow descent rate of approximately 2 m/s with engine at 2,500 rpm. (Imre Mitter Archive)

Equipment of a Military Ar 79

No.	Equipment	Instrument Range	Requisition/Equipment Number
1	SUM AP 8* starter injection pump		8-4505 A
2	Tank switch and fuel cock		
3	Undercarriage indicator (four lamps)		Fl 32526
4	Ignition switch		Fl 21118
5	Turn and bank indicator		Fl 22402
6	Airspeed indicator	50 – 350 km/h	Fl 22228
7	FK 38 magnetic compass		Fl 23233
8	Statoscope -vertical speed indicator	+10/-10 m/sec	Fl 22381
9	Air pump for fuel gauge		
10	Fine and coarse altimeter	0 – 10000 m	Fl 22320
11	RPM indicator	600 – 3,600 rpm	Fl 20222-3
12	Fuel pressure gauge	0 – 1 kg/cm^2	Fl 20504 or 20505
13	Fuel gauge	0 – 120 l	Fl 20704
14	Electrical system automatic switch	Fl 32408 (?)	

* not in photograph

Fritz Ulmer's Instrumentation from 1962

No.	Equipment	Instrument Range	Requisition/Equipment Number
1	Undercarriage warning light		
2	Electrical system main switch		
3	Fire warning light		
4	Fuel gauge	0 – 120 l	Fl 20704
5	Ignition switch		Fl 21118
6	Tank selector switch and fuel cock		
7	Mechanical undercarriage position indicator	(similar to Bf 109 E)	
8	Bo-UK 1 clock		Fl 23885
9	Airspeed indicator	50 – 250 km/h	Fl 22227
10	Turn and bank indicator		Fl 22402
11	Fine and coarse altimeter	0 – 10000 m	Fl 22320
12	FK 38 magnetic compass		Fl 23220
13	Vertical speed indicator (Winter, post 1945)		
14	Radio equipment (Friebe, post 1945)		
15	Airspeed indicator	60 – 450 km/h)	Fl 22229
16	RPM indicator	600 – 3,600 rpm	Fl 20222-3
17	Oil temperature gauge	0 - 160°	Fl 20308
18	Navigation lights warning lamp		
19	Deviation table		
20	Parking brake		
21	Fuel pressure gauge	0 – 1 kg/cm2	Fl 20504-1
22	Air pump for fuel gauge		Fl 20742-1
23	Starter injection pump		

(see photo Page 76)

Instrumentation of Ar 79 D-ECUV following overhaul in 1962. Note the two "female passengers".

No.	Equipment	Instrument Range	Requisition/Equipment Number
1	Electrical system switch		
2	Parking brake		
3	Fire warning lamp		
4	Ignition switch		Fl 21118
5	Tank switch and fuel cock		
6	Radio controls		
7	Clock		
8	Deviation table		
9	Airspeed indicator	0 – 450 km/h / 0 – 250 knots	
10	Radio frequency selector		
11	Magnetic compass		Hamilton
12	Undercarriage indicator lights		
13	Artificial horizon		
14	Inclinometer for bank indicator		Winter
15	RPM indicator	600 – 3,600 rpm	Fl 20222-3
16	Electrical system fuses		
17	Multiple indicator for		
	oil temperature	0 - 150°	
	oil pressure	0 – 200 lb/sq.in.	
	fuel pressure	0 – 25 lb/sq.in.	
18	Fine and coarse altimeter	0 – 20,000 feet	
19	Cylinder head temperature gauge		
20	Vertical speed indicator	-6,000 / +6,000 feet/min	
21	Fuel gauge	0 – full	Sky Sports
22	Low fuel warning lamp		
23	Starter injection pump		

Lufthansa instrumentation following restoration and re-registration for flight operations in 1996. (P. Selinger)

Bücker Bü 131 *Jungmann*

Among the many pilots seeking work after the First World War was Carl Clemens Bücker, a former naval aviator. Because of the terms in the Versailles Treaty which limited aviation in Germany, Bücker first went to Sweden, where he established an aircraft factory.

In 1933 Bücker returned to Germany with his chief designer, A.J. Andersson. In his baggage were the plans for a small two-seat biplane which would one day make aviation history. That aircraft, the Bücker Bü 131 *Jungmann*, remains to this day one of the best known and most popular German sporting aircraft,

After just four months of construction work, in April 1934 the first aircraft took off on its maiden flight. The first contracts for the Bü 131, a fully aerobatic training aircraft, were issued while the aircraft was still under test. The first large-scale operator of the type was the *Deutsche Luftsportverband*. In the years that followed, the type was exported to more then twenty countries. It was also built under license in Switzerland (88), Spain (555), the CSSR (260), Hungary and Japan. Worldwide, a total of approximately 4,000 Bücker Bü 131s was built.

The *Jungmann* had a long career as a training aircraft. In Switzerland it was flown by the military until 1971 and in Spain into the 1980s. Most aircraft continued flying after they were retired by the military and some have survived as treasured vintage aircraft or as sporting machines.

Astonishingly, the *Jungmann* achieved its greatest successes after the Second World War, winning numerous aerobatic championships in the 1960s.

In the course of its development a number of versions of the *Jungmann* were built, these differing mainly in the type of engine installed. The version built in the greatest numbers was the Bü 131 B equipped with a 105-H.P. Hirth HM 504. Today most have Lycoming horizontally-opposed engines. While these do little to improve the aircraft's appearance, there is no spares problem.

With about 350 surviving examples, the *Jungmann* is the most common vintage German aircraft. As well, in recent years about twelve copies have been built.

The photographs presented here depict a variety of Bü 131s built in Germany, Switzerland and Spain.

The layout of the Bü 131 was typical for a two-seat biplane of the 1930s with two tandem open cockpits, the pilot occupying the rear one and the student or observer seated in front. In the airman's jargon of the day the pilot was nicknamed *Emil* and the observer *Franz*.

Beautifully restored Bü 131 in historically-accurate finish. D-EAVV was originally registered in Switzerland (HB-UUB) and was probably built by Bücker in Rangsdorf.

Pilot's cockpit of D-EAVV, a Bü 131 B. Care was taken during restoration to ensure authenticity. Some concessions had to be made to modern flight requirements, however, such as the radio on the cockpit floor.

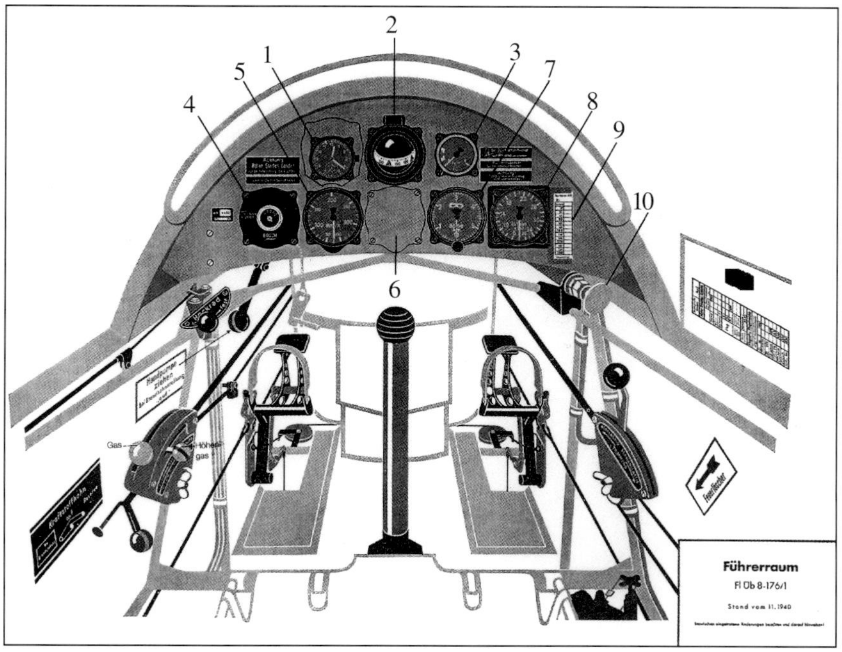

Drawing of the Bü 131 cockpit as it appeared in November 1940.

Rear cockpit instrument panel of a Swiss Bü 131 B (HB-UUL). The instrument panel was originally painted black and was only repainted in light gray when the aircraft entered civilian service.

Bü 131 D, Equipment in the Pilot's Cockpit (rear):

No.	Equipment	Instrument Range	Requisition/Equipment Number
1	Clock		Fl 23885 and others
2	Lke 6 "small Emil" magnetic compass		Fl 23226
3	Fuel pressure gauge	0 – 1 kg/cm²	Fl 20504-1
4	Ignition switch		Fl 21109
5	Airspeed indicator	50 – 350 km/h	Fl 22228
6	Cover plate (planned location for turn and bank indicator)		
7	Altimeter	0 – 6000 m	Fl 22316-6
8	RPM indicator	600 – 3,600 rpm	Fl 20220
9	Nav Vordruck K 6 deviation table		Fl 23906
10	SUM AP 8 starter injection pump		8-4505 A

Bü 131 D, Equipment in Observer's Cockpit (front):

No. Equipment	Instrument Range	Requisition/Equipment Number
• Cover plate (for compass, etc.)		
• Ignition switch	Fl 21109	
• Airspeed indicator	50 – 350 km/h	Fl 22228
• Altimeter	0 – 6000 m	Fl 22316-6
• RPM indicator	600 – 3,600 rpm	Fl 20220

These titles were sometimes also used by the manufacturers of aircraft compasses (navigator's compass Franz or Fränzchen, depending on size, and master compass Emil). The term "*verfranzen*", to lose one's way due to poor navigation, is still used today.

The instrumentation installed in the production Bü 131 was limited to what was absolutely necessary, as the aircraft was intended for initial training in visual flight. For that reason, instrumentation in the forward cockpit was limited to an airspeed indicator, altimeter, RPM indicator and in come cases a compass. It was felt that the student should concentrate more on flying the aircraft than on scanning instruments. Throttle levers and trim controls were present in both cockpits.

An overview of the pilot's (rear) cockpit dated November 1940 depicts in detail the standard equipment installed in the Bü 131 D. The fuel level indicator was a gauge glass located on top of the fuselage in front of the forward cockpit. Its measuring range was 0 to 80 liters.

Front cockpit instrument panel of a Swiss Bü 131 B (HB-UUA). Note the RPM indicator mounted outside the cockpit.

Rear cockpit of the CASA 1.131 E (EC-DJL). With the exception of the radio equipment, the instrumentation is all original and is largely similar to that of German aircraft in 1940. Visible on the lower right is the trim lever. (P.F. Selinger)

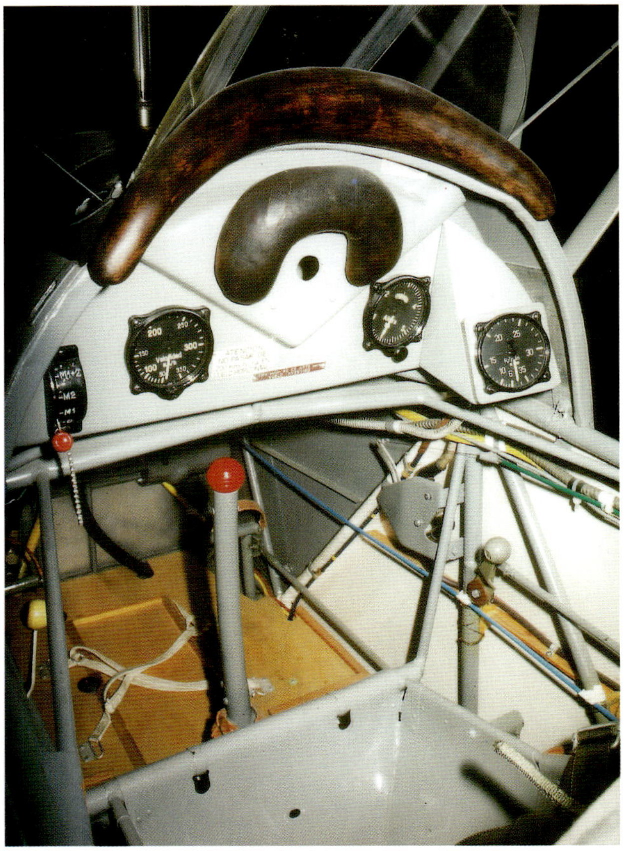

Front cockpit of the CASA 1.131 E (E.3B-555) in the Deutsches Museum. The cockpit has been restored to its original condition.

Bücker Bü 131 (Dornier), Equipment in Rear Cockpit:

No.	Equipment	Instrument Range	Manufacturer
1	Vertical speed indicator	+10/-10 m/sec	Askania
2	Lke 11 "Large Emil" magnetic compass	Askania	
3	Clock	Revue	
4	Ignition switch	Scintilla	
5	Airspeed indicator	80 – 450 km/h	Bruhn
6	Turn and bank indicator	Thommen	
7	Altimeter	0 – 10000 m	Thommen
8	Fuel pressure gauge	0 – 1 kg/cm²	
	later replaced by a multiple indicator for:		
	Fuel pressure	0 – 25 lb	
	Oil pressure	0 – 200 lb	
	Oil temperature	0 - 120° C	
9	Accelerometer	+ 10 / - 3 g	Peravia
	(installed during later overhaul)		

The fuel gauge was a sight glass on the fuselage spine in front of the forward cockpit. Other equipment was later installed, for example switches for navigation lights and instrument panel lighting for night flight.

(see Page 79, top right)

Bücker Bü 131 B (Dornier), Equipment in Forward Cockpit:

Equipment	Instrument Range	Manufacturer
Ignition switch	Scintilla	
Airspeed indicator	80 – 450 km/h	Bruhn
Clock		Revue
Altimeter	0 – 6000 m	Utz (Askania)
RPM indicator	0 – 3,500 rpm	Alpha

(mounted externally beneath a fairing on the right side of the fuselage)

In comparison, the equipment of the license-built version produced by CASA in Spain more closely resembled the German original. Even the German paint finish and color markings were retained.

Instrumentation of the CASA 1.131 in the Rear Cockpit:

No.	Equipment	Instrument Range	Manufacturer
1	Cover panel (for clock or V.S.I.)		
2	A 200 magnetic compass		Telmar
3	Fuel / oil pressure gauge	0-0.5 / 0-10 kg/cm^2	Bressel
4	Deviation table		
5	SH/ZH 2/1 ignition switch (similar to Fl 21118)		Bosch
6	Airspeed indicator	50 – 350 km/h	
7	Oil temperature gauge	0 – 120 ° C	Bressel
8	Altimeter	0 – 6000 m	Telmar (Askania)
	or	0 – 3000 m	
9	RPM indicator	600 – 3,600 rpm	Bressel
10	Starter injection pump		

The replacement parts list dated June 1979 includes additional instrumentation:

Vertical speed indicator	+ 2,000 / - 2,000 ft/min
Turn and bank indicator	
Accelerometer	+ 6 / - 3 g
Clock	

The fuel gauge was a gauge glass mounted on the fuselage spine in front of the forward cockpit.

Instrumentation of the CASA 1.131 E in the Forward Cockpit:

Equipment	Instrument Range	Manufacturer
SH/ZH 2/1 ignition switch		Bosch
Airspeed indicator	50 – 350 km/h	
Altimeter	0 – 6000 m	Telmar (Askania)
or	0 – 3000 m	
RPM indicator	600 – 3,600 rpm	Bressel

Additional instrumentation:

A 200 magnetic compass	Telmar
Vertical speed indicator	+2,000 / - 2,000 ft/min

Several placards gave instructions and warnings for operating the aircraft:

> Attention
> For Taxiing, Takeoff, Landing
> ensure that the lever is in the
> "TAILWHEEL LOCKED" position
>
> secure belts in the passenger seat

> When fuel remaining reaches 20 liters
> switch to reserve

> Maximum duration of inverted flight
> 2 minutes

> Attention !
> Do not exceed 3,300 rpm
> in diving flight

In military and civilian service the aircraft were modified or modernized to meet changing requirements. For reasons of safety and the availability of spare parts, many of the Bü 131s still flying have been reequipped with modern equipment and instruments.

The nature and arrangement of the equipment often reflects the individual tastes of the owner, for the military's insistence on standardization for supply reasons no longer exists.

The items listed above correspond to those installed in standard production aircraft. Other equipment was installed at the request of the customer, especially export aircraft and those with special equipment for experimental or record flights.

Bü 131s built under license had their own instrumentation, however for technical reasons this was usually comparable to the German. The Swiss had their own aircraft instrument industry, and Bü 131 B aircraft built under license by Dornier in Altenrhein were almost completely equipped with domestic instruments.

Former Swiss *Bü 133 C in the colors of a Luftwaffe training aircraft. The stripes are green with a red outline.*

Bücker Bü 133 *Jungmeister*

Utilizing entire components from the Bü 131, such as the tail, undercarriage and parts of the wings, Bücker's designer A.J. Andersson developed the single-seat Bü 133. Initially it was powered by the Hirth HM 506 inline engine (Bü 133 A). All subsequent variants, however, were equipped with the 160 H.P. Siemens Sh 14 radial engine. This small maneuverable biplane attracted interest all over the world, and it soon became obvious that Andersson had produced a classic design.

Beginning in 1937, the *Jungmeister* won just about every major aerobatic competition there was, including the German championship in 1937 and 1939, the competition in Cleveland, USA and the Governor-General of Mozambique's prize in 1938, the Romanian championship in 1939, and the International Aerobatic Competition in Cuba in 1940. In 1937 Bücker chief pilot Arthur Benitz crossed the Andes in a Bü 133.

It is less well known that the *Luftwaffe* maintained an aerobatic squadron equipped with the *Jungmeister* in 1938-39. It enjoyed great popularity in and outside Germany. Its high point was a demonstration at the Zurich Air Meet in 1939, where the squadron flew a

The instrument panel of G-AEZX, a Bü 133 C, is original with numerous placards in German, although several instruments, such as the airspeed indicator, have been replaced by modern ones. The arrangement of the instruments is largely similar to that of later production aircraft. (Vanhee)

Instrument panel of an early civil Bü 133 from a Bücker company brochure. Note the liquid bank indicator in the center, a design originating from the First World War. (Hafner Archive)

Equipment of an Early Civilian Bü 133 Based on a Company Brochure:

No.	Equipment	Instrument Range	Requisition/Equipment Number
1	ZVZ 12/122 ignition switch		
2	Altimeter	0 – 6000 m	Fl 22310 or Fl 22316-6
3	Lk 6 magnetic compass		Fl 23226
4	Lu 3 r clock		
5	Airspeed indicator	80 – 450 km/h	Fl 22229
6	Bank indicator (Goerz)		
7	RPM indicator	600 – 3,600 rpm	Fl 20210 or 20213
8	Fuel pressure gauge	0 – 0.5 kg/cm²	Fl 20504 or 20505
9	SUM AP 8 starter injection pump	8-4505 A	
10	Fuel gauge (on engine cowling)		Fl 20703-2

An illustration from a brochure produced by Askania shows the instrument panel in a later version of the Bü 133. There are some minor deviations from the Bü 133's standard instrumentation. (Soppa Collection)

program with its aircraft connected to each other by ropes.

The end of the war by no means ended the *Jungmeister*'s career. It won the first five German aerobatic championships and in the 1950s the Swiss pilot Albert Ruesch even crossed the Alps in inverted flight.

By the time production ended in 1940, Bücker had built slightly less than 200 examples of the *Jungmeister*, primarily for the German Air Sports Association and the *Luftwaffe* for use as an aerobatic aircraft and advanced trainer. The aircraft was exported to Switzerland, Lithuania, Poland and Spain.

In 1936 the Swiss air force decided to procure the Bü 133 for air combat training. At least three machines were purchased from Rangsdorf, however all the rest of the total of 52 Bü 133 C trainers were built under license by Dornier in Altenrhein. The aircraft proved so successful that they remained in service until 1968. Another 25 aircraft were built under license by CASA in Spain.

The *Jungmeister* was undeniably the best aerobatic aircraft in the world for a period of three decades. While its numbers have shrunk, the aircraft is still flown enthusiastically by its owners. In 1968 a small series of aircraft was built by Bitz in Augsburg and Hirth in Nabern.

Altogether some 70 *Jungmeister* have survived to the present day. Since its conception, the legendary design has inspired almost a dozen copies.

The equipment installed in a production Bü 133 is revealed by the company brochure and the replacement parts list. Historical photographs reveal that there were some changes in the instrumentation and arrangement of the instruments.

The arrangement of the aircraft's controls and instruments is largely in keeping with German standards of the 1930s. Since the Bü 133 was designed as an advanced trainer and for aerobatics training, its equipment includes instruments such as a bank indicator or turn and bank indicator.

Radio equipment was not installed as a rule. Not until the 1960s were radios available that were small and light enough to fit into the tiny single-seater.

The interior shots presented here are of two Bü 133 Cs which are still flying. One is an original Bü 133 C built in Rangsdorf (*Werknummer* 1018), which was delivered to Spain in 1939 and which is now based in England and wears the registration G-AEZX. The aircraft is finished as a *Luftwaffe* training aircraft (LG+03).

Instrument panel of U-95, a Swiss Bü 133 C. Most of the instruments are Swiss in origin.

Equipment of a Later Bü 133

No.	Equipment	Instrument Range	Requisition/Equipment Number
1	Ignition switch		Fl 21119
2	Altimeter	0 – 6000 m	Fl 22310 or Fl 22316-6
3	Magnetic compass		Fl 23226
4	Lu 3 r clock (Askania)		
5	Airspeed indicator	80 – 450 km/hr	Fl 22229
6	Turn and bank indicator		Fl 22402
7	RPM indicator	600 – 3,000 rpm	Fl 20210 or Fl 20213
8	Fuel pressure gauge	0 – 0.5 kg/cm^2	Fl 20504 or 20505
9	Oil pressure gauge	0 – 10 kg/cm^2	Fl 20606
10	Vapor pressure thermometer	0 - 160° C	Fl 20314-2 ?
11	SUM AP 8 starter injection pump		8-4505 A
12	Fuel gauge (on the engine cowling)		Fl 20703-2

In most cases a deviation table (Fl 23906) was placed to the right of the ignition switch. The replacement parts list reveals that there were later deviations in production aircraft:

No.	Equipment	Instrument Range	Requisition/Equipment Number
4	Statoscope-vertical speed indicator	+10/-10 m/s	Fl 22381-10
8	Bo UK 1 clock		Fl 23885
9	Twin pressure gauges for fuel and oil	0-1 / 0-10 kg/cm^2	Fl 20512-1

The equipment listed above is typical of a standard production Bü 133. During the type's production life and in later use there were, of course, further changes which resulted from the supply situation and the wishes of the aircraft's pilots (see illustration bottom of Page 83). After 1945, many privately-owned Bü 133s were fitted with custom instrumentation incorporating modern instruments to suit the wishes of their owners.

The Swiss **Bü 133 C**s built by Dornier in Altenrhein were equipped with Swiss instruments. As they were intended mainly for aerobatic and air combat training, the Swiss instrumentation included an accelerometer.

No.	Equipment	Instrument Range
1	Throttle lever	
2	Mixture lever	
3	Fuel cock	
4	Tailwheel locking lever	
5	Pre-heat handle	
6	Deviation table	
7	Manufacturer's placard	
8	Cylinder head temperature gauge	0 - 350° C
9	Clock	
10	Ke 11 magnetic compass (Askania)	
11	Accelerometer	
12	Oil temperature gauge	0 - 140° C
13	Ignition switch	
14	Visual indicator for cable coupling (glider towing)	
15	Fine and coarse altimeter	0 – 10000 m
16	Airspeed indicator	80 – 450 km/h
17	RPM indicator	400 3,200 rpm
18	Oil pressure gauge	0 – 6 kg/cm^2
19	Fuel pressure gauge	0 – 600 psi
20	Starter injection pump	
21	Fuel gauge (on the engine cowling)	

The second is a Bü 133 C (*Werknummer* 42) built by Dornier in Altenrhein. It served as U-95 with the Swiss air force. The aircraft later passed to owners in Switzerland, Germany and France and today flies in England with a beautifully restored Swiss finish as U-95 (G-BVGP).

HB-SEX, the last surviving Erla 5 A, in Switzerland. (A. Schätti)

Erla 5

At the beginning of the 1930s in Germany an effort was launched to develop a "Peoples Airplane", one which would open up flying to a broad spectrum of the population.

Engineer F.X. Mehr of the Erla GmbH located in the Erz Mountains designed the Me V a, later the Erla 5 A. It was a small single-seat, low-wing monoplane which was easy to disassemble for transport. The aircraft was powered by a 20 H.P. DKW two-stroke engine. A later variant, the Erla 5 D, was powered by a 50 H.P. Zundapp and was capable of aerobatics. It achieved two notable feats in 1939. It flew over three continents (Europe-Africa-Asia-Europe) and set a range record for aircraft in the two-liter class by flying from Lake Constance to Northern Sweden, a distance of 1909.83 km.

Only 23 Erla 5s were built. The aircraft's price tag, 4,000 RM, proved too high and multi-seat aircraft were preferred for economic reasons. The Erla GmbH was later absorbed into the Erla Maschinenwerk Leipzig GmbH, which went on to produce more than 12,000 Bf 109s under license. The last design produced by the company was the Erla 6 A high-wing monoplane in 1937.

Only one Erla 5 A has survived. Registered D-YBIT in 1934, today it appears on the Swiss registry as HB-SEX.

The Erla 5 is a very small aircraft with an open cockpit. Consequently its instrumentation is limited and optimized for visual flight.

A company brochure contained the following description of the equipment installed in an Erla 5 A equipped with the 20 H.P. DKW FL 600 W two-stroke engine:

Equipment	Instrument Range	Manufacturer/Remarks
RPM indicator	0 – 4,000 rpm	DKW
Airspeed indicator	50 – 250 km/h	Bruhn or Lambrecht
Altimeter	0 – 4000 m	Lufft?
Clock		
Lke 6 "Small Emil" magnetic compass		Askania
Coolant temperature gauge	0 – 100° C	
Ignition switch		Bosch
Fuel gauge	0 – 25 l	Maximall
Fuel gauge air pump		
Fire extinguisher with manometer		

Also offered as special equipment:
Turn and bank indicator
Pitch indicator
Fine altimeter
Vertical speed indicator
Instrument panel lighting

In spite of the small number of aircraft built, photographs of four different machines reveal four different instrumentations. In several cases the instruments are the same but the layout is different. Presumably each purchaser was able to select his own instrumentation.

The first Erla Me Vs had non-standard round instruments, which were common in the 1920s. Two examples of this are the Me V, D-2378, which flew for the Auto-Union in 1932-33, and the Me Va, D-2585, which was completed in 1933 and retained by the company for its own use.

D-2378 had a Plath magnetic compass in a bell mount on top of the fuselage in front of the cockpit, obscuring much of the view through the small windscreen. The airspeed indicator range was 0 to 120 km/h, while the altimeter's maximum reading was 4000 m.

Photograph of the Erla 5 A's instrument panel from a company brochure. Note the modified fuselage cross-section and technical improvements over the Erla Me V. (Feige Collection)

Cockpit of the Erla Me V, D-2378. Most of the instrumentation had its origins in the 1920s. (Feige Collection)

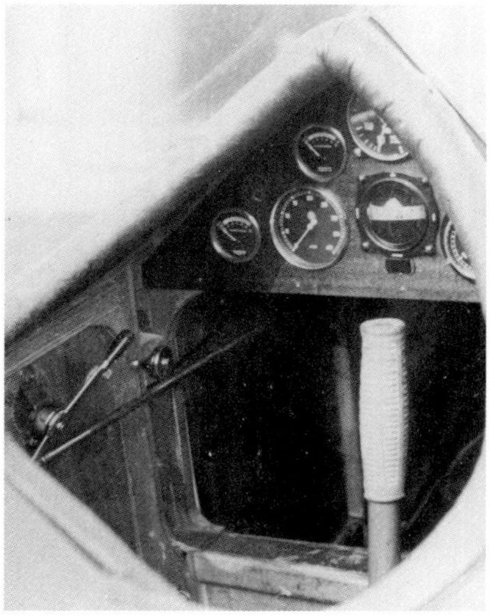

Instrument panel of the Erla Me Va, D-2585. On the left is the throttle lever. Note the rubber stick grip, similar to the grips seen on the handlebars of a bicycle. (Feige Collection)

Instrumentation of the Erla 5 D (D-YMOP) with Standard Instruments:

No.	Device	Instrument Range	Requisition/Equipment Number
•	Ignition switch (Bosch)		Fl 21119
•	Clock (Kienzle 8 day)		Fl 23886
•	Altimeter (Lufft)	0 – 8000 m	Fl 22308
•	Airspeed indicator	50 – 250 km/h	Fl 22206
•	Z7gk magnetic compass (Plath)		Fl 23220
•	Electric turn and bank indicator (Horn ?)		Fl 22413-1
•	Vertical speed indicator	+5/-5 m/s	(Askania)
•	Fuel/oil pressure gauge (beneath the instrument panel behind the control stick)	0-1/0-10 kg/cm^2	Fl 20512-2
•	Fuel gauge, sight gauge on top of fuselage		

Compared to this historic instrumentation, Erla 5 A HB-SEX, which is flown as a vintage aircraft, has conventional international instrumentation. Some of the equipment was installed as a result of changing from the original DKW to a VW engine.

Device	Instrument Range	Manufacturer/Remarks
Type 2300 magnetic compass		USA
Altimeter	0 – 10000 m	Utz, Bern
Altimeter	0 – 4000 m	Aera, Paris
Airspeed indicator	30 – 200 km/h	Thommen, Switzerland
Bank indicator		Winter, Germany
Oil pressure gauge	0 – 80 lbs (?)	USA ?
Cylinder head temperature gauge	0 - 350° C	Ref. 6A/1305, U.K.
Oil temperature gauge	20 - 120° C	Draeger, Germany
Lv7r vertical speed indicator	-5/+5 m/sec	Askania, Germany
RPM indicator	0 – 3,500 rpm	USA

The arrangement of the instruments seems rather arbitrary and unplanned, for the usual grouping with the flight instruments on the left and center and the engine instruments on the right was not adopted by Erla until later. It would appear that the RPM indicator was considered the most important instrument, for it was always installed in the center of the instrument panels of the first Erla Vs.

Two standard instruments were installed in the Erla Me V D-2585: the airspeed indicator (now to 250 km/h) and the magnetic compass, a "Small Emil" by Askania. The latter was installed in the instrument panel, improving the pilot's view through the windscreen. A second temperature gauge was also installed, probably for the oil.

The Erla 5 A variant built in 1935-36 featured a redesigned fuselage which was slightly larger with more rounded contours. This created more space for the instrument panel.

The illustration from the company brochure still shows several non-standard instruments but also two electrical switches, probably for cockpit lighting or navigation lights. The fuel gauge was now a sight gauge on top of the fuselage behind the engine.

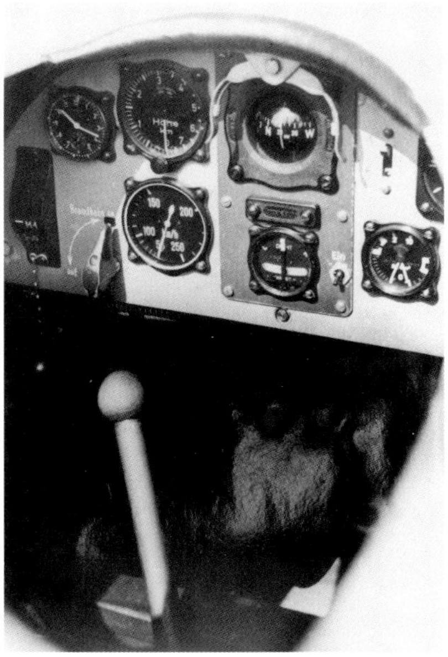

Instrumentation of the Erla 5 D, D-YMOP, with standardized instruments. The electric turn-and-bank indicator was powered by a flashlight battery and was only switched on when needed. The RPM indicator beneath the instrument panel is concealed by a cover or leather jacket. (Feige Collection)

Built in 1938, the Erla 5 D was the last and most capable version. It was powered by a 50 H.P. Zundapp 9-091 engine and had a reinforced airframe.

The aircraft's somewhat more extensive instrumentation consisted entirely of standard instruments. The equipment carried by the Erla 5 D is illustrated by aircraft D-YMOP.

The list of instruments for the Erla 5 HB-SEX was compiled from a photograph taken in 1980. Some of the aircraft's original instruments were replaced by modern types, presumably because replacements for the vintage types were not available.

Cockpit of the only Erla 5 A still flying, HB-SEX. Note the "international" instrumentation.

Beautifully restored Fw 44 J in original factory finish. D-EMOF was built under license by ASJA in Sweden.

Focke Wulf Fw 44 *Stieglitz* (Goldfinch)

In 1932 aircraft designer Kurt Tank became technical director of Focke Wulf in Bremen. The first aircraft which he designed in this capacity was the *Stieglitz*, which was to become one of the most famous sporting aircraft anywhere. The impetus for the design came from the aerobatic pilot Gerd Achgelis, who later conducted an impressive tour of the USA with the Fw 44.

The Fw 44 was a two-seat staggered biplane of mixed construction. It very quickly proved to be an outstanding aerobatic airplane, winning prizes in numerous international competitions and holding the world aerobatics championship for many years.

The *Stieglitz* was built in several versions, with the Fw 44 B powered by a 150 H.P. Siemens Sh 14a engine produced in the greatest numbers. This version had been redesigned to the smallest detail to facilitate mass production.

Instrument panel from the rear cockpit of a Finnish Fw 44 J (SZ-26) with German instruments added.

Many *Stieglitze* were specially equipped for aerobatics. For example, the oil system of the standard Fw 44 D was designed for inverted flight. The conventional rigid suction line was replaced by a pendulum pipe, enabling it to reach the oil supply in any attitude. A floatless carburetor designed for inverted flight could also be installed if required.

Easily mastered, the Fw 44 served as a training aircraft with the German air transport schools and later the *Luftwaffe*. Production reached such levels that other manufacturers had to be brought into the program. The Fw 44 J for Finland and the several aircraft for Sweden were built by CKD in Prague under license from Focke Wulf.

Pilot's cockpit of Fw 44 J, D-EMOF. Most of the instruments date from before 1945. Added to the instrument panel, however, was a vibration-proof mount for the airspeed indicator, turn-and-bank indicator, vertical speed indicator and compass. Other concessions to modernity are circuit breakers at the bottom of the instrument panel and a radio.

Instrument panel of a restored Fw 44 J (D-EGBR) which was formerly registered in Finland. The historical instrumentation was retained, however some equipment has been supplemented or replaced by modern devices such as a clock, vertical speed indicator, RPM indicator, altimeter and radio. Visible next to the flying helmet is an accelerometer.

The Fw 44 J export variant was built in large numbers and delivered to Bolivia, Bulgaria, Chile, China, Finland, Romania, Slovakia and Turkey. It was also built under license in Argentina, Brazil and Sweden. Most of the surviving *Stieglitze*, many of which are still flying, originated in Scandinavia.

The Focke Wulf Fw 44 is a classic two-seat biplane of the 1930s and 40s. The pilot occupied the rear cockpit and consequently had more extensive instrumentation than the observer or student sitting in the front cockpit.

Late production variants and repaired aircraft were equipped with more modern instruments, for example the FK 5 (Fl 23211) or FK 38 (Fl 23233) compass.

As a rule, export aircraft were equipped with German instruments with faces and placards in the language of the destination country. License-built machines, such as those built by ASJA of Sweden, had their own instrumentation and cockpit layout. The Fw 44 J trainers operated by Sweden and Finland served for more than two decades and afterwards flew for many years in the hands of private owners. Often, during repairs, the aircraft's instrumentation was updated or supplemented through the addition of vertical speed indicators or turn and bank indicators.

Most of the Fw 44s still flying today are equipped according to the wishes of their owners. Only rarely have attempts been made to install historically accurate instrumentation. This often depends on the availability of suitable vintage equipment. As well, present-day aviation regulations also play a role or perhaps pilots do not wish to sacrifice the convenience of a GPS system.

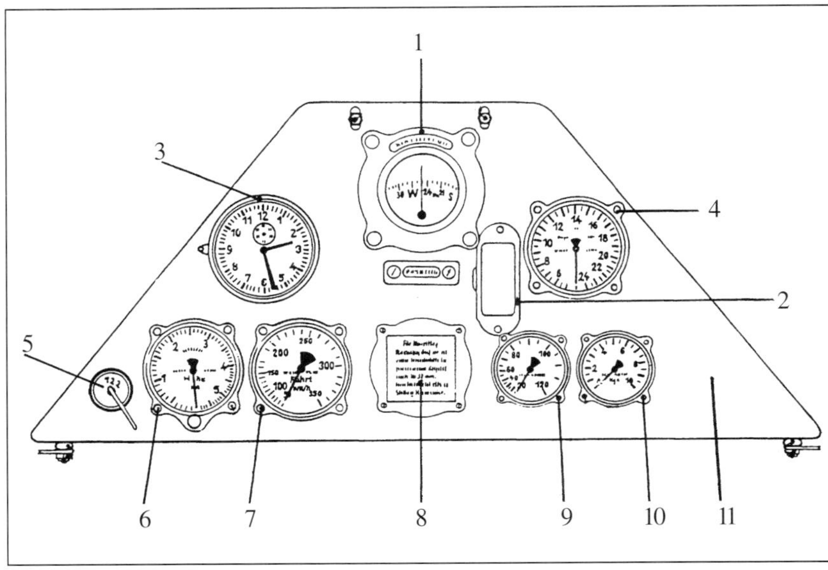

Arrangement of instruments in the rear cockpit panel of the Fw 44 D to G. (Hafner Archive)

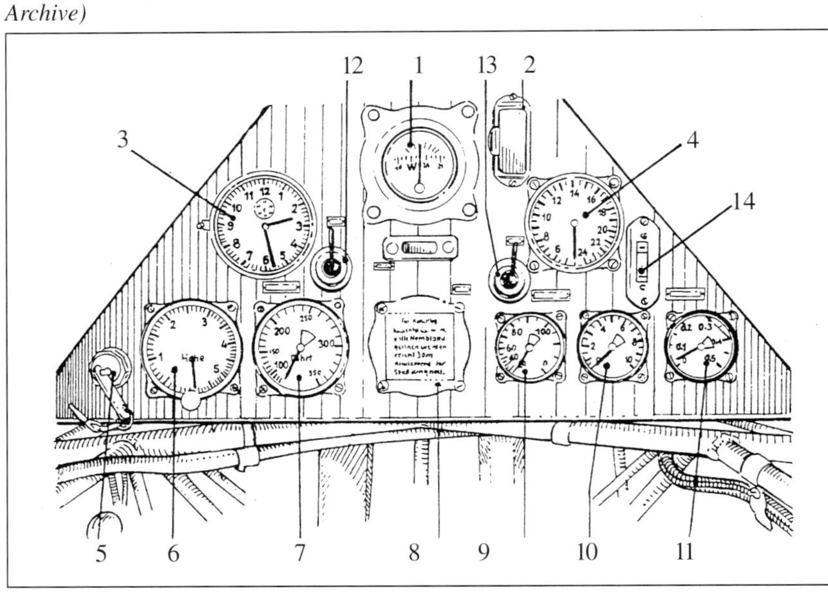

Arrangement of instruments in the rear cockpit panel of the Fw 44 J. (Hafner Archive)

Arrangement of instruments in the front cockpit of the Fw 44 E to J. (Hafner Archive)

Standard equipment installed in the Fw 44 D, E, F, G and J based on the replacement part lists.

Equipment installed in the pilot cockpit (rear) of the Fw 44 D to J:

No.	Equipment	Instrument Range	Requisition/Equipment Number
1	Plath magnetic compass with compensation		Fl 23227
2	Nav Vordruck K 6 deviation table		Fl 23906
3	Clock		Fl 22602
4	RPM indicator	500 – 2,400 rpm	Fl 20212
5	Bosch ignition switch		Fl 21110
6	Altimeter	0 – 6000 m	Fl 22310
7	Airspeed indicator	50 – 350 km/h	Fl 22221
8	Turn and bank indicator (planned) (otherwise blanking plate with placard)		Fl 22402
9	Oil temperature gauge	20 - 120° C	Fl 20308
10	Oil pressure gauge	0 – 10 kg/cm²	Fl 20606
11	Fuel pressure gauge (from Fw 44 E)	0 – 0.5 kg/cm²	Fl 20504

The fuel gauge was a sight gauge to 130 l (Fl 20703-1) on top of the fuselage in front of the forward cockpit.

The placard on the cover plate (8) contained instructions for aerobatic flight:

> For aerobatics:
> Aerobatics must only be begun
> with a full bottom tank.
> Fuel is then sufficient
> for 30 min. flying time.
> The fuel cock must be in the
> "MAIN TANK" position at all times.

The Fw 44 J and several of the Fw 44 E to G variants were equipped with an instrument panel lighting system as well as navigation lights and a landing light. The appropriate switches were installed in the instrument panel:

No.	Equipment	Instrument Range	Requisition/Equipment Number
12	Navigation light switch (Bosch SSH 507/1Z)		Fl 26643
13	Lighting switch (Bosch SSH 507/1Z)		Fl 26643
14	Landing light switch		Fl 32316

The forward cockpit of the Fw 44 was much less well equipped in almost every variant. Two small instrument panels were installed on the left and right:

No.	Equipment	Instrument Range	Requisition/Equipment Number
1	Left instrument panel		
2	Right instrument panel		
3	Bosch ignition switch		Fl 21110
4	Airspeed indicator	50 – 350 km/h	Fl 22221
5	Altimeter	0 – 6000 m	Fl 22310
6	Clock		Fl 22602
7	RPM indicator	500 – 2,400 rpm	Fl 20212

He 46 photographed on a training flight before the war.

Heinkel He 46

Although the *Luftwaffe* did not officially come into being until 1935, efforts to procure suitable aircraft began in 1933. The only way this could be done was to produce existing aircraft in the greatest possible numbers.

At that time Heinkel was able to offer two biplanes for the tactical reconnaissance role, with prototypes already in the test phase. The He 45 design was accepted and placed into production, however the He 46, which had been designed as an artillery spotter, was developed into a high-wing monoplane to improve the downwards view.

Both types became standard *Luftwaffe* reconnaissance aircraft until replaced by the Hs 126 in 1938. Although a few He 46s were still flying operationally at the time of the Polish Campaign, by then most had been passed on to the flying schools.

Pilot's instrument panel of an He 46 C or E (D-IGYK). Note the coarse altimeter at the top of the panel.

Pilot's Instrument Panel:

No.	Equipment	Instrument Range	Requisition/Equipment Number
1	SSH 32/2Z ignition switch		Fl 21110
2	Instrument panel lighting		
3	Electrical system cutout switch	Fl 32301	
4	Fine altimeter (Fuess)	0 – 1000 m	Fl 22306
5	SSH 507/1Z switch for instrument panel lighting?		Fl 26643
6	FK 5 magnetic compass (Ludolph)	Fl 23211	
7	Coarse altimeter (Fuess)	0 – 8000 m	Fl 22308
8	Lkz 5p course indicator (Askania)	Fl 22354	
9	Reflector sight cutout switch		
10	Statoscope-vertical speed indicator	+10/-10 m/s	Fl 22381-10
11	Airspeed indicator (Bruhn)	80 – 450 km/h	Fl 22229
12	Turn and bank indicator (Askania)	Fl 22402	
13	RPM indicator (Deuta)	600 – 2,400 rpm	Fl 20206
14	Oil temperature gauge – inlet	0 - 120° C	Fl 20308-?
15	Oil temperature gauge – outlet	0 - 120° C	Fl 20308-?
16	Oil pressure gauge	0 – 10 kg/cm²	Fl 20606
17	Fuel pressure gauge	0 – 0.5 kg/cm²	Fl 20504 or 20505
18	Fuel cock with tank selector switch		
19	Landing light switch		Fl 32303
20	SUM AP 8 starter injection pump	8-4505 A	
21	Electrical switchbox with fuses and dimmers for pitot heat, navigation lights and instrument lights		(Arado)
22	Lreg 5 sensitivity control for turn and bank indicator		Fl 22405
23	Operating instructions placard		
24	Boost pressure gauge	0.2 – 1.2 atm	Fl ?
25	Clock (Junghans)		Fl 22600
26	Fuel gauge	0 – 400 l	Fl 20704
27	Air pump for fuel gauge		Fl 20742-1
28	Camera controls ?		
29	Lkg 2r course selector (Askania) for the remote-reading compass	Fl 23300	
30	Fuel hand pump		

The He 46 D incorporated a number of changes:
No reflector sight

No.	Equipment	Instrument Range	Requisition/Equipment Number
24	Boost pressure gauge	0.6 – 1.8 atm	Fl 20550
28	Clock instead of camera control	Fl 22600	

An additional placard provided information on flight endurance:

2 hrs. flight endurance at cruising speed

Installed in the observer's cockpit were:

Equipment	Instrument Range	Requisition/Equipment Number
Coarse altimeter (Fuess)	0 – 8000 m	Fl 22308
Airspeed indicator (Bruhn)	80 – 450 km/h	Fl 22229
Clock (Junghans)	Fl 22600	
Sch A2 antenna current indicator	0 – 10 A	Fl 26749
Lkz 5p course indicator (Askania)	Fl 22354	
Lkg 2r course selector (Askania) for the remote-reading compass		Fl 23300
FuG I radio (beneath instrument panel)		

The equipment lists provided above are just two examples of the equipment installed in the He 46. Further changes occurred during development and operational use as a result of technical advances, changes in role and the spares situation.

In 1943 a small number of He 46s returned to operations, serving as night harassment aircraft on the Eastern Front.

A total of 481 machines was built by Heinkel and various licensees. In addition to serving with the *Luftwaffe*, the He 46 was also flown by Bulgaria, Spain and Hungary. Variants were the He 46 A biplane and the He 46 B to F high-wing monoplanes. The main production version was the He 46 C powered by a Siemens SAM 322 B engine producing 650 H.P.

The French operated a number of captured German aircraft from La Martinerie airfield near Chateauroux, including a He 46 D built in 1934 with the *Werknummer* 8146 and the manufacturer's code ??+BL. The aircraft was only flown on special occasions, and each time the crew were uncomfortably aware of the absence of the exhaust system.

The He 46 was retired in October 1945 and later went to the Musée de Trois Guerres in Diors. In 1982 it was acquired by the Musée de l'Air in Paris in exchange for a MS.505 and has since been in storage awaiting restoration. It is the only surviving He 46 and it is the subject of some of the interior photographs displayed here.

These photographs and two historical photos depict well the equipment installed in standard production aircraft. It is apparent, however, that there were deviations in instrumentation and the arrangement of equipment.

The arrangement of the controls and instruments followed standard German practices of the 1930s. On the left were the throttle lever and ignition switch, in the center flight instruments, and on the right engine instruments. The pilot's two-piece instrument panel was taken from the He 45 with some modifications. The radio operator/observer had his own instrumentation. The instruments were in-

The observer's station. Visible at the bottom is the receiver of the FuG 1 radio set. (F. Selinger Archive)

Pilot's instrument panel in the last surviving He 46 D in Paris. Visible at the bottom is the fire extinguisher.

The bottom part of the instrument panel with operating data placard. Missing on the right is the clock. The instruments associated with the fuel system are marked in yellow as per regulations. (Couderchon)

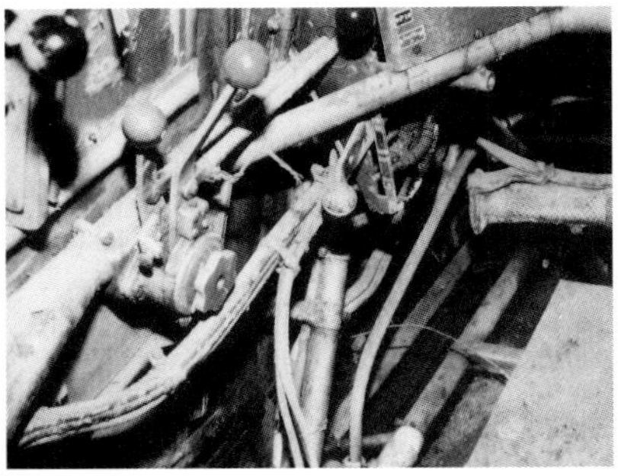

The left side of the pilot's cockpit of the He 46 D with (from left) the throttle and mixture levers in yellow, the fuel cock in red and the oil cooler lever in brown. (Couderchon)

stalled in the instrument panel from behind, which was standard Heinkel practice at that time.

Two historical photographs depict the equipment of a He 46 C or E. This version was armed with a fixed MG 17 machine-gun and was therefore equipped with a reflector sight. The list of equipment has been reconstructed from available photographs. Several pieces of equipment have not been identified with certainty.

Rear cockpit instrument panel of an early He 72. (Rohrbach Collection)

Heinkel He 72 *Kadett*

In 1933 the RLM issued a contract to Heinkel for the He 72 *Kadett* training aircraft. It was to be used for the initial training of airline and air force pilots. The RLM specification described a classic slightly staggered, single-bay biplane of mixed construction with open tandem cockpits. The principal power plant was the 160 H.P. Siemens Sh 14 A radial engine.

Even the lower-powered variants of the He 72 exhibited good, balanced handling characteristics. The version with the Sh 14 A was built in the largest numbers and was often mistaken for the Fw 44 *Stieglitz*, which it resembled. Several hundred He 72s were built, however none has survived to the present day. The last one flew in France until 1958, when it was scrapped.

In 1996 at the collectors auction in Stuttgart a dealer offered a complete original instrument panel from a He 72 C. It had probably come from an airman who had removed the item as a souvenir at the end of the war. Several missing instruments had been replaced with similar items and the panel had been mounted on a wooden base for display. Photos of the instrument panel illustrate this chapter.

The pilot's and observer's cockpits were equipped in a conventional fashion for that time. The pilot occupied the rear cockpit and the trainee or observer the front. The equipment installed in the cockpits was listed in a description dated December 1941:

- left: throttle lever, mixture lever, fuel cock, electrical system cutout and ignition switch.
- center: flight and navigation instruments
- right: engine instruments, trim and starter pump.

The arrangement of equipment and types of instruments installed could vary from one variant to another.

Also installed was instrument panel lighting and a speaking tube for communication with the trainee or observer. In the early 1930s most aircraft manufacturers still preferred to install instruments from the back of instrument panels. This meant, however, that if repairs were necessary the entire panel had to be removed.

Lineup of newly-completed He 72s waiting to be delivered.

The *Kadett* was produced in the following versions with various types of power plant:

He 72 A	139 H.P. Argus As 8B
He 72 B	160 H.P. Siemens Sh 14 A, built in several versions
He 72 BW	Float-equipped version with improved Sh 14 A 4
He 72 B-3	"*Super Kadett*" with engine cowling, wheel pants, from it was later developed the He 172
He 72 C	Special version of the He 72 B-2 with improved undercarriage
He 72 D	Designation for all versions of the He 72 which flew in German and European competitions

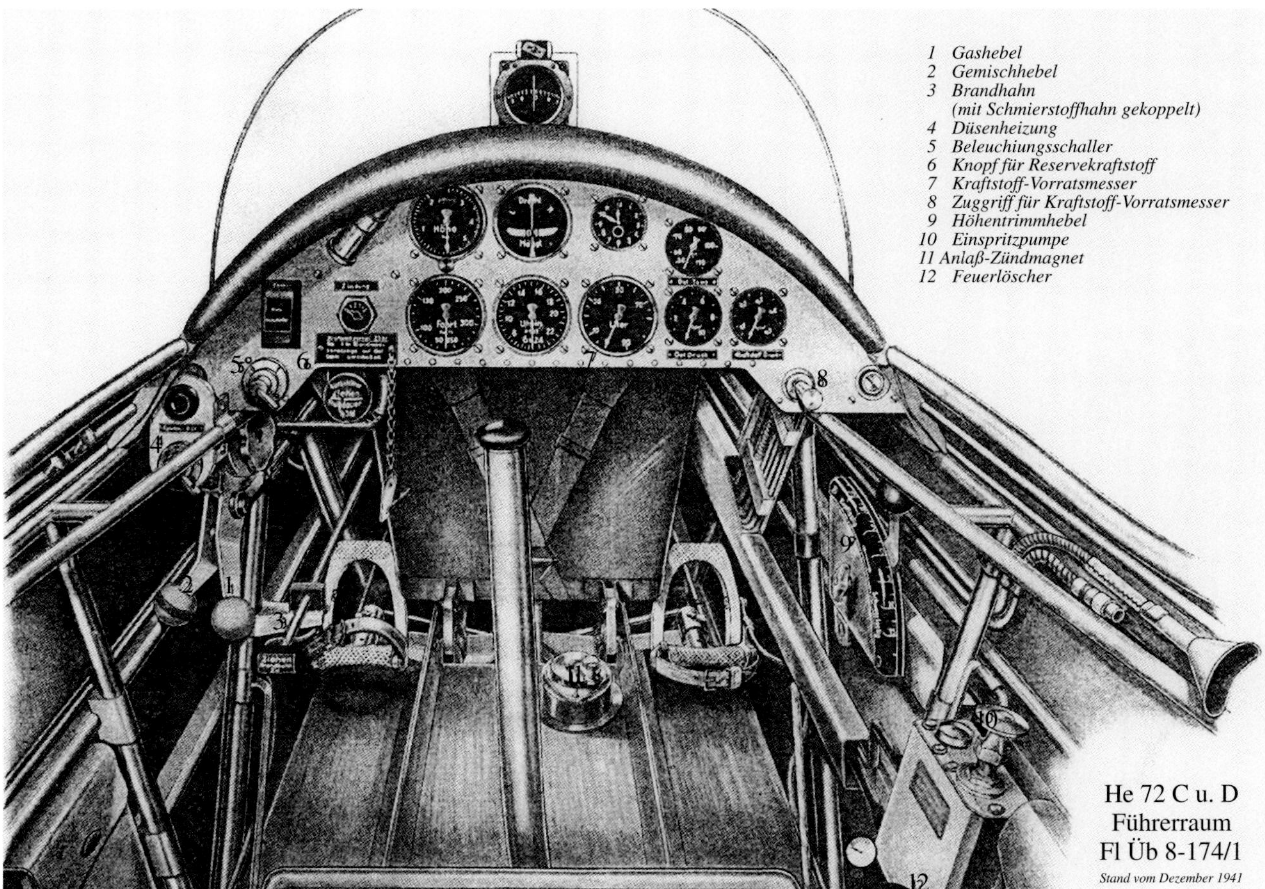

Drawing of the cockpit of the He 72 C and D dated December 1941.

Intact instrument panel from an He 72 C at a collector's auction. The three vibration-damping mounts for installation in the fuselage are still present.

Illustration of the pilot's instrument panel taken from a series of instructional photographs for the He 72. The type of compass installed suggests that this is an early series aircraft.

Illustration of the observer's panel from a series of instructional photographs.

Equipment in the rear cockpit of the He 72 C and D, based on survey dated December 1941:

Equipment	Requisition/Equipment Number
Map pocket	
Throttle lever	
Mixture lever	
Fuel cock, coupled with oil cock	
SSH 507/1Z switch for pitot heat	Fl 26643
Visual indicator or lamp for pitot heat	

Pilot's Instrument Panel:

No.	Equipment	Instrument Range	Requisition/ Equipment Number
1	Switch for navigation lights SSH 507/1Z		Fl 26643
2	Electrical system emergency cutout switch		Fl 32301
3	Instrument panel lighting		
4	SSH 32/2 Z ignition switch		Fl 21110
5	Instruction placard for changing tanks:		

Fuel Capacity 25 l
When fuel gauge indicates 5 liters
switch to emergency tank

Pilot's Instrument Panel:

No.	Equipment	Instrument Range	Requisition/
6	Reserve fuel knob		
7	Coarse altimeter	0 – 6000 m	Fl 22310
8	Airspeed indicator	50 – 350 km/h	Fl 22228
9	FK 38 magnetic compass (in front of windscreen)	Fl 23233	
10	Turn and bank indicator	Fl 22402	
11	RPM indicator	500 – 2,400 rpm	Fl 20212
12	Clock, e.g. Kienzle 8 Day	Fl 23886-1	
13	He 72 fuel gauge	0 – 90 liters	Fl 20710
14	Oil temperature gauge	0 – 110° C	Fl 203??
15	Oil pressure gauge	0 – 10 kg/cm²	Fl 20606
16	Fuel pressure gauge	0 – 0.5 kg/cm²	Fl 20504 or 20505
17	Air pump for fuel gauge		Fl 20742-1

Right side:

Equipment	Requisition/Equipment Number
• Elevator trim lever	
• APB 6 starter injection pump with tank	8-4506 A
• Fire extinguisher	
• Speaking tube	
• AM 1 B 2 starter magneto (on floor)	Fl 21201
• Tool pouch	

Trainee's or Observer's Instrument Panel:

No.	Equipment	Instrument Range	Requisition/Equipment Number
4	SSH 32/2 Z ignition switch		Fl 21110
7	Coarse altimeter	0 – 6000 m	Fl 22310
8	Airspeed indicator	50 – 350 km/h	Fl 22228
9	FK 38 magnetic compass (in front of windscreen)		Fl 23233
11	RPM indicator	500 – 2400 rpm	Fl 20212
15	Oil pressure gauge	0 – 10 kg/cm²	Fl 20606

Compared to the description dated December 1941, illustrations from a series of instructional photographs show deviations in the equipment of the pilot's cockpit:

No.	Equipment	Instrument Range	Requisition/Equipment Number
	The instrument panel lighting and switch are absent, as is the placard with instructions for switching tanks		
8	Airspeed indicator	0 – 250 km/h	Fl 22227
9	Plath Z 4 g st MC		
10	No turn and bank indicator		
12	Clock (Kienzle 8 Day, large version)		Fl 22602

The surviving instrument panel shows a second layer of paint, at least on the front side. It was either applied during a repair before the end of the war or after 1945 during preparations for display. The original equipment and the instruments installed later show further variations:

Equipment	Instrument Range	Requisition/Equipment Number
• Coarse altimeter	0 – 10000 m	Fl 22316-10
• Airspeed indicator	0 – 250 km/h	Fl 22227
• Fuel capacity placard		

Operating fuel	90 l
Reserve fuel	20 l
Total fuel	110 l

Reserve fuel = 25 minutes flying time

The instruction placard for switching tanks is absent.
The following items were added later to replace missing original equipment:

Equipment	Instrument Range	Requisition/Equipment Number
Warning light, red (replacement for instrument panel lighting)		
Oxygen pressure gauge (replacement for clock)	0 – 250 kg/cm²	Fl 30496
Trim indicator (replacement for temperature gauge)		Fl 22855
Fuel pressure gauge	0 – 1 kg/cm²	Fl 20504-1

The hand pump for the fuel gauge had a modified grip.

The Mücke after completion of restoration work.

Mücke (Mosquito) Motorized Glider (Dr. Hübner)

Dr. Hübner, a brewmaster in Mosbach, constructed aircraft in the period 1910 to 1912. In 1929, following a lengthy hiatus caused by the First World War, he returned to his old passion. Using several gliders of his own design, he became one of the co-founders of the Mosbach Aviation Groups.

In 1935 he produced a small powered glider. The light single-seat biplane was equipped with a Kroeber M 4 horizontally-opposed engine producing 18 H.P. and was intended to facilitate the transition from gliders to motorized flight. The design consisted of a steel-tube fuselage and wooden wings with fabric covering. Painted blue and ivory, the sported the Olympic rings in honor of the 1936 Olympic Games. The aircraft bore no markings and was flown without a registration.

The machine was initially flown by Master Mechanic Hugo Wild from the brewery and Dr. Hübner's son Walter. They flew the extremely forgiving aircraft with no training in powered flight, but also without the knowledge of the authorities. The meadows beside the Neckar River near Obrigheim served as a landing field.

Handling was extremely simple. Transported in a trailer towed by an automobile, the aircraft could be assembled in a few minutes. The engine was started using a pull-cord in the same manner as a lawnmower.

Following a demonstration for a *Luftwaffe* committee in Mannheim, the press proclaimed "The mosquito actually flies!" The authorities threatened to ban it from the air. When Dr. Hübner died in 1938 his "Mosquito" disappeared into one of the brewery buildings in Mosbach. In 1983 it resurfaced, together with the 1912 monoplane. Restored by the Kornwestheim Aviation Group, in 1984 it went on display in the Auto and Technical Museum in Sinsheim.

The "Mosquito" is an example of a simply equipped homebuilt aircraft for visual flight in good weather conditions. Consequently

Historical photograph of the motorized glider during flight operations from a meadow near the River Neckar. Note the installation of the engine and the fairing atop the fuselage, which is absent from the restored aircraft. The instruments are visible but cannot be identified in this photo. Note the throttle lever on the left. (Hübner Collection)

The cockpit after restoration. Little consideration was given to pilot comfort. The throttle lever is missing as no original could be found. While the RPM indicator and altimeter date from the 1930s, they are not the same types originally installed.

The Kroeber M 3 engine. The RPM indicator had an instrument range of 0 to 2,500 rpm. As installed in the Mücke the propeller shaft was considerably longer. (B. Lange Archive)

its instrumentation is limited to what is absolutely necessary.

Contemporary photographs make it possible to reconstruct the instrumentation, although their quality leaves several uncertainties. The instruments were arranged from left to right around the pilot's seat and in the instrument panel.

During restoration the instrument panel was refurbished, because all of the original equipment was missing with the exception of the ignition switch. Available vintage instruments with standard housings were used, although their arrangement differed from the one in the photographs. As the altimeter could not be identified and the RPM indicator for the Kroeber M 4 is very rare, vintage instruments matching their instrument ranges were used:

- mechanical RPM indicator (Deuta) 600 – 3,000 rpm
- altimeter (Scholz) 0 – 6000 m
- airspeed indicator (Bruhn) 20 – 150 km/h
- vertical speed indicator (Askania) –5 / +5 m/sec

In spite of these substitutions the restored aircraft gives a good impression of a homebuilt powered glider of the 1930s.

Equipment of Dr. Hübner's "Mosquito"

- Engine control lever for the Kroeber M 4 engine
- Altimeter: probably an older instrument or a converted barometer. The instrument range is not known, but must have had a maximum of between 3000 and 5000 meters.
- Airspeed indicator: because of the aircraft's low airspeed, an Airspeed indicator such as that made by DBU with a maximum indicated speed of 120 km/h could have been used.
- Ignition switch: A Bosch type for the Kroeber M 4 required two magnetos.
- Vertical speed indicator: As the Mosquito could be flown as a powered glider, a vertical speed indicator with a range of + 5 to – 5 m/sec was installed (e.g. Askania Lv7r).
- RPM indicator: the shaft-driven device was an accessory of the Kroeber M 4 and probably came from an automobile supplier as its housing did not fit the aeronautical standard. Its range was probably in the area of 0 to 3,000 rpm. Earlier versions of the Kroeber engine (M 3) were equipped with a RPM indicator with a range of up to 2,500 rpm.
- Pitot intake in the nose of the aircraft.

Junkers W 34 hi, D-OPUY, in civilian service.

Cockpit of the W 34 hi with double instrumentation. (Richter Collection)

Junkers W 34

The W 34 was among the most successful of all German multipurpose aircraft. A total of about 2,000 was built, in more than 70 variants, and the aircraft was exported all over the world. The W 34 was powered by a variety of engines, mainly radials, including the 420 H.P. Gnôme Rhône Jupiter VI, the 550 H.P. Pratt & Whitney (or BMW) Hornet, the 520 H.P. Siemens Sh 20 and the 715 H.P. BMW Bramo 322 H.

The aircraft's performance enabled it to establish speed and payload records in 1929 and in May of the same year it established a world altitude record of 12739 meters.

As well as serving with *Lufthansa*, the W 34 was operated on wheels, skis and floats in Canada, Sweden, Persia, Bolivia and New Guinea, carrying freight, mail and passengers and serving as a photo-survey aircraft and air ambulance. The aircraft's versatility was such that it remained in service in Canada and Sweden until 1961.

A military version of the W 34, the K 43, was produced in 1927. It differed from the W 34 only in detail and in its power plant. These aircraft, which could also operate on floats, were exported to Sweden, Finland, Argentina and Portugal. The *Luftwaffe* employed the W 34 as a training and liaison aircraft and a glider tug until 1945. The most widely used variants were the W 34 hi powered by the BMW Hornet and the W 34 hau with a Bramo engine and four-blade propeller.

Only three complete W 34s and parts of three others have survived.

The aircraft operating manual and a color overview of the cockpit produced in 1941 provide detailed information on the standard equipment installed in the cockpit of the W 34. Photographs reveal, however, that there were deviations in the instrumentation and layout of equipment.

The arrangement of the controls and instruments was largely in keeping with German standard practice for aircraft with dual controls produced in the 1930s. The instrument panel was in three parts, with two sets of flight instruments, left and right, and the engine instruments and control levers in the center, allowing them to be reached from both seats.

As a rule, the radio equipment was installed in the rear cabin. Only in aircraft with simplified instrumentation was it installed up front on the right instrument panel. When this was done the clock and course selector were relocated elsewhere.

A Junkers W 34 hau in service with the Luftwaffe. Visible on the fuselage are the antenna mast, DF loop, generator and venturi tube. The four-blade propeller was a feature of the W 34 hau.

Cockpit of the W 34 hau, probably the same machine illustrated above. The instrument panel was painted Black-Gray 66. The temperature and pressure gauges were installed from the back of the instrument panel.

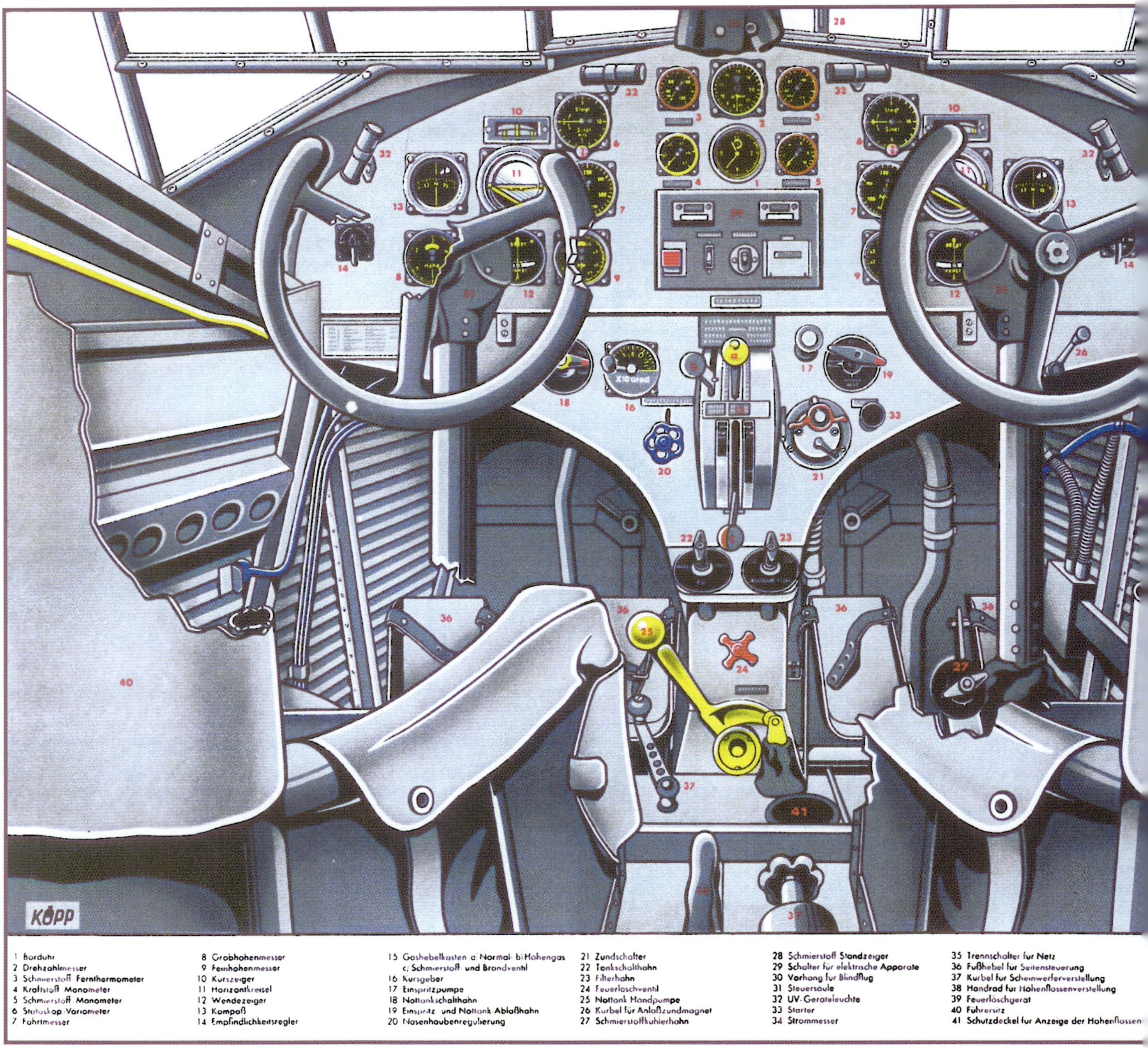

Instrument panel of a Junkers W 34 hi. Color was probably Gray 02. (Schneider Collection)

The instrumentations depicted here are only examples. There were changes during the course of the aircraft's production life and as a result of the changing supply situation.

The W 34s flown in Canada and Sweden until 1961 were ultimately equipped with American instruments. One such aircraft was serial number 2835, a W 34 h which was built under license in Sweden in 1935. First flown by the Swedish air force, in 1961 it was flown as SE-BYA in Lapland, carrying mail and supplies. Today the aircraft is on display in Stockholm-Arlanda. The aircraft's equipment and instrument layout has changed little, with the flight instruments on the left, engine instruments and controls in the center and the radio equipment on the right.

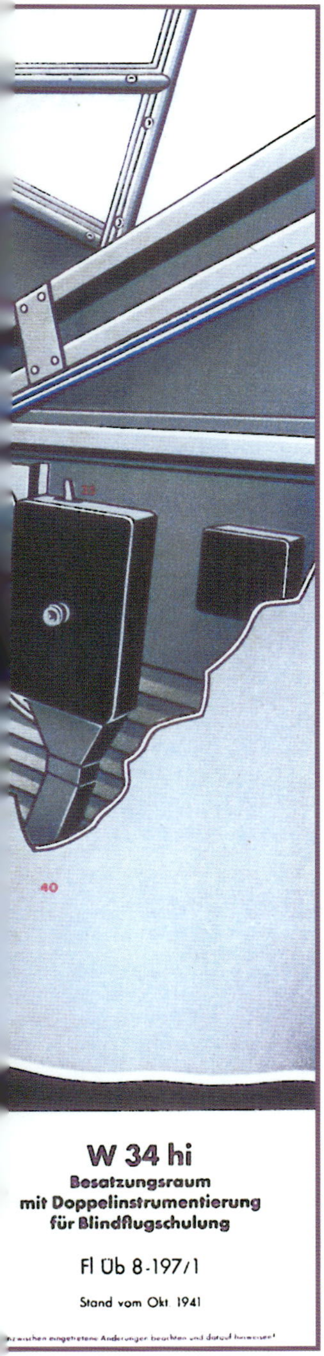

Equipment of a Junkers W 34 hi in October 1941

No.	Equipment	Instrument Range	Requisition/Equipment Number
1	Clock		Fl 22600 or 22602
2	RPM indicator	600 – 2,400 rpm	Fl 20206
3	Oil temperature gauge	30 – 120° C	Fl 20308 ?
4	Fuel pressure gauge	0 – 0.5 kg/cm^2	Fl 20504 or 20505
5	Oil pressure gauge	0 – 10 kg/cm^2	Fl 20606
6	Statoscope-vertical speed indicator	+10/-10 m/s	Fl 22381-10
7	Airspeed indicator	50 – 350 km/h	Fl 22207 or 22209
8	Coarse altimeter	0 – 6000 m	Fl 22310 or 22316-6
9	Fine altimeter	0 – 1000 m	Fl 22306 or 22316-1
10	Course indicator		Fl 23351
11	Artificial horizon (Sperry)		Fl 22326
12	Turn and bank indicator		Fl 22402
13	Zürn Z 7g magnetic compass		Fl 23227
14	Turn and bank indicator sensitivity control		Fl 22405
15	Throttle lever box (a = normal, b = altitude c = oil and fuel valve)		
16	Course selector		Fl 23300
17	SUM AP 8 starter injection pump		8-4505 A
18	Emergency tank selector cock		
19	Injection and emergency jettison cock		
20	Cowling control		
21	ZSH 5/3Z ignition switch		Fl 21112
22	Tank selector switch		
23	Filter switch		
24	Fire extinguisher valve		
25	Emergency fuel tank pump		
26	Starter crank		
27	Oil cooler switch		
28	Oil level indicator (on cowling)		
29	Electrical system switch with electrical system cutout (left)		Fl 32301
	2 warning lights		
	2 landing light switches		Fl 32303
30	Curtain for blind flying training		
31	Control columns		
32	UV instrument lighting		
33	Starter		
34	Ammeter		
35	Electrical system circuit breaker		
36	Rudder pedals		
37	Searchlight position control crank		
38	Tailplane incidence control wheel		
39	Fire extinguisher		
40	Pilot seats		
41	Protective cover for tailplane incidence indicator		

A photograph of the cockpit of a Junkers W 34 hau reveals several changes:

No.	Equipment	Instrument Range	Requisition/Equipment Number
1	Boost pressure gauge	0.6 – 1.8 atm	Fl 20550
16	Fuel gauge		Fl 20704
	Fuel gauge air pump		Fl 20742-1
	Switch for two measuring positions		Fl 20754-2?
29	2 visual indicators instead of lights		Fl 32525
	one switch deleted		

The Lufthansa tradition aircraft is a good example of a Ju 52/3m in civilian service. (Lufthansa)

Junkers Ju 52

The most important versions of the Ju 52:

fe	commercial aircraft operated by Lufthansa
g1e, g2e	commercial aircraft for Lufthansa with BMW 132 engines
g3e	bomber
g4e	transport with large cargo door on starboard side
g5e	similar to g4e, but with hot-air deicing, some on floats
g6e	transport with revised radio equipment
g7e	similar to g5e, but with larger cargo door and autopilot
g8e	similar to g6e, but with autopilot
g9e	tropical version of the g4e
g10e	transport with revised cargo door
g11e	similar to g10e, but with hot-air deicing
g12e–g14e	transport, multipurpose aircraft, some with armor
g4e-g6e	minesweeper versions

At 57, the number of surviving Ju 52s is relatively high, and around the world examples may be viewed of aircraft built in Germany as well as some of the 415 built under license in France (Amiot AAC.1) and the 170 produced in Spain (CASA 352 L).

The three-engined "*Tante Ju*" (Auntie Ju) is probably the most famous German aircraft of all time. In the course of decades it has safely carried thousands of passengers and countless tons of freight to destinations all over the world. Today, more than sixty years after its maiden flight, examples of this indestructible corrugated-skin aircraft are still flying.

The Ju 52's career actually began with a failure. In 1930 Ernst Zindel designed a large single-engine cargo aircraft using Junkers' proven method of corrugated metal skinning. His objective was to create an aircraft which would make possible profitable commercial air transport without subsidies. Procurement costs were kept low and ease of servicing was stressed. Although this Ju 52/1m variant was very capable— in Canada one machine continued flying until 1947—it was not a great commercial success.

With multi-engine aircraft gaining in popularity, not least for reasons of safety, Zindel designed a three-engine version of the Ju 52. Performance was improved significantly and the aircraft won its category at the Zurich Air Meet in 1932, where it was shown publicly for the first time. The Ju 52/3m established further records, setting the stage for its success all over the world. Lufthansa made the Ju 52/3m its standard aircraft and airlines in more than 20 countries placed orders for the type. The Ju 52/3m's career continued after the Second World War. A number of companies, some of which had never owned Ju 52s before, now flew captured German aircraft or examples built under license after the war. The last Ju 52/3m in regular commercial service was not retired until the 1960s. The military career of the "*Tante Ju*" lasted much longer than Hugo Junkers had foreseen. It was first used in a military role in the Gran Chaco War in 1934, when it served as a transport and makeshift bomber. Then came the Spanish Civil War, however the type's hardest test was undoubtedly the Second World War.

The stories of lucky and tragic missions in countless transport and rescue flights are as legion as the number of airmen from many nations who flew in the Ju 52. The aircraft continued in military service until 1981, when it was retired by the Swiss air force. The three aircraft had been purchased by Switzerland in 1939.

It is impossible to say when the Ju 52/3m will cease flying, for examples of this robust machine continue to fly in Germany, Switzerland and South Africa, appearing at air shows and participating in air meets.

A total of slightly less than 5,000 Ju 52s was built, and the number of individual variants can scarcely be estimated, as equipment and power plants varied from customer to customer. The most familiar version, however, is the one powered by three 660 H.P. BMW 132 radial engines, which gave the Ju 52/3m its unmistakable appearance.

The interior photographs presented here depict the following machines:
Ju 52/3m g4e, WNr. 6610, HB-HOP based in Dübendorf, Switzerland
Ju 52/3m g4e, WNr. 6693, DB+RD based at Wunstorf air base
Ju 52/3m g8e, WNr. 130714, D-CDLH (D-AQUI) of Lufthansa
CASA 352 L, serial number 50, RJ+NP in the Auto + Technik Museum, Sinsheim

With its two large wooden control wheels, the cockpit of the Ju 52 brings to mind an aircraft from the pioneering days of aviation rather than a modern passenger aircraft of the 1930s. The extensive glazing provided the pilots with a good view from the cockpit, and the instruments and controls were well illuminated, at least by day. As usual, the pilot sat on the left and the flight engineer sat on the right. As the aircraft was equipped with dual controls, the latter could take over and relieve the pilot.

The large instrument panel was divided into three parts and as a rule was arranged with the flight and navigation instruments on the left in front of the pilot, the engine instruments in the center, and additional engine controls for the flight engineer on the right. In the center of the cockpit there was a large console housing the engine control levers.

In the beginning the Ju 52 was relatively sparsely equipped with a number of non-standard circular instruments. Later instrumentation became more extensive and an automatic pilot by Askania or Siemens and distant-reading compass systems became standard. In many military and civil versions of the Ju 52 double was standard.

The number of variations in instrumentation is unknown, mainly because foreign customers often installed non-German instruments to suit their own requirements. Even *Lufthansa* operated numerous versions, from simply equipped aircraft to

Instrumentation of a Ju 52/3m airliner with Askania distant-reading compass.

Instrumentation of a civil Ju 52/3mg from 1938-39:

No.	Equipment	Instrument Range	Requisition/Equipment Number
1	Lkz 1p course indicator		Fl 23351
2	Homing indicator ?		
3	Clock (Junghans)		Fl 22600
4	Airspeed indicator	50 – 250 km/h	Fl 22209
5	Lg 14r turn and bank indicator, pneumatic		Fl 22402
6	Lgab 8 artificial horizon (Sperry)	Fl 22426	
7	Lv 7r vertical speed indicator	-10/+10 m/s	Fl 22370
8	Fine altimeter ?	0 – 1000 m	Fl 22306
9	Altimeter	0 – 6000 m	Fl 22310
10	Lkg 2r course selector		Fl 23300
11	Fuel pressure gauges (3)	0 – 0.5 kg/cm^2	Fl 22505 ?
12	RPM indicator	0 – 2,400 rpm	Fl 20276 ?
13	RPM indicators (2)	600 – 2,400 rpm	Fl 20218 ?
14	Boost pressure gauges (3)	0.5 – 1.5 atm	
15	Oil pressure gauges (3)	0 – 10 kg/cm^2	Fl 20605 ?
16	Oil temperature gauges (intake) (3)	0 - 120° C	Fl 20308
17	Oil temperature gauges (outlet) (3)	0 – 120° C	Fl 20308
18	Outside air temperature indicator	-40/+40° C	
19	Double pressure gauge for wheel brakes	0 – 10 kg/cm^2	Fl ?
20	Double pressure gauge for wheel brake pressure reducing valve	0 – 20/0 – 200 kg/cm^2	Fl 20511
21	Fire extinguisher pressure gauge	0 – 10 kg/cm^2	Fl 20625 ?
22	Propeller blade deicing switch		
23	FK 10/32 navigator's compass	Fl 23210	
24	Landing light switch	Fl 32303	
25	Lreg 10 sensitivity control for negative pressure device		
26	Selector switch for suction device (distant-reading compass)		
27	Pull handle for rudder setting in case of engine failure		
28	Central console		
29	Auxiliary panel with engine controls		
30	Cockpit lighting		

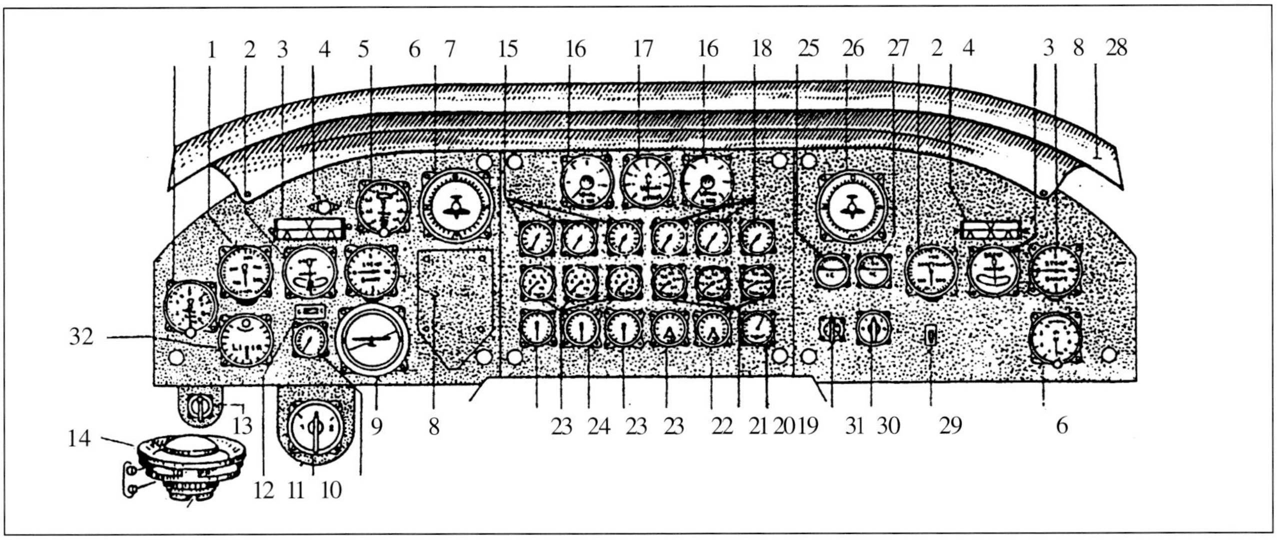

Instrumentation of the Junkers Ju 52/3mg5e.

examples with the Askania three-axis autopilot. For this reason the instrument groupings described here should be seen as examples.

Descriptions are provided for two pre-1939 civil versions and three military models. For sake of comparison the modern equipment installed in the Lufthansa Ju 52 (D-AQUI) is also depicted.

The Ju 52/3mg5e was a military transport version with hot air deicing and a Patin distant-reading compass system. Some of the flight instruments were duplicated. As the military transport and, in particular, the float-equipped versions were usually operated at low level, boost gauges were deleted.

The Ju 52/3mg4e, which is also illustrated here in several photos, differed from the subsequent g5e only in having the Askania distant-reading compass system and absence of the hot-air deicing system and fuel flow meter.

Compared to these earlier variants, the instrumentation of the Ju 52/3mg14e, the last production version of the Ju 52, was considerably simplified. As a pure transport aircraft, its instrumentation was relatively simple. Apart from a complete set of flight instruments, it had a reduced complement of engine instruments and double indicators were also used. A Siemens K4ü autopilot eased the pilot's workload on long flights. The g14e was also the model for the AAC.1., which was built under license in France.

Instrument panel of a Ju 52/3mg5e:

No.	Equipment	Instrument Range	Requisition/Equipment Number
1	Coarse altimeter	0 – 10000 m	Fl 22316-10
2	Airspeed indicator	80 – 450 km/h	Fl 22210
or	60 – 550 km/h	Fl 22230	
3	Turn and bank indicator, pneumatic	Fl 22402	
4	Course indicator	Fl 22592	
5	Landing probe indicator light	Fl 33262	
6	Fine and coarse altimeter	0 – 10000 m	Fl 22320
7	Patin PFK/f3 pilot's repeater compass	Fl 23338	
8	Vertical speed indicator	-10/+10 m/s	Fl 22382-10
9	Artificial horizon (Sperry)	Fl 22426	
10	Pressure-suction gauge	0.5 – 2 atm 200 – 2000 mmWS	Fl 20553
11	Suction pump selector switch		
12	Pitot tube heat visual indicator	Fl 32525	
13	Air relief cock for equalizing line		
14	FK 10 navigator's compass		
15	(3) Distant-reading oil temperature gauges (inlet)	0 - 120° C	Fl 20308
16	Electrical distant-reading RPM indicators	(2) 0 – 2,400 rpm	Fl 20276 ?
17	Mechanical RPM indicator	500 – 2,400 rpm	Fl 20218 ?
18	Distant-reading oil temperature gauges (3) (outlet)	0 – 120° C	Fl 20308
19	Fire extinguisher pressure gauge	0 – 10 kg/cm²	Fl 20625 ?
20	Fuel pressure gauges (3)	0 – 0.5 kg/cm²	Fl 22505 ?
21	Double pressure gauge for the wheel brake pressure reduction valve	0 – 20 / 0 – 200 kg/cm	Fl 20511
22	Double pressure gauge for wheel brakes	0 – 10 kg/cm²	Fl ?
23	Fuel flow meters (3)	80 – 180 l/hr ?	Fl 20772 ?
24	Oil pressure gauges (3)	0 – 10 kg/cm²	Fl 20625 ?
25	Hot air deicing temperature gauge	?	
26	Observer's Patin PFK/b3 repeater compass		Fl 23339
27	Outside and intake air temperature gauge	–60/+40° C	Fl 20349
28	Instrument panel shade		
29	Propeller deicing switch		
30	Position switch (4 positions) for 27	Fl 32336-1	
31	Position switch (2 positions) for 25	Fl 32331	
32	Indicator for AFN 1 radio navigation	Ln 27000	

The main instrument panel and central console of Ju 52/3mg4e, DB+RD, give a good impression of the cockpit of a military Ju 52. The care taken during restoration is clearly evident. (IG Ju 52)

The right side of the cockpit of DB+RD with the switchboard at the bottom right. The cockpit interior is painted RLM Gray 02. (IG Ju 52)

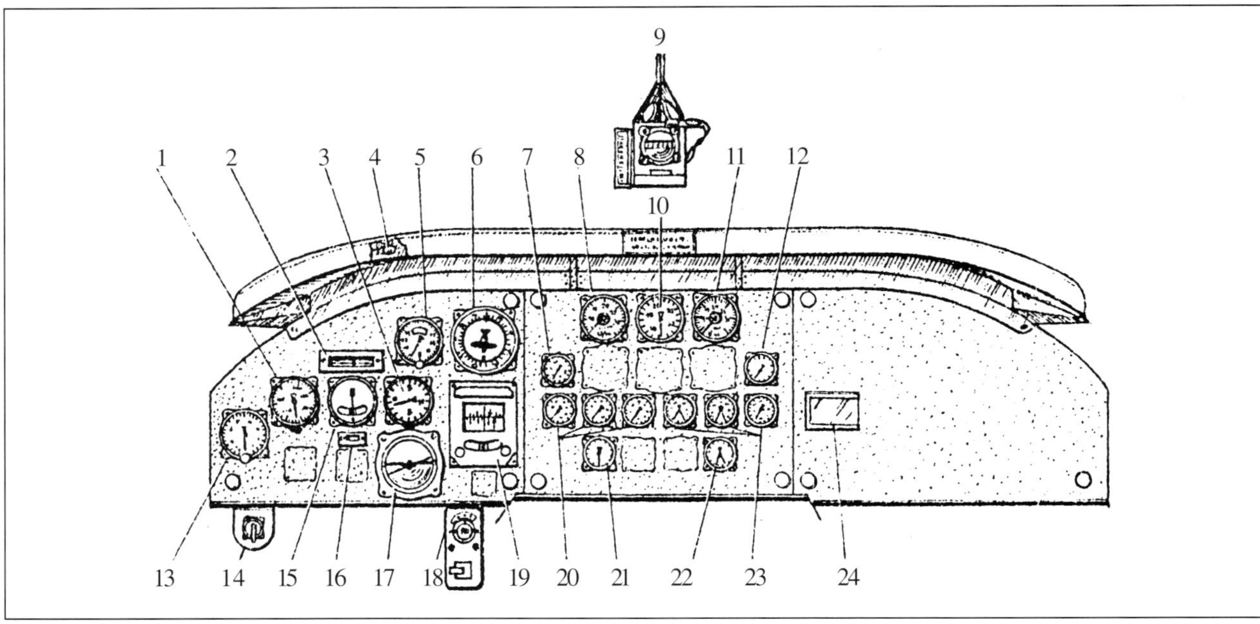

Instrumentation of the Junkers Ju 52/3mg14e.

Cockpit of CASA 352 L, RJ+NP, in the Auto and Technik Museum in Sinsheim. This license-built machine from Spain provides a good impression of the instrumentation of a German-built machine as the equipment was almost identical.

Instrument panel of the Ju 52/3mg14e:

No.	Equipment	Instrument Range	Requisition/Equipment Number
1	Airspeed indicator	60 – 550 km/h	Fl 22230
2	Lkz 3 course indicator	Fl 22562	
3	Statoscope-Vertical speed indicator	-10/+10 m/s	Fl 22381-10
4	Instrument panel shade		
5	Fine and coarse altimeter	0 – 10000 m	Fl 22320
6	Patin PFK/f3 pilot's repeater compass	Fl 23338	
7	Double pressure gauge for wheel brakes	0 – 10 kg/cm^2	Fl ?
8	Electrical distant-reading RPM indicator	300 – 3,600 rpm	Fl 20286-3
9	FK 38 magnetic compass	Fl 32333	
10	Mechanical RPM indicator	500 – 2,400 rpm	Fl 20218 ?
11	Electrical distant-reading RPM indicator	300 – 2,600 rpm	Fl 20286-3
12	Double pressure gauge for the wheel brake pressure reduction valve	0 – 20 / 0 – 200 kg/cm^2	Fl 20511
13	Coarse altimeter	0 – 10000 m	Fl 22316-10
14	Switch for pressure reduction device	Fl 22476 ?	
15	Turn and bank indicator, electric	Fl 22412	
16	Pitot heat visual indicator	Fl 32525	
17	Artificial horizon (Sperry) or turn and bank indicator combined with artificial horizon		Fl 22426 or Fl 22427 Fl 22411-1
18	Headset socket	Fl 27876	
19	Lku 4 gyro compass	Fl 22561	
20	Distant-reading oil temperature gauges (3)	0 – 120 ° C	Fl 20308
21	Outside air temperature gauge	-60 / + 40° C	Fl 20349
22	Fire extinguisher pressure gauge	0 – 10 kg/cm^2	Fl 20625 ?
23	Fuel/oil pressure gauge	0-10 / 0-10 kg/cm^2	Fl 20512-1
24	Mount for autopilot operating instructions		

Some aircraft were also equipped with a FuG 101a radio altimeter. In such a case an Ln 28330-1 indicator (0 - 150 / 0 – 750 m above ground) was also installed in the instrument panel.

Cockpit of HB-HOP, a Swiss Ju 52/3mg4e. Taken in 1981, this photograph allows many original instruments to be seen. Since then, however, most have been replaced by more modern instruments during overhaul.

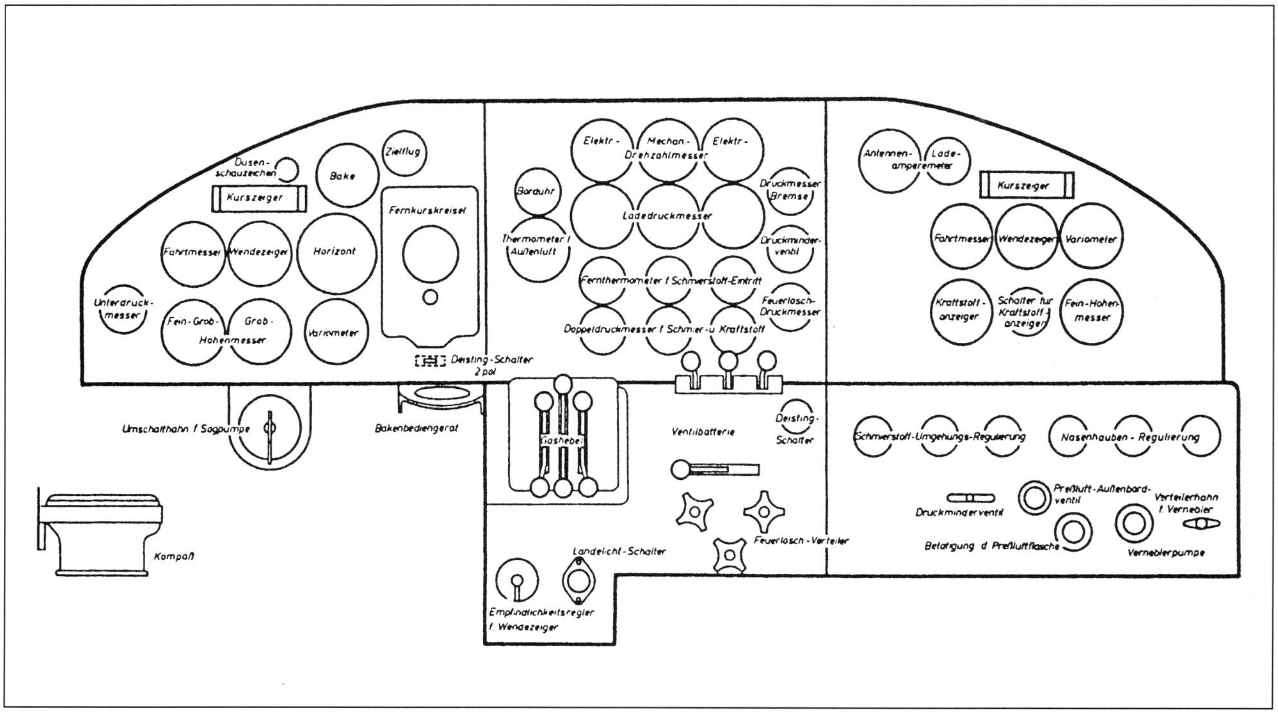

Equipment of a civil Ju 52/3m as illustrated in a company brochure. (Hafner Archive)

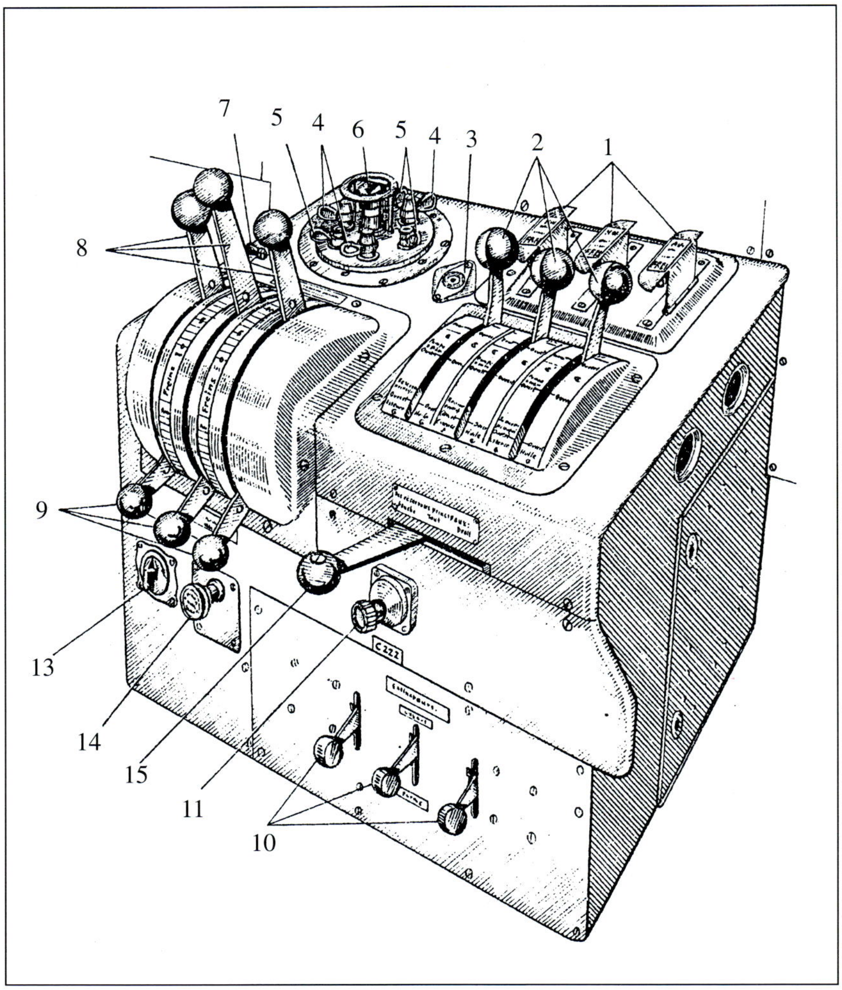

Central console of the Ju 52/3mg14e.

The cockpit of the Lufthansa Ju 52/3m with modern instruments

The central console of the Ju 52/3m, which housed the engine control levers, remained virtually unchanged in all versions. Most of the changes that did occur were related to the installation of the autopilot and distant-reading compass systems or more modern instruments.

No.	Equipment	Requisition/Equipment Number
1	3 starter switches	Fl 21214
2	Mixture setting lever	
3	Electrical system cutout	19-6829 A
4	ZSH 1/5 Z magneto switch	Fl 21111
5	Ignition timing adjustment lever	
6	Ignition cutout switch	
7	Throttle lever position limiter	
8	Throttle lever	
9	Levers for altitude throttle	
10	Fire extinguisher levers	
11	Illumination dimmer	Fl 32416
12	left blank	
13	Autopilot master switch	Fl 22559-1
14	Autopilot emergency disengage button	Fl 22557
15	Fuel tank selector lever	

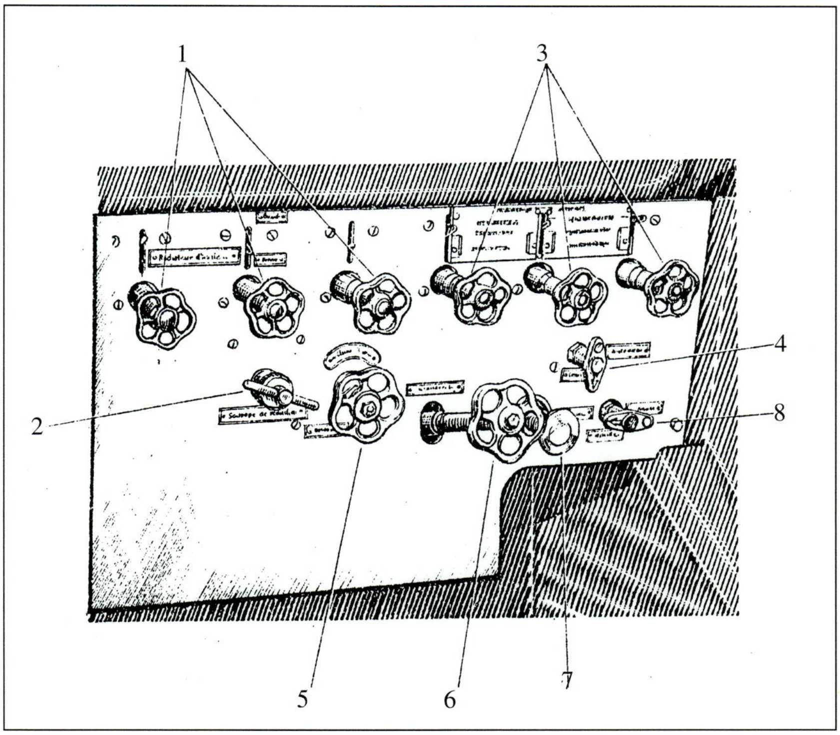

Switch panel on the bottom right of the Ju 52/3mg14e's instrument panel.

Under the starboard section of the main instrument panel was the control panel for the coolers, starter fuel and the compressed air system. With its large turning handles it was reminiscent of a locomotive engineer's station. This control panel remained virtually unchanged through all versions of the Ju 52.

1 Turning handles for the oil cooler
2 Valve for compressed air pressure reduction
3 Turning handles for carburetor pre-heat
4 Turning handles for the starter fuel distributor
5 Valve for the compressed air external coupling
6 Valve for the compressed air bottles
7 Starter injection pump
8 Starter injection selector switch

Another view of the instrument panel of the Lufthansa Ju 52. Most of the instruments comply with current international standards. (Kleikamp)

Instrumentation of the Lufthansa Ju 52/3mg:

No.	Equipment	Instrument Range
1	Magnetic compass and deviation table	
2	Airspeed indicator	20 – 190 kts/50 – 350 km/h
3	Artificial horizon	
4	Fine and coarse altimeter	0 – 30,000 feet
5	Radio compass	
6	VOR indicator	
7	Radio and navigation systems controls	
8	Vertical speed indicator	-4,000/+4,000 ft/min
9	Turn and bank indicator	
10	Navigation equipment	
11	3 RPM indicators	0 – 2,800 rpm
12	Engine warning lights and indicators	
13	Outside air temperature gauge	-20/+50° C°
14	3 boost pressure gauges	5 – 45 in HG abs
15	3 oil pressure gauges	0 – 120 psi
16	3 fuel pressure gauges	0 – 10 psi
17	3 oil temperature gauges (inlet) (adjustable for outside air temperature)	-10/+120° C
18	3 cylinder head temperature gauges	0 – 300° C
19	3 carburetor temperature gauges	-20/+50° C
20	3 exhaust gas temperature gauges	0 – 1,000° C
21	Clock	
22	Throttle levers	
23	High-altitude throttle levers	
24	Fuel mixture levers	
25	Fuel tank selector switch	
26	Carburetor pre-heat cranks	

The equipment installed in the Lufthansa Ju 52/3mg, D-AQUI, is illustrated for comparison with the vintage instrumentation described earlier. For safety reasons the aircraft has been equipped with modern instruments, some of which are also used in Airbus aircraft. Virtually none of the aircraft's original instrumentation remains. Some of the instrument ranges are determined by the aircraft's Pratt&Whitney Wasp engines.

Klemm L 25 D VII R, D-EJOL, at a flying meet in 1979.

Instrument panel from a Klemm L 25 c. The panel is complete with all original instruments.

Equipment of a Klemm L 25 c (from left to right:

No.	Equipment	Instrument Range	Requisition/Equipment Number
1	Bosch SVZ 14/3M6 ignition switch		
2	Askania Lr 19r airspeed indicator	50 – 250 km/h	Fl 22208
3	Zürn Z7A magnetic compass		
4	Lufft C 4/60 altimeter	0 – 5000 m	
5	Maximall fuel gauge for L 25c	0 – 40 l	
6	Air pump for fuel gauge		(Fl 20740)

The list is based on the equipment installed in a surviving original instrument panel. As a rule, the Klemm L 25 C was powered by the 60 H.P. BMW Xa, the 70-80 H.P. Hirth HM 60/R or the 85 H.P. Pobjoy R.

Klemm L 25

The L 25, which was developed from the L 20, was probably the best known aircraft produced by Hans Klemm. By 1939 total of approximately 600 had been built for customers worldwide. Thus for an entire decade the L 25 was the standard aircraft of sports fliers.

A two-seater with a plywood fuselage, over the years the L 25 was built in a multitude of versions, often differing only in the engine installed: Mercedes F 7502, Salmson AD 9, Armstrong-Siddeley Genet, BMW X, Hirth HM 60, Pobjoy R, Siemens Sh 13 or Argus As 8, a performance spectrum of from 20 to 95 H.P. The wishes of the customers had no bounds, resulting in the monoplane being delivered with and without a cockpit canopy, floats, skis, high- and low-pressure tires, rubber shocks or oil-damped shock struts.

It is unlikely that any other sporting aircraft won as many prizes and victories as Klemm's L 25: International Light Aircraft Competition Paris-Orly in 1928, a German distance record in 1929, the contest for the Belgian King's Cup in the same year, participation in the Europa Rundflug in 1929 and 1930, a high-altitude record for light aircraft and an endurance record in France, the International Light Aircraft Competition in Brussels in 1930, participation in the Deutschlandflug and many more.

Forward cockpit of D-EJOL. The airspeed indicator and RPM indicator were mounted on the outside of the fuselage.

Rear cockpit of D-EJOL. The instrument panel is original with the exception of some added equipment. Below right is the fire extinguisher. The radio has been removed. Visible on the bottom left is the hand pump.

Standard simple instrumentation in the rear cockpit of a Klemm L 25 D. The version at the top is for an aircraft with hand pump, the one at the bottom for a machine with engine-driven pump. (Hafner Archive)

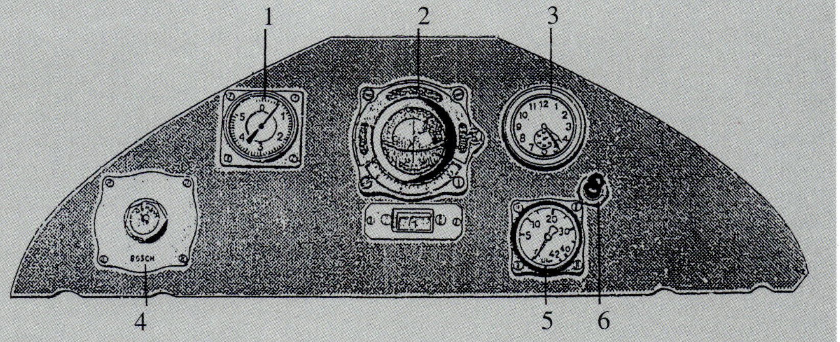

Simple instrumentation for L 25 D with engine-driven pump and mixture ignition: rear cockpit (see illustration below):

No.	Equipment	Instrument Range	Requisition/Equipment Number
1	Lufft C4/60 altimeter	0 – 5000 m	
2	Zürn Z7g magnetic compass with compensation		Fl 23220
3	Fuel pressure gauge	0 – 0.5 kg/cm²	Fl 20505
4	Bosch SSH 32/8 Z ignition switch		Fl 21107
5	Junghans clock		Fl 22600
6	Maximall fuel gauge	0 – 42 / 0 – 48 l	Fl 20704
7	Air pump for fuel gauge		Fl 20740
8	Three-position cock for the measuring line with placards "Header Tank" and "Side Tank"		

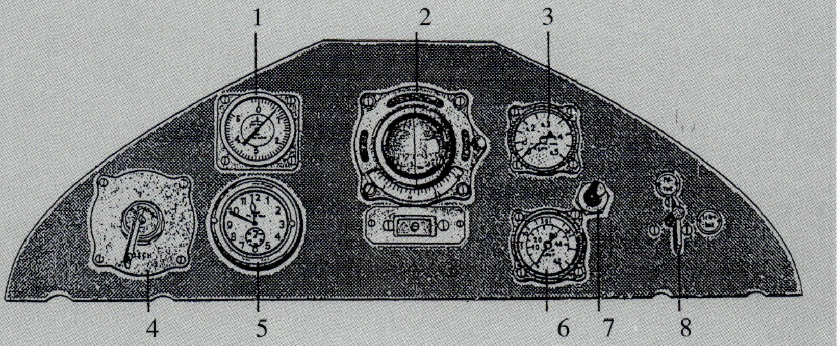

Forward Cockpit

No.	Equipment	Instrument Range	Requisition/Equipment Number
•	Airspeed indicator (left side fuselage exterior beneath fairing)	50 – 350 km/h	Fl 22221
•	Bosch SSH 32/8 Z ignition switch (left side of instrument panel)		Fl 21107
•	Veigel F 80 RPM indicator or Deuta (right side fuselage exterior beneath fairing)	0 – 2,500 rpm 600 – 3,000 rpm	Fl 20207

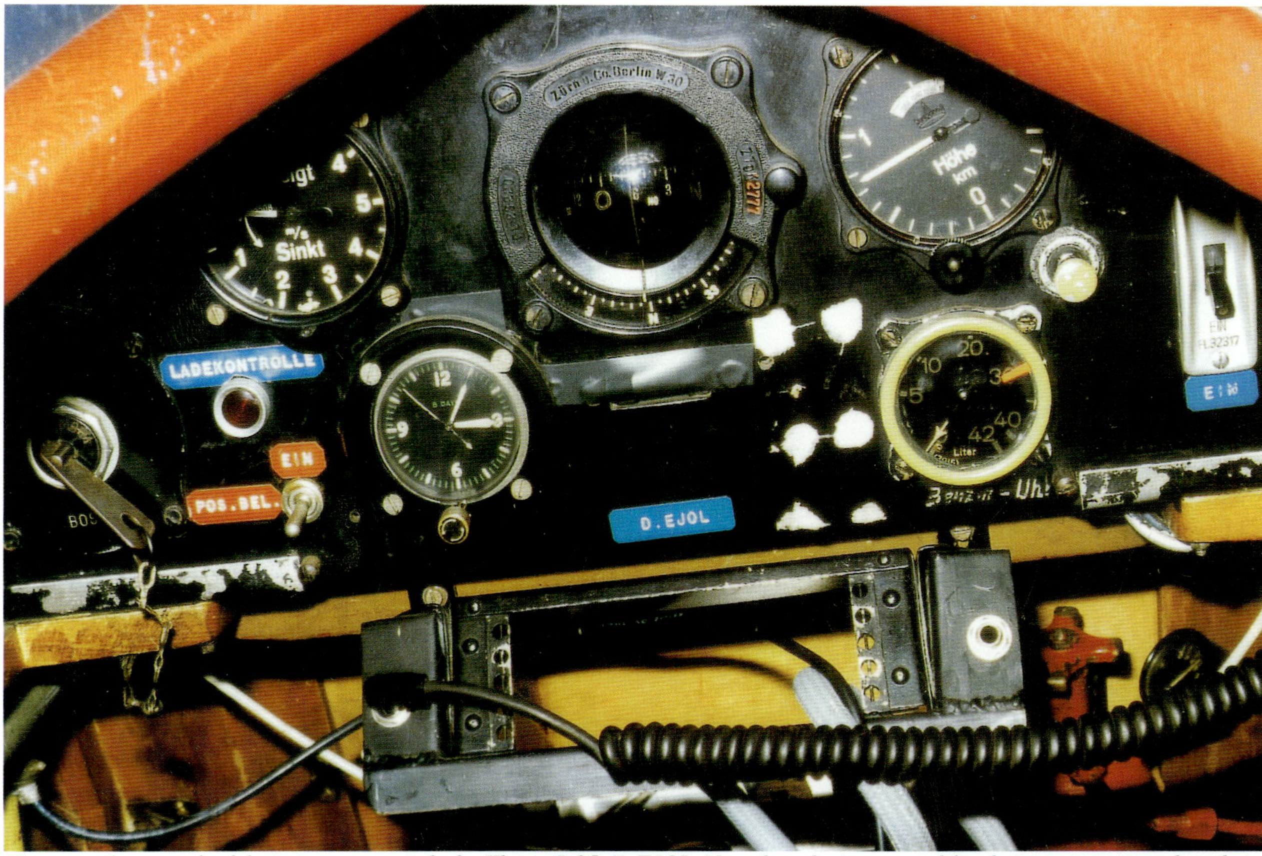

Close-up photograph of the instrument panel of a Klemm L 25, D-EJOL. Use of synthetic material for the instrument panel made it a simple task to install additional equipment.

Other original examples are provided for the replacement part lists for the Klemm L 25 D, of which the VII and VIIr versions with the 70-80 H.P. Hirth HM 60/R were built in the greatest numbers. The two versions differed in that one had simplified instrumentation—mainly in the rear cockpit—and the other duplicated instrumentation in the two cockpits.

Simple instrumentation for L 25 D with hand pump and battery ignition: rear cockpit (see illustration at top right of Page 116):

No.	Equipment	Instrument Range	Requisition/Equipment Number
1	Lufft C4/60 altimeter	0 – 5000 m	
2	Zürn Z7g magnetic compass with compensation		Fl 23220
3	Junghans clock	Fl 22600	
4	Bosch SSH 32/8 Z ignition switch		
5	Maximall fuel gauge	0 – 42 l	Fl 20704
6	Air pump for fuel gauge		Fl 20740

Forward cockpit:

No.	Equipment	Instrument Range	Requisition/Equipment Number
•	Airspeed indicator (left side fuselage exterior beneath fairing)	50 – 350 km/h	Fl 22221
•	Bosch SSH 32/4 Z ignition switch (left side of instrument panel)		
•	Veigel F 80 RPM indicator	0 – 2,500 rpm	
	or Deuta (right side fuselage exterior beneath fairing)	600 – 3,000 rpm	Fl 20207

The aircraft was also used for expeditions to Iceland, Spitzbergen, North America and an attempted crossing of the Atlantic. Famous names such as Robert Lusser, Wolf Hirth, Elly Beinhorn, Theo Osterkamp and Heinz Rühmann are associated with the Klemm L 25. The aircraft also appeared in a number of films. Ernst Udet flew it in "SOS Iceberg" and "The White Hell of Piz Palü".

Although production officially ceased in 1939, deliveries of a few machines continued until 1943. The aircraft was built under license in the U.K. by the British Klemm Company and British Aircraft and in the USA by Aeromarine. Of the 600 aircraft built, thirteen L 25s have survived complete as well as parts of three others.

Designed to be undemanding and cheap to operate, the instrumentation of the L 25 was correspondingly simple. The basic aircraft had instrumentation only in the rear cockpit, which was usually occupied by the pilot. The forward cockpit's equipment was limited to a second ignition switch plus airspeed indicator and RPM indicator, with the latter installed beneath hoods on each side of the cockpit.

The replacement part list does provide a standard instrumentation, however with the many vari-

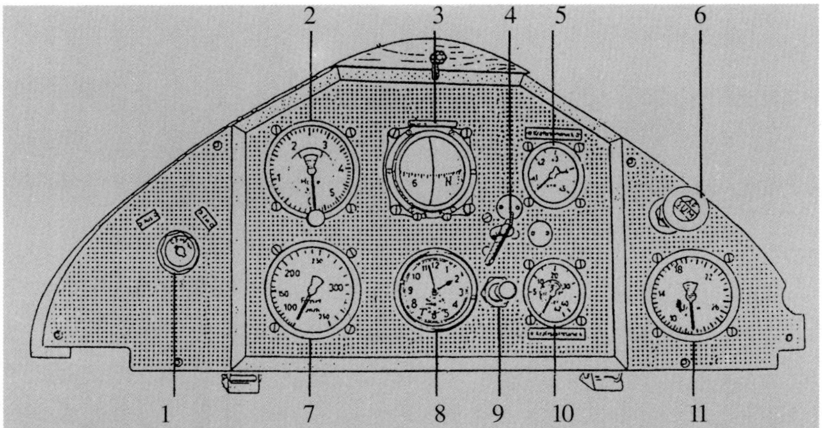

Rear cockpit (see illustration above):

No.	Equipment	Instrument Range	Requisition/Equipment Number
1	Bosch SSH 32/8 Z ignition switch		Fl 21107
2	Lufft AN 6000 altimeter	0 – 6000 m	Fl 22310
3	Ludolph FK 5 magnetic compass		Fl 23220
4	Three-position cock for measuring line ("Header Tank" / "Side Tank")		
5	Fuel pressure gauge	0 – 0.5 kg/cm²	Fl 20505
6	SUM AP 8 starter injection pump ?		Fl 20592
7	Airspeed indicator	50 – 350 km/h	Fl 22221
8	Junghans clock	Fl 22600	
9	Air pump for fuel gauge	Fl 20740	
10	Maximall fuel gauge	0 – 42 l	Fl 20704
11	Deuta RPM indicator	600 – 3,000 rpm	Fl 20207

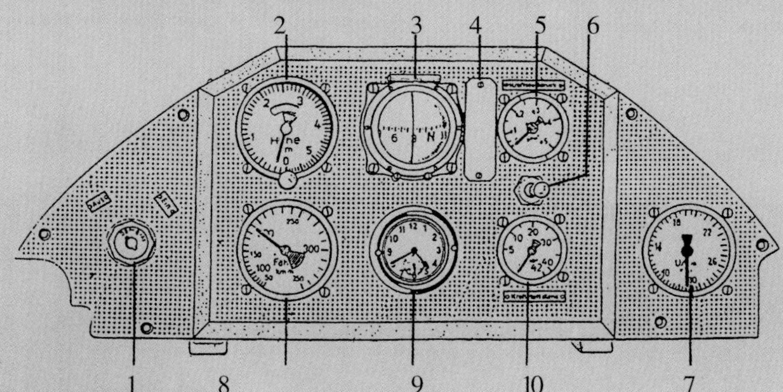

Forward Cockpit:

No.	Equipment	Instrument Range	Requisition/Equipment Number
1	Bosch SSH 32/8 Z ignition switch		Fl 21107
2	Lufft AN 6000 altimeter	0 – 6000 m	Fl 22310
3	Ludolph FK 5 magnetic compass		Fl 23220
4	Deviation table		
5	Fuel pressure gauge	0 – 0.5 kg/cm²	Fl 20505
6	Air pump for fuel gauge	Fl 20740	
7	Deuta RPM indicator	600 – 3,000 rpm	Fl 20207
8	Airspeed indicator	50 – 350 km/h	Fl 22221
9	Junghans clock	Fl 22600	
10	Maximall fuel gauge	0 – 42 l	Fl 20704

(Illustrations Hafner Archive)

ants there were also numerous deviations. For this reason the descriptions offered here must serve as examples only. Export aircraft were equipped with standard foreign instruments, depending on the nation to which they were sold.

Some Klemm L 25s were flown for decades. In some cases new or additional equipment was installed during overhauls at the request of their owners. The instrument panels of the standard L 25 were made of black Pertinax, a synthetic material. It is rare to find a Klemm L 25 still flying or in a museum with original instrumentation. Either foreign instruments have been installed, especially in the case of export machines, or additional instruments were added to ease operation.

One example is Klemm L 25 D VII R, D-EJOL, built in 1934, which now belongs to the city of Böblingen. It was originally equipped with simple instrumentation with hand pump. The original equipment was partly replaced with comparable vintage instruments or supplemented by equipment required for ease of operation, such as a vertical speed indicator and two switches for the electrical system in the rear cockpit. Klemm L 25s built prior to 1945 were not usually equipped with radios. Added to the front cockpit were an altimeter and a magnetic compass.

The Klemm L 25 with duplicated instrumentation was rather more extensively equipped. In such aircraft the instrument panels were made of metal and wood.

Klemm Kl 35 D, D-EFTG, of the Flugschule Koch in the colors of a Luftwaffe training aircraft.

Cockpit of D-EFTG. Instrumentation is typical for a Luftwaffe aircraft with some minor deviations. Additions include a cylinder head temperature gauge and an accelerometer for aerobatics.

Klemm Kl 35

Klemm's best known light aircraft, the L 25, was followed by the more modern Kl 35, a fully aerobatic low-wing monoplane with a steel tube fuselage and wooden wings. By 1945 more than 2,000 examples of this popular two-seat trainer and sporting aircraft had left the assembly halls in Böblingen, making it the most produced Klemm aircraft. The most important variants were:

Kl 35 A: Basic version with an 80 H.P. Hirth HM 60 R.

Kl 35 B: First production version with a 105 H.P. Hirth HM 504 A.

Kl 35 D: Final series, mainly used as training aircraft by the *Luftwaffe*.

Kl 35 D: Special version produced after the war for aerobatic competition.

The Kl 35 was exported to Hungary, Romania, Lithuania and Czechoslovakia. One of the type's major foreign users was the Swedish air force, which purchased a total of 75 Kl 35 Ds in 1940. The Swedes operated the type, which they designated SK.15, until 1947.

The surviving aircraft were initially transferred to the Swedish civil registry and later most were sold to foreign buyers. For this reason, all but one of the surviving Klemm Kl 35s are former Swedish air force machines.

The standard equipment installed in the Klemm Kl 35 B and D is shown in detail by the illustrations in the pilot notes. The rear cockpit was usually occupied by the pilot or instructor, while the forward

Equipment in the pilot's cockpit (rear) of the Klemm Kl 35:

No.	Equipment	Instrument Range	Requisition/Equipment Number
1	Altimeter	0 – 6000 m	Fl 22316-6 or 22310
	or	0 – 10000 m	Fl 22316-10 or 22311
2	FK 5 or	Fl 23211	
`	FK 38 magnetic compass	Fl 23233	
3	Placard:		

Maximum allowable speeds and revolutions		
215 km/h	in level flight	2,530 rpm
340 km/h	in diving flight	3,300 rpm
185 km/h	in poor visibility at low level	2,360 rpm

4 Placard:

Main tank	60 l	at cruising revs	2,530 rpm
Header tank	31 l	fuel consumption	25 l/hr
Oil tank	4.25 l	oil consumption	0.25 l/hr
Endurance	3 1/2 hr		

No.	Equipment	Instrument Range	Requisition/Equipment Number
5	Label: "Fuel Pressure"		
6	Fuel pressure gauge	0 – 0.5 kg/cm²	Fl 20504 or 20505
or	0 – 1 kg/cm2	Fl 20504-1	
7	Air pump for fuel gauge	Fl 20742-1	
8	Fuel gauge	0 – 31 l	Fl 20704
9	Placard: "Contents Header Tank"		
10	Placard: "Contents Main Tank"		
11	Fuel gauge	0 – 60 l	Fl 20704
12	RPM indicator	600 – 3,000 rpm	Fl 20207
13	Airspeed indicator	50 – 350 km/h	Fl 22228
14	Keinzle 8-Day	Fl 23886-1	
	or Junghans Bo-UK-1 clock	Fl 23885	
15	Ignition switch	Fl 21118	
16	Deviation table "Nav. Vordruck K 6"	Fl 23906	

Equipment in the observer's position (front cockpit):

No.	Equipment	Instrument Range	Requisition/Equipment Number
1	Altimeter	0 – 6000 m	Fl 22316-6 or 22310
	or	0 – 10000 m	Fl 22316-10 or 22311
2	FK 5 magnetic compass	Fl 23211	
	or FK 38	Fl 23233	
3	Deviation table "Nav Vordruck K 6"	Fl 23906	
4	RPM indicator	600 - 3,000 rpm	Fl 20207
5	Placard with maximum allowable speeds and revolutions (same as No. 3 on the pilot's instrument panel)		
6	Airspeed indicator	50 – 350 km/h	Fl 22228
7	Ignition switch		

Instrument Panel of a Kl 35 with Askania Small Instruments:

No.	Equipment	Instrument Range	Type
1	Altimeter	0 – 3000 m	Lh 1K
2	Pitch indicator	+15 / -15°	La 1K
3	Airspeed indicator	0 – 200 km/h	Lr 1K
4	Battery box for turn and bank indicator		
5	Electric turn and bank indicator	Lge 1K	
6	Turn and bank indicator switch		
7	Magnetic compass		Lke 1K
8	Vertical speed indicator	-5/+5 m/s	Lv 7r
9	Clock	Lu 1k	
10	Gyro compass		
11	Compensator for the vertical speed indicator		

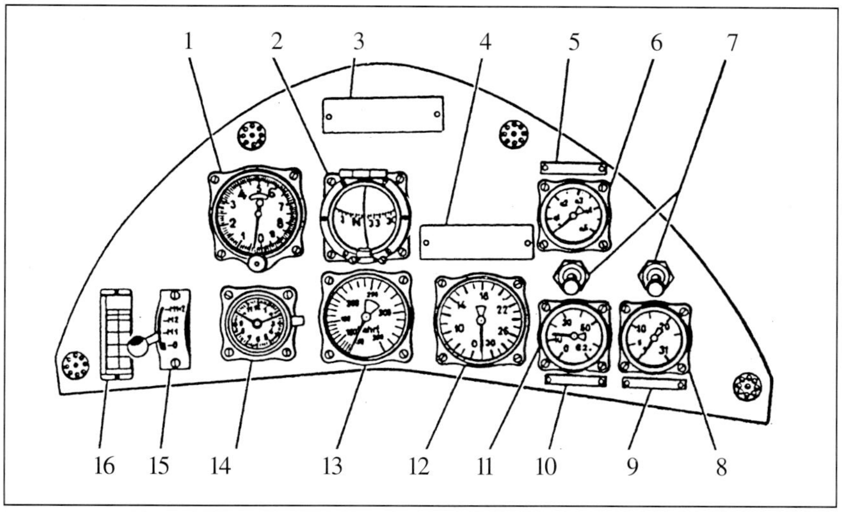

Arrangement of instruments in the pilot's panel of the Kl 35. (Hafner Archive)

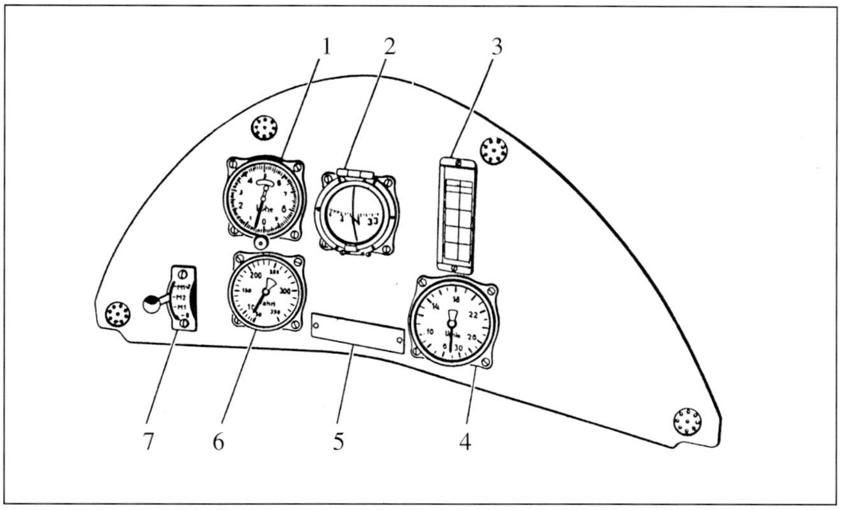

Arrangement of instruments in the observer's panel of the Kl 35. (Hafner Archive)

Instrument panel of a Kl 35 with Askania small instruments. (Soppa Collection)

cockpit accommodated the observer, trainee pilot or passenger. For this reason, the forward cockpit was less well equipped than the rear.

The equipment described above corresponds to the standard equipment installed in the Kl 35 B or D. There were variations at the request of customers, especially for export machines and specially-equipped aircraft built for attempts at records or experimental use.

One example of this is provided by an illustration from the catalogue of Askania, the instrument maker. As there are no engine instruments, it must be the instrument panel from the observer's position. Most of the instruments are "Askania Small", meaning instruments with a diameter of 66.7 mm, designed for installation in the small instruments of gliders.

Typically, vintage aircraft on the civilian registry are equipped and painted in a way which suits the personal requirements of their owners. Usable vintage instruments are often difficult to come by and in most cases have been replaced with technically similar foreign or new instruments. Only in a few cases have owners, who in most cases are more interested in flying the aircraft, strived to accurately restore the aircraft's instrumentation and paint scheme.

One example of this is the Swedish Klemm Kl 35 D of the Koch Flying School, which most recently was registered in England as G-BWRD. Previously it was flown from Augsburg as D-EFTG.

The owners have attempted to restore the aircraft as a *Luftwaffe* training machine. The machine is painted inside and out in a color which resembles RLM 02 (gray). The instrument panel is painted black. Almost all of the instruments are vintage devices and German-language placards have replaced the original Swedish ones.

Cockpit of a Swiss Bf 108 B-1 with variable-pitch propeller. (Fliegermuseum)

Messerschmitt Bf 108 *Taifun*

The Messerschmitt Bf 108 Taifun was originally developed for the 1934 *Europa-Rundflug*, and it subsequently came to be regarded as a classic example of the four-seat tourer. The *Taifun* was Willy Messerschmitt's first all-metal design and it incorporated a number of advanced features which would become standard in his later designs: retractable undercarriage, automatic leading edge slats and stressed skin construction. The design of the Bf 108 resulted in an aircraft with excellent handling characteristics and, thanks to its 240 H.P. Argus As 10 C engine, a high cruising speed. The *Taifun* was ahead of its time and even today, more than 60 years after its maiden flight, it does not look out of place amongst modern sporting aircraft.

The main production versions were the Bf 108 B, a touring aircraft, and the Bf 108 D, a courier aircraft for the *Luftwaffe*. In 1942 production was transferred to the French company S.N.C.A. du Nord,

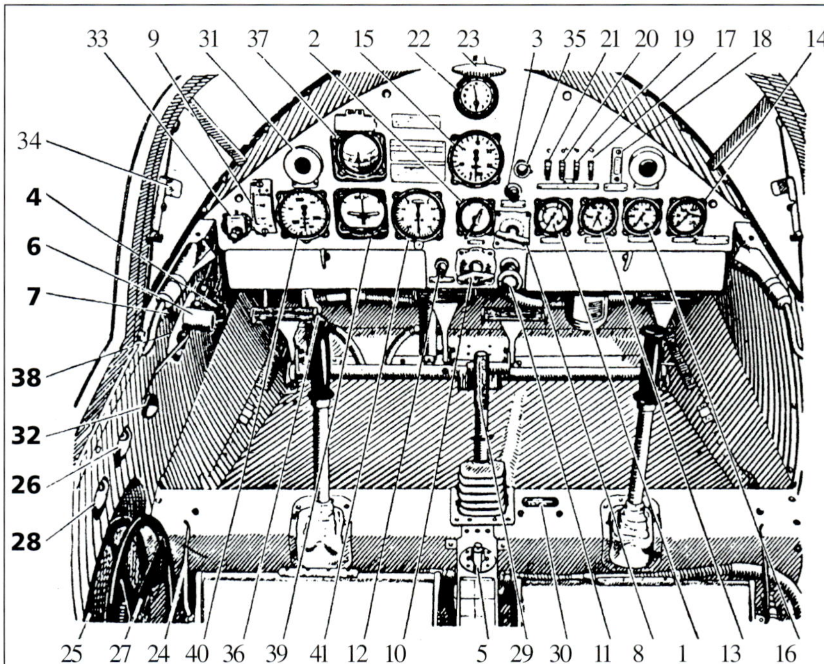

Bf 108 with blind-flying instrumentation. (Soppa Collection)

The pilot's notes and equipment guide of March 1939 provides an impression of the **equipment of the Bf 108 B-1**:

	Equipment	Instrument Range	Requisition/Equipment Number
1	Fuel contents gauge	0-60 l rear 0-90 l front	Fl 20704
2	Fuel contents gauge selector switch		Fl 20754-2
3	Fuel contents gauge pump		Fl 20742-1
4	Fuel cock lever		
5	Fuel tank selector switch (5 position)		
6	Throttle lever		
7	Selector switch for automatic switch with remote control		
8	Fuel hand pump		
9	Ignition switch		Fl 21118
10	Compressed air valve handle		
11	SUM AP 8 starter injector pump	8-4505 A	
12	Starter button	Fl 21212	
13	Fuel/Oil pressure gauge	0-0.5/0-10 kg/cm² or 0-1/0-10 kg/cm²	Fl 20512 Fl 20512-1
14	Compressed air pressure gauge	0 – 250 kg/cm²	Fl 20519
15	RPM indicator	600 – 3,000 rpm	Fl 20219
16	Oil temperature gauge	0 – 120° C	Fl 20308-2
17	Pitot tube heat switch		Fl 32316
18	Pitot tube heat visual indicator		Fl 32525-3
19	Instrument panel lighting switch		Fl 32316
20	Navigation lights switch		Fl 32316
21	Landing light switch		Fl 32316
22	Junghans clock		Fl 22600
23	Central canopy handle		
24	Seat adjustment lever		
25	Land flap adjustment wheel		
26	Landing flap position visual indicator		
27	Tailplane incidence control wheel		
28	Tailplane incidence visual indicator		
29	Undercarriage control lever		
30	Undercarriage position mechanical indicator		
31	Ventilation port		
32	Throttle lever locking nut		
33	Electrical system cut-out switch		Fl 32315-2
34	Canopy jettison lever		
35	Fire extinguisher handle		
36	Control lock ring		
37	Lke 6 "Kleiner Emil" magnetic compass		Fl 23226-1
38	Circuit breaker panel		
39	Lg 14 r turn-and-bank indicator		Fl 22402
40	Airspeed indicator	50 – 350 km/h	Fl 22228
41	Lh 22r-10 altimeter	0 – 10000 m	Fl 22319

which after the war continued to produce the aircraft for the French air force. The French designation for the Bf 108 B was Nord 1000 with the Argus engine and Nord 1001 or 1002 with a 223 H.P. Renault engine. In French service the type was dubbed "*Pingouin*". The most obvious external difference between the Argus- and Renault-powered machines was the revised engine cowling of the French version.

During the war Nord was also tasked with continuing development of the *Taifun*. Under German direction it produced the Me 208, which differed from the original design in having a slightly larger airframe and a tricycle undercarriage. After the war the type was produced for the French air force as the Nord 1100 and 1101 "*Noralpha*" and was used in the communications and liaison roles.

A total of 887 *Taifuns* were built by 1945 and another 285 by Nord in France. Eleven Bf 108s have survived and several are still flying, such as the Bf 108 B-1, D-ESBH, of the Messerschmitt Foundation and the Bf 108 B-1, D-EBEI, of Lufthansa.

More than forty examples of the Nord 1002 have survived and several of these built continue flying, mainly in France.

The Bf 108 had a roomy cabin with two seats in the front and a bench seat in the rear. Most of the instruments were arranged in front of the pilot, with the flight instruments grouped on the left and the engine instruments in the center and left. The aircraft was equipped with dual controls, but there was only one throttle lever and fuel cock, on the left side.

The compressed air system for starting the engine was not installed in all variants of the Bf 108. The compressed air pressure gauge was not fitted in aircraft which lacked this system.

Cockpit of a Swiss Bf 108 B-1 with variable-pitch propeller. (Fliegermuseum)

Bf 108 with blind-flying instrumentation. (Soppa Collection)

Equipment of the Bf 108 D:

No.	Equipment	Instrument Range	Requisition/Equipment Number
1	RPM indicator	600 – 3,600 rpm	Fl 20222-2
2	Starter switch		Fl 21212
3	Oil temperature gauge	0 – 120 or 0 - 160° C	Fl 20308-2
4	Fuel / oil pressure gauge	0 – 1 / 0 – 10 kg/cm²	Fl 20512-1
5	Ignition switch		Fl 21119
6	SUM AP 8 starter injection pump		8-4505 A
7	Compressed air pressure gauge	0 – 250 kg/cm²	Fl 20519
8	Compressed air starter button		
9	Handle for compressed air valve	108-901.017	
10	Cockpit ventilation pipe		
11	Hand crank with position indicator for Me P 7 propeller	108-919.07	
12	Airspeed indicator	80 – 550 km/h	Fl 22230
13	Visual indicator for pitot heat		Fl 32525-3
14	Fine and coarse altimeter	0 – 10000 m	Fl 22320
15	Statoscope-vertical speed indicator	-10/+10 m/s	Fl 22381-10
16	Turn and bank indicator		Fl 22402
17	FK 38 magnetic compass		Fl 23233
18	Deviation table		Fl 23906
19	Bo-UK 1 clock		Fl 23885
20	Fire extinguisher		
21	Button for fire extinguisher valve		
22	Cockpit canopy jettison levers		
23	Electrical system cutout switch		Fl 32315-2
24	Cockpit ventilation slide		
25	Left control stick		
26	Handle for fuel hand pump		108-709.024
27	Undercarriage indicator		
28	Undercarriage lever		
29	Ring on cable for rudder lock		
30	Right control stick		
31	Map holder		
32	Vertical speed indicator compensator		Fl 32350
33	Toggle switch		
34	Throttle lever		
35	Electrical panel with circuit breakers for generator, landing light, navigation lights, cabin lighting, pitot heat, undercarriage warning horn, instrument panel lighting.		
36	Fuel gauge		
37	Fuel cock lever		
38	Trim wheel with indicators for tailplane and landing flap position		

Instrumentation of the Bf 108 D

The cockpit featured numerous placards containing instructions for operation of the engine and operating limits for various systems:

Engine Start
Cold engine: prime twice
Warm engine: do not prime

Attention! Quick-Release Harness
Secure before takeoff.

Maximum speed with flaps
fully lowered
190 km/h

Landing Flap Position:		Tailplane Incidence
Takeoff	15°	0°
Landing	50°	

Cruising revs	1,820 rpm
Cruising speed	265 km/h
Range	1000 km
Endurance	3 hr 50 min

Maximum allowable continuous engine speed
1,880 rpm

Canopy Jettison
1 Reduce to minimum possible speed
2 Open the top central grip
3 Advance the side jettison lever.
Both doors can than be lifted off to the rear

In flight tank cock in Position 1 or 3
In the event of loss of fuel pressure in Position 1, move through Position 2 to 3.
In the event of loss of fuel pressure in Position 3, move through Position 2 to 1.

If fuel pressure does not increase, wait approximately 1 min. then move tank cock to Position 2 (reverse) and after 20 minutes make an emergency landing.

Instrument panel of Bf 108 B-1, D-EBEI. (Lufthansa)

Some Bf 108 Bs were equipped with expanded instrumentation and an Askania distant-reading compass for instrument flying. In this case the following equipment was installed:

Equipment Number	Instrument Range	Requisition/Part
• Lkg 2r course selector		Fl 23300
• Lkz 1p course indicator		Fl 23351
• Lgab 8 artificial horizon		Fl 22426
• Statoscope-vertical speed indicator	+10/-10 m/s	Fl 22381-10
• Sensitivity control for suction devices		

Equipment of the Lufthansa Bf 108 B-1

No.	Equipment	Instrument Range	Requisition/Equipment Number
1	Magnetic compass		
2	Deviation table		
3	Ventilation		
4	Undercarriage indicator		
5	Boost pressure gauge	0.4 – 1.4 atm	
6	RPM indicator	0 – 2,800 rpm	
7	Fuel pressure gauge	0 – 1 kg/cm²	
8	Low pressure gauge	0 – 10 inches HG	
9	Clock		
10	Outside air temperature gauge	-20 / +50° C	
11	Oil temperature and pressure gauge	0 - 120° C/0-10 kg/cm²	
12	Fuel gauge	0 – 60 / 0 – 90 l	Fl 20704
13	Fuel gauge air pump	Fl 20742-1	
14	Fuel gauge tank selector cock	Fl 20754-2	
15	Electric fuel pump switch		
16	Fuel reserve warning light		
17	Ammeter / voltmeter	-30 / + 100 A / -10 / + 30 V	
18	Pitot battery power switch		
19	Electrical system master switch		
20	Intercom volume control		
21	Turn and bank indicator		
22	Airspeed indicator	0 – 250 kts / 0 – 450 km/h	
23	Artificial horizon		
24	Altimeter	0 – 30,000 ft	
25	Vertical speed indicator	+ 6,000 / - 6,000 ft/min	
26	Gyrocompass		
27	Correction table for fuel gauge		
28	Radio controls		
29	Circuit breakers		for the electrical system
30	for the fuel system		
31	for the instruments		
32	for the starter system, etc.		
33	for the radio systems		
34	for cockpit lighting		
35	Tank selector switch with fuel cock		
36	Undercarriage signal lights – landing position		
37	Propeller pitch control switch		Messerschmitt
38	Operating data placard		
39	VOR indicator		
40	Mixture control lever		
41	Fuel hand pump		
42	Battery warning light		
43	Battery switch		
44	Ignition switch		Fl 21118
45	Starter switch		
46	Electrical system master switch		
47	Generator switch		
48	Pitot heat switch		
49	Cockpit lighting switch		
50	SUM AP 8 starter injection pump		8-4505 A
51	Parking brake		
52	Map holder		

It is unlikely that any other Bf 108 was better equipped than this aircraft.

Reconstructed instrument panel of a Bf 108 B. In fact, however, the aircraft is a Nord 1002, a built-built version of the Bf 108 D on display in Hermeskeil.

There were surely other variations and deviations in instrumentation, since civil aircraft were often fitted out according to the wishes of the purchaser.

The Bf 108 D-1 was the last production version of the *Taifun* and was built until 1945 for the liaison role with the *Luftwaffe*. As production proceeded, more modern instruments were installed. Production was ultimately transferred to Nord in France, as Messerschmitt was overburdened with fighter production. After the war the Bf 108 D-1 became the Nord 1000 "*Pingouin*" and early machines continued to use German instruments.

The Bf 108 B-1 operated by *Lufthansa* (D-EBEI) has much more comprehensive instrumentation incorporating modern radio and navigational equipment. Some of the flight instruments have been replaced with modern ones and only six original instruments remain.

Rear view of the Hungarian Siebel 202, HA-MAE. Note the no-slip walkway on the wing root. (Imre Mitter Archive)

Siebel Si 202 *Hummel* (Bumblebee)

First appearing in 1938, the Si 202 Hummel was designed to be an economical single-engine sporting aircraft for two persons, with emphasis on ease of handling. Built entirely of wood, it possessed innocuous handling characteristics, making it a safe aircraft to fly, even for relatively inexperienced pilots.

At the beginning of 1939 the Si 202 set two world altitude records of 5982 meters with two persons and 7043 meters with one person. Later the aircraft reached 7500 meters. The small aircraft also won first place in its class in numerous air races, rallies and endurance flights.

The aircraft was powered by a variety of engines, including Hirth and Zündapp inline engines and Salmson radials, with a power range of from 50 to 60 H.P. This was sufficient to provide the aircraft, which weighed just 290 kilograms empty, with an excellent performance and good fuel consumption.

Only sixty examples of the "Bumblebee", which sold for 6,000 RM, were built. Most of these remained in Germany, although a few were exported, to Hungary for example.

Not a single Si 202 has survived; fortunately, however, there are color photographs of the exterior and interior of one of the aircraft delivered to Hungary. These come from the archive of the Hungarian aviation historian Imre Mitter.

These photographs depict a simply-equipped aircraft with only the most important flight and engine instruments, which were more than adequate for visual flight.

At the bottom of the instrument panel are two additional openings for small standard instruments (57 mm installed diameter). The one on the left probably housed a clock, while the other was used for another engine instrument, probably a fuel pressure gauge, an oil temperature gauge or a fuel gauge. The large openings on both sides of the instrument panel were probably used to store aviation charts.

The aircraft depicted in the color photographs, HA-MAE, was finished in an overall gray color, probably RLM 02, with Hungarian national colors on the tail surfaces and a yellow fuselage band similar to that applied to Axis aircraft on the Eastern Front. The legend "Siebel Hummel" appears on the side of the fuselage in front of the cockpit, at least on the port side.

Suspended from the roof of the cockpit is the FK 5 (Fl 23211) magnetic compass. The small metal instrument panel, which was painted black, housed the following instruments:

Instrument	Part no.
Coarse altimeter to 6000 m	Fl 22316-6
Airspeed indicator 50-250 km/h	Fl 22227
RPM indicator, mechanical, 600-3,000 rpm	Fl 20207
Ignition lock	

Cockpit of Hummel HA-MAE. Note the red and white limit markings on the instruments. (Imre Mitter Archive)

The Second World War, 1939-1945

The standards from the 1930s were initially retained at the start of the Second World War. As the war went on, however, raw materials shortages and supply bottlenecks began to make themselves felt, and these also had an effect on aircraft instruments. In the beginning there was an upturn in the German aviation industry and many new types were developed and placed in service while development of older types continued. Increasingly powerful engines and more comprehensive equipment meant resulted in an increase in the number of instruments which had to be accommodated in instrument panels.

In an effort to save space, combined and multipurpose instruments were adopted, for example:

- Turn and bank indicator combined with artificial horizon
- RPM indicator combined with boost pressure gauge
- Two-position propeller pitch indicator
- Triple trim indicator
- Oxygen indicator (pressure gauge and oxygen control)

As well, 1944 saw the introduction of another small instrument standard with an installed diameter of 40 mm. As a rule they were electrical indicators (temperature and pressure gauges and various position indicators) with a simple pressed metal housing.

Instruments continued to be produced in the previous large and small standard sizes, such as electric turn and bank indicators and radio navigation indicators.

In aircraft with fully glazed noses, such as the Do 217, He 111, He 177 and Ju 188, the instruments were distributed among several consoles and instrument panels in order to avoid restricting the pilot's view. A few types, such as the Hs 129, Ju 88 and Bf 110, had instruments mounted in the engine nacelles for space reasons.

The standard blind flying panel was introduced in 1944, in particular in fighter aircraft and bombers such as the Ar 234, Ju 388, Bf 109 K, Me 163 and Me 262. Constructed mainly of plywood, the blind flying panel housed the six most important flight and navigation instruments.

The airspeed indicator, combined turn and bank indicator and artificial horizon, vertical speed indicator and repeater compass were installed in the familiar T arrangement. On the bottom left and right of the panel were the coarse altimeter and the radio navigation indicator.

This was comparable to the English "Basic Six", which was be found in almost every RAF aircraft from the end of the 1930s and consisted of airspeed indicator, artificial horizon, vertical speed indicator, altimeter, directional gyro and turn and bank indicator.

During the latter stages of the war strategic materials such as metals were replaced by wood or synthetic materials such as Bakelite. By then most instrument panels and consoles were made of plywood, constructed by furniture or glider makers. One well-known material was *Formholz*, layers of birch glued and together and pressed into shape. Compared to aluminum instrument panels, production time was cut in half and costs were thirty percent lower.

In the course of conservation and refinement measures, complicated devices were replaced by simpler ones and, in some cases, instruments not absolutely vital to the operational use of the aircraft were deleted. Several examples:

- Combined turn and bank indicator and artificial horizon:
  replaced by electric turn and bank indicator
- Distant-reading compass:
  replaced by simple magnetic compass
- Round counter:
  replaced by simple visual indicator
- Fuel warning light: deleted
- Clock: deleted
- Undercarriage position indicator:
  replaced by clear-view panel and mechanical indicators
- Wiring:
  shielding deleted

Another measure that was adopted to shorten development times and lower costs was the use of components from existing aircraft types. For example, the He 162 employed undercarriage components from the Bf 109, switches from the He 111 and fuel gauges from the He 177.

When the war broke out, the systems for painting and marking of aircraft interiors contained in the 1936 directives continued in use. From the end of 1941, however, the RLM introduced a change, ordering that all surfaces visible through canopies and glazed areas should be painted Black-Gray 66.

Later in the war units mixed their own colors for application during repairs and eventually not even the manufacturers could guarantee uniform colors.

An Arado Ar 96 B-1 in service with a flying school. Here an instructor is seen giving final instructions to a student pilot. (Schmid)

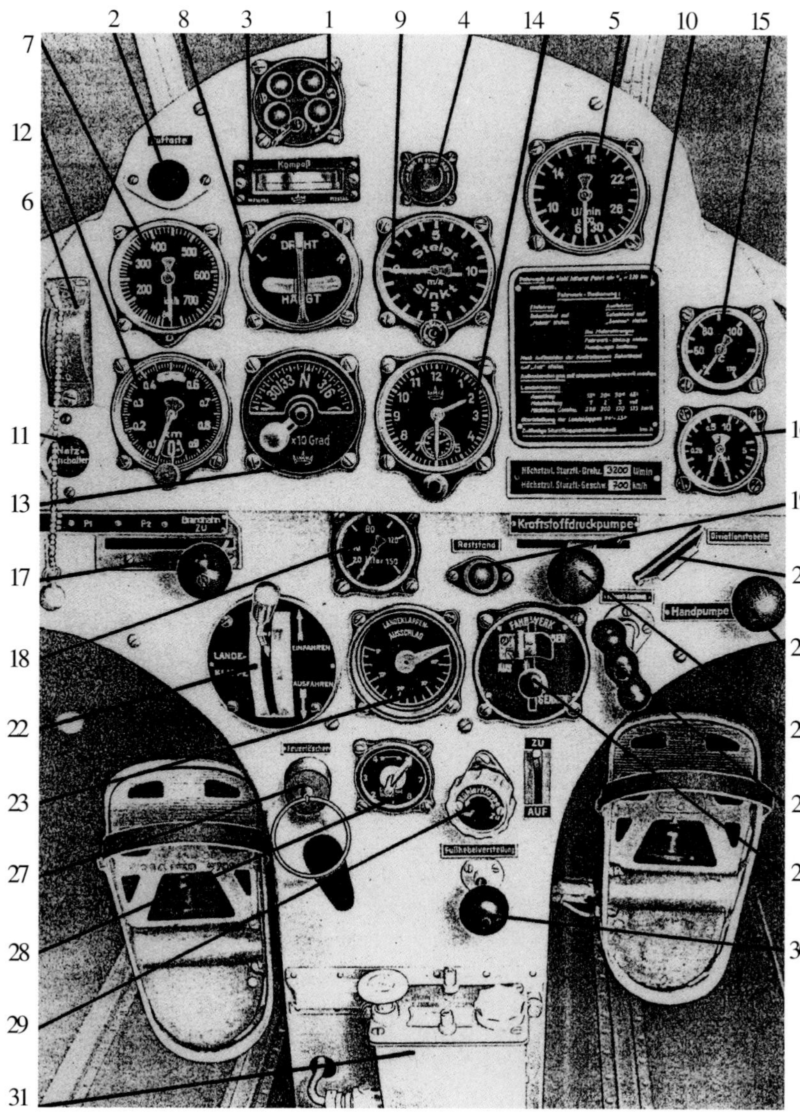

Instrumentation of the Ar 96 A with Askania distant-reading compass.

Other changes resulted from materials shortages late in the war. As service aircraft had relatively short lives, internal surfaces which were not externally visible, especially those made aluminum, were not painted.

A comparison of photographs of museum aircraft and contemporary Second World War photos will often reveal deviations in the equipment installed and the arrangement of instruments. The reason for this is that a considerable amount of time often passed from when the manuals were produced and the aircraft actually went into production. Changes were introduced on the production line, while others resulted from requests from combat units and shortages of materials.

Arado Ar 96

The 1930s were characterized by a breakthrough in aircraft construction. Relatively slow biplanes of mixed-construction were replaced by fast low-wing monoplanes of all-metal construction. This trend also affected military training aircraft and one of the first German types to reflect this was the Arado Ar 96, a robust two-seat design which made its debut in 1936.

The monocoque fuselage included a fully enclosed cockpit, and the entire airframe was flush riveted. Other features were a one-piece wing, retractable wide-track undercarriage, Argus variable-pitch propeller and extremely pleasant handling characteristics.

More than 11,500 examples of the Ar 96 B, which was powered by a 564 H.P. Argus As 410 engine, were built, making it one of the most produced German aircraft. Other sources suggest that only 3,400 were built, however. The Ar 96 also served with the air forces of Bulgaria, Romania and the CSSR, and the last examples were not withdrawn from service until the 1960s.

As a result of the war situation, the succeeding Ar 296 and Ar 396 were of mixed and wooden construction, respectively. The Ar 396 was produced in France as the S.I.P.A. S.10, of which approximately 200 were built. The all-metal French version was used as a training aircraft and as a light bomber in the war in Algeria.

Though the Ar 96 and its successors were built in large numbers, no complete aircraft has survived. Fragments and partial wrecks of approximately five aircraft remain and one machine has been completely restored in Norway.

One of the instrument panels shown here is from Arado Ar 96 B-1 WNr. 4210 (PD+EJ), which is currently in storage in Landshut. The restored forward instrument panel is in possession of the Musée de l'Air in Paris.

Forward instrument panel from an Ar 96 B with Askania distant-reading compass:

No.	Equipment	Instrument Range	Requisition/Equipment Number
1	Undercarriage indicator		Fl 32526
2	Radio transmit button		
3	Course indicator for distant-reading compass		Fl 23345
4	Dimmer		Fl 3402-1
5	RPM indicator	600 – 3,000 rpm	Fl 20207?
6	Ignition switch		Fl 21118
7	Airspeed indicator	80 – 750 km/h	Fl 22231
8	Turn and bank indicator		Fl 22402
9	Statoscope-vertical speed indicator	+10/-10 m/s	Fl 22381-10
10	Undercarriage and landing flaps operating instructions placard		
11	Electrical system cutout switch		Fl 32315-2
12	Fine and coarse altimeter	0 – 10000 m	Fl 22320
13	Course selector for distant-reading compass		Fl 23300
14	Clock (Askania)		Fl ?
15	Oil temperature gauge	30 - 120° C	Fl 20308
16	Fuel/oil pressure gauge	0-0.5 / 0-10 kg/cm^2	Fl 20512
17	Fuel cock		
18	Fuel gauge	0 – 150 l	Fl 20704
19	Fuel warning light, red		Fl 32262-1
20	Fuel pressure pump lever		
21	Slide with aircraft data placard and deviation table		Fl 23501
22	Landing flap control lever		
23	Landing flap indicator	0 - 45°	
24	Undercarriage selector switch		
25	Emergency undercarriage handle		
26	Hand pump for emergency lowering of UC		
27	Fire extinguisher pull ring		
28	Sensitivity control for turn and bank indicator		Fl 22405
29	Radiator flap control		
30	Rudder pedal adjustment lever		
31	ABP 6 starter injection pump with tank		8-4506 A

Historical photograph of the forward instrument panel of an Ar 96 B-1. (via Wildmoser)

Historical photograph of the forward cockpit of an Arado Ar 96 B-2 with armament. The arrangement of the instruments was modified to accommodate a Revi C/12 reflector gun sight. Visible at the top of the photo are the gun sight connector plug and the attachment cable.

Restored forward instrument panel of the Ar 96 B-1 in the Musée de l'Air. (Couderchon)

As an advanced trainer, the Ar 96 was equipped with instrumentation in the front cockpit similar to that of a fighter aircraft. Noteworthy are the numerous operating instructions on the instrument panel. Some Ar 96s were equipped with a fixed gun armament.

The instrument panel in the rear cockpit, which was occupied by the instructor or observer, was more sparsely equipped.

Two main types of instrumentation are known for the Ar 96, an earlier version in the Ar 96 A with Askania distant-reading compass and a later one from the Ar 96 B with Patin distant-reading compass system.

The text from the placard containing operating instructions for the undercarriage and landing flaps is reproduced below.

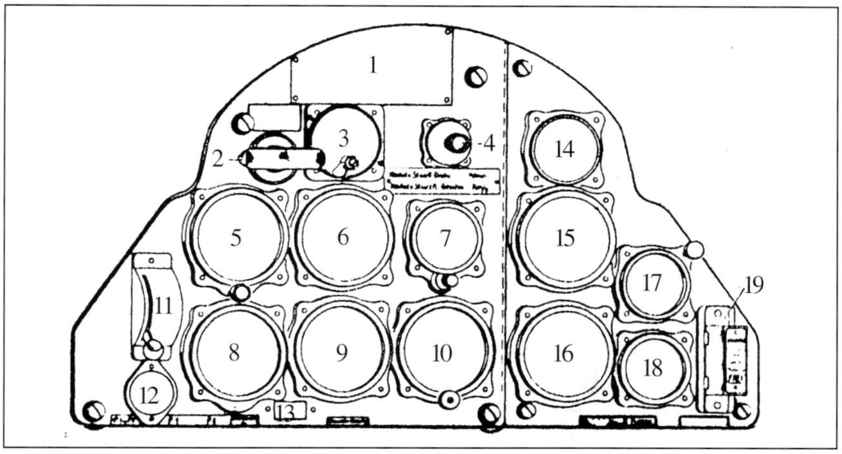

The forward main instrument panel of the Ar 96 B-1.

Forward main instrument panel:

No.	Equipment	Instrument Range	Requisition/Equipment Number
1	Undercarriage operating instructions		
2	Propeller pitch control		
3	Undercarriage indicator		Fl 32526
4	Dimmer		Fl 32402-1
5	Fine and coarse altimeter	0 – 10000 m	Fl 22320
6	PFK/f2 master compass indicator		Fl 23334
7	Bo-UK 1 clock		Fl 23885
8	Airspeed indicator	80 – 750 km/h	Fl 22231
9	Electric turn and bank indicator		Fl 22406
10	Statoscope-vertical speed indicator	+10/-10 m/s	Fl 22381-10
11	Ignition switch		Fl 21118
12	Electrical system cutout switch		Fl 32315-2
13	Pitot tube heat visual indicator		Fl 32525-3
14	Fuel gauge	0 – 175 l	Fl 20723
15	Boost pressure gauge	0.6 – 1.8 atm	Fl 20550
16	RPM indicator	600 – 3,600 rpm	Fl 20222-3
17	Oil temperature gauge	0 - 120° C	Fl 20342-2
18	Fuel-oil pressure gauge	0 – 1 / 0 – 10 kg/cm²	Fl 20512-1
19	Starter	Fl 21212-1	

Do not lower **undercarriage** at speeds exceeding 220 km/h

Undercarriage – Operation

Retraction:	Extension:
Move control lever to "RAISE"	Move control lever to "LOWER"

In case of engine failure
Pull emergency undercarriage handle
Operate hand pump
After indicator lights come on move control lever to "OFF"
Forced landings with undercarriage retracted, set flaps:

Deflection	15°	20	30°	45°
Lever position	1	2	3	full
Max. allowable speed	230	200	170	135 km/h
Landing flap position for takeoff		20° - 30°		
Maximum allowable diving speed		700 km/h		

Later Ar 96 B-1s had the Patin distant-reading compass system. The following description of the Ar 96 B-1's instrumentation is from the equipment list.

Various photographs illustrated that there were other variations during production and resulting from the replacement parts situation. The Ar 96 B-2 was a fighter trainer with fixed armament for gunnery practice. The aircraft was equipped with a Revi C/12 gun sight for that purpose.

The lettering associated with the electrical system of the Ar 96 B was usually applied in red.

The instrument panel was made of 5 mm aluminum sheet, which made it possible to cut the threads for the instrument attachment bolts directly into the panel and thus eliminate the plate nuts.

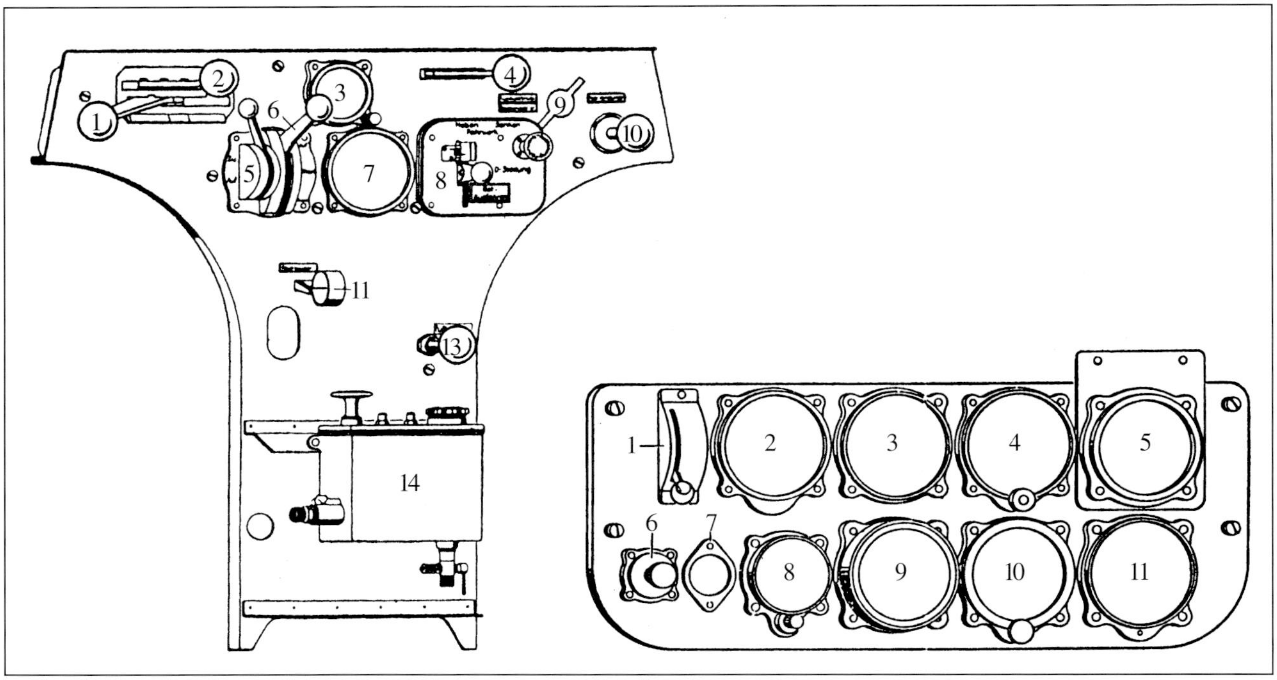

The forward auxiliary instrument panel and the rear observer's panel of the Ar 96 B-1.

Forward auxiliary panel:

No.	Equipment	Instrument Range	Requisition/Equipment Number
1	Tank selector lever		
2	Fuel cock selector lever		
3	Ammeter and voltmeter	+30 / -30 A/V	Fl 32502-4
4	Fuel pressure hand pump		
5	Leading edge slat locking lever		
6	Landing flap selector switch		
7	Landing flap indicator	0 - 6	
8	Undercarriage selector switch		
9	Slide with aircraft data placard and deviation table		Fl 23501
10	Hydraulic hand pump		
11	Pull lever for fire extinguisher		
13	Rudder pedal adjustment lever		
14	ABP 6 starter injection pump with tank		8-4506 A

Rear cockpit panel:

No.	Equipment	Instrument Range	Requisition/Equipment Number
1	Ignition switch with remote control		Fl 21124
2	Airspeed indicator	80 – 750 km/h	Fl 22231
3	Electric turn and bank indicator		Fl 22406
4	Statoscope-vertical speed indicator	+10 / -10 m/s	Fl 22381-10
5	RPM indicator	600 – 3,600 rpm	Fl 20222-3
6	Dimmer switch		Fl 32402-1
7	Electrical system cutout switch		Fl 32315-2
8	Bo-UK 1 clock		Fl 23885
9	PFK/f2 master compass indicator		Fl 23334
10	Fine and coarse altimeter	0 – 10000 m	Fl 22320
11	Boost pressure gauge	0.6 – 1.8 atm	Fl 20550

Factory-fresh Ar 234 B-2. Note the bomb racks under the engine nacelles. (Griehl Collection)

Arado Ar 234 *Blitz* (Lightning)

Port console of the Ar 234 B-2 in the NASM. Some of the items of equipment listed in the operating manual were obviously not installed in this machine. (R.P. Lutz)

In 1941, after the failure of the German air offensive against Great Britain, Arado received a contract to develop a fast long-range reconnaissance aircraft. It was specified that the new turbojet engines would power the aircraft, as existing piston engines would not enable it to achieve the specified performance.

And so the Arado Ar 234 took shape on the drawing boards: a cantilever shoulder-wing monoplane with a streamlined fuselage and fully glazed nose housing the pilot, the sole crewmember. The two Jumo 004 turbojets were slung in pods beneath the wings, simplifying maintenance. The initial A series was designed to take off on a jettisonable trolley and land on retractable skids.

Technical difficulties delayed the first flight until the summer of 1943. Soon afterwards, the prototypes began flying test missions over England. Meanwhile plans were being made to use the type as a high-speed bomber, which resulted in the Ar 234 B with a retractable undercarriage. The aircraft's handling characteristics were excellent and, because the design was in a more advanced state of development, were even superior to those of the Me 262. Care was required when taxiing, however, due to the type's narrow track undercarriage.

By mid-1944 Allied air superiority had become so marked that it was almost impossible for the *Luftwaffe* to fly reconnaissance missions with conventional aircraft. The Ar 234 was the only answer. And so, in spite of Allied air superiority, the Arados were able to carry out their missions at altitudes in excess of 10000 meters, out of reach of enemy fighters. The

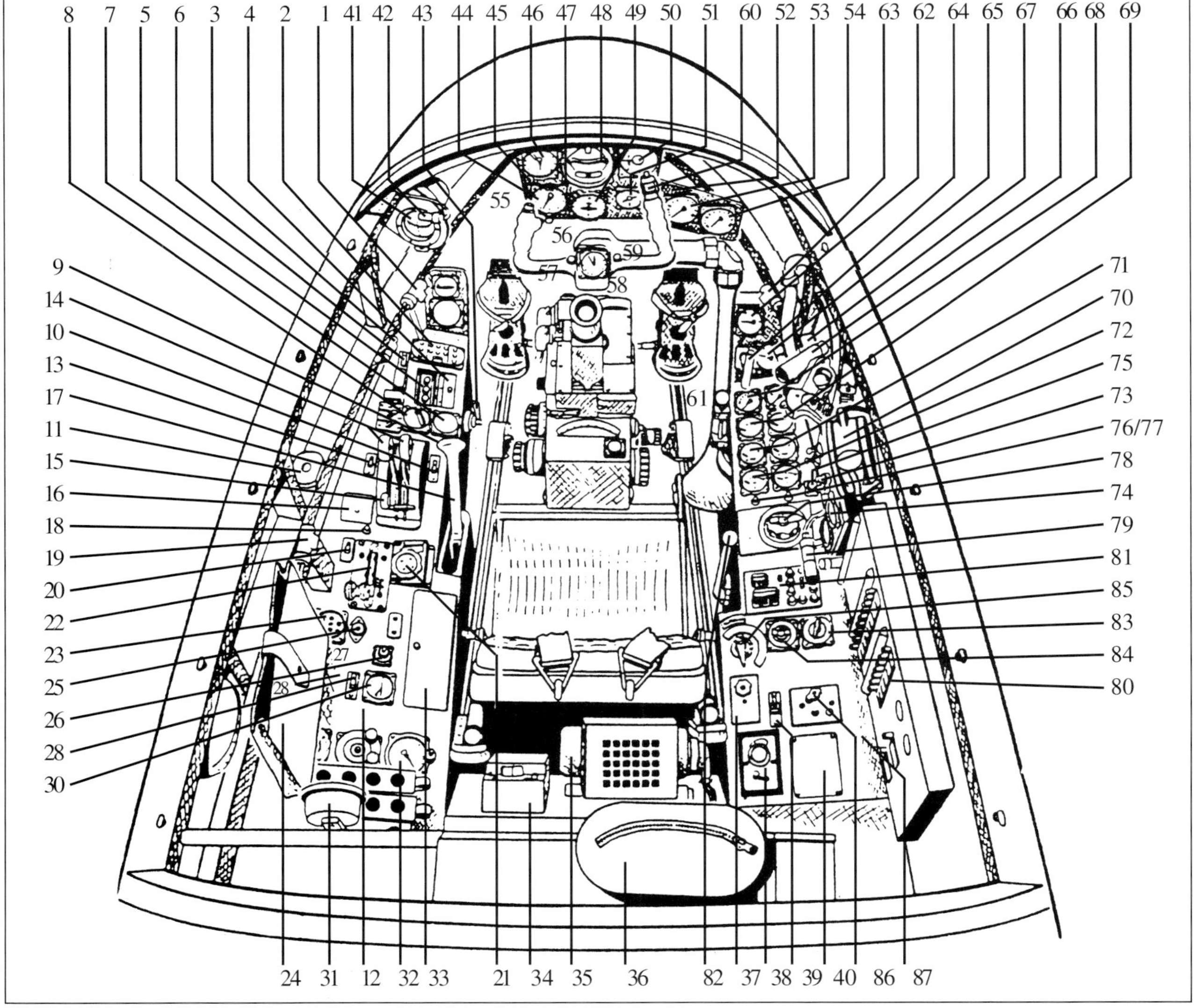

Drawing of the cockpit of the Ar 234 B from the pilot's notes.

Arados provided the German command with clear photographs of the Allied preparations to invade Europe.

More advanced versions, such as the four-engine Ar 234 C and a night fighter, appeared shortly before the end of the war. Wind tunnel tests were being carried out with swept wings of laminar profile and crescent wings with decreased sweep outboard, however neither of these interesting projects was completed.

The Allies were of course very interested in the Ar 234. Eleven were taken to the U.K., four to the USA and an unknown number to Russia. Only one of the approximately 250 Ar 234s which were built has survived, in the USA. It is Ar 234 B-2 *Werknummer* 140312, formerly of III./KG 76. The aircraft was re-

The right side of the cockpit with oxygen system and the main electrical panel. As this is an Ar 234 B-2 bomber, the camera controls are absent. (R.P. Lutz)

Ar 234 B-2 Cockpit Equipment (based on illustration in handbook):

No.	Equipment	Instrument Range	Requisition/Equipment Number
1	Equipment lighting		
2	Undercarriage and landing flap position i ndicators (12 light unit)		Fl 32532
3	Ultra-violet cockpit lighting		
4	Undercarriage selector switch		
5	DSK-C/2 landing flap switch		19-9206 A-1
6	Instrument homing switch		Fl 32345
7	Pressure gauge for hydraulic system	0 – 160 kg/cm²	Fl 20516-3
8	Switch for Patin three-axis autopilot		127-180 B
9	Electrical system emergency cutout switch		19-5836 A-1
10	Landing light switch		Fl 32346
11	Spirit level		
12	Port console		
13	Landing light switch		Fl 32350
14	Throttle levers		
15	Throttle friction damper lock		
16	Ignition switch		
17	Tailplane incidence operating lever		
18	Ignition warning light (red)		Fl 32529-1
19	Equipment lighting		
20	Switch for auxiliary tanks		Fl 32350
21	Rudder trim hand wheel		
22	Tank selector lever		
23	Takeoff-assist rocket switchbox		
24	Map pocket		
25	Takeoff-assist rocket jettison switch		
26	Lighting dimmer switch		Fl 32402
27	Rev selector switch		
28	Exhaust nozzle control switch		Fl 32350
29	Ignition switch		Fl 32345
30	Outside air temperature gauge	-60 / +40° C	Fl 20349
31	Bosch warning horn		
32	Contact altimeter to the left HKG 1	0 – 6000 m	Fl 22317
	altitude corrector (air pressure) associated with the bomb-aiming system	0 – 10 km / 950 – 1050 mb	
33	Navigation equipment stowage		
34	SWA 10/X/I automatic bombing switchbox		Fl 50959
35	Ignition transformer		
36	Flashlight pocket		
37	FBG 16 remote control unit		Ln 27188
38	Helmet plug socket		
39	Radio equipment demolition switch		
40	Hand crank for remote control of cameras (reconnaissance version)		
41	FK 38 magnetic compass		Fl 23233
42	Compass lighting		
43	Heating switch		
44	Fine and coarse altimeter	0 – 10000 m	Fl 22320
45	Pitot tube heat visual indicator		Fl 32530-6
46	Airspeed indicator	100 – 1000 km/h	Fl 22245
47	Standard blind flying panel		Fl 22000
	to the left in many aircraft: double boost pressure gauge	2 x 0.6 – 1.8 atm	Fl 20556
48	Combined turn and bank indicator and artificial horizon		Fl 22411
49	PFK/f2 master compass indicator		Fl 23334

stored by the National Air and Space Museum in Washington and is on display in the markings of F1+GS. Several of the photographs displayed here depict the interior of this aircraft.

The cockpit of the Ar 234 was completely faired into the fuselage nose, which resulted in extremely clean lines. The extensive glazing provided the pilot with a virtually unobstructed view in all directions except to the rear. A PV 1 B periscope was provided to cover that area.

Most instruments and controls were housed in two large side consoles to the left and right of the pilot. The only obstructions to the pilot's forward view were the standard blind flying panel and two small auxiliary panels. In the Ar 234 B-2 bomber version a Lotfe 7 K bombsight was positioned between the legs of the pilot. The Ar 234 B-1 was a reconnaissance aircraft.

The standard instrumentation of an Ar 234 B-2 is well depicted in the operating manual from 1944. Additional engine instruments were added at a later date, as was a Patin autopilot.

Restored cockpit of the Ar 234 B-2, serial number 140312 in the National Air and Space Museum. (R.P. Lutz)

50	Vertical speed indicator	+ 15 / - 15 m/s	Fl 22384
	or	+ 30 / - 30 m/s	Fl 22386
51	AFN 2 radio navigation indicator		Ln 27002
52	Auxiliary instrument panel		
53	RPM indicator	2,000 – 15,000 rpm	Fl 20266
54	as 53		
55	Bomb release button		
56	Ultra-violet cockpit lighting		
57	Transmit button		
58	Bo-UK 1 clock		Fl 23885
59	Clock illumination button		
60	Autopilot course-setting control		
61	Control column release knob		
62	Fuel burner pressure gauge	0 – 60 kg/cm²	Fl 20516-1
or	0 – 160 kg/cm2		Fl 20516-3
63	Panel lighting		
64	Emergency bomb release		
65	as 62		
66	Flare pistol		
67	Ultra-violet cockpit light		
68	Two fire-warning temperature gauges	0 - 200° C	
69	Two oil pressure gauges	0 – 15 kg/cm²	Fl 20504-15
70	Oxygen system		Fl 30403-1
71	Two jet pipe temperature gauges	300 – 1000° C	Fl 20338
72	Fuel gauge (left)	0 – 1800 l	Fl 20723
	Fuel gauge (right)	0 – 2000 l	Fl 20703
73	Panel lighting		
74	Oxygen system, consisting of:		
	Oxygen pressure gauge	0 – 250 kg/cm²	Fl 30496
	Oxygen flow indicator		Fl 30489
	Oxygen valve		Fl 30508
75	Cockpit lighting dimmer switch		Fl 32402
76	Fuel warning light (red)		Fl 32529-1
77	as 76		
78	ZSK 244 A-2 bomb arming panel		Fl 50869
79	Ultra-violet cockpit light		
80	Main electrical switch panel with automatic circuit-breakers		
81	ASK 234 bomb sequence selector panel		
82	Emergency hydraulic hand-pump		
83	Radio system mode selector switch		19-5843
84	Frequency selector switch		19-5843
85	Flap and undercarriage emergency hydraulic selector switch		
86	BG 25a IFF control switch		Ln 28810
87	Starboard console		

The two empty openings on the left beneath the magnetic compass were intended for a repeater horizon and the Patin autopilot target speed indicator.

The equipment listed above represents that installed in the standard production version of the Ar 234 B-2. Modification directives and replacement part problems resulted in variations.

Bachem Ba 349 *Natter* (Adder)

By the beginning of 1944 the *Luftwaffe* had largely lost air superiority over Germany. When the production of conventional fighter aircraft no longer sufficed, as part of the "Emergency Fighter Program" a requirement was issued for a small fast fighter aircraft to be constructed of non-strategic materials and which could be considered expendable.

In addition to well-known manufacturers such as Heinkel, Junkers and Messerschmitt, a proposal was submitted by Erich Bachem, who had a small aircraft factory in Bad Waldsee. His design, the BP-20, was initially rejected as "technically and tactically doubtful".

Bachem had come up with the idea for this rocket-propelled aircraft in August 1944, when a formation of American bombers overflew Bad Waldsee on a clear sunny day, totally unmolested. The name "*Adder*" came from a line in Shakespeare's "Julius Caesar".

Bachem's design was a vertical-takeoff interceptor powered by a Walther 109-509 engine producing 1500 kg of thrust. Built entirely of wood, the aircraft took approximately 1,000 hours to construct. Armament consisted of a battery of 24 Föhn rockets in the nose of the aircraft. Takeoff was made from a launch tower with guide rails, with additional power provided by four jettisonable solid-fuel rockets, and the small fighter was capable of reaching 10000 meters within one minute of takeoff. After firing his

Reconstructed from original parts, the Bachem Ba 349 M 17 in the Deutsches Museum. The M 17 was an unmanned prototype.

The sparse instrument panel of the Ba 349 M1 prototype. (Lommel Collection)

Instrument panel of the Ba 349 M24. At the bottom is the gyro-horizon. (Lommel – from an instructional film)

rockets, the pilot was supposed to dive away and jettison the forward fuselage, from which he would then parachute to safety. The aft fuselage with the rocket engine would also be lowered to the ground by parachute so that it could be used again.

Bachem required support from the very highest level to secure the contract. An initial series of 23 prototypes was used for trials, initially towed aloft by a He 111 and later from a launch tower at the Heuberg troop training grounds. The only manned rocket-powered flight took place at the beginning of 1945, with pilot Lothar Sieber losing his life in the process.

In spite of its primitive construction, the Ba 349 was a well-thought-out design with quite promising handling characteristics. It pioneered the use of solid-fuel takeoff-assist rockets (called booster rockets today), ribbon parachutes and radar guidance to the target.

Equipment in the M 24 Prototype:

Equipment	Instrument Range	Requisition/Equipment Number
Airspeed indicator	100 – 1000 km/h	Fl 22241
Fine and coarse altimeter	0 – 13000 m	Fl 22322
Turbine RPM indicator	0 – 12500 (= 100%)	Fl 20265
Turbine pressure gauge	0 – 6 kg/cm^2	Fl 20521?
Chamber pressure gauge	0 – 25 kg/cm^2	Fl 20521?
Gyro-horizon	(Fl 22561)	

Cockpit of a Ba 349 A-1 replica. (Kuncze via Lommel)

The jettisonable nose section of the Ba 349 A-1 in the National Air and Space Museum. Only the instrument plugs remain. Note the primitive ventilation flap built into the windscreen. (P. Selinger)

Production totaled 35 prototypes and eight Ba 349 A service aircraft. Two have survived, a Ba 349 A-1 in the National Air and Space Museum (NASM) in Washington, USA and a reconstructed prototype (M17) in the Deutsches Museum. In keeping with its simple overall design, the instrumentation and systems of the Ba 349 was restricted to what was absolutely essential. Photographs reveal at least three instrument arrangements and there were more in the prototypes and service aircraft.

Aft fuselage section of the Ba 349 B-1. There were few concessions to pilot comfort. On the right is the throttle lever and behind it a toggle switch and a electrical system circuit breaker. (P. Selinger)

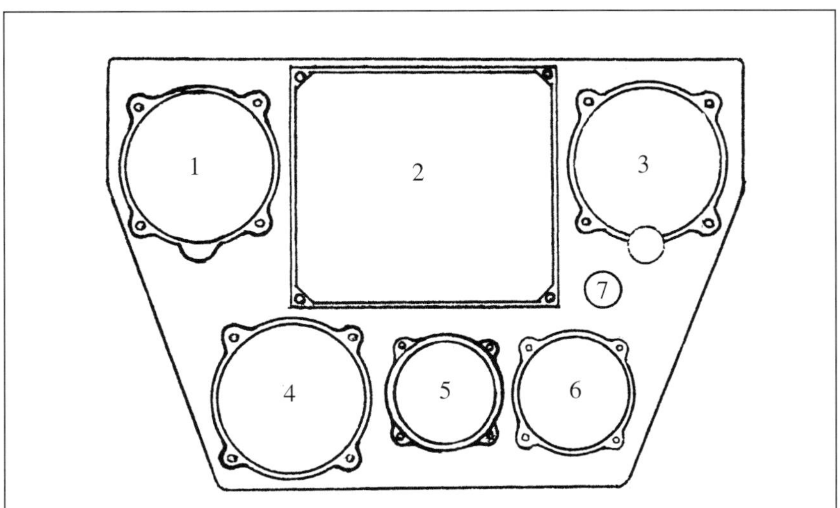

Equipment in the Ba 349 A-1 Service Aircraft:

No.	Equipment	Instrument Range	Requisition/Equipment Number
1	Airspeed indicator	100 – 1000 km/h	Fl 22241
2	Gyro-horizon		(Fl 22561)
3	Fine and coarse altimeter	0 – 13000 m	Fl 22322
4	Turbine RPM indicator	0 – 12500 (= 100%)	Fl 20265
5	Turbine pressure gauge	0 – 6 kg/cm^2	Fl 20521?
6	Chamber pressure gauge	0 – 25 kg/cm^2	Fl 20521?
7	Visual indicator (fuel warning)		19-6824 B-1

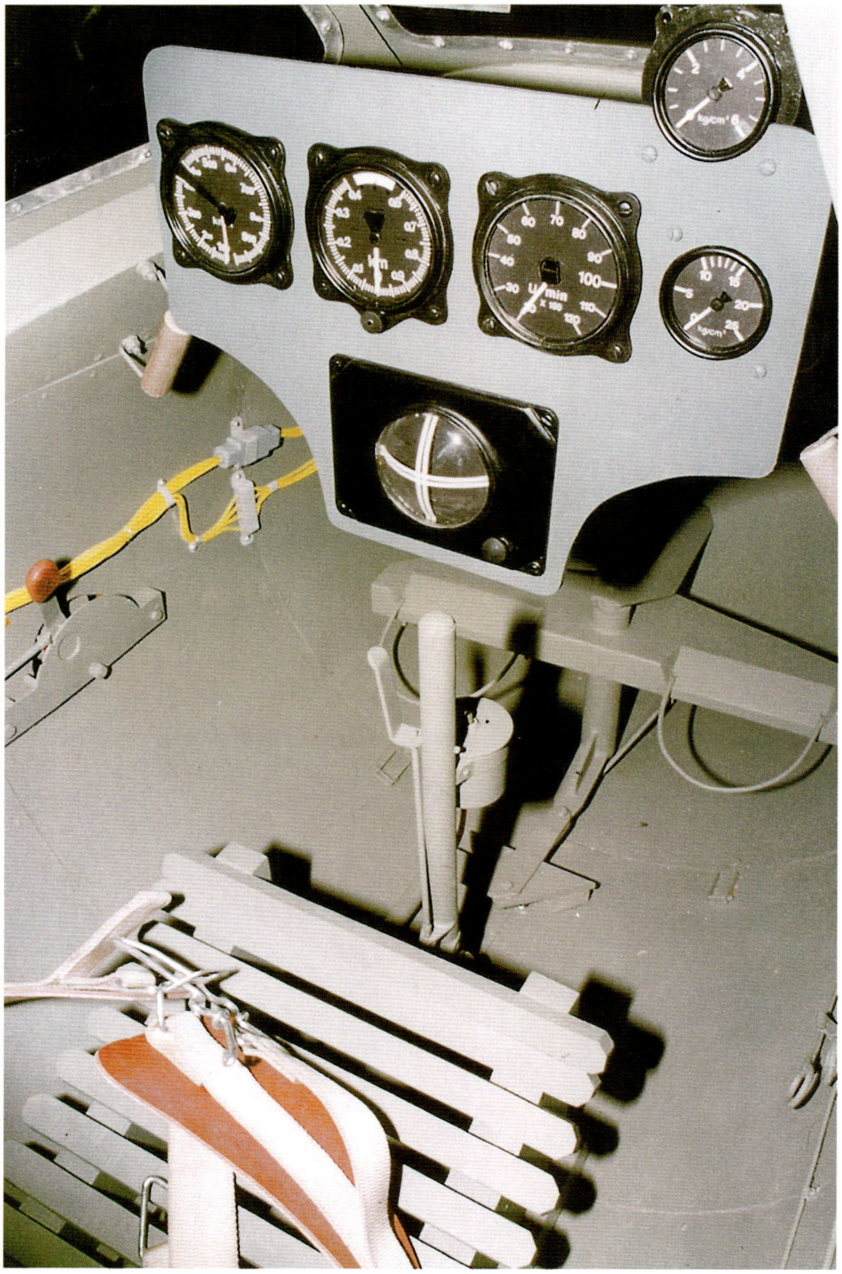

The Ba 349 replica in the Planes of Fame Museum in Chino, USA is actually a mixture of a Ba 349 A-1 operational aircraft and the instrumentation of the M 24 prototype.

The first variation was used by the M 1 prototype, which on 3 November 1944 was towed aloft by a He 111. The aircraft's instrumentation consisted of an airspeed indicator with a range of 50 to 350 km/h (Fl 22228), two toggle switches and an automatic switch for the electrical system, and a crank for the trim weight in the nose.

The **M 24** prototype, which was supposed to be test flown from Heuberg, was much more extensively equipped, however after the crash of the M 23, in which the pilot lost his life, no flights were made.

There is a film of the M 24 which was made for training purposes, in which the instrument panel is visible. With the HWK 109-509 rocket motor installed, engine instruments were similar to those found in the Me 163 B. One interesting instrument was the gyro-horizon, which was based on the Lku 4 gyro compass (Fl 22561) by Siemens.

The Planes of Fame Museum in Chino, California has on display a replica of a Ba 349 A-1 production aircraft based on the Natter stored by the NASM. For lack of historical documents, however, the aircraft has been fitted with an instrument panel identical to that of the M 24.

The instrument panel of the **Ba 349 A-1** service aircraft, which was powered by an HWK 109-509 A-2 engine producing 1700 kg of thrust, was laid out differently. The shape can be determined from aircraft under construction, however the instruments used must be reconstructed from documents. Other equipment was added for the planned radio equipment and armament. These additional controls and instruments included:

- Timer for automatic takeoff system and control of fuel consumption
- Firing button for rocket engine on left forward hand-grip
- Progressive switch mechanism on control stick for firing rockets
- Rocket firing button
- Automatic switch for the 19-5000 electrical system

The aircraft lacked a vertical speed indicator, however it was planned to install one in the Ba 349 B, which would have had engines for takeoff and cruise. A vertical speed indicator was installed in one of the prototypes. With an instrument range of – 250 to + 250 meters per sec, it was a minor sensation in its day.

The pilot carried his own oxygen supply and none was built into the aircraft.

Blohm & Voss Bv 155

In 1941 Messerschmitt was tasked by the RLM to develop a single-seat high-altitude fighter with a pressurized cockpit. The project was initially based on the airframe of the Bf 109 G-5 with a new wing of increased span. Components of the Me 209 and Ju 87 were used and the design incorporated features of the North American Mustang.

The project was subsequently designated Me 155, however Messerschmitt lacked the capacity to continue development and in 1943 it was handed over to Blohm & Voss. The documentation provided by Messerschmitt was incomplete, and Blohm & Voss engineers were forced to calculate the missing data. It soon turned out that the design would have to be completely reworked. The wing, fuselage, tail section, engine systems and main undercarriage were all redesigned.

After some weeks nothing was left of the original Messerschmitt design and the Bv 155 was a completely new aircraft. It was pow-

The incomplete Bv 155 V2 at Farnborough in late 1945. (Griehl Collection)

The left side of the cockpit of the Bv 155 V1 with equipment console and throttle quadrant.

Close-up of the instrument panel depicting the engine instruments.

Left side of cockpit:

No.	Equipment	Instrument Range	Requisition/Equipment Number
1	Aileron locking switch		Fl 32346
2	Turbine automatic control switch		Fl 32350
3	Trim position indicator		Fl 20855
4	Fore and aft trim switch		Fl ?
5	Push-button flap control		
6	Electrical system cutout switch		19-5836 A-1
7	Push-button undercarriage control		
8	Switch for manual/automatic drive (propeller pitch?)		Fl ?
9	Ignition switch		Fl 21118
10	Flap visual indicator (UP / DOWN)		19-6824 B-1
11	Undercarriage visual indicators (UP / DOWN)		19-6824 B-1
12	Undercarriage door visual indicators		Fl 32530
13	Throttle lever with thumb switch for propeller pitch control		Fl 32337
14	Fuel cock		
15	Throttle brake		
16	Cockpit ventilation control ?		

ered by a DB 603 U with a Hirth TKL 15 turbosupercharger, producing 1,810 H.P. The exhaust gases needed to drive the turbosupercharger were directed through pipes on the fuselage sides. Air was bled from the turbosupercharger through a special blower to the pressurized cockpit.

The Bv 155 was subjected to countless changes and the maiden flight of the first prototype was delayed until February 1945. After a few flights the aircraft was irreparably damaged in a forced landing. After the war the Allies discovered two unfinished prototypes, the Bv 155 V2 and V3, in Finkenwerder. Additional variants proceeded no farther than the project phase.

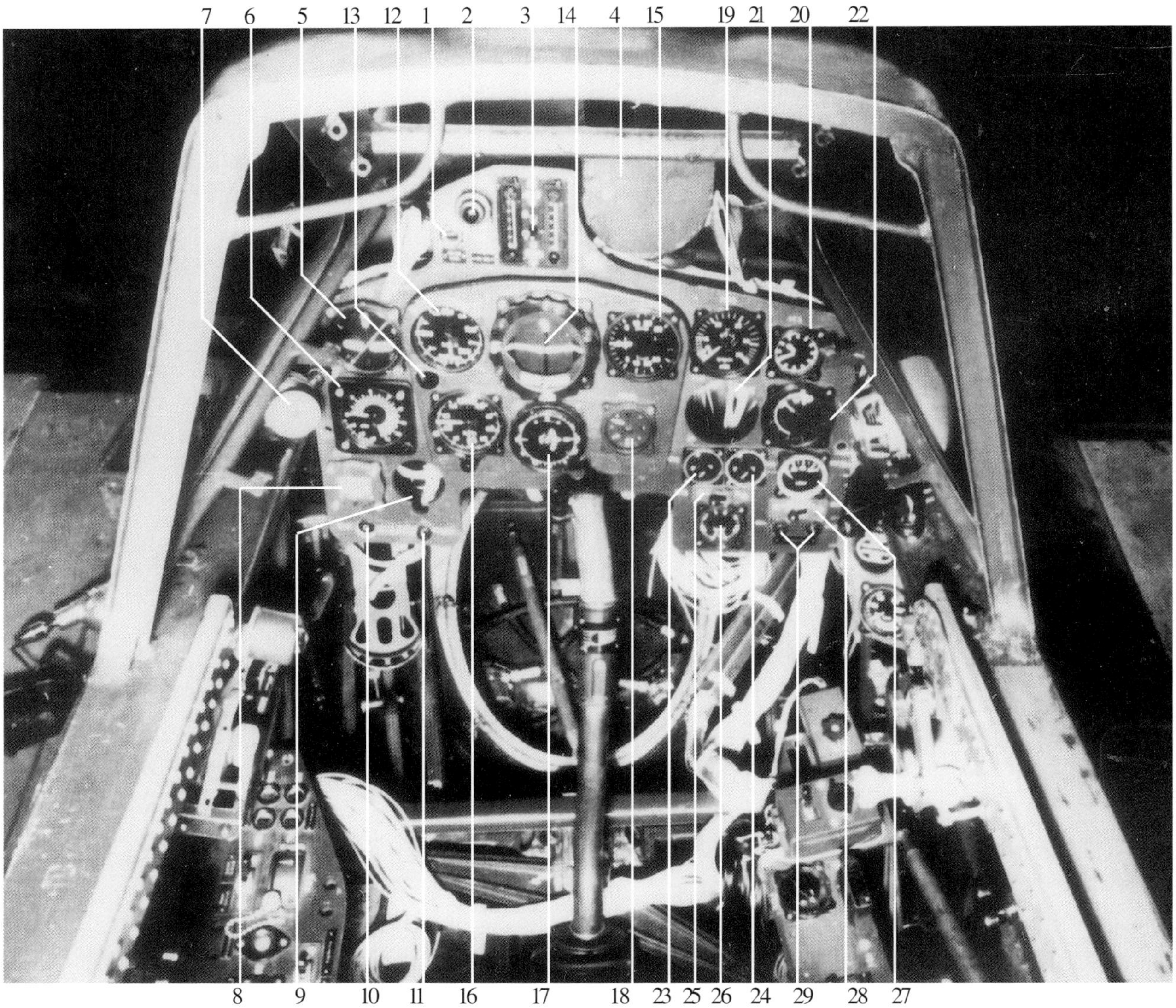

The cockpit of the Bv 155 V1 during the final construction phase. Some instruments remain to be installed.

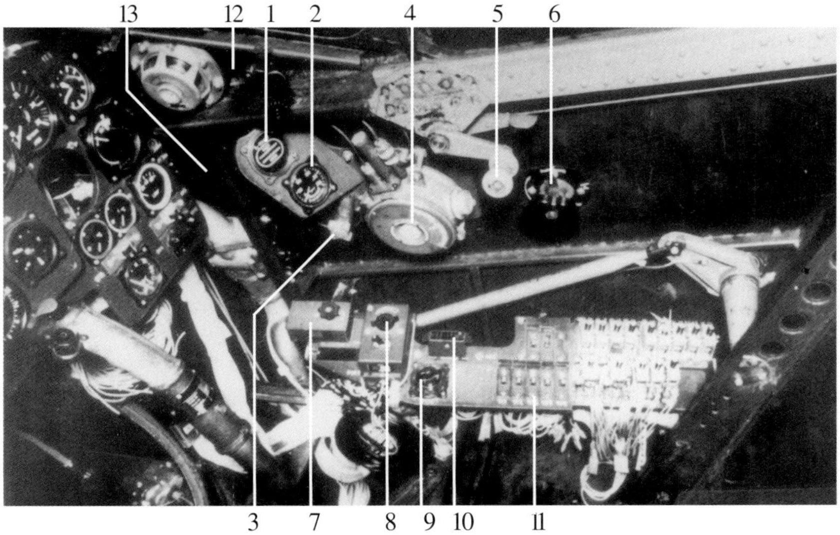

The right side of the cockpit of the Bv 155 V1.

The Bv 155 V2 was taken to Farnborough for tests and in 1946 was delivered to the USA. Today it is in storage in the National Air and Space Museum.

The Bv 155 was a relatively large single-engine aircraft whose turbosupercharger and pressurized cockpit required special equipment. The configuration was typical of 1944-45 standards.

The throttle lever, trim controls, undercarriage and flap levers were all positioned on the left side of the cockpit, and the number of electric drives was unusual. In the center of the instrument panel was the standard blind flying panel (Fl 22000) and on the right the engine instruments. On the right side of the cockpit was the pilot's oxygen system, the radio controls and switches and circuit breakers for the electrical system.

Instrument Panel:

No.	Equipment	Instrument Range	Requisition/Equipment Number
1	Engine cannon breech control visual indicator		19-6824 B-1
2	Engine cannon cocking button		Fl 26872 ?
3	SZK K 2 round counter		Fl 47317
4	Revi 16 B reflector gun sight also planned was the EZ 42 (Fl 52218) or the ZFR-3A telescopic sight (Fl 52513-2)		Fl 52955
5	Electric turn and bank indicator		Fl 22407 or Fl 22412
6	Cockpit pressure gauge	0 – 15 km / 0 – 0.6 atm	Fl 22325
7	AP 20 starter injection pump		8-4511 A-1
8	Altitude alerter		
9	Bo-UK 1 clock		Fl 23885
10	Fire extinguisher push-button control		
11	Fire warning light (red)		Fl 32529-1
12	Airspeed indicator (altitude compensating)	100 – 1000 km/h	Fl 22241
13	Pitot tube heat visual indicator		Fl 32530
14	Combined turn and bank indicator and artificial horizon		Fl 22415-1
15	Vertical speed indicator	+30 / -30 m/s	Fl 22386
16	Fine and coarse altimeter	0 – 13000 m	Fl 22322
17	PFK/f2 master compass indicator		Fl 23334
18	AFN 2 radio navigation indicator		Ln 27002
19	RPM indicator	500 – 3,600 rpm	Fl 20269 ?
20	Propeller pitch indicator		Fl 20841
21	Turbine RPM indicator	2,200 – 15,000 rpm	Fl 20266
22	Boost pressure gauge	0.6 – 1.8 atm	Fl 20555
23	Oil temperature gauge	0 - 130° C	Fl 20358
24	Coolant temperature gauge	0 - 130° C	Fl 20358
25	Oil temperature gauge selector switch		Fl ?
26	Fuel / oil pressure gauge	0 – 3 / 0 – 15 kg/cm²	Fl 20512-3
27	Fuel gauge	0 – 700 l ?	Fl 20723
28	Fuel measuring point selector switch		Fl ?
29	Fuel warning light (red)		Fl 32529-1

Right side of cockpit:

No.	Equipment	Instrument Range	Requisition/Equipment Number
1	Oxygen flow indicator		Fl 30489
2	Oxygen pressure gauge	0 – 250 kg/cm²	Fl 30496
3	Oxygen valve		Fl 30508
4	Oxygen supply connector		Fl 30403-1
5	Cockpit canopy hand-crank		
6	Cockpit ventilation control ?		
7	Remote control for FuG 16 (FBG 16)		Ln 27188
8	Helmet connector socket		
9	FuG 16 frequency selector		19-5843
10	Starter		Fl 21214
11	Switch (Fl 32350 ?) and automatic switch (19-5000) for the electrical system		
12	Ultra-violet cockpit light		
13	Undercarriage emergency control		

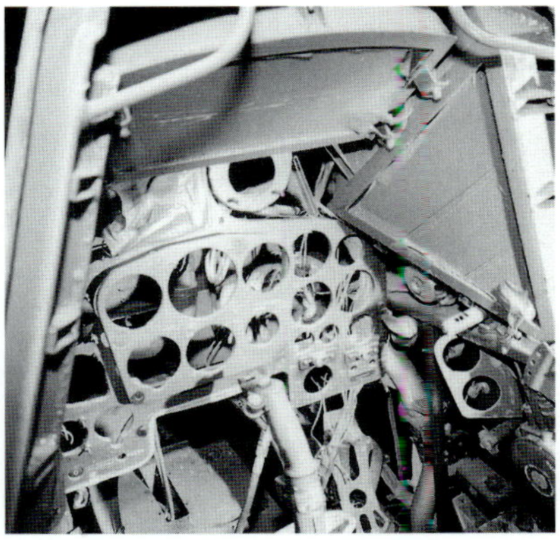

The cockpit of the Bv 155 V2 stored in Washington. All instruments have been removed. Some panels have been uncovered, probably in preparation for once planned restoration work. (R.P. Lutz)

Factory photographs, probably of the Bv 155 V1, and several photos of the stored Bv 155 V2 make it possible to reconstruct the instrumentation. All of the instruments have been removed from the Bv 155 V2 stored in the USA, making it impossible to say with certainty if these were identical to those of the V1, however the arrangement of the openings in the instrument panel suggest that they were.

Bücker Bü 181 *Bestmann*

The Bü 181 was the last aircraft type produced by the Bücker company. Used by the *Luftwaffe* mainly as a primary trainer, it began replacing the earlier Bücker types in 1940.

More than 4,500 examples of this popular machine were built for the *Luftwaffe* by Bücker and other manufacturers. Powered by a 105 H.P. Hirth HM 504 engine, it was fully aerobatic and was employed in the training, courier and liaison roles. The Bü 181 was also built under license in Sweden (120), by Hägglund and Sons, and Czechoslovakia (180) and continued flying in both countries in military and civilian service

Bü 181 C, SV+NJ, following restoration. (Couderchon)

long after the war. The *Bestmann* was also used by the Swiss *Fliegertruppe* and the Royal Air Force, which used the type as a liaison aircraft.

In 1950 the CSSR transferred its production license to Egypt. The National Aircraft Factory in Heliopolis built the type as the *Gomhouria*, powered by a 145 H.P. Continental engine. More than 200 were built in six versions and the aircraft was exported to a variety of African states.

In 1955 the Federal Republic of Germany was allowed to resume aviation activities. Sweden had just retired its *Bestmann* trainers, giving many aviation enthusiasts the opportunity to procure an aircraft. The *Bestmann* became the first equipment of many sports fliers after the war.

Today the *Bestmann* has become rare, but the survivors are still flown by their owners. The *Gomhouria* remains in active service in Egypt, where it still used as a training aircraft. The first retired *Bestmann* arrived in Germany in 1988. The Bü 181 is thus one of the longest-lived German designs and also one of the most-built German light aircraft ever.

Only sixteen original Bü 181s have survived to the present day, along with 17 Swedish, 7 Czechoslovakian and approximately 40 Egyptian aircraft.

The standard equipment installed in a Bü 181 B-1 is well-depicted in illustrations from the replacement parts list of October 1942. The instrument panel was divided into three sections. On the left were the instruments required by the pilot. In the center, accessible from both seats, were the engine instruments

The cockpit of SV+NJ was largely restored according to Luftwaffe manuals. The flash has made the black-gray interior appear lighter. A contact altimeter from a Ju 87 was installed as an original could not be found.

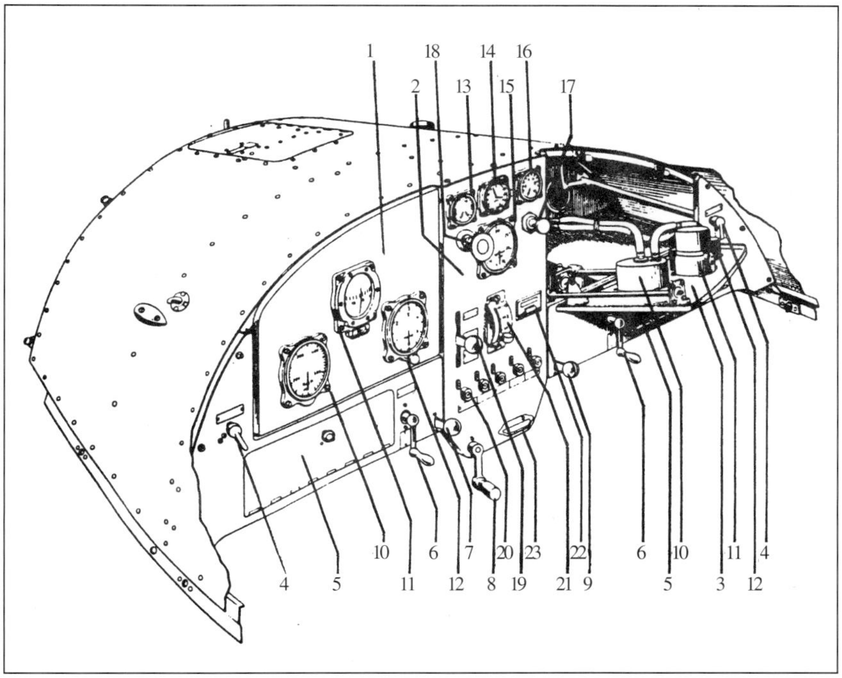

Equipment of the Bü 181 B-1:

No.	Equipment	Instrument Range	Requisition/Equipment Number
1	Left instrument panel		181.18-06
2	Center instrument panel		181.18-08
3	Right instrument panel (folded down)		181.18-07
4	Door locks, left and right		181.18-20 and 21
5	Map cases, left and right		181.18-15 and 16
6	Rudder pedal adjustment crank		181.41-04
7	Pull-cord for fire extinguisher		181.18-23 HO5
8	AMP 1 starter magneto crank		9-4064 A
9	Pull-cord for the hand pump		181.18-23 HO4
10	Airspeed indicator	80 – 550 km/h	Fl 22230
11	FK 38 master compass		Fl 23233
12	Altimeter	0 – 6000 m	Fl 22316-6
13	Double pressure gauge for fuel and oil	0 – 1 / 0 – 10 kg/cm²	Fl 20512-1
14	Clock (Kienzle 8-day)		Fl 23886-1
15	RPM indicator	500 – 3,600 rpm	Fl 20222-3
16	Fuel gauge	0 – 100 l	Fl 20704
17	Air pump for fuel gauge		Fl 20742-1
18	SUM AP 8 starter injection pump		8-4505 A
19	Fuel cock lever		181.18-18
20	4 automatic switches		Fl 32404-1
	1 automatic switch (left, master switch)		Fl 32404-3
21	Ignition switch		Fl 21118
22	Lighting system visual indicator		Fl 32525-3
23	Sliding tray for operating data placard and deviation table		Fl 23501

The equipment list above was standard for the Bü 181 B-1 used in the training role with double instrumentation. Aircraft used in the liaison role usually had simplified instrumentation on the left side only.

and controls. Training aircraft were equipped with an identical set of flight instruments on the right side. As a rule the type was not equipped with a radio.

The photographs offered here depict the instrumentation of a *Luftwaffe* Bü 181 C and two surviving built-built machines. While an effort was made to accurately recreate a 1944-45 aircraft during restoration of the Bü 181 C, the other aircraft were used as sporting machines for many years and during that time were instrumented in various ways to suit their owners, for whom flying came first.

The **Bü 181 C-3 *Werknummer* 330884** belongs to the Musée de l'Air in Paris. Delivered in 1944, the aircraft was initially flown as a liaison aircraft on the Eastern Front bearing the manufacturer's code SV+NJ. After the war it was operated by the RAF as a liaison aircraft, and in 1955 it was registered in France as F-BBNA. During the course of its restoration, which was completed in 1985, the French made every effort to return the aircraft to its original state as delivered to the *Luftwaffe* in 1944.

Bü 181 B-1 serial number Fv25071 is a Swedish-built machine which was flown as a trainer (Sk 25) by the Swedish air force bearing the registration 5-271. The aircraft was sold in Germany and in recent years has been restored in its original Swedish colors with orange wings and dark green fuselage.

The instrumentation is a typical mix of original equipment and mainly American instruments. The arrangement of the instruments has also been changed to allow for the installation of radio and navigational equipment.

***Gomhouria* MK.6 serial number 184** is an Egyptian-built copy of the Bü 181 or Zlin Z.381. Today registered in Germany as D-EGBA, it was flown for many years by the Egyptian air force as a training aircraft with the registration SU-346. This is reflected in the Arabic script to be found in the cockpit.

The cockpit of D-EDUB, a former Swedish Bü 181 B-1 with extensive use of leather. Many instruments are of Swedish origin. Note the boost pressure gauge on the right.

The instrument panel of the Egyptian Gomhouria is largely similar in layout to that of the Czech Z. 381. D-EGBA features a mixture of German and foreign instruments and equipment. Note the accelerometer at the bottom center of the panel, probably left over from its service in Egypt as a training aircraft. Many placards with Arabic text remain.

Gomhouria MK. 6, D-EGBA. The aircraft is finished in the bright yellow of the Egyptian air force. The only external difference from the German Bü 181 is the horizontally-opposed engine.

DFS 230 A-2 replica now on display in the Luftwaffe Museum. When this photo was taken the aircraft was still in Oberschleissheim.

DFS 230

In 1933-34 the Rhön-Rossitten Gesellschaft became the *Deutsche Forschungsinstitut für Segelflug* (German Research Institute for Gliding Flight). In the years that followed, the institute made major contributions to the development of aviation technology. Tailless aircraft, towed glider methods, combined aircraft (better known as *Mistel*) and high-speed rocket aircraft were all researched and developed there.

While the activities of the DFS were initially of a civilian nature, in 1936 it broadened its field of endeavor when glider designer Hans Jacobs developed the "DFS Braking Flap", which was actually conceived as a dive brake for gliders. At that time in Germany thought was being given to the use of the transport glider for military purposes. The RLM's Technical Department subsequently initiated the L.S. 1 development program, through which the DFS was tasked with designing a transport glider under the greatest secrecy.

The prototype of the ten-seat shoulder-wing glider, which had been designated the DFS 230, first flew in January 1937. By the time the Second World War broke out, the transport gliders were operational. The type then gained fame in the spectacular capture of the Belgian fortress of Eben-Emael and the costly invasion of Crete. For the rest of the war the DFS 230 was used mainly in transport missions on all fronts. The DFS found the aircraft to be an ideal platform with which to test various new concepts, towing methods and other experimental systems. As the nature of

Cockpit of the DFS 230 A-2 replica. Visible on the left side of the cockpit are placards containing operating information (deviation table, electrical system schematic, loading diagram, instrument panel schematic) and the instrument panel lighting. Flare cartridges are stowed on the right. A French turn-and-bank indicator was installed as a suitable German item could not be found.

Instrument panel of the DFS 230 A:

No.	Equipment	Instrument Range	Requisition/Equipment Number
1	Turn and bank indicator (Askania)		Fl 22402
2	Airspeed indicator (Bruhn)	50 – 350 km/h)	Fl 22228
3	Fine altimeter (Fuess)	0 – 1000 m	Fl 22316-1
4	FK 38 magnetic compass (Ludolph)		Fl 23233
	or FK 5 in earlier versions		Fl 23211
5	Coarse altimeter (Fuess)	0 – 6000 m	Fl 22316-6
6	Vertical speed indicator (Horn)	-15 / +15 m/s	Fl 22382
7	Pull-handle for tow coupling		
8	Pitot tube heat visual indicator		Fl 32525-3
9	5 automatic switches for the electrical system		Fl 32404-1
	From left: master switch, landing light, navigation lights, instrument panel lighting, pitot tube heat		
10	Dimmer switch for instrument panel lighting		Fl 32402-1
11	Clock (Kienzle 8-day)		Fl 23886-1
	or Bo-UK 1 (Junghans)		Fl 23885

A placard on the instrument panel stated maximum allowable speeds:

Maximum allowable speed while under tow and in free flight in turbulence:	180 km/h
Maximum allowable speed in a dive:	290 km/h

Other items of equipment were:

	Item	Number
•	Instrument panel light	Fl 32266
•	Compensator for the vertical speed indicator	Fl 23360
	Pitot	Fl 22260
•	Feed nozzle for the turn and bank indicator gyro	Fl 23400
•	Pressure regulator	Fl 22652

The position of the clock varied, while in earlier versions it was absent.

Instrument panel of an early DFS 230 built under license by Hartwig in Sonneberg. The compass is the earlier FK 5 type and there is no clock. ((F. Selinger Archive)

Instrument panel from a late-PO DFS 230 finished in Schwarzgrau 66. Some instruments have been replaced as shown by the statoscope-vertical speed indicator on the right, which does not quite fit.

the transport glider's role made them more or less expendable, few survived. Out of a total of 1,591 aircraft built, just 10 partial airframes, mainly fuselage frameworks, have survived and are now in museums in Germany, France and Serbia.

One of these fuselage frameworks formed the basis for the reconstruction of a complete DFS 230 A-2 in 1986-1990. Hans Jacobs, who is still alive, helped reconstruct plans for the wings. The newly-constructed glider is now on display in the *Luftwaffenmuseum* in Berlin-Gatow as KA+1-52, an aircraft of *Verbindungskommando (S) 4*, a supply unit based on the Eastern Front. Some of the photographs presented here are of this aircraft.

The DFS 230 was essentially a large glider with a electrical system, thus the instrumentation is equivalent to that of a well-equipped glider. The accompanying list of equipment is based on a Gotha Waggonfabrik replacement parts list dated September 1941.

The versions of the DFS 230 equipped with a braking parachute had two additional pull-handles for:

- parachute open (below 170 km/h)
- parachute disreef (below 180 km/h)

Several other switches were included in aircraft with braking rockets in the fuselage nose.

The DFS 230's instrument panel was of aluminum sheet and the instruments were attached with clinch nuts.

Dornier Do 24

In 1935 the Dutch began seeking a successor to their now-obsolescent *Wal* flying boats. As the *Wal* had proved a success, particularly in the Dutch East Indies, they turned to Dornier once again. The Dutch specification called for a three-engine flying boat with a crew of six and defensive positions capable of high-seas operation.

The first prototype was completed in 1937. Whereas the Dutch machines were delivered with Wright-Cyclone radial engines, Dornier's own prototype was powered by the somewhat unreliable Jumo 205 diesel engine. As a result, the *Technische Amt* was initially uninterested, although the Wright-Cyclone powered Do 24 displayed an impressive performance during trials on the North Sea, even under the most adverse conditions.

The Do 24 T-3 in the Museo del Aire in Madrid. (A. Flores)

Production began simultaneously in Germany and the Netherlands, and by the time of the German occupation twenty-two Do 24 Ks had been delivered to the Dutch East Indies, where they distinguished themselves even under the most difficult operational conditions. Following the Japanese conquest of the East Indies the surviving Do 24s flew with the RAAF until they were grounded by lack of spare parts.

When the requirement for a suitable air-sea rescue aircraft became acute in Germany, the *Luftwaffe* turned to the Do 24, which was in its element in that role. Powered by three 1,000 H.P. BMW Bramo 323 engines, with its roomy cockpit, great range and outstanding seaworthiness, the Do 24 T operated over every sea and ocean. Air-sea rescue crews saved the lives of more than 11,000 personnel, both friend and foe.

In 1942 S.N.C.A. du Nord of France was involved in the production of the Do 24 and after the war it continued building the aircraft for the French navy, which operated the type until 1953. Spain received twelve Do 24 Ts for air-sea rescue in 1944, the last ones flying from Mallorca until 1969.

Main instrument panel of the Do 24 V1. (Couderchon Collection)

The Dornier ATT photographed during a test flight.

Instrument panel of the Do 24 V1 with Siemens autopilot:

No.	Equipment	Instrument Range	Requisition/Equipment Number
1	Nav. Vordruck K 6 deviation tables		Fl 23906
2	Kle 6 "Small Emil" magnetic compass (Askania)		Fl 23226
3	Instrument panel lighting		
4	Windscreen wiper		
5	Lkz 3 course indicator		Fl 22562
6	Outside air temperature gauge	-40 / +40° C	Fl 20342-1
7	Autopilot visual indicator		Fl 32525
8	Pitot tube heat visual indicator		Fl 32525
9	Airspeed indicator	60 – 550 km/h	Fl 22230
10	Turn and bank indicator		Fl 22402
	or electric turn and bank indicator		Fl 22406
11	Statoscope-vertical speed indicator	-10 / +10 m/s	Fl 22381-10
12	Pfk/f3 master compass indicator		Fl 23338
13	Landing flap indicator lights ?		
14	Fine and coarse altimeter	0 – 10000 m	Fl 22320
15	Artificial horizon (Sperry)		Fl 22426
16	Indicator for AFN 1 radio navigation		Ln 27000
17	Lku 4 directional gyro		Fl 22561
18	Automatic switch		
19	Propeller pitch selector	9-9502 B	
20	Landing flap control lever		
21	Warning light		
22	Warning light for landing probe		
23	Electrical system cutout switch		Fl 32315-2
24	Autopilot master switch		Fl 22559-1
25	Autopilot emergency disengage button		Fl 22557
26	Pull handle		
27	Electric RPM indicator	400 – 2,400 rpm	Fl 20283 ?
28	Electric quad temperature gauge for coolant (top) and oil (bottom). For oil divided lower (left) and upper (right) crankshaft	0 - 160° C	Fl 20360
29	Electric quad fuel / oil pressure gauge	3 x 0 – 10 kg/cm² and 1 x 0 – 0.5 kg/cm²	Fl 20560
30	Electric propeller pitch indicator		Fl 20841
31	Fuel gauges for left and right tanks	0 – 1600 l	Fl 20723
32	ASK-L bomb sequence selector panel		Fl 50962
33	Bo-UK 1 clocks in the control wheels		Fl 23885
34	Course selector for the autopilot		

The Do 24, of which 294 were built, represented the apex of flying boat design for decades, and long after it was first flown the aircraft formed the basis for an advanced new design. Dornier modified an old Do 24 T fuselage and fitted it with a new wing mounting three Pratt & Whitney shaft turbines and the undercarriage from the Do 31. The prototype began flight trials in 1983-84.

The Do 24 TT, as it was initially dubbed—later the ATT (Amphibious Technology Testbed)—represented a symbiosis of old and new and displayed very promising characteristics. The test program was ended, however, because the flying boat fuselage was no longer aerodynamically suitable. The Do ATT (D-CATD) was ultimately placed in storage at Leipheim.

The four surviving Do 24s are all ex-Spanish aircraft. As well, pieces of three other machines have survived.

Some of the photographs here depict a former Spanish Do 24 T currently in the Militaire Luchtvaart Museum in Kamp van Zeist in Holland, while others illustrate the Do ATT.

The three-engine Do 24 was a relatively large aircraft which was quite comprehensively equipped. The main instrument panel included duplicated instruments for the pilot and copilot, with secondary panels for the flight engineer and radio operator.

The customary arrangement of engine controls in a central console was not possible as a passageway to the nose was located in the front of the cockpit. Instead the engine control levers were positioned on the side walls beside the two pilots.

Standard equipment included an autopilot by Askania or Siemens to relieve the pilots during long search missions. The different engine types—diesel or air-cooled radials—required specialized instruments. Multiple indicators were used to save space on the instrument panel and make scanning easier.

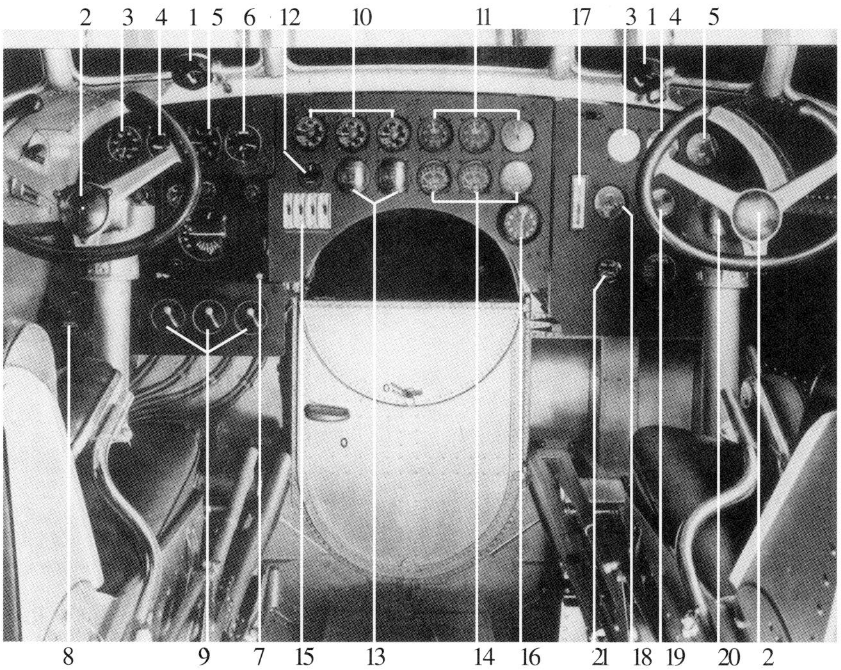

Instrument panel of a Dutch Do 24 K. Most of the instruments are American or British in origin. (Company Brochure)

Instrument panel of a Dutch Do 24 K:

No.	Equipment	Instrument Range	Manufacturer
1	Windscreen wiper		
2	Control wheels		
3	Airspeed indicator	40 – 260 mph ?	
4	Lg 14 r turn and bank indicator		Askania
5	Lv 7 r vertical speed indicator	–15 / +15 m/s	Askania
6	Lh 22 r fine and coarse altimeter	0 – 10000 m	Askania
7	Master reference gyro for the Askania (Sperry) A-2 autopilot with compass card, horizon, banking indicator and low pressure gauge		
8	Component with the control speed valves and oil pressure gauge for the master reference gyro		Askania
9	Ignition switch		American
10	RPM indicator	0 – 2,500 rpm	American
11	Boost pressure gauge	10 – 50 inches of mercury	Pioneer
12	KJ 130 N DF loop indicator	AEG	
13	Fuel-air mixture indicator	Camebridge	
14	Cylinder head temperature gauge	0 - 350° C	Weston
15	4 switches for cockpit lighting, navigation lights, landing light, etc.		
16	Clock		
17	Clinometer (climb/descent)	+20 / -20°	English
18	Lh 19 r coarse altimeter	0 – 10000 m	Askania
19	Lgc 3 directional gyro (Sperry)		Askania
20	Fine altimeter ?		
21	Pressure gauge for low-pressure equipment	0 – 3000 mm WS	Askania
22	Magnetic compass (suspended from cockpit roof)		

Based on contemporary Dornier company brochure.

The flight engineer's panel from a Do 24 T with engine instruments.

The available sources have made it possible to reconstruct four different instrument layouts, although there were surely other variations:

- Do 24 V1 with Junkers diesel engines and Siemens autopilot
- Do 24 K export version with Askania (Sperry) three-axis autopilot
- Do 24 T with radial engines and Askania autopilot
- Do 24 T with Siemens autopilot

Compared to these, the Dutch Do 24s with their air-cooled Wright Cyclone engines were instrumented differently. A number of American and British instruments were fitted. The most significant feature, however, was the Askania (Sperry) three-axis autopilot.

As the most-produced variant, the Do 24 T powered by Bramo radial engines was operated with several variations in instrumentation with Askania or Siemens autopilots.

The Spanish Do 24s were fitted with a Siemens autopilot. As these were relatively late production Do 24 T-3s, they were fitted with equipment then standard in the *Luftwaffe* (1944):

- Electric RPM indicators
  500 – 3,600 rpm Fl 20286-3
- Combined turn and bank indicator and artificial horizon
  Fl 22411
- Radio altimeter
  (FuG 101 A)
  0 – 150 / 0 – 750 m Ln 28330-1

The instrument layout of the original Do 24 was simple, but easily viewed. As this photograph of the cockpit of the Do ATT shows, little of the original instrumentation remains, apart from the clock in the control horn. As an experimental aircraft, instrumentation is more extensive than that of a production aircraft. Deletion of the nose position has made it possible to add a large central console.

The cockpit of the restored Do 24 T-3 in Kamp van Zeist, Holland. Although some items of equipment are missing, this is a lovely example of a Do 24 T with Siemens autopilot. (Militaire Luchtvaart Museum)

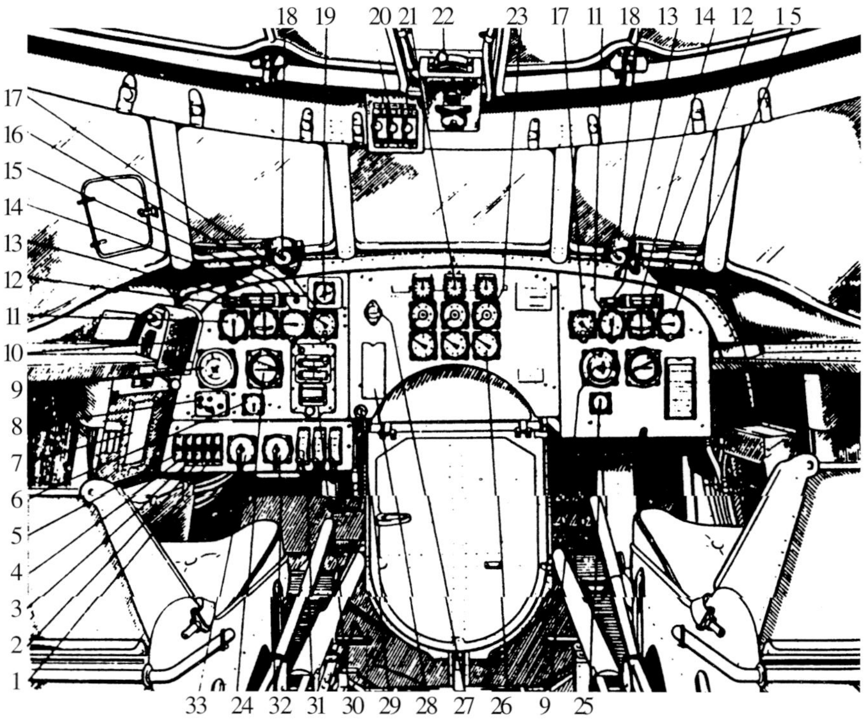

Instrument panel of a Do 24 T with Askania autopilot:

No.	Equipment	Instrument Range	Requisition/Equipment Number
1	Gyro compass heat switch		
2	Ultra-violet light switch		
3	Navigation lights switch		
4	Nose light switch		
5	Formation lights switch		
6	Suction pressure gauge	0 – 3 kg/cm²	Fl 22471
7	Deviation table		
8	Controls for FuG 25 (BG 25a)		Ln 28810
9	PfK/f3 master compass indicator		Fl 23338
10	Landing light switch		
11	Airspeed indicator	60 – 550 km/h	Fl 22230
12	Turn and bank indicator		Fl 22402
	or electric turn and bank indicator		Fl 22406
13	Pitot tube heat visual indicator		Fl 32525
14	Lkz 1p course indicator		Fl 22592
15	Statoscope-vertical speed indicator	-10 / +10 m/s	Fl 22381-10
16	Landing flap indicator lights		Fl 32262
17	Fine and coarse altimeter	0 – 10000 m	Fl 22320
18	Windscreen wiper		
19	AFN 2 radio navigation indicator		Ln 27002
20	Propeller pitch switches (3)		9-9502 B
21	Electric propeller pitch indicators (3)		Fl 20841
22	Landing flap setting lever		
23	Electric RPM indicators (3)	400 – 2,400 rpm	Fl 20283?
24	Artificial horizon (Sperry)		Fl 22426 or Fl 22427
25	Suction gauge	200 – 2500 mm WS	Fl ?
26	Boost pressure gauges (3)	0.6 – 1.8 atm	Fl 20555
27	Electrical system cutout switch	(Do 24 T-2 only)	Fl 32315-2
28	Air navigation table		
29	Autopilot emergency disengage button		Fl 22557
30	Lfgk gyro compass		Fl 22500
31	Ignition switches (3)		Fl 21119
32	Selector switch (pressure)		
33	Selector switch (suction)		
34	Bo-UK 1 clocks (in control wheels)		Fl 23885

The flight engineer was provided with an instrument panel located behind the cockpit and containing the following engine instruments:

- Fuel gauge (Tank I)
  0 – 280 l Fl 20723
- Fuel gauge (Tank II)
  0 – 485 l Fl 20723
- Fuel gauge (Tank III)
  0 – 540 l Fl 20723
- Fuel gauge (Tank IV)
  0 – 540 l Fl 20723
- Fuel gauge (win tank)
  0 – 1000 l Fl 20723
- Measuring point selector switch
- Outside air temperature gauge
  -50 / +20° C Fl 20349
- 3 fuel / oil pressure gauges
  0 – 2 / 0 – 10 kg/cm² Fl 20512-2
- 3 oil temperature gauges
  0 – 130° C Fl 20342

(see illustration on Page 154)

The French Do 24 T was also largely equipped with German instruments.

Dornier Do 335 A-02, VG+PH, at a Dornier open house in 1983. In the background is a Dornier Do 31.

Dornier Do 335 *Pfeil* (Arrow)

The twin-engined Do 335 first flew on 26 October 1943. This large aircraft was propelled by a conventional tractor propeller and a pusher propeller at the rear driven by means of an extension shaft. Drag was thus the same as that of a single-engine aircraft. The pilot was provided with an ejection seat and the cockpit, with its many instruments, was reminiscent of later jet cockpits.

Flight tests confirmed the potential of the "Anteater", as the machine was dubbed on account of its unconventional appearance. The counter-rotating propellers made it comfortable to fly and the Do 335's performance made it one of the fastest piston-engined aircraft ever built.

Of the approximately forty aircraft which were completed, only the second pre-production aircraft, the Do 335 A-02, has survived. This aircraft, WNr. 240102, manufacturer's code VG+PH, was built for equipment testing.

Replica of a Do 335 A instrument panel. The arrangement of the temperature and pressure gauges for the two engines differs from that of the original, with a broad stripe dividing the indicators for the two power plants. Those on the left are for the forward engine, those on the right for the rear power plant.

Original right portion of the main instrument panel from a Do 335 A housing the engine instruments. The panel is displayed in the Dornier Museum in Merseburg.

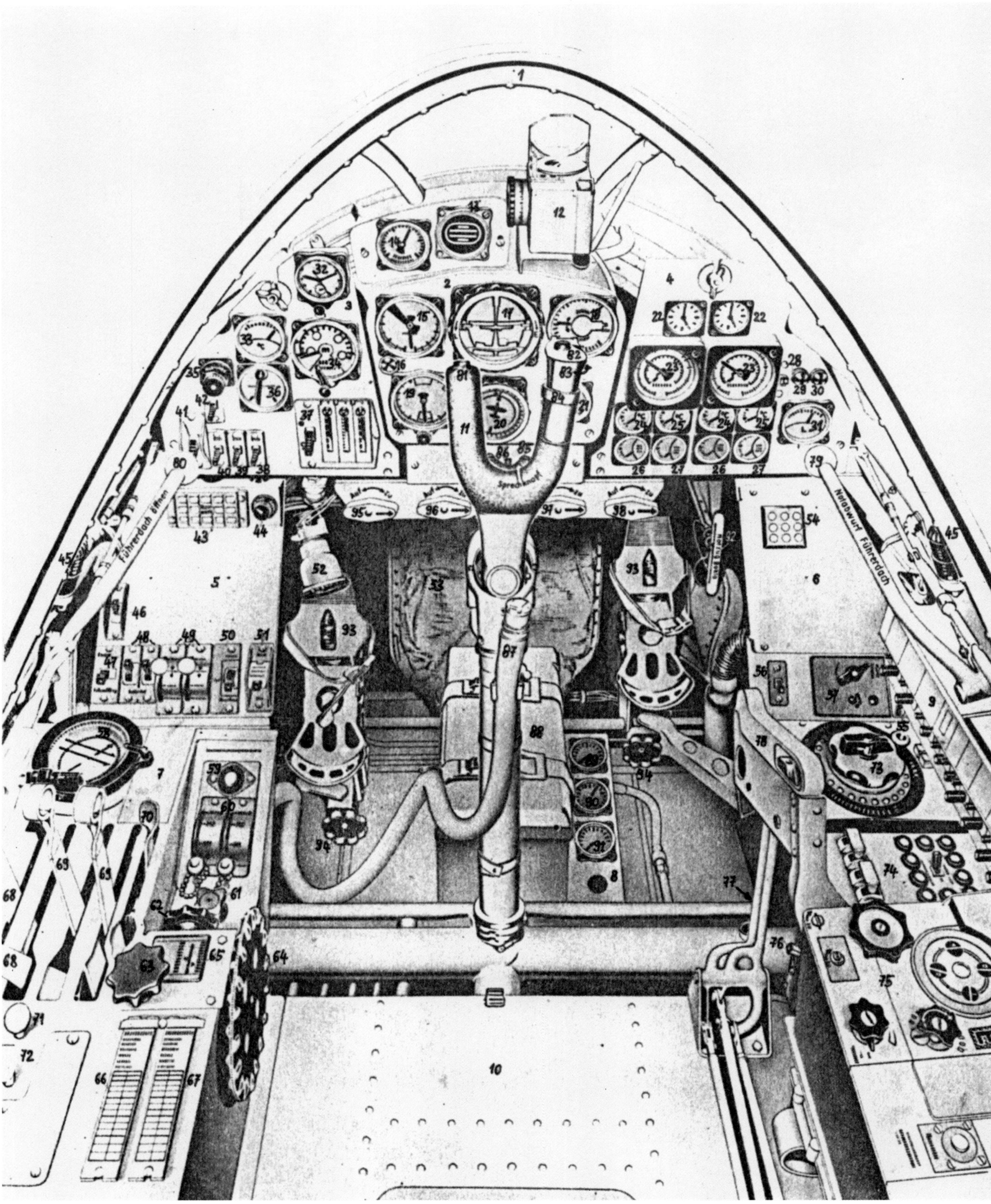

Drawing of the Do 335 A-0 and A-1 cockpit as it appeared in September 1944. (Dornier Archive)

Equipment of the Do 335 A-0 and A-1 as of September 1944:

No.	Equipment	Instrument Range	Requisition/Equipment Number
1	Windscreen		
2	Main instrument panel – blind flying panel		Fl 22000
3	Main instrument panel – left section		
4	Main instrument panel – right section		
5	Left auxiliary panel		
6	Right auxiliary panel		
7	Left console		
8	Equipment Support		
9	Electrical control panel		
10	Seat base		
11	Pivoting control grip		
12	Revi 16 D gun sight		Fl 52598
13	Oxygen flow meter		Fl 30489
14	Oxygen pressure gauge	0 – 250 kg/cm^2	Fl 30496
15	Airspeed indicator	100 – 900 km/h	Fl 22234
		or 100 – 1000 km/h	Fl 22245
16	Pitot tube heat visual indicator		Fl 32530-7
17	Combined turn and bank indicator and artificial horizon		Fl 22410-1
			or Fl 22411-1
18	Vertical speed indicator	+30 / -30 m/s	Fl 22386
19	Fine and coarse altimeter	0 – 13000 m	Fl 22322
20	PFK/f2 master compass indicator		Fl 23334
	or KT/f3 if autopilot installed		127-118 A
21	AFN 2 homing indicator		Ln 27002
22	Propeller pitch indicator		Fl 20845
23	RPM indicator-boost pressure gauge	500 – 3,600 rpm	Fl 20569
		0.6 – 1.8 atm	
24	Coolant temperature gauge	0 - 160° C	Fl 20358
25	Oil temperature gauge	0 - 160° C	Fl 20358
26	Fuel pressure gauge	0 – 3 kg/cm^2	Fl 20582
27	Oil pressure indicator	0 – 15 kg/cm^2	Fl 20584
28	Fuel transfer switch (leading edge tanks)		
29	Low temperature warning light (white)		Fl 32529
30	Fuel warning light (red)		Fl 32529-1
31	Fuel gauge	0 – 1200 l	Fl 20723
32	Bo-UK 1 clock		Fl 23885
33	Outside air temperature gauge	-60 / +40° C	Fl 20349
34	Radio altimeter (FuG 101 A)	0 – 150 / 0 – 750 m	Ln 28330-1
35	Ultra-violet lighting dimmer switch		Fl 32416
36	PSH 17 gyro monitoring switch	128-180 B	
37	SZK K 3 switch, counter and control box		Fl 47318
38	Pitot tube heat switch		Fl 32350
39	Instrument panel lighting switch		Fl 32350
40	Navigation lights switch		Fl 32350
41	Landing light switch		Fl 32350
42	Backup navigation lights switch		Fl 32350
43	Five-light indicator for undercarriage and flaps		19-6822 A
44	Compass lighting dimmer switch		Fl 32402-1
45	Ultra-violet lights		Fl 32269-1
46	Propeller jettison switch (belly landing)		Fl 32349-2
47	Control transfer switch		19-5834 A
48	Propeller selector switch		Fl 32346-1
49	Propeller manual pitch control switch		Fl 18502-2
50	DKS-C switch for landing flaps		19-9206 A-1
51	Undercarriage switch		Fl 32349-2
52	Pivoting lamps		Fl 32260-2
53	Engine cannon cover		
54	Fire warning device		
55	Jettison switch (emergency bail-out)		Fl ?
56	Autopilot axis selector switch		Fl 32350
57	IFF controls (FuG 25a)		Ln 28810

Dornier company photograph of the cockpit of a Do 335 A-0. (F. Selinger Archive)

In April 1945 it was flown from the Rechlin test station to the Dornier airfield in Oberpfaffenhofen, where it was captured by the Americans. The machine was subsequently flown to Cherbourg, from where it was shipped to the USA along with other captured German aircraft aboard the aircraft carrier HMS Reaper. The Do 335 was examined at the Patuxent River Naval Air Station, however a lack of spares prevented it from being flown.

Placed in storage in Norfolk in 1947, in 1961 the Do 335 was transferred to the National Air and Space Museum in Washington. In 1974 the aircraft was returned to Germany, where it was restored by Dornier. It was subsequently displayed in the Deutsches Museum in Munich from 1984 to 1989, after which it was returned to the United States. One of the interior shots included here is of this aircraft.

58	OK 42 emergency compass with light		Fl 23238
59	Electrical system cutout switch		Fl 32315-2
60	Ignition switch		Fl 21118
61	Oxygen flow valve		Fl 30508
62	Aileron trim wheel		
63	Rudder trim wheel		
64	Elevator trim wheel		
65	Trim indicator		
66	Emergency compass deviation table		Fl 23906
67	Master compass indicator deviation table		Fl 23906
68	Fuel cock lever		
69	Throttle levers		
70	Throttle lever friction lock		
71	Fire extinguisher knob, forward engine		
72	Fire extinguisher knob, rear engine		
73	ZSK 246 bomb arming panel		Fl 50596
74	ASK 335 bomb sequence selector panel		Fl ?
75	FuG 16 Z(Y) control box		
76	Radio system mode selector switch		
77	Location for installation of FBG 2 remote control		Fl 26604 ?
78	Ejection seat firing handle		
79	Canopy jettison lever		
80	Canopy closing handles		
81	Bomb release button		
82	Engine cannon firing button		
83	MG 151 firing button		
84	Course indicator for Lri 3 autopilot		127-237
85	Transmit button		
86	Autopilot engage switch		19-9300 A
87	Oxygen connection		
88	Battery		
89	Hydraulic system pressure gauge	0 – 160 kg/cm^2	Fl 20516-3
90	Emergency compressed air pressure gauge	0 – 160 kg/cm^2	Fl 20516-3
91	Ejection seat system pressure gauge or	0 – 160 kg/cm^2 0 – 250 kg/cm^2	Fl 20516-3 Fl 20519
92	Bomb bay doors emergency opening switch		
93	Rudder pedals		
94	Rudder pedal adjustment wheel		
95	Undercarriage emergency switch		
96	Flaps emergency switch		
97	Control transfer emergency switch		
98	Bomb doors emergency switch		

Replica of a Do 335 V instrument panel. The instrument panels of many prototypes included an electric turn-and-bank indicator on the left. (Bende)

The cockpit of the Do 335 was very roomy and by the standards of 1943-44 was quite advanced and well-laid-out.

The main instrument panel included the standard blind flying panel introduced in 1943, which included the most important flight instruments. Above the main panel were mounted the reflector sight and instruments associated with the oxygen system.

Located to the left of the blind flying panel were other flight and navigation instruments, controls for the Patin autopilot and the round counters.

The engine instruments were grouped on the right and were separated with those for the forward engine on the left and the rear engine on the right. To save space, instruments with the new square housings were used almost exclusively, especially the small electric indicators with an installed diameter of 40 mm and the combined RPM indicator-boost pressure gauges.

The port auxiliary instrument panel and console housed the engine throttle levers, trim controls, ignition switches, the emergency compass and undercarriage and flap controls and indicators.

Grouped in the **starboard auxiliary instrument panel and console** were the fire warning lights, radio system controls (FuG 16 and FuG 25), bomb sequence selector panel and the firing handle for the compressed-air ejection seat. Above them was the main electrical panel with automatic circuit breakers.

A comparison of contemporary photographs with the cockpit of the restored Do 335 A-02 reveals a number of changes. Some original instruments had to be replaced with similar, or in the case of the toggle switches, modern equipment during restoration.

The rear (instructor's) cockpit of the two-seat training version was equipped with much-simplified instrumentation consisting of the standard blind flying panel and two small rectangular instrument panels to the left and right. The port panel housed two RPM indicator-boost pressure gauges and the right the oxygen flow meter and oxygen pressure gauge, arranged one above the other.

Cockpit of the restored Do 335 A-02. The original main instrument panel was missing and had to be replaced. Compromises had to be made in the equipment used, with some of the instruments being historically similar or modern items (low fuel warning light and toggle switches). As well, the Phillips-head screws used did not exist in Germany in 1944-45. Note the Revi 16 B gun sight at the top of the photograph. (Wildmoser)

The instrument panel of a Do 335 prototype seen from the right. (F. Selinger Archive)

The B-series differed from the A only in detail, as required by the later version's modified equipment. There were significant changes when compared with the early prototypes, however, such as the V3 or the V8. The prototypes made extensive use of older Small Standard engine instruments with an installed diameter of 57 mm.

No original Do 335 prototype has survived, however there are replicas of instrument panels from a Do 335 prototype in collectors circles.

Differences in Equipment in the Do 335 Prototypes Compared to the Do 335 A-0/A-1 Production Aircraft:

Equipment		Instrument Range	Requisition/Equipment Number
5	with selector switch for camera equipment and unidentified visual indicator		Fl 32525
12	Gunsight replaced by FK 38 magnetic compass		Fl 32333
15	Airspeed indicator	100 – 750 km/h	Fl ?
18	Vertical speed indicator	+15/-15 m/sec	Fl 22384
22	the propeller pitch indicators were arranged one above the other		
23	Double RPM indicator	500 – 3,600 rpm	Fl 20274-2 ?
	Double pressure gauge (right)	0.6 – 1.8 atm	Fl 20556
	24-27 from left to right (pairs of instruments arranged vertically):		
	Temperature gauges (coolant)	0 - 130° C	Fl 20342
	Temperature gauges (oil)	0 - 130° C	Fl 20342
	Fuel/Oil pressure gauges	0 – 3 kg/cm² 0 – 10 kg/cm²	Fl 20572
34	Deleted, in some cases replaced by electric turn-and-bank indicator		Fl 22407 or 22412
36	Deleted, replaced by two deviation tables		Fl 23906
37	Deleted, replaced by toggle switch with safety cover		
48	Two propeller pitch control switches		Fl 18502-2
49	DKS-C switch for landing flaps		19-9206 A-1
50	Undercarriage switch		Fl 32349-2
51	Electrical system cut-out switch		Fl 32315-2
56	Deleted		
59	Deleted		
73	Deleted, replaced by FuG 25a control panel		Ln 28810
74	Deleted		
95-98	Deleted		

A placard beneath the blind-flying panel advised of maximum allowable speeds

	Maximum Speed	
Undercarriage down Landing flaps in takeoff position	340 km/h	Flaps in landing position 270 km/h

The manned Fi 103 A-1/Re 4 in the military museum in Delft, Netherlands. (Wildmoser)

A firing range was set up on the island of Usedom, where the first catapult launch was made in December 1942. A Walter catapult was later adopted and each time it was fired the piston was ejected from the catapult, resulting in the nickname "Cherry Pit" for the Fi 103.

Fieseler rushed the V 1 into production in 1943, which resulted in numerous setbacks. In some cases the missiles disintegrated when launched, while maximum speed was considerably below calculated values.

A total of 32,000 V 1s were built, most by forced labor working under inhuman conditions. Of these, approximately 22,400 were launched from catapults and later from aircraft. Of these 59% reached their targets, London and Antwerp. The rest were shot down or lost through technical failure. The damage inflicted by the unmanned missiles was sometimes considerable, but not even the V 1 could prevent the defeat of the Nazis.

Fieseler Fi 103 *Reichenberg*

By 1941-42 the Allied bombing offensive against German cities had become a serious threat. With the *Luftwaffe* overextended and largely relegated to a defensive role, the German command began seeking a "revenge weapon" with which to respond.

The result, the *Vergeltungswaffe 1* (Revenge Weapon 1) or V 1, was an unmanned missile of very simple design. It was a cantilever monoplane with the wing located mid-fuselage. Power was provided by a single pulse-jet, a relatively primitive type of power plant. The V 1 was controlled by an autopilot consisting of an attitude gyro, two rate-of-turn gyros, a compass and an altimeter. Distance flown was measured by the revolutions of a small propeller in the nose of the aircraft.

In the winter of 1943-44 consideration was given to a manned version of the Fi 103 for suicide missions. Approximately 175 missiles were converted for use in "Operation Götterdämmerung", an attack against Allied shipping and troop concentrations. The manned version, or Fi 103 A-1/Re 4, was dubbed "Reichenberg". There was also an unarmed two-seat trainer version.

The Allied invasion of France precluded the planned operation and the target was switched to Russian industrial facilities. The pilot of the Reichenberg was supposed to steer his machine toward the target and bail out before it entered its final dive. His chances of survival were poor, however, for the aircraft's cockpit was cramped and located directly in front of the air intake. The Fi 103 also suffered from poor stability, which meant that the pilot would have to delay bailing out until relatively late to be sure of hitting the target.

View of the empty, but original, instrument panel of an Fi 103 A-1/Re 4 in Wilrijk, Belgium. The device on the lower left was part of the fuel system. (Vanhee)

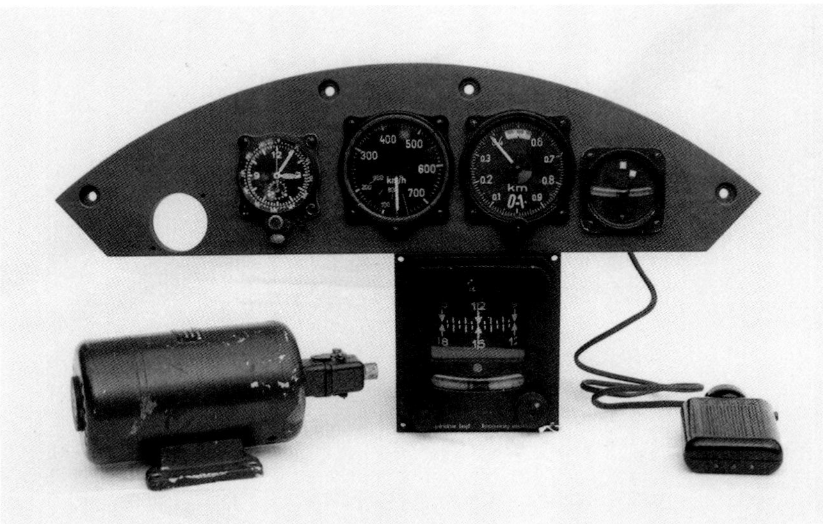

Reconstructed instrument panel of the Fi 103 A-1/Re 4 with instruments. Seen at the bottom are a transformer, Siemens Lku 4 gyro compass and the battery box for the turn-and-bank indicator.

Equipment for the Fi 103 A-1/Re 4:

No.	Equipment	Instrument Range	Requisition/Equipment Number
1	Armament master switch		
2	Bo-UK 1 clock		Fl 23885
3	Airspeed indicator	100 – 900 km/h	Fl 22234
4	Fine and coarse altimeter	0 – 10000 m	Fl 22320
5	Electric turn and bank indicator		Fl 22414
6	Battery box for turn and bank indicator		Fl 22414-3
7	Gyro-compass		
8	Ignition button		
9	Air cock		
10	Fuel cock		

A placard on the instrument panel instructed the pilot what to do when starting the engine and in event of engine failure:

Start:	Air cock on, throttle up, depress button
Flame-Out:	Wait 20 seconds, then re-start

After the end of the war in Europe the Americans continued work on the unmanned Fi 103 for possible use against the Japanese. While the American version differed little from the original V 1, it was twenty times as expensive as the German original. It was, however, rather more reliable. Approximately 1,200 were built but none was ever used in action.

The V 1 initiated the age of the long-range self-guided missile and it began a process which culminated in today's intercontinental ballistic missiles.

The notoriety of the V 1 has resulted in the survival of approximately 60 German- and American-built versions, including four of the manned variety.

The cockpit of the Fi 103 A-1/Re 4 was one of the most primitive ever produced by the German aviation industry. To create the manned version of the Fi 103 A-1, a hole approximately 40 x 50 cm was cut in the top of the fuselage in front of the engine air intake. The resulting tiny cockpit was fitted with a seat, controls and a small instrument panel.

The cockpit was enclosed by a canopy. Colored lines were painted on the side panels to assist the pilot in judging the dive angle. The only concession to pilot comfort was a headrest and a primitive ventilation pipe in the cockpit canopy.

The gyro-compass sat in a vibration-dampened mount on the floor between the pilot's knees. It was probably a modified Siemens Lku 4 directional gyro, Fl 22561, with a transformer and power supply.

Empty holes in the instrument panels of Fi 103 A-1/Re 4s in photographs suggest that a clock was planned but not installed. The aircraft was not equipped with an oxygen system or radio.

D-EBGY, a Fi 156 C-3 in a tropical camouflage scheme, photographed at an old-timers meet in Degerfeld. The aircraft is now registered as D-EZZZ.

Fieseler Fi 156 *Storch* (Stork)

The Fieseler *Storch* is probably the best known short takeoff and landing aircraft in the world to date. In calm wind conditions the aircraft's minimum speed is just 51 km/h while losing none of its controllability. With a light headwind the takeoff run is 50 meters and landing run an astonishingly short 15 meters.

The secret of its excellent slow-flying characteristics is a large rectangular wing of constant profile, full span leading edge slats and large split flaps which are coupled with the ailerons. The aircraft also has a wide-track undercarriage with capable oil shock absorbers which allows it to endure hard landings. It is powered by a 240 H.P. Argus As 10 engine which provides adequate power reserves, even in extreme flight attitudes. The high wing configuration combined with extensive glazing provides the pilot with an excellent view from the cockpit.

The stories and legends which surround the Storch are as legion as the famous personalities who have flown in it. The Fi 156 was flown in military and civilian guises in more than fifteen nations outside Germany. A total of approximately 2,600 Storks were built by 1945, with the most important variants being the Fi 156 C communications aircraft and the Fi 156 D air ambulance.

In addition to the aircraft built by Fieseler, 150 Storks were built by Mràz for the Czech air force as the Cap K-65, while the French company Morane Saulnier built 156 as the MS.500 Criquet. With no more Argus engines available, Morane Saulnier used inline engines (MS.501), and later radial engines by Salmson (MS.502) and Jacobs (MS.504 and MS.505). A total of 756 MS.500 to MS.505 was built. A number of MS.500s were later converted to later variants by replacing the engine.

Historical photograph of the instrument panel of a Fi 156 C. The white markings and inscriptions on the electrical systems were hand-painted. (Hampel Collection)

The instrument panel of D-EFTY, an MS.505. The arrangement of the instruments is largely similar in to that of the Fi 156. Most of the instruments are modern French or American items. Also present is a cylinder head temperature gauge and a boost pressure gauge on the right. At the bottom are the controls for the radio and navigation equipment. The rudder pedals are standard Luftwaffe types.

The cockpit of the Fi 156 C (MS.500) in the Musée de l'Air in Paris is painted pale gray with the instrument panel in black-gray. It thus provides a good impression of a Fi 156 prior to 1941. With the exception of the RPM indicator, the instruments are French-made.

NMS.505 of Flugschule Koch, photographed in Augsburg circa 1987. An authentic French paint scheme was applied during restoration. Many of the MS.505s still flying have been painted in Luftwaffe markings.

For years the Fi 156 was widely used as a glider tug, a task for which it was extremely well suited. Today a number are still flown and lovingly cared for. Approximately 90 Storks of all versions have survived, with Morane Saulnier the most numerous, with about 60 still in existence.

The photographs presented here depict the following aircraft:

- A Swiss Fi 156 C, photographs of whose instrument panel were taken in flight. The identity of the machine is not known, however the black-gray finish of the cockpit interior suggests that it was a *Luftwaffe* aircraft which was interned during the war.

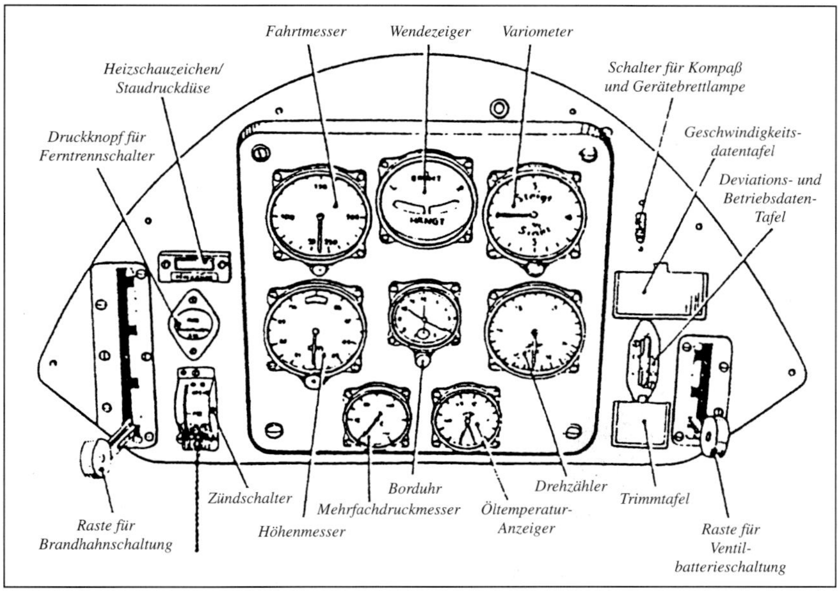

Drawing of the instrument panel of the Fi 156 from the pilot's notes. (Hafner Archive)

Equipment of the Fi 156 C:

No.	Equipment	Instrument Range	Requisition/Equipment Number
1	FK 38 magnetic compass		Fl 23233
	or FK 5		Fl 23211
	plus Nav Vordruck K 6 deviation table		Fl 23906
2	Fuel cock selection lever		
3	Starter warning light (above 4)		Fl 32529
4	Pitot tube heat visual indicator		
5	Electrical system cutout switch		Fl 32315-2
6	Ignition switch		Fl 21118
7	Dimmer switch (above 10)		Fl 32402-1
8	Airspeed indicator	50 – 200 km/h	Fl 22209
	or	50 – 350 km/h	or 22228
	or	60 – 400 km/h	Fl 22233
9	Fine and coarse altimeter	0 – 10000 m	Fl 22320
10	Turn and bank indicator		Fl 22402
11	Kienzle 8-day clock		Fl 23886-1
	or Junghans Bo-UK 1		Fl 23885
12	Statoscope-vertical speed indicator	+10 / -10 m/s	Fl 22381-10
13	RPM indicator	600 – 3,600 rpm	Fl 20222-3
14	Oil temperature gauge	0 - 120° C	Fl 20330
	or	0 - 130° C	Fl 20342
	or	0 - 160° C	Fl 20343
15	Double pressure gauge	0 – 1 /	Fl 20512-1
	for fuel and oil	0 – 10 kg/cm^2	
19	Compass light toggle switch		19-?
20	Speed placard		
21	DBS 1 sliding tray for operating data		Fl 23501
22	Trim information placard		
23	Valve accumulator adjustment lever		
24	AP 8 starter injection pump (beneath 22)		8-4505 A
25	Starter		Fl 21211
26	Toggle switch for advanced / delayed ignition		Fl 32350
27	5 circuit breakers for the electrical system		Fl 3240?
28	Fuel gauge (sight glasses beneath the wings)		Fl 20712

* Not in all aircraft

- Fi 156 C-3, D-EBGY (now D-EZZZ), owned privately. A former *Luftwaffe* aircraft, during the war it was interned in Sweden, where it was used as a training and liaison aircraft. After its return to Germany in 1961, it was rebuilt using parts from two other Fi 156s from Sweden and for many years was flown by the Unterwössen Alpine Gliding School.
- MS.500 of the Musée de l'Air in Paris. This former French military aircraft is displayed as a German air ambulance with the civilian registration D-EMAW.
- MS.505, D-EFTY, of the Koch Flying School. After it was retired from French military service it was owned by a French flying club for many years.

The cockpit of the Fi 156 was sparsely equipped. A two-part metal instrument panel was placed in front of the pilot beneath the large windscreen. The flight and engine instruments were housed in a special vibration-proof panel in the center. All instruments were attached to the panel by lens-head bolts and retaining nuts on the back side. The magnetic compass was installed in a special mount in a central position above the windscreen, where it was least likely to be affected by electrical fields or metal parts. The throttle lever was situated on the left side of the cockpit, while the electrical system's circuit breakers were mounted on the right side of the pilot's seat.

There were minor differences in the arrangement of equipment between individual variants. In some cases this was influenced by the spares situation and the wishes of the pilot.

In the Fi 156s built by Morane after the war—the MS.500 and its successors—the arrangement of the instruments and switches was largely unchanged, although French instruments were more frequently used as production went on. The cockpit was painted to French standards. Most of the Storks still flying today are equipped to suit the wishes of their owners. Only a few machines have historically correct equipment and paint schemes. In later years flight safety became increasingly important, and modern or overhauled instruments were installed.

Rare color photograph of the instrument panel of a Swiss Fi 156 C. The photograph was apparently taken while the aircraft was on approach to land: airspeed just above the minimum speed marking of 80 km/h, -4 m/s rate of descent, altitude approximately 30 meters, revolutions 1,200 rpm, mid-range temperature of approximately 70°C, fuel and oil pressure in the upper ranges. (Gamperle Collection)

The Fi 156 C handbook describes the instruments originally installed in the aircraft. A comparison of this with contemporary photographs reveals that there were some deviations, however, in the equipment and arrangement of instruments.

The drawing also shows that a number of minor errors were made in the creation of the handbook or that changes in equipment were not recorded. In the drawing the positions of the pressure gauge and oil temperature gauge are reversed.

Ultra-violet lighting with a dimmer switch was installed for the magnetic compass and instrument panel.

An experimental version of the Fi 156 C was built with equipment for the carriage of bombs. An additional circuit breaker was installed in the cockpit, along with a ZSK 244 bomb arming panel.

Focke Wulf Fw 190 V5K, one of the predecessors of the A-series.

Photograph of the cockpit of Fw 190 A-3 serial number 313. This aircraft became the first Fw 190 to fall into the hands of the RAF when its pilot became lost and landed in the U.K. In early versions of the Fw 190 there was a cover panel over the front of the main instrument panel. (via Couderchon)

Focke Wulf Fw 190

The *Luftwaffe* had hoped to adopt the Bf 109 as its standard fighter aircraft, however as early as 1937, during the Spanish Civil War, the type exhibited a number of shortcomings. As a result, a competition was begun for a new fighter aircraft.

Focke Wulf was the successful bidder and in the summer of 1937 Kurt Tank began work on the single-seat fighter which would become the Fw 190. He selected the 1,550 H.P. BMW 139 twin-row radial engine to power the aircraft, as it was at a more advanced stage of development than comparable inline engines. A wide-track undercarriage gave the aircraft excellent handling qualities on the ground, and its flight characteristics were outstanding. In June 1939 the RLM requested the installation of the more powerful BMW 801 radial engine. Subsequent flight testing was a near disaster, as the new engine proved extremely troublesome.

The RLM wanted to cancel development, but the *Luftwaffe* was convinced of the new fighter's potential. Finally, after many changes, in mid-1941 the Fw 190 was ready for action. From the very outset it proved superior to the best Allied fighters then in service. As time went on the Fw 190 was overtaken by technical developments, however it remained the best German piston-engined fighter until the end of the war.

The most important variants were the Fw 190 A fighter and the Fw 190 F and G fighter-bombers, all powered by versions of the BMW 801. When the radial-engined versions of the Fw 190 proved unable to keep pace with new Allied fighter aircraft, Focke Wulf began installation of more powerful inline engines, such as the 1,750 H.P. Jumo 213, in the proven airframe of the Fw 190. The fuselage had to be lengthened fore and aft of the wing, which was unchanged.

The "Longnose Fw 190" had an excellent top speed and was extremely maneuverable. It was highly respected by Allied fighter pilots even though it was built in relatively small numbers.

Approximately 19,500 Fw 190s of all versions were built. Of these 16 complete and 10 partial airframes have survived. Since 1999 a small number of Fw 190 A-8 replicas has been built, equipped with Russian or American radial engines.

Some of the photographs here depict the following museum aircraft:

Fw 190 A-6/R6, WNr. 550214, PN+LU, in the National War Museum in Johannesburg, South Africa.

Fw 190 F-8/R1, WNr. 931884, White 7, in the NASM in Washington.

Fw 190 D-9, WNr. 601088, Black 1, in the USAF Museum in Dayton, Ohio.

Fw 190 A-8 reconstruction, Yellow 11, in the Laatzen Aviation Museum.

Compared to the cockpit of the Bf 109, that of the Fw 190 was relatively roomy. The view from the cockpit, with its blown hood, was outstanding. The only exception to this was the view forward while taxiing, as the bulky radial engine blocked the pilot's view.

The instrument panel of the Fw 190 was divided into three parts. On the fuselage sat a windscreen frame of cast aluminum, which supported the windscreen and the main instrument panel. It also housed the round counters, the reflector gun sight and the clock, or the radio navigation homing indicator.

The main instrument panel, which was made of thick aluminum sheet, housed the flight and navigation instruments as well as the most important engine instruments. The remaining engine instruments were mounted in an auxiliary panel attached to a fuselage frame (equipment frame). Other items of equipment were located on two large consoles on either side of the pilot.

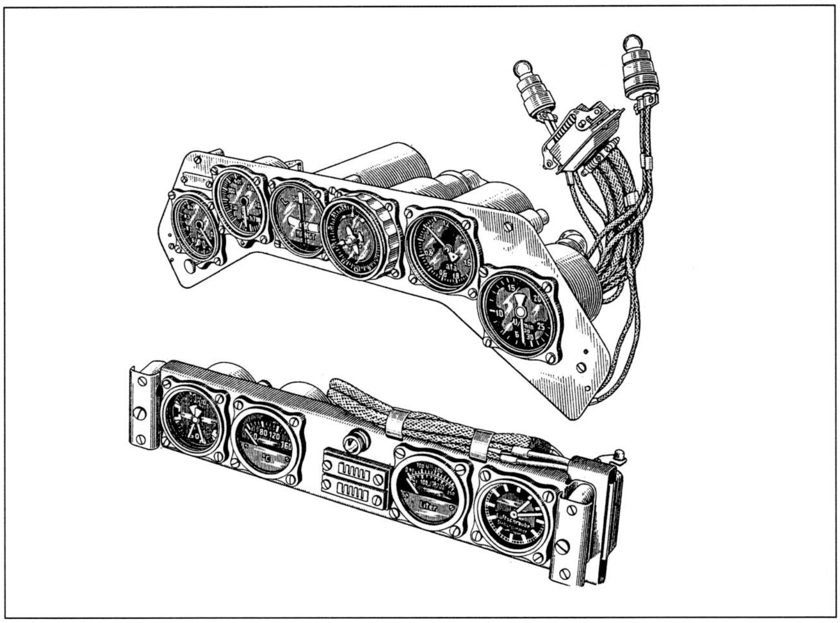

Detail drawing of the main instrument panel and the panel behind the equipment frame of the Fw 190 A-2 to A-4. (Hafner Archive)

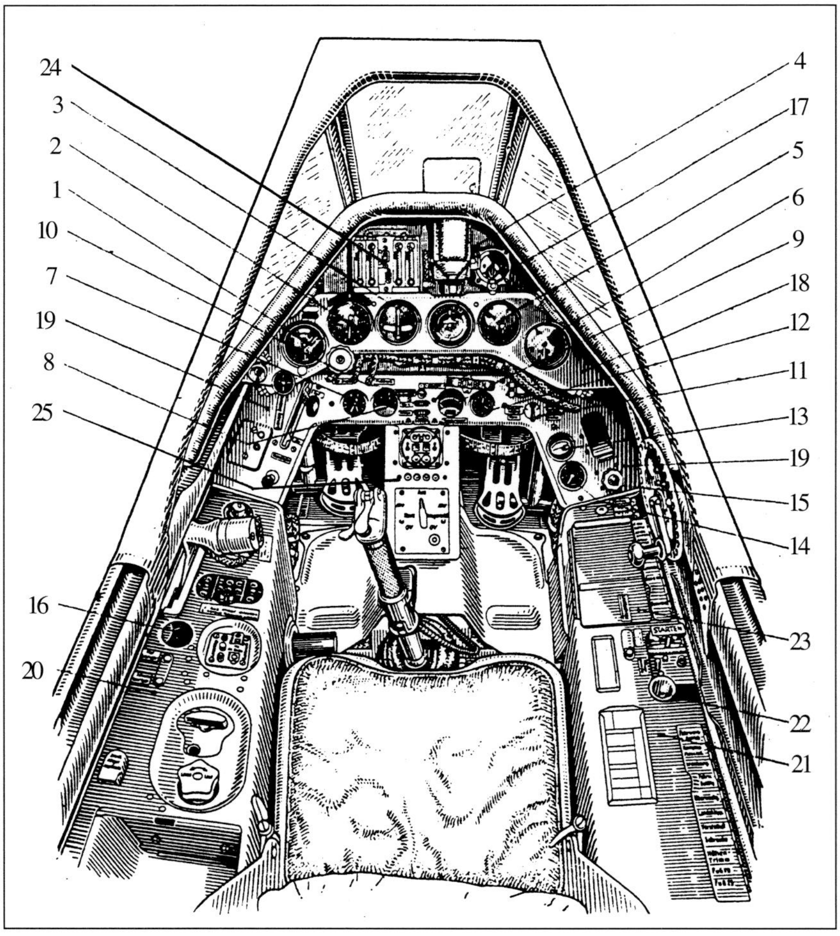

Cockpit of the Fw 190 A-1. The cockpits of the A-2 to A-4 differed only in detail. (Hafner Archive)

Equipment of the Fw 190 A-1 to A-4

No.	Equipment	Instrument Range	Requisition/Equipment Number
1	Fine and coarse altimeter	0 – 10000 m	Fl 22320
2	Airspeed indicator	80 – 750 km/h	Fl 22231
	with pitot tube heat visual indicator		Fl 32525-3
3	Electric turn and bank indicator		Fl 22406
4	Pfk/f2 master compass indicator		Fl 23334
5	Boost pressure gauge	0.6 – 1.8 atm	Fl 20555
6	RPM indicator	600 – 3,000 rpm	Fl 20222-2
7	Fuel/oil pressure gauge	0 – 2 / 0 – 10 kg/cm²	Fl 20512-2
	from Fw 190 A-2	0 – 3 / 0 – 15 kg/cm²	Fl 20512-3
8	Oil temperature gauge	0 - 120° C	Fl 20342-2
9	Fuel gauge	0 – 300 l / 0 – 230 l	Fl 20723
10	Fuel warning light (red)		Fl 32529-1
	beneath it two visual indicators for the fuel pumps (the Fw 190 A-4 had another indicator for the pump serving the auxiliary fuel tank)		Fl 32525
11	Fuel gauge selector switch		Fl 32331
12	Mechanical propeller pitch indicator		Fl 18503-2
13	Oxygen flow indicator		Fl 30489
14	Oxygen pressure gauge	0 – 250 kg/cm²	Fl 30496
15	Oxygen valve		Fl 30508
16	Tailplane trim indicator		Fl 22855
17	Bo-UK 1 clock		Fl 23885
18	Main instrument panel		
19	Equipment frame with, left and above:		
	Undercarriage emergency lowering handle		
	Fuel cock control lever		
	BG 25a control panel for FuG 25 (IFF)		Ln 28810
	Engine starter brushes withdrawal button		
	Bomb manual release handle		
20	Port console with following equipment (from top)		
	Cockpit lighting dimmer switch		Fl 32401
	Propeller pitch control selector switch AUTOMATIC/MANUAL		Fl 32327
	Electrical system cutout switch		Fl 32315-2
	Ignition switch		Fl 21118
	Throttle lever with propeller pitch control thumb switch		Fl 32337
	Undercarriage and flap position indicators (12 lights)		Fl 32532
	Undercarriage and flap actuating buttons		
	Tailplane trim switch		
	Asr 1 headset socket (replaced by newer type from Fw 190 A-2)		Fl 26517-4
	APB 6 starter injection pump with tank		8-4506 A
21	Starboard console with following equipment (from top)		
	Circuit breakers for the electrical system		
	Starter switch		Fl 21212
	Nav. Vordruck K 6 deviation table		Fl 23906
	Operating data table		
22	Flare pistol holder		
23	Flare box		
24	Windscreen superstructure with:		
	SZK K 4 round counter		Fl 47319
	Revi C 12/D reflector gun sight		Fl 52095
25	Auxiliary instrument panel with:		
	ZVK-FF round counter for MG FF cannon		
	Bomb release warning lights (4)		Fl 32529
	ZSK 244 A bomb arming panel (fighter-bombers only)		Fl 50869

Fighter-bomber versions featured an additional panel mounted low in the center of the equipment frame. This housed the bomb sequence selector panel.

This configuration remained unchanged in all versions of the Fw 190 up to the Ta 152. Only the instruments were changed as new equipment became available or as required by new variants.

Compared to the Bf 109 the Fw 190 also had a much more extensive electrical system and used more electrically-driven equipment.

The first production version was the **Fw 190 A-1** powered by the 1,560 H.P. BMW 801 C-1. The subsequent **Fw 190 A-3 to A-5** used the more powerful BMW 801 D and had a revised armament. A revised undercarriage was introduced beginning with the **Fw 190 A-4**.

The most important changes in instrumentation between these variants was the installation of a double pressure gauge with a greater instrument range and new sockets and controls for the radio equipment in the port console.

The **Fw 190 A-5** and **A-6** had an improved airframe, and the installation of the more powerful BMW 801 D resulted in an increase in length. In the cockpit the arrangement of the instruments in the main panel was revised, as the turn and bank indicator was replaced by a combined turn and bank indicator and artificial horizon and a homing indicator for the radio navigation system was added.

The **Fw 190 A-8** had increased fuel tankage and was by far the most produced version of the Fw 190. It also formed the basis for the Fw 190 F-8 fighter-bomber version and the Fw 190 S-8 two-seat conversion trainer, which had simplified instrumentation for the second cockpit. As well, the Fw 190 A-8 was used as the upper half of a Mistel combination together with a Ju 88 bomber.

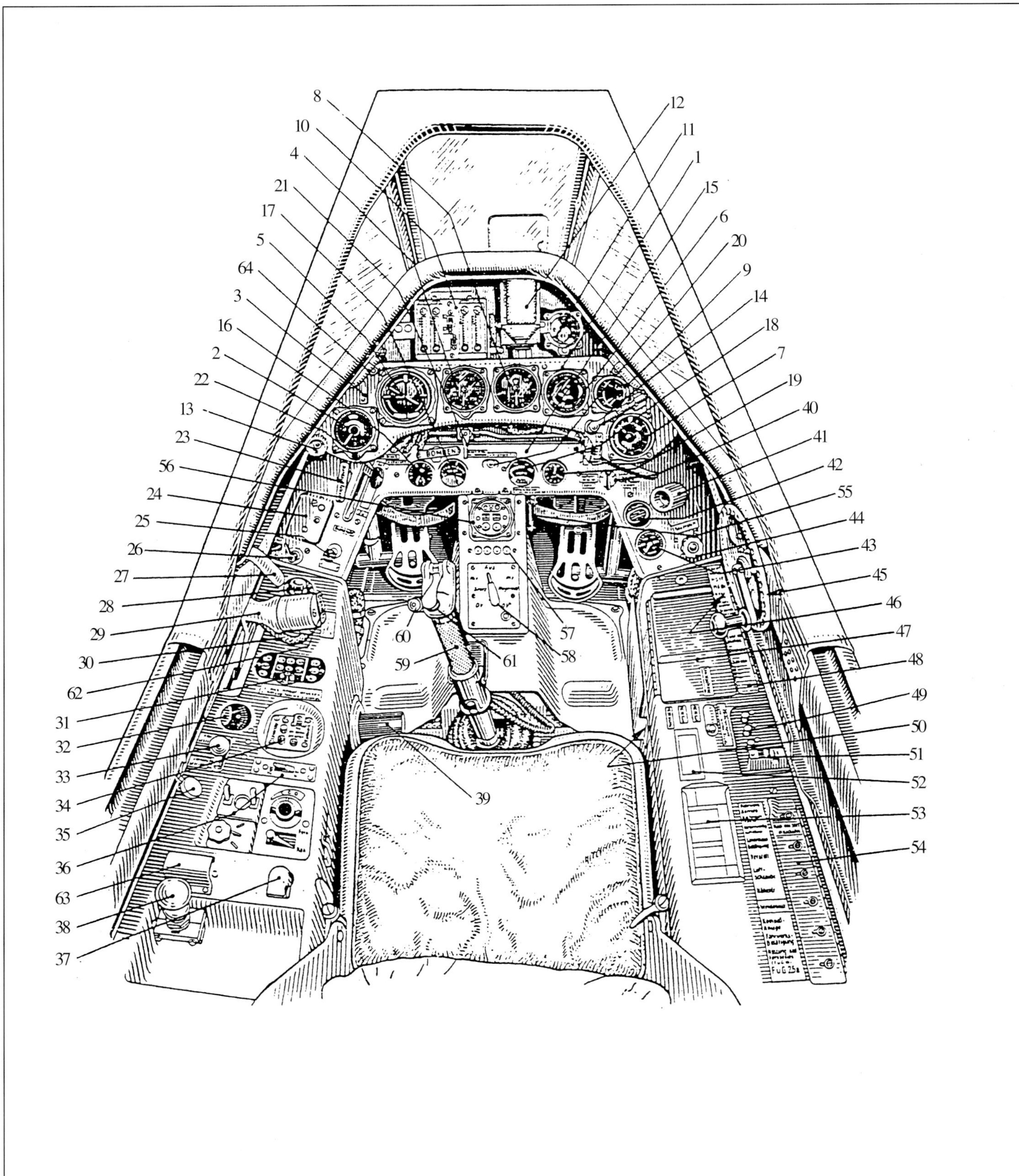

Cockpit equipment of the Fw 190 A-5 and A-6. (Hafner Archive)

Equipment of the Fw 190 A-5 and A-6

1 Main instrument panel
2 Fine and coarse altimeter
3 Pitot tube heater light
4 Airspeed indicator
5 Combined turn and bank indicator and artificial horizon
6 Master compass indicator
7 Boost pressure gauge
8 Direct reading RPM indicator
9 Homing indicator
10 Round counter and control box for MG 17 and MG 151 (SZKK 4)
11 Clock
12 Reflector gun sight
13 Cockpit ventilation control knob
14 Hand crank for operation of cooling gills (engine cooling control)
15 Auxiliary instrument panel
16 Double pressure gauge (fuel and oil)
17 Electric oil temperature gauge
18 Electric fuel gauge
19 Mechanical propeller pitch position indicator
20 Fuel warning light
24 FuG 25a controls
25 Engine starter brushes withdrawal button
26 Stop cock control lever
27 Hand-grip for tropical filter flap operation
28 Instrument panel lighting dimmer switch
29 Throttle lever
30 Ignition switch (hidden by throttle lever)
31 Undercarriage and landing flap position indicators
32 Tailplane trim position indicator
33 Tailplane trim switch
34 Undercarriage and landing flap actuator switches
35 Mixture control
36 FuG 16 Z control panel
37 Headset socket
38 SUM primer pump handle AP 11
39 Throttle friction knob
40 Fuel gauge selector switch
41 Flare pistol holder
42 Oxygen flow indicator
43 Oxygen pressure gauge
44 Oxygen flow valve
45 Canopy actuator drive
46 Circuit breakers for MG 17, MG 151 and bomb-dropping equipment
47 Flare box
48 Forward circuit breaker cover
49 Fuel pump circuit breakers
50 Circuit breakers for MG FF (A-5 series) or MG 151 (outer wings) and camera equipment (A-6 series)
51 Starter switch
52 Deviation table
53 Operating data table
54 Rear circuit breaker cover
55 Cockpit ventilation control
56 Ammunition counter and breech control (ZVK-FF) (up to A-5)
57 Bomb status indicators
58 ZSK bomb arming panel
59 Control stick
60 Bomb release button
61 Outboard cannon firing button
62 Propeller pitch control thumb switch
63 Toggle switch for FuG 25a destruct charge
64 Instrument panel lighting

Cockpit of the restored Fw 190 A-8 in the Laatzen Aviation Museum. Some components such as the rudder pedals, control stick grip and side consoles, have yet to be installed. (Rienecker)

Fw 190 A-8 (NC.900) in the Musée de l'Air in Paris bearing the markings of "Pips" Priller's aircraft.

Cockpit of the Fw 190 A-6 in South Africa. Some items of equipment are missing and most of the instruments have been replaced with British ones. In spite of this, the arrangement of the instruments is easily discernable. A radar scope was installed at the top left in place of the SZK K 4 bomb fusing panel. (National War Museum)

The main instrument panel of the Fw 190 F-8 in the NASM prior to restoration. Some items are missing, however the cockpit is largely in original condition. (R.P. Lutz)

The cockpit of a Fw 190 A-8, part of a Mistel combination. Engine instruments for the Ju 88 were installed at the bottom of the auxiliary instrument panel. (F. Selinger Archive)

Changes in equipment of the Fw 190 A-5 and A-6:

Equipment	Requisition/Equipment Number
2 "Armed" indicator lights for MG 151 in windscreen superstructure	Fl 32529
Combined turn and bank indicator and artificial Horizon (replaced turn and bank indicator)	Fl 22410
Homing indicator for AFN 2 radio navigation	Ln 27002
Fuel pump visual indicators deleted	
AP 11 starter injection pump without tank	
ZVK-FF round counter for MG FF in the Fw 190 A-5 only	

Cockpit of the Fw 190 D-9 in the USAF Museum. (Photo R.P. Lutz)

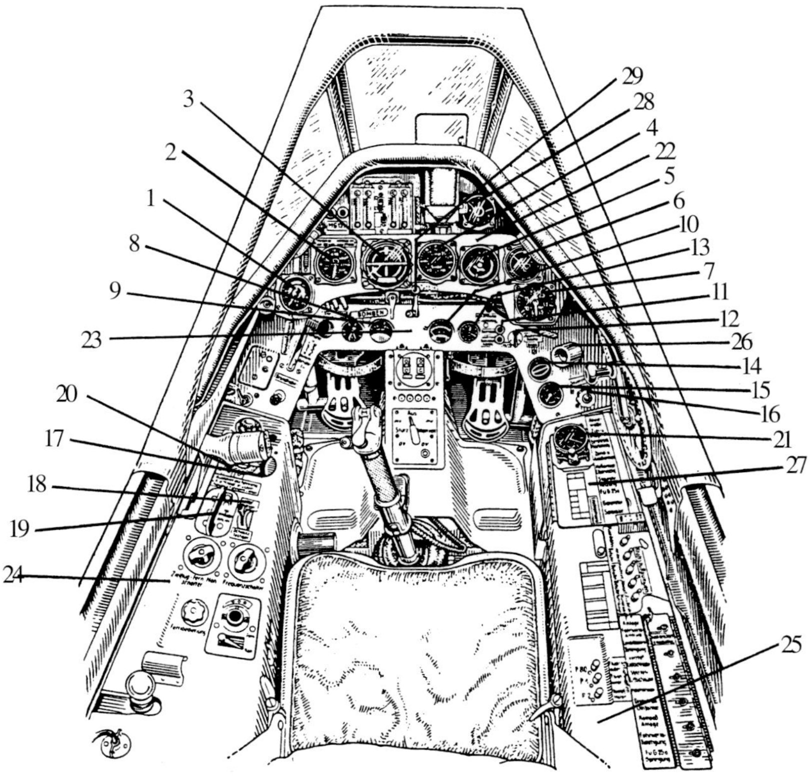

1 Fine and coarse altimeter
2 Airspeed indicator
3 Electric combined turn and bank indicator and artificial horizon
4 Vertical speed indicator
5 Master compass indicator
6 Boost pressure gauge
7 RPM indicator
8 Double pressure gauge for fuel and oil
9 Oil temperature gauge
10 Fuel gauge
11 Fuel warning light
12 Fuel gauge selector switch
13 Mechanical propeller pitch indicator
14 Oxygen flow meter
15 Oxygen pressure gauge
16 Oxygen flow valve with rapid release
17 Tailplane trim indicator
18 Tailplane trim button
19 Undercarriage and landing flap actuator switches
20 Undercarriage and landing flap position indicators
21 Clock
22 Main instrument panel
23 Auxiliary instrument panel
24 Port console
25 Starboard console
26 Flare pistol holder
27 Flare box
28 Radio navigation homing indicator
29 Ventilation flap crank

Cockpit of the Fw 190 A-7 to A-9. (Hafner Archive)

The last production version was the **Fw 190 A-9** powered by the 2,000 H.P. BMW 801 F. The A-7 to A-9 versions introduced further changes in instrumentation, especially in the main panel. Further changes resulted from the adoption of new versions of the FuG 16.

In aircraft modified for use as Mistel command machines, the bomb sequence selector panel in the auxiliary instrument panel was replaced by instruments with which to monitor the engines of the Ju 88:

- two-position indicator for the propellers, 127-1092 A
- 2 combined RPM indicators and boost pressure gauges, Fl 20569

The ASK 190 C-1, a bomb sequence selector panel designed specially for the Fw 190, was installed above the fusing selector box in the **Fw 190 F-8**.

The following speed limits placard appeared on the main instrument panel:

Undercarriage down
Over 200 km/h
Flaps down
Below 295 km/h

The Fw 190 A-8 replica built by the Flug Werk company is identical to the original, however it is equipped with modern instruments of the now standard dimensions.

The last and most potent version of the series was the **Fw 190 D** equipped with the Jumo 213 inline engine. Some aircraft were equipped with MW 50 water-methanol injection for increased performance, consequently, instrumentation differed somewhat from that of A-series aircraft.

Changes in equipment of the Fw 190 A-7 to A-9:

Equipment	Instrument Range	Requisition/Equipment Number
AFN 2 homing indicator in windscreen superstructure		Ln 27002
Airspeed indicator	100 – 900 km/h	Fl 22234
Combined turn and bank indicator and artificial horizon		Fl 22415
Vertical speed indicator	-30 / +30 m/s	Fl 22386
RPM indicator	500 – 3,600 rpm	Fl 20222-3
Oil temperature gauge	0 - 130° C	Fl 20342
2 fuel warning lights (red) for the fore and aft tanks		Fl 32529-1
Bo-UK 1 clock in starboard console		Fl 23885
2 frequency selectors for the FuG 16 in port console		19-5843

The Fw 190 D-9 in Dayton, USA. (USAF Museum)

Replica of the instrument panel from a Fw 190 D-9. (Rienecker)

The left side of the Fw 190 D-9's cockpit and instrument panel. The arrangement of instruments was changed from that of the Fw 190 A-8. (R.P. Lutz)

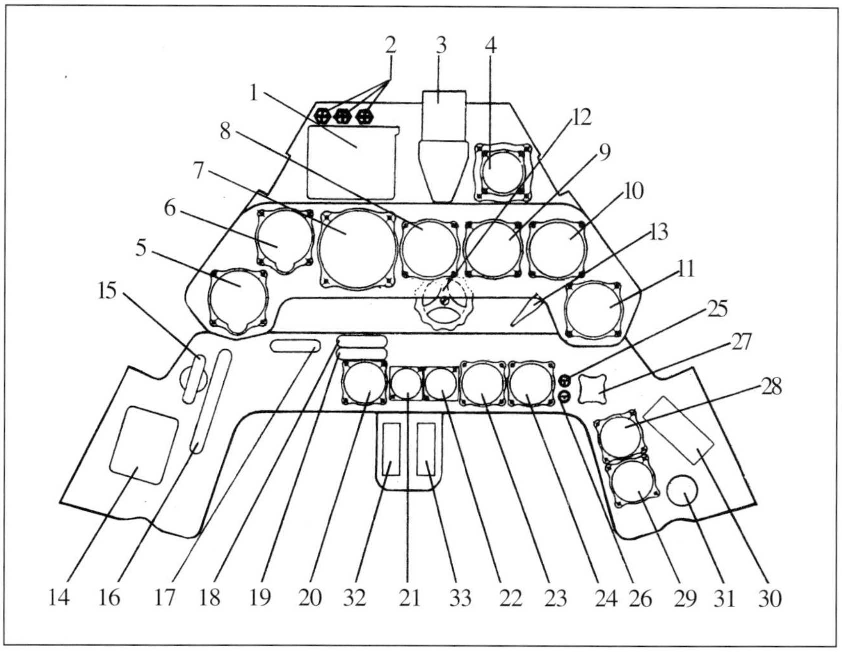

Instrumentation of the Fw 190 D-9:

No.	Equipment	Instrument Range	Requisition/Equipment Number
1	SZK K 4 round counter		Fl 47319
2	3 "Armed" indicators		Fl 32530
3	Revi 16 B gun sight		Fl 52955
4	AFN 2 homing indicator		Ln 27002
5	Fine and coarse altimeter	0 – 13000 m	Fl 22322
6	Airspeed indicator	100 – 900 km/h	Fl 22234
7	Combined turn and bank indicator and artificial horizon		Fl 22415
8	Vertical speed indicator	-30 / +30 m/s	Fl 22386
9	PFK/f2 master compass indicator (the positions of 8 and 9 were sometimes reversed)		Fl 23334
10	Boost pressure gauge	0.5 – 2.5 atm	Fl 20554
11	Electric RPM indicator	500 – 3,600 rpm	Fl 20269
12	Radiator cooling gills control wheel		
13	Windscreen washer lever		
14	BG 25a control panel for the FuG 25		Ln 28810
15	Undercarriage manual control handle		
16	Fuel cock control lever		
17	Operating systems emergency release		
18	Fuselage bomb emergency release		
19	Wing bombs emergency release		
20	Fuel / oil pressure gauge	0 – 3 / 0 – 15 kg/cm^2	Fl 20512-3
21	Fuel temperature gauge	0 - 130° C	Fl 20385
22	Oil temperature gauge	0 - 130° C	Fl 20385
23	MW 50 system pressure gauge	0 – 1 kg/cm2	Fl 20504-1
24	Fuel gauge	0 – 300 / 0 – 230 l	Fl 20723
25	Fuel warning light (red) for forward tank		Fl 32529-1
26	Fuel warning light (red) for rear tank		Fl 32529-1
27	Fuel gauge selector switch		Fl 32331
28	Oxygen flow meter		Fl 30489
29	Oxygen pressure gauge	0 – 250 kg/cm^2	Fl 30496
30	Flare pistol holder		
31	Oxygen flow valve		Fl 30508
32	Toggle switch (safety)		Fl 32346
33	Toggle switch (WGR 21 rockets)		Fl 32346
34	ZSK 244 A bomb arming panel (below 32,33)		Fl 50869

The Ta 152 C (V7). This fighter-bomber differed from the Ta 152 H mainly in its use of the DB 603 engine. Instrumentation was almost identical. (F. Selinger Archive)

Focke Wulf Ta 152

After the Fw 190 D demonstrated an outstanding performance in 1943, Focke Wulf continued development of the type for the high-altitude fighter role. The type designation was changed to Ta 152, reflecting the name of its designer, Kurt Tank. The design was based on the Fw 190 D-9, however numerous changes and aerodynamic improvements were made to the airframe.

The principal variants were the Ta 152 A, B, C and E, for the fighter, fighter-bomber and photo reconnaissance roles. Depending on the series, the aircraft was powered by a DB 603 E or Jumo 213. The Jumo 222 was also proposed as a power plant for the aircraft.

The final version produced was the Ta 152 H high-altitude fighter with increased wingspan, a pressurized cockpit and three-stage supercharger. Next to the Do 335 it was the fastest German piston-engined fighter aircraft. A total of 215 was built, however only a few saw action, mainly defending bases used by jet fighter aircraft.

The sole surviving machine is a Ta 152 H-0 which was delivered in January 1945 with the *Werknummer* 150010 and the manufacturer's code CW+CJ. When the war ended, "Green 4" was on the strength of Stab/ JG 301 and was captured by the Allies at Tirstrup, Denmark.

The aircraft was subsequently taken to the United States, where it was assigned the Foreign Equipment Number FE-112 and later T2-112. Today it is part of the collection of the National Air and Space Museum and is stored in Silver Hill. Most of the photographs presented here are of this aircraft. Another photo depicts a replica of an instrument panel from a Ta 152 H which was built with reference to a technical description dated January 1944.

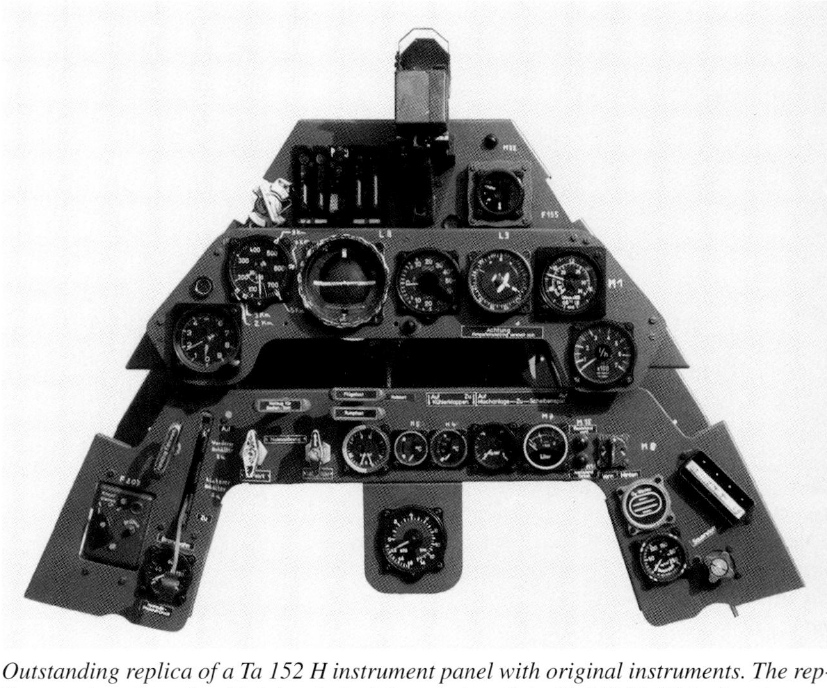

Outstanding replica of a Ta 152 H instrument panel with original instruments. The replica was based on the official technical description of the Ta 152 H. (T. Lederer)

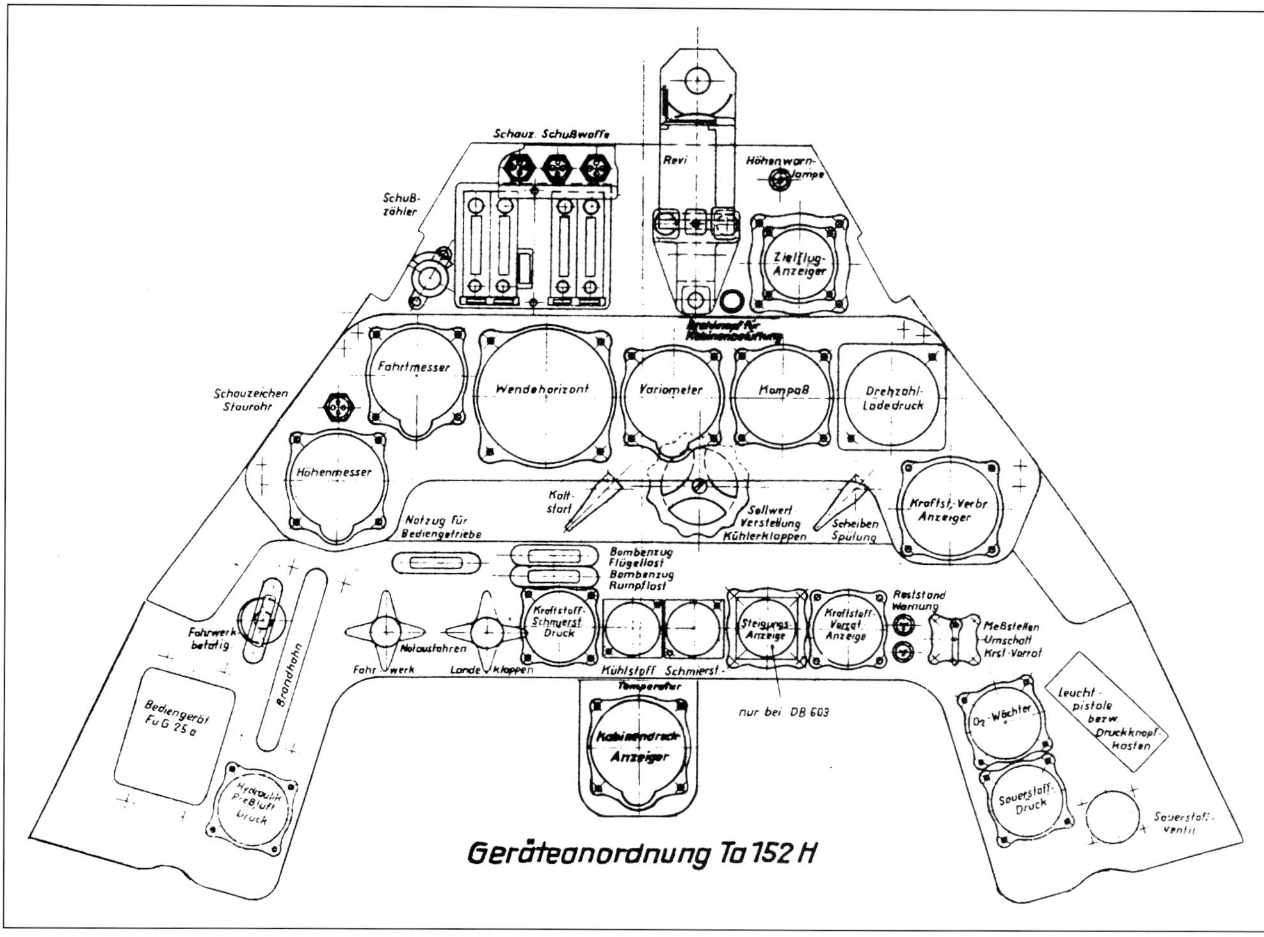

Drawing of the Ta 152 H instrument panel from the technical description.

Cockpit of the Ta 152 H-0 in storage at the National Air and Space Museum. The control panel for the FuG 25 is missing as is the undercarriage emergency lowering handle. Missing from the main instrument panel are the altimeter and combined turn-and-bank indicator and artificial horizon. (R.P. Lutz)

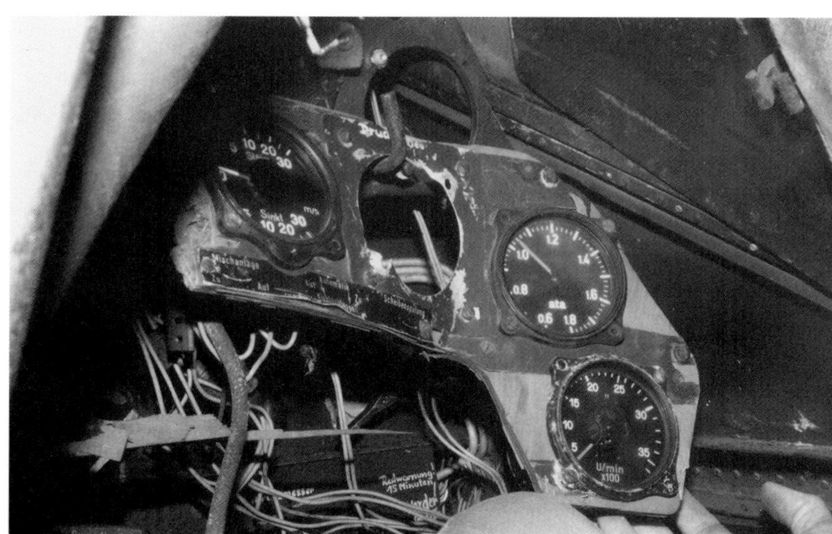

The right side of the cockpit of the Ta 152 H-0. The wooden main instrument panel is broken and will have to be repaired during restoration. The repeater compass is missing. The instrument panel was probably designed for the large repeater compass of the fighter autopilot, as a metal panel has been installed over the original opening, reducing it to a diameter of 80 mm. (R.P. Lutz)

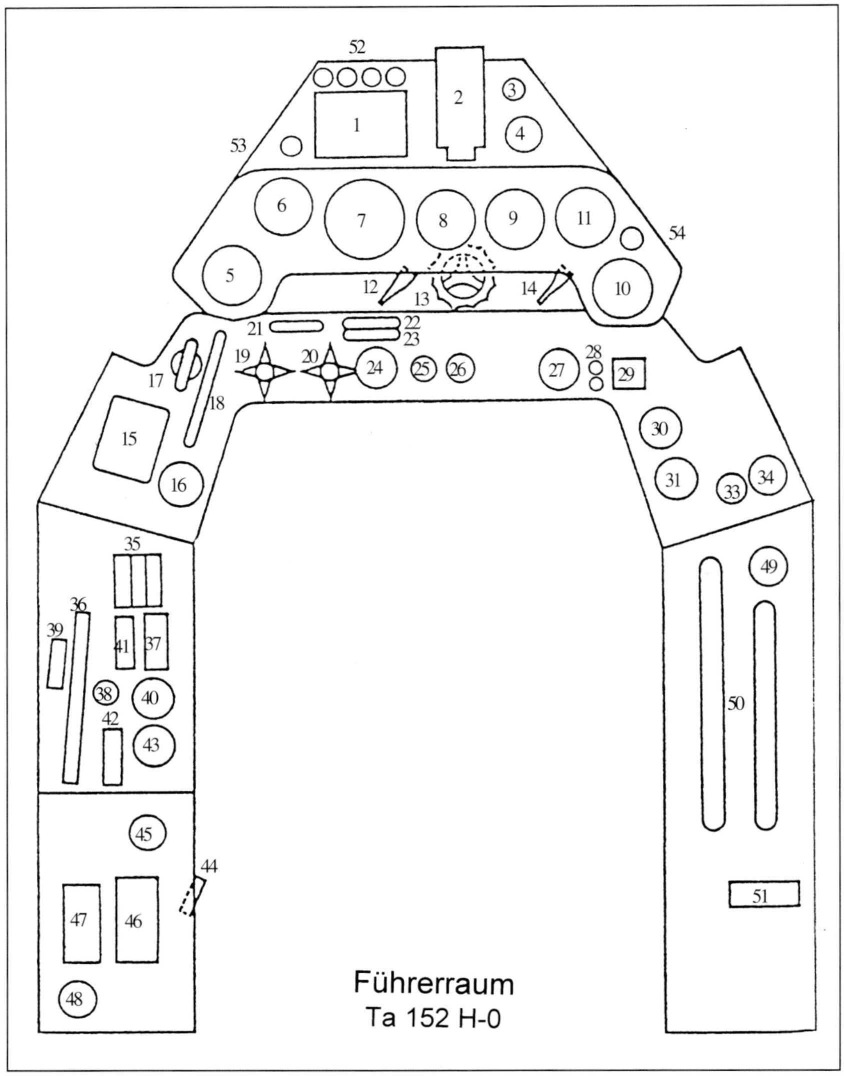

Drawing from the pilot's notes for the Ta 152 H-0.

Equipment in the cockpit of the Ta 152 H-0:

No.	Equipment	Instrument Range	Requisition/Equipment Number
1	SZK K 4 ammunition counter		Fl 47319
	with 3 SZ 100 round counters		Fl 47314
2	Revi 16 B reflector gun sight		Fl 52955
3	Altitude warning light (red)		Fl 32529-1
4	AFN 2 homing indicator		Ln 27002
5	Fine and coarse altimeter	0 – 16000 m	Fl 22326
6	Airspeed indicator	100 – 900 km/h	Fl 22234
7	Combined turn and bank indicator and artificial horizon		Fl 22411-1
8	Vertical speed indicator	+30 / -30 m/s	Fl 22386
9	Master compass indicator		Fl 23334
10	Electric RPM indicator	500 – 3,600 rpm	Fl 20265
11	Boost pressure gauge	0.6 – 1.8 atm	Fl 20555
12	Cold start lever		
13	Handwheel for setting position of cooling gills		
14	Windscreen washer lever		
15	FuG 25a control panel (BG 25a)		Ln 28810
16	Compressed air pressure gauge	0 – 200 kg/cm²	Fl 20516-4

17	Undercarriage handle		
18	Fuel cock		
19	Undercarriage manual lowering handle		
20	Landing flaps manual lowering handle		
21	Emergency release for engine operating system		
22	Emergency release for fuselage stores		
23	Emergency release for wing stores		
24	Fuel-oil pressure gauge	0 – 3 kg/cm^2 and 0 – 15 kg/cm^2	Fl 20512-3
25	Coolant temperature gauge	0 - 130° C	Fl 20385
26	Oil temperature gauge	0 - 130° C	Fl 20385
27	Fuel gauge*	0 – 280 / 0 – 230 l	Fl 20723
28	2 fuel warning lights (red) for fore and aft tanks		Fl 32529-1
29	Fuel gauge selector switch		Fl 32331
30	Oxygen flow meter		Fl 30489
31	Oxygen pressure gauge	0 – 250 kg/cm^2	Fl 30496
32	missing		
33	Oxygen flow valve		Fl 30508
34	Camera window wiper (photo reconnaissance aircraft only)		
35	Undercarriage and landing flap indicators		
	3 red indicator lights		Fl 32529-1
	3 green indicator lights		Fl 32529
36	Throttle lever		
37	Ignition switch		Fl 21118
38	Venting for GM-1 system (push-button)		Fl 50911
39	On-Off switch for GM-1 system		19-5824 A
40	Electrical system cutout switch		19-5836-2
41	Selector switch for special fluid system (not on H-0)		
42	Tailplane trim switch		Fl 32346-2
43	Tailplane trim indicator		Fl 22855
44	Connection for heated flight suit		
45	FuG 16 ZY mode selector switch		19-5843 W
46	Connector socket for FuG 16 ZY (AD 16ZY)		Ln 27266-2
47	FuG 16 ZY remote control (FBG 16)		Ln 37188
48	AP 20 starter injection pump		8-4511 A
49	Cockpit lighting dimmer switch		Fl 32401-5
50	Circuit breakers for the electrical system		
	2 with automatic release		19-5002 H
1	19-5001 A		
2	19-5000 E		
3	19-5000 C		
10	19-5000 B		
17	19-5000 A		
51	Starter		Fl 21212
52	3 "Armed" indicators**		Fl 32529
53	Cocking button for MK 108 (DKUP-1)		
54	Warning light for special fluid (red)		Fl 32529-1

* In the case of the stored Ta 152 H-0, *Werknummer* 150010, the fuel gauge was moved to the left, and an outside air temperature gauge was installed next to it on the right (-60 to +40° C, Fl 20349).

** The drawing in the handbook shows four lights, although only three weapons were planned.

The cockpit of the Ta 152 was based on the relatively roomy cockpit of the Fw 190 and was similar in design. Some equipment changes were made, in keeping with the Ta 152's technical and tactical requirements. The instrument panel was a three-part structure and was made of metal as a rule. A windscreen superstructure of cast aluminum sat on the fuselage and accommodated the windscreen, the anti-glare shield, the main instrument panel and several items of equipment such as the gun sight.

In production Ta 152s the main instrument panel was made of birch plywood and housed the flight instruments and most important engine instruments. Beneath it was a fuselage frame of aluminum sheet which served as an auxiliary instrument panel, accommodating most of the engine instruments. The remaining equipment was installed in two large consoles to the left and right of the seat.

The two electric temperature gauges on the auxiliary panel were small standard types with an installed diameter of 40 mm. These small instruments were developed in 1944 to save space on increasingly crowded instrument panels. As a rule they were electric indicators with a simple pressed metal housing and were used as temperature and pressure gauges and propeller pitch indicators.

The list of equipment presented here is based on the Ta 152 H-0 handbook dated January 1945, the technical description for the Ta 152 H, the equipment list for the Ta 152 H-1 (device numbers) plus wartime photographs and photos of the surviving aircraft.

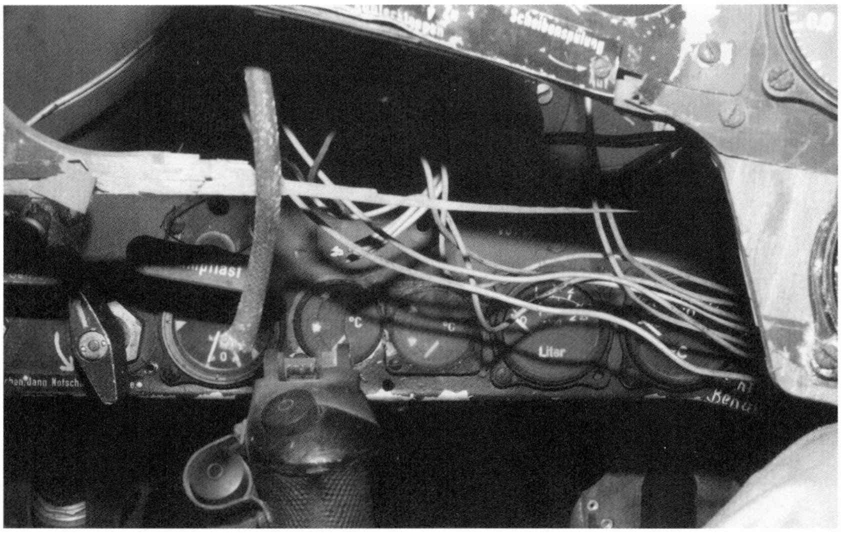

The engine instruments in the auxiliary instrument panel. The fuel contents gauge was moved to the left on this Ta 152 H-0 and an outside air temperature gauge was installed to its right. Decades in storage have resulted in rust forming on the temperature gauge's metal housing. It is interesting to note that the left temperature gauge was attached to the instrument panel from behind, while the one on the right was attached from the front. (R.P. Lutz)

Differences in the Ta 152 H technical Description of January 1944:

No.	Equipment	Instrument Range	Requisition/Equipment Number
5	Fine and coarse altimeter	0 – 16000 m	Fl 22321-16
7	Combined turn and bank indicator and artificial horizon		Fl 22415-1
8	Vertical speed indicator	+50 / -20 m/s	Fl 22383
9	Fuel gauge	0 – 700 l/h	127-1115 G
	or		127-1122 G
16	Double pressure gauge		Fl 20512-6
11	Boost pressure gauge and RPM indicator	600 – 3,600 rpm 0.6 – 1.8 atm	Fl 20569
35	2 sets of indicator lights for undercarriage and landing positions		19-6825 A-1
52	3 "Armed" rotary indicator lights		19-6824
54	deleted		

The technical description listed additional equipment:

For the windscreen superstructure:
Control knob for cockpit ventilation
For the main instrument panel:
Pitot tube heat visual indicator 19-6824 M-1
For the auxiliary instrument panel:
Cockpit pressure gauge 17 bz 0 – 15 km / 0 – 0.6 atm Fl 22325
(or in windscreen superstructure)
Propeller pitch indicator for DB 603 Fl 20845
Push-button box Befa 4 Ln 24515
or flare pistol
For the port console:
Push-button for propeller pitch control (DB 603) Fl 50911
For the starboard console:
Bo-UK 1 clock Fl 23885
Deviation table Fl 23906
Altitude alerter to 8 km

It is to be assumed that there were further differences in production aircraft and because of the strained spares situation.

Gotha Go 229 (Horten H IX)

When the Allies advanced into Germany in early 1945, they discovered in the dispersed factories and hidden design bureaus aircraft which seemed to have sprung from science-fiction novels. There were jet aircraft with variable-geometry wings, delta winged aircraft, and manned rockets. Several were about ready to make their maiden flights, while others existed only in mockup form or on paper.

Of all the advanced German designs which had reached the construction stage, probably none was more fantastic than the one the Americans discovered in the Gothaer Waggonfabrik. In an abandoned workshop was a flying wing constructed entirely of wood, a single-seater powered by two turbojet engines and equipped with a braking parachute.

Together with Alexander Lippisch, the Horten brothers were pioneers in the field of all-wing aircraft. Their first design, the H I glider, appeared in 1933. It was followed by other designs, the best known of which was the H IV high-performance glider. Their first powered aircraft, the H V, was built in 1936-37, making use of synthetic materials.

Other Horten projects included transports, trainers, supersonic aircraft and a trans-Atlantic machine, however none proceeded beyond the design stage. In 1943 state support was terminated and design work continued at the company's own expense.

The last Horten aircraft to fly before the end of the Second World War was the H IX, a single-seat fighter powered by two Jumo 004 engines each producing 890 kg of thrust. The RLM's interest was reawakened and the type was immediately ordered into production. The first prototype was flown as a glider, as no engines were available. In spite of this, valuable flight data was accumulated. The second prototype was equipped with jet engines and a retractable undercarriage.

The *Luftwaffe* command was so impressed by the test flights that further development was passed on to the Gothaer Waggonfabrik, where it was to be produced in quantity as the Go 229. The only aircraft to be completed before the end of the war, however, was the Go 229 V3, which was similar to the Go 229 A production variant.

The uncompleted V3 was found by the Americans in a furniture factory in Friedrichsroda and was taken to the test station at Freeman Field in the USA. It was estimated that 15,000 man hours were required to put the aircraft in flyable condition. Some work was obviously begun, as some equipment in the cockpit appears to be associated with the installation of American radio equipment. Finally, in 1946 the Go 229 V3 was set up for display purposes and finally

Cockpit of the Go 229 V3. Several instruments are missing. Note the thickness of the plywood used in the instrument panel. To which the instruments were secured with wood screws. (P.F. Selinger)

placed in storage without ever having flown. At the present time the machine is in the hands of the National Air and Space Museum in Washington.

Restoration would probably be very expensive, as much of the aircraft's plywood skinning has deteriorated. If such s restoration was completed, it would offer the first view of the Go 229 V3, as the aircraft was never completely assembled. The close-up photographs presented here are of this aircraft.

Overall, the cockpit of the Go 229 seems rather primitive. Like many other types designed or built in early 1945, the equipment and materials used were determined by sheer practicality and availability.

The arrangement of controls and instruments is conventional. On the left are the throttle levers and trims, in the center the plywood instrument panel and on the right the main electrical panel with circuit breakers.

The center-section of the stored Go 229 with the cockpit and power plants. T2-490 is the captured aircraft code assigned to this machine. (P.F. Selinger)

Reconstruction of the instrument panel of a Go 229 A with complete instrumentation. (Rienecker)

Close-up of the cockpit. The three switches on the left are part of the radio system installed by the Americans. The control stick grip is missing. (R.P. Lutz)

Instrumentation was similar to that of other German jet aircraft, but was limited to what was absolutely necessary.

As the aircraft was never completed, it is uncertain as to which equipment is missing and which cover panels remained to be installed, for the left and right sides of the cockpit are dominated by the two Jumo engines and the tubular steel framework of the fuselage.

It is possible to reconstruct the original instrumentation of the Go 229 V3 from historical photos and pictures of the stored aircraft. The replica of the instrument panel in the photo at the tope of the page is somewhat different, containing some features which might have been included in production aircraft.

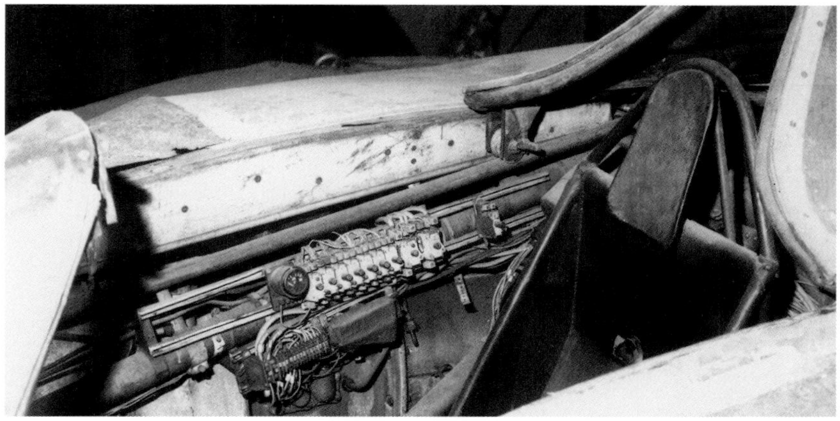

Right side of the Go 229 V3's cockpit showing the pilot's seat and the main electrical panel. (R.P. Lutz)

Equipment of the Go 229 V3:

No.	Equipment	Instrument Range	Requisition/Equipment Number
1	Combined turn and bank indicator and artificial horizon		Fl 22415-1
2	Vertical speed indicator	-30 / +30 m/s	Fl 22386
3	Airspeed indicator	100-900 km/h	Fl 22234
4	Pitot tube heat visual indicator		Fl 32525
5	Fine and coarse altimeter	0 – 16000 m	Fl 22326
6	Master compass indicator		Fl 23338
7	AFN 2 homing indicator		Ln 27002
8	2 fuel gauges (probably taken from a Fw 190)		Fl 20723
9	2 fuel warning lights (red)		Fl 32529-1
10	Undercarriage position indicator lights		Fl 32262?
11	Electrical system cutout switch		Fl 32315-2
12	2 ignition switches		Fl 32350
13	Landing flap position indicator lights		Fl 32262?
14	2 injection pressure gauges	0 – 160 kg/cm²	Fl 20516-3
15	2 gas temperature gauges	300 - 1000° C	Fl 20338
16	2 RPM indicators	2,000 – 15,000 rpm	Fl 20266
17	Oxygen pressure gauge	0 – 250 kg/cm²	Fl 30496
18	Oxygen flow meter		Fl 30489
19	Unidentified (clock?)		
20	Outside air temperature gauge	-60 / +40° C	Fl 20349

The following instruments and equipment were installed on the cockpit side-walls:

Item	Instrument Range	Requisition/Equipment Number
Port side:		
Compressed-air pressure gauge	0 – 250 kg/cm²	Fl 20519
On the main electrical panel, starboard side:		
Voltmeter	18 – 30 V	Fl 32510
10 circuit breakers (total number unknown)		19-5000

Other equipment, such as radios and armament, would have been installed in service aircraft. Further changes would have been almost certain as production went on.

In comparison to the above, the instrumentation of the unpowered prototype, the Horten H IX V1, was simple and easy to read:

No.	Equipment	Instrument Range	Requisition/Equipment Number
1	Airspeed indicator	80 – 550 km/h	Fl 22230
2	Turn and bank indicator		Fl 22402
3	Vertical speed indicator	-30 / +30 m/s	Fl 22386
4	Fine and coarse altimeter	0 – 10000 m	Fl 22320
5	FK 38 magnetic compass		Fl 23233

A Heinkel He 111 G-0 equipped with BMW VI inline engines. (F. Selinger Collection)

Heinkel He 111

In 1932 Swissair began operating a new American-made high-speed transport aircraft, the Lockheed Orion. Not wanting to be left behind, *Lufthansa* requested the development of high-speed commercial aircraft, resulting in the single-engine Ju 60 and He 70 *Blitz* (Lightning).

In 1934-35 Heinkel followed this up with the He 111 *Doppelblitz* (Double Lightning). In keeping with its name, the aircraft had also been designed for two purposes. As it was realized that *Lufthansa* would require only a relatively small number of aircraft, Heinkel also designed a military version in order to recover some of the development costs.

While the He 111 C and G commercial transports were built in relatively small numbers, more than 7,000 of the military version were produced for use as bombers, transports, glider tugs and training aircraft.

The initial military versions (He 111 A, B, E, F and J) entered service beginning in 1936. All had the long glazed nose and characteristic elliptical wing. In 1937 several machines were sent to Spain, however by the outbreak of war the early variants had been largely replaced by the He 111 H and P variants, both of which had a revised, fully-glazed nose and a revised wing with straight leading edge.

The He 111 P was powered by two DB 601 engines, however as the Daimler Benz engine was required for fighter production, the He 111 H vari-

Cockpit of an He 111 C airliner. The instrumentation of the He 111 G was similar.

Equipment of an He 111 C based on an historical photograph:

No.	Equipment	Instrument Range	Requisition/Equipment Number
1	Course indicator for the distant-reading compass		Fl 23351
2	Pitot tube heat visual indicator ?		
3	Airspeed indicator	100 – 550 km/h	Fl 22230 ?
4	Turn and bank indicator, pneumatic		Fl 22402
5	Vertical speed indicator	-10 / +10 m/s	Fl 22370
6	Course selector for the distant-reading compass		Fl 23300
7	Fine altimeter	0 – 1000 m	Fl 22306
8	Artificial horizon (Sperry)		Fl 22426
9	Coarse altimeter	0 – 8000 m	Fl 22308
10	Landing flaps position indicator		Fl 22853
11	Gyro monitoring switch		Fl 22505-1 ?
12	Suction devices sensitivity control (concealed)		Fl 22478 ?
13	FK 10-11 navigators compass (Ludolph)		
14	Operating data placard		
15	Undercarriage position indicator		Fl 32526
16	Landing light switch		Fl 32303
17	Landing flaps reset valve		
18	RPM indicator, electric	0 – 1,800 rpm	Fl 20282 ?
19	Outside air temperature gauge	-40 / +40° C	Fl 20400 ?
20	Clock (Junghans)		Fl 22600
21	ZSH 5/3Z ignition switch		Fl 21112
22	Electrical system cutout switch		Fl 32301
23	Coolant temperature gauge (inlet)	30 - 180° C	Fl 20331
24	Coolant temperature gauge (outlet)	30 - 180° C	Fl 20331
25	Oil temperature gauge	20 - 120° C	Fl 20308
26	Fuel pressure gauge	0 – 0.5 kg/cm^2	Fl 20505 ?
27	Oil pressure gauge	0 – 10 kg/cm^2	Fl 20625
28	Telefunken 378 F (FuG XXI) radio equipment		
29	Ammeter for the radio equipment		
30	Throttle lever		
31	Mixture lever		
32	Starter switch		
33	Tank selector switch outer = fuel pump selector inner = oil tank selector		
34	Hand-pumps		
35	Propeller pitch control levers below pressure gauge	0 – 10 kg/cm^2	Fl 20625 ?
36	Hand-pump for manual lowering of the undercarriage		
37	Hand-pumps for the cooling gills		
38	Starter system controls		
39	Trim wheel		

The last surviving He 111 E, on display in the Museo del Aire in Madrid. (A. Flores)

ant, which was powered by various versions of the Junkers Jumo 211, was built in much larger numbers.

The most interesting version was undoubtedly the five-engined He 111 Z, which combined two He 111 H airframes and was used as a glider tug for the Me 321 glider.

Although it was already more or less obsolete by 1941, the He 111 remained in service until the end of the war, serving as a transport and launch platform for V 1 rockets in the final stage of the war.

After the Second World War the He 111 was built under license in Spain as the CASA 2.111. A total of 236 aircraft was built by 1956. When the German Jumo 211 became unavailable, the Spanish found an alternate power plant in the Rolls Royce Merlin 500. The built-built Spanish aircraft never matched the production quality or reliability of the German aircraft, especially the Jumo-powered variants. Nevertheless, the Spanish aircraft soldiered on until 1973, last serving in the transport role. Some of these machines gained fame in 1968, appearing in the British-produced film "The Battle of Britain".

Although production in Germany and Spain exceeded 7,000 machines, today only three complete He 111s and twelve CASA 2.111s remain, along with a number of wrecks.

Some of the photographs presented here depict the following museum specimens:

He 111 H-20, WNr. 701152, NT+SL, in the RAF Museum, London.

CASA 2.111 B, G1+AD in the *Luftwaffe* Museum in Berlin-Gatow.

Essentially the various versions of the He 111 were equipped with four main variants of instrumentation, all of which are listed:

- the civil He 111 C and G
- the military He 111 A, B, E, F and J with stepped fuselage nose
- the He 111 D, P and early H
- most versions of the He 111 H, including the CASA 2.111

Cockpit of an He 111 E or F. (Hafner Archive)

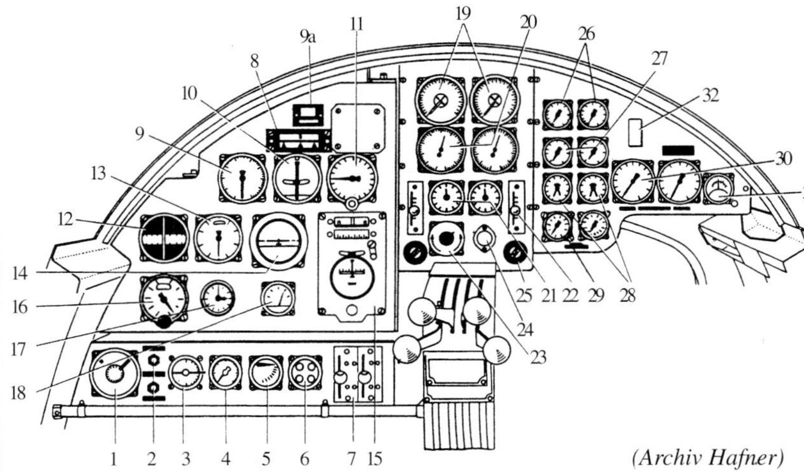

(Archiv Hafner)

The **Heinkel He 111 C and G** commercial transports were equipped with instrumentation then standard for twin-engined aircraft. The flight and navigation instruments, which included an Askania distant-reading compass system, were arrayed on the left in front of the pilot. In the center, between the two seats, were the engine instruments and control levers. Installed on the right side were the remaining engine instruments and the radio equipment.

The selection of engine instruments depended on the type of engines installed, BMW VI liquid-cooled engines on the He 111 C and G and BMW 132 radials on the late-production He 111 G.

The installation of an Askania autopilot was planned.

The first military versions, such as the **He 111 E or J**, had a passageway to the nose compartment on the right side of the cockpit. As a result, the radio equipment was relocated to the rear, in the area of the dorsal gun position. A pneumatic autopilot by Askania was part of the standard equipment.

It was planned to install an AFN 1 homing indicator (Ln 27000) above the vertical speed indicator. The autopilot system's emergency disengage button (Fl 22557) was located beneath the instrument panel in the area of the double switch for the autopilot.

Instrument Panel of an He 111 E or F:

No.	Equipment	Instrument Range	Requisition/Equipment Number
1	Selector switch and damping control for the Lv 194 turn and bank indicator		Fl 22475
2	2 air pumps for the fuel gauges		Fl 20742-1
3	Double switch for the Lzs 3r autopilot		Fl 22505
4	Autopilot pressure gauge	0 – 3 kg/cm²	Fl 22471
5	LaKZ landing flaps position indicator		Fl 22853
6	Undercarriage position indicator		Fl 32526
7	2 switches for propeller pitch control		9-9500.20
8	Lkz 1p course indicator		Fl 23351
9	Airspeed indicator	60 – 550 km/h	Fl 22230
9a	LmA 1 pitot tube heat visual indicator		Fl 32525-3
10	Lg 14r turn and bank indicator, pneumatic		Fl 22402
11	Statoscope-vertical speed indicator	-10 / +10 m/s	Fl 22381-10
12	Lke 6 "Small Emil" magnetic compass (Askania)		Fl 23226
13	Fine and coarse altimeter	0 – 10000 m	Fl 22320
14	Lgab 8 artificial horizon (Sperry)		Fl 22426
15	Lfgk 2/24 directional gyro		Fl 22500-2
16	Coarse altimeter	0 – 8000 m	Fl 22316-8
	or	0 – 10000 m	Fl 22311
17	Bo-UK 1 clock		Fl 23885
18	Outside air temperature gauge	-40 / +40° C	Fl 20342-1
19	Two electric RPM indicators	0 – 3,000 rpm	Fl 20284-1
20	2 LpA 3 boost pressure gauges	0.6 – 1.8 atm	Fl 20550
21	2 propeller pitch indicators		9-9500.60
22	2 SSH 45/7Z ignition switches		Fl 21118
23	Cockpit lighting dimmer switch		Fl 32401-2
24	Electrical system cutout switch		Fl 32315-2
25	2 SUM AP 8 starter injection pumps		8-4505 A
26	2 coolant temperature gauges	0 - 120° C	Fl 20308
27	2 double oil temperature gauges	30 - 180° C	Fl 20330-8
28	2 fuel pressure gauges	0 – 0.5 kg/cm²	Fl 20504
	or 2 fuel pressure gauges	0 – 1 kg/cm2	Fl 20504-1
	or 2 double pressure gauges	0 – 1 / 0 – 10 kg/cm²	Fl 20512
29	2 oil pressure gauges	0 – 10 kg/cm²	Fl 20625
	(deleted when double pressure gauges installed)		
30	2 fuel gauges	0 – 700 l	Fl 20710
31	Ammeter/Voltmeter	-30 / +30 A/V	Fl 20710
32	2 SSH 35/1Z ignition switches	Fl 21207	

The restored He 111 P, 5J + CN, in Gardemoen, Norway. (Wildmoser)

Instrument panel of an He 111 P, photographed in flight at an altitude of approximately 2600 meters. Visible on the right is the outside air temperature gauge. (Griehl Collection)

The adoption of a fully glazed nose, beginning with the **He 111 D and P**, made it necessary to completely revise the arrangement of equipment in the cockpit. A large equipment console was installed to the pilot's left, this accommodating all the engine controls plus trim controls, ignition switches and the propeller pitch indicators.

A new instrument panel covered the entire width of the cockpit roof and housed all flight, navigation and engine instruments. The control column could be folded out of the way to allow the bomb aimer to relieve the pilot. An airspeed indicator and altimeter were installed in the bomb-aimer's position to provide the necessary data for the bomb sight. On the right side of the cockpit were the bomb sequence selector box and the large DF repeater compass. The radio equipment was installed further aft in the fuselage beneath the dorsal gun position.

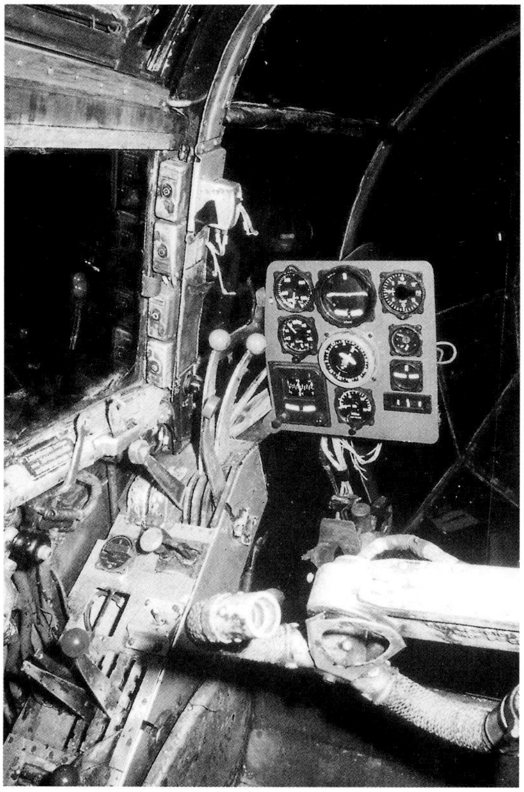

This photograph of the cockpit of the He 111 H-20 in the RAF Museum shows the rebuilt main instrument panel. Further restoration work remains to be done.

A Siemens K4ü autopilot was now standard equipment.

In the earlier versions the outside air temperature gauge was installed in Position 22 and the fuel-oil double pressure gauge was placed on the center frame of the cockpit canopy. In later versions the positions of these instruments were reversed as a result of operational experience.

Additional instruments were housed in the auxiliary instrument panel in front of the port console and on the center frame of the cockpit canopy.

In later versions, beginning with the He 111 H-6, the arrangement of the instruments was again revised, as the large panel in front of the pilot seriously restricted his view forward and above. A smaller instrument panel containing the flight and navigation instruments was positioned directly in front of the pilot, while the engine instruments were placed in a new console on the right side of the cockpit.

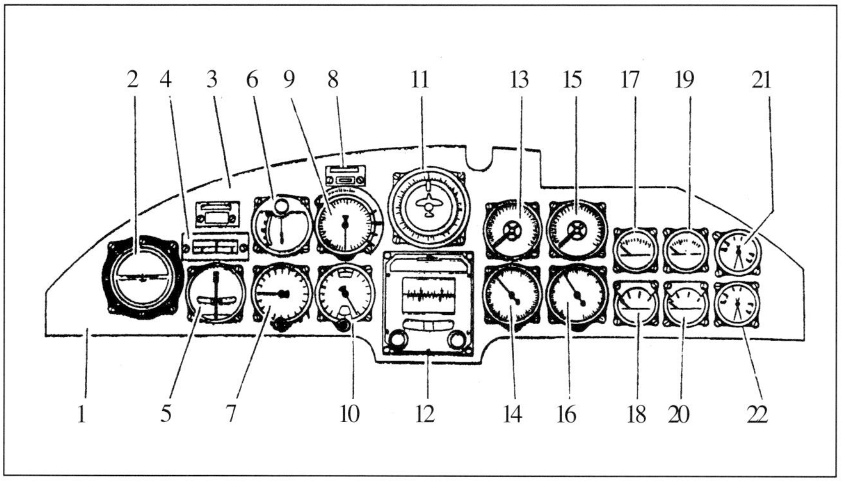

(Archiv Hafner)

Instrument panel of the He 111 D, P, H-1 and H-2:

No.	Equipment	Instrument Range	Requisition/Equipment Number
1	Bo-UK 1 clock (in control column yoke in later versions)		Fl 23885
2	Artificial horizon (Sperry)		Fl 22426
3	Autopilot visual indicator		Fl 32525
4	Lkz 3 course indicator		Fl 22562
5	Electric turn and bank indicator		Fl 22406
6	AFN-1 homing indicator		Ln 27000
7	Statoscope-vertical speed indicator	-10 / +10 m/s	Fl 22381-10
8	Pitot tube heat visual indicator		Fl 32525-3
9	Airspeed indicator	60 – 550 km/h	Fl 22230
10	Fine and coarse altimeter	0 – 10000 m	Fl 22320
11	PfK/f3 master compass indicator		Fl 23338
12	Lku 4 gyro compass		Fl 22561
13	RPM indicator, port engine	500 – 3,000 rpm	Fl 20284 ?
14	Boost pressure gauge, port engine (Fl 20550 in early versions)	0.6 – 1.8 atm	Fl 20555
15	RPM indicator, starboard engine	500 – 3,000 rpm	Fl 20284 ?
16	Boost pressure gauge, starboard engine (Fl 20550 in early versions)	0.6 – 1.8 atm	Fl 20555
17	Oil temperature gauge, left (indicates outlet temperature, could be set to inlet)	0 - 160° C	Fl 20343
18	Coolant temperature gauge, left	0 - 120° C	Fl 20342-1
19	Oil temperature gauge, left (indicates outlet temperature, could be set to inlet)	0 - 160° C	Fl 20343
20	Coolant temperature gauge, starboard	0 - 120° C	Fl 20342-2
21	Double pressure gauge, port	0 – 2 / 0 – 10 kg/cm^2	Fl 20512-2
22	Double pressure gauge, starboard	0 – 2 / 0 – 10 kg/cm^2	Fl 20512-2

Heinkel He 111 H-20 in the RAF Museum.

Auxiliary panel:

No.	Equipment	Instrument Range	Requisition/Equipment Number
a	Throttle lever box on port console		
b	Auxiliary instrument panel		
f	Electric propeller pitch indicator, starboard engine		Fl 20841
g	Electric propeller pitch indicator, port engine		Fl 20841
h	Landing flaps position indicator		Fl 22853
i	Undercarriage position indicator		Fl 32526
m	Cockpit lighting dimmer switch		Fl 32401-2
w	Cockpit lighting		

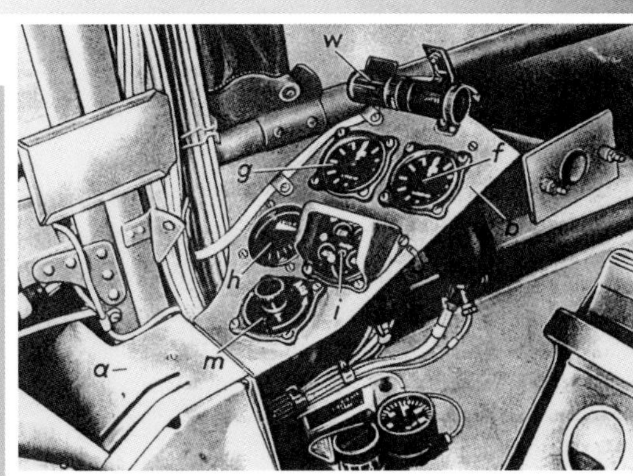

Auxiliary instrument panel in an He 111 P, located on the throttle quadrant. (Hafner Archive)

Equipment on the cockpit canopy center frame (early version):

No.	Equipment	Instrument Range	Requisition/Equipment Number
a	Center frame		
b	Fuel gauge selector switch		Fl 32331
c	2 fuel warning lights (red)		Fl 32262-1
d	2 fuel gauges for the port and starboard tanks		Fl 20723
e	2 fuel-oil pressure gauges	0 – 2 / 0 – 10 kg/cm²	Fl 20512-2
f	Push-button		
g	Cockpit lighting dimmer switch		Fl 32402

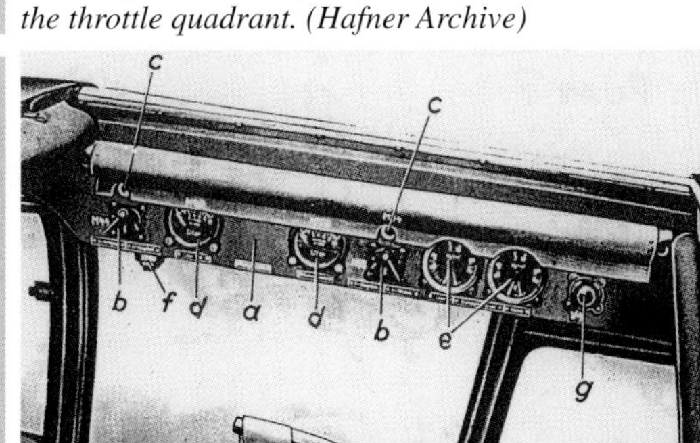

Instruments mounted on the center canopy frame of an He 111 P. (Hafner Archive)

Console on the left side of the He 111 H-20's cockpit. (Hafner Archive)

Equipment of the He 111 H-20:

Port console:

No.	Equipment	Instrument Range	Requisition/Equipment Number
1	Throttle levers		
2	RPM selector lever		
3	Propeller pitch control switch		9-9502 B
4	Ignition switches		Fl 21118
5	Supercharger selector switch		
6	Ignition switch		Fl 21212
7	Oil cooler flap control lever		
8	Fuel cock lever		
9	Fuel transfer pump system selector lever		
10	Fuel transfer pump system switch		
11	Fuel transfer pump system indicator lights		Fl 32262
12	Automatic mixture control switch		
13	Automatic mixture control switch indicator light		Fl 32262
14	Aileron trim wheel		
15	Ammeter/Voltmeter	-120 / +120 A/V	Fl 32501
16	Electrical system cutout switch or		Fl 32315-2 19-6829 A
17	Undercarriage switch		
18	Snap switch		
19	Landing flaps control lever		
20	Emergency handle for autopilot		Fl 22557
21	Autopilot master-switch		Fl 22559-1
22	Pitot tube heat switch		
23	Auxiliary navigation lights switch		
24	Navigation lights switch		
25	Landing light switch		
26	Compass lighting switch		
27	Compass support switch		
28	Starter pumps		
29	Cockpit lighting dimmer switch		Fl 32401-2
30	Undercarriage position indicators		Fl 32526
31	Landing flap position indicators		Fl 22853

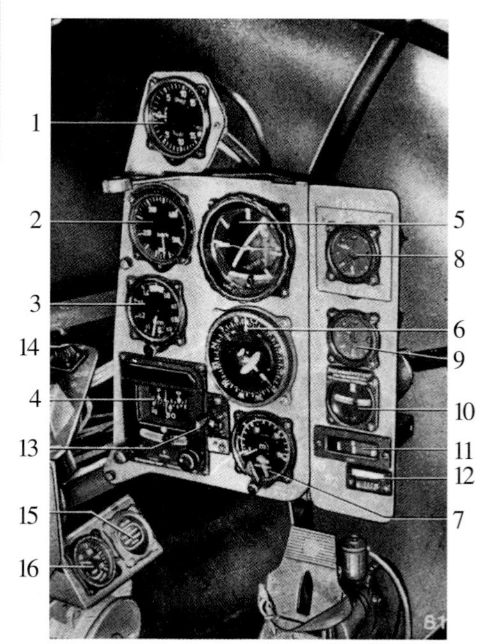

Pilot's instrument panel of the He 111 H-20. (Hafner Archive)

The cockpit of the Spanish-built CASA 2.111 is largely similar to that of an He 111 H-16. The engine instrument panel on the right has been reduced in size through the use of multiple indicators.

This arrangement is illustrated using the He 111 H-20 as an example. This variant's instrumentation differed from that of its predecessors only in detail. Once again the K4ü autopilot was standard equipment. Some late-production aircraft were also equipped with a FuG 101 radar altimeter.

The **CASA 2.111**, which was based on the He 111 H-16, had comparable equipment, although the instruments were built-built German types or similar English devices. The instrumentation was technically simpler than the German, with no autopilot, for example, this being replaced by a built-built Askania distant-reading compass.

Right side of the He 111 H-20's cockpit with the panel housing the engine instruments. (Hafner Archive)

Instrument panel in front of pilot:

No.	Equipment	Instrument Range	Requisition/Equipment Number
1	Vertical speed indicator	-15 / +15 m/s	Fl 22384
2	Airspeed indicator	60 – 550 km/h	Fl 22230
3	Fine and coarse altimeter	0 – 10000 m	Fl 22320
4	Lku 4 gyro compass		Fl 22561
5	Combined turn and bank indicator and artificial horizon		Fl 22411
6	PfK/f3 master compass indicator		Fl 23338
7	FuG 101a indicator	0 – 150 / 0 – 750 m	Ln 28330-1
8	FuG 16 Z homing indicator (installed similar to AFN 2) (the vertical speed indicator was installed here in earlier versions)		Ln 27002
9	AFN 2 homing indicator		Ln 27002
10	Backup turn and bank indicator		Fl 22414-1
11	Lkz 3 course indicator		Fl 22562
12	Pitot tube heat visual indicator		Fl 32525-3
13	Equipment destruct switch		Fl 32350 ?
14	Cockpit lighting dimmer switch		Fl 32402
15	Oxygen flow meter		Fl 30489
16	Oxygen pressure gauge	0 – 250 kg/cm^2	Fl 30496

Equipment on starboard side of cockpit:

No.	Equipment	Instrument Range	Requisition/Equipment Number
1	Engine instrument panel		
2	2 electric RPM indicators	500 – 3,500 rpm	Fl 20284 ?
3	2 electric fuel consumption gauges 0 – 500 l/hr		Fl 20812
4	2 fuel / oil pressure gauges	0 – 2 / 0 – 10 kg/cm^2	Fl 20512-2
5	2 coolant temperature gauges	0 - 130° C	Fl 20342
6	2 oil temperature gauges	0 - 130° C	Fl 20342
7	Double boost pressure gauge	0.6 – 1.8 atm	Fl 20556
8	Oxygen pressure gauge (bomb-aimer) 0 – 250 kg/cm2		Fl 30496
9	Oxygen flow meter (bomb-aimer)		Fl 30489
10	2 switches for fuel tank pumps, each with indicator light		Fl 32408 ? Fl 32525
11	Patin PFA/R DF indicator		Fl 23470
12	Flare cartridge box		
13	Intercom connector socket		
14	BG 25 a control device for FuG 25 A		Ln 28810
15	ZSK 244 A bomb arming panel		Fl 50869

On the right, beneath the DF indicator, was a retractable hand-lamp.

Instruments on the cable shaft under the cockpit roof of the He 111 H-20. (Hafner Archive)

Control column of the He 111 H-20. (Hafner Archive)

Equipment on the port side of the wiring channel on the cockpit ceiling:

No.	Equipment	Instrument Range	Requisition/Equipment Number
1	Fuel gauge for port fuel tanks	0 – 700 / 0 – 1025 l	Fl 20723
2	Fuel gauge selector switch for port tanks		Fl 32331
3	Fuel gauge for starboard fuel tanks	0 – 700 / 0 – 1025 l	Fl 20723
4	Fuel gauge selector switch for starboard tanks		Fl 32331
5	Fuel gauge for fuselage tank	0 – 835 l	Fl 20723
6	Warning light (red) for port relief tank		Fl 32262-1
7	Warning light (red) for starboard relief tank		Fl 32262-1
8	Outside air temperature gauge	-40 / +40° C	Fl 20342-1
9	Cockpit lighting dimmer switch		Fl 32402

Equipment on the control column:

No.	Equipment	Instrument Range	Requisition/Equipment Number
1	Bomb release button		
2	Bo-UK 1 clock		Fl 23885
3	Autopilot system turn control		
4	Intercom connector socket		
5	RSS 6a control switch		Ln 28665
6	Control box for takeoff-assist rockets		
7	FAR-NEAR switch for FuG 16		
8	FuG 10, FuG 16 selector switch		Fl 32345
9	Remote-control panel for FuG 16		Ln 27188

Heinkel He 162 *Salamander*

In late 1944, with the military situation becoming ever more precarious for the German Reich, the *Luftwaffe* command introduced the Emergency Fighter Program. Its purpose was to rationalize fighter production and introduce jet fighter aircraft into service as quickly as possible. As a result of the program, Heinkel was awarded a contract to develop a jet fighter, which was designated the He 162. The first prototype flew on 6 December 1944, after just three months of development work.

The ambitious production program called for 1,000 machines to be completed in April 1945. Production was later supposed to rise to 3,000 aircraft per month, with final assembly taking place at the air bases.

The He 162 was a small shoulder-wing monoplane with a BMW 003 turbojet mounted on the spine of an all-metal fuselage. This design resulted in the incorporation of an ejection seat and twin fins and rudders. The undercarriage and some other components were taken from other aircraft.

It was anticipated that the "*Volksjäger*" (People's Fighter) would be flown by young pilots with little training. The aircraft's performance was good, however engine problems plagued the design until the end of the war. Overall, the He 162 proved a stable weapons platform.

In the end, only about 270 machines were built. The only unit to be equipped with the He 162 was I./JG 1, which flew a number of sorties against Allied tactical aircraft from its base in Leck. When the war ended the unit's 45 aircraft were handed over to the English. Of these seven have survived in various museums.

The interior photographs presented here are of the He 162 A-2 with the *Werknummer* 120223, which is displayed in the Musée de l'Air in Paris. It served with I./JG 1 as "Yellow 1" and was later test-flown by the Armée de l'Air at Mont-de-Marsan. The aircraft was restored as "Yellow 1" and great care was taken to ensure that the cockpit, in particular, was depicted accurately. As a result, this aircraft has the most authentic cockpit of any of the surviving He 162s.

The aircraft is displayed without armament, and therefore two weights have been placed in the cockpit to prevent the machine from sitting on its tail. The weights may be recognized as a large rectangular block on the starboard side and a semicircular part in the seat tub.

Heinkel He 162 A-2, serial number 120223, in the Musée de l'Air in Paris.

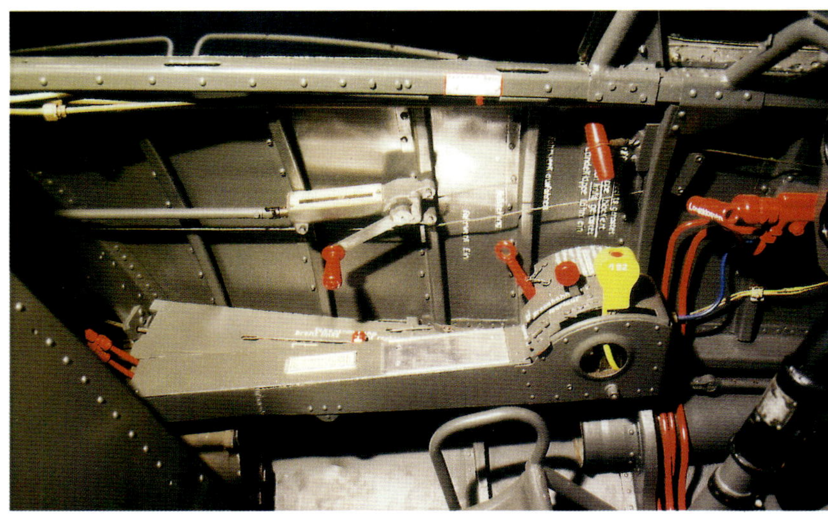

Left side of the cockpit with trim, flap and throttle levers.

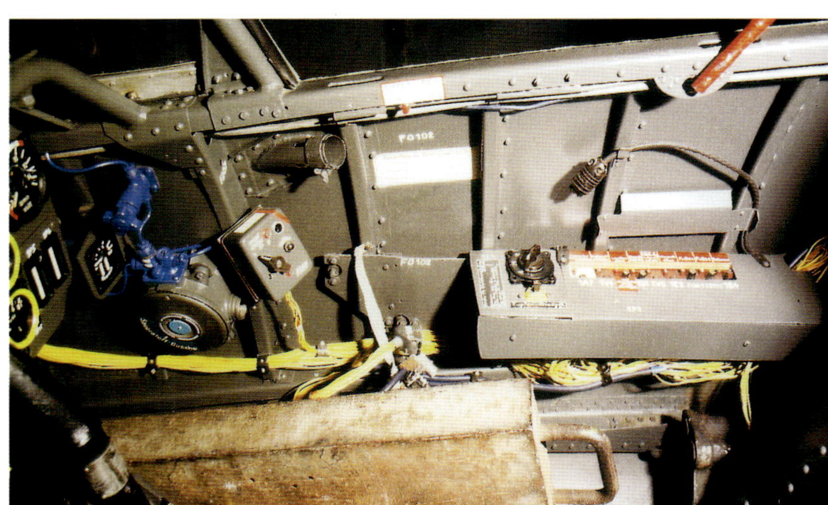

Right side of the cockpit with oxygen system, control panel for the FuG 25 and circuit breakers. The control panel for the FuG 24 is missing. Visible in the center is a placard with instructions for use of the ejection seat.

The cockpit of He 162 A-2, 120223. The large block on the right is iron ballast installed to compensate for the weight of the armament, which was removed.

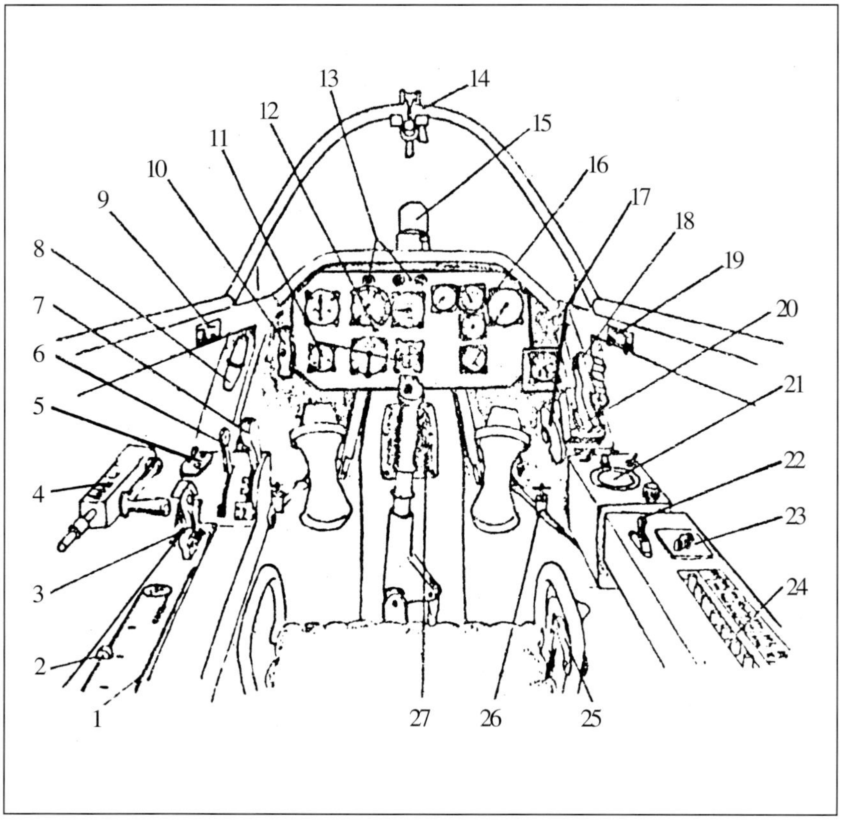

Drawing from the pilot's notes illustrating the cockpit of the He 162 A.

The cockpit of the He 162 and its equipment reflected the *Luftwaffe* standards of 1944-45. The instruments and control elements were arranged as follows:

- port side of the cockpit:
  throttle lever, trims, landing flap and undercarriage levers
- instrument panel:
  flight and navigation instruments on the left, engine instruments on the right
- starboard side of cockpit:
  main electrical panel, radio and oxygen system controls.

The overall impression one gains from the He 162's cockpit is one of the simple and in some cases primitive production methods employed in the final phase of the war.

Equipment was kept simple and was selected for functionality. In some cases control cables and rods run uncovered through the cockpit. Covers were only installed where absolutely necessary.

Several components were taken from other aircraft and modified for use in the He 162. These included the main undercarriage (Bf 109 G), the undercarriage selector switch (He 111) and the fuel gauge (He 177).

The instrument panel was roughly sawn from plywood sheet, and the instruments were attached to it with wood screws. Most instruments were held in place by just two screws to save materials.

It was anticipated from the beginning that the He 162 would be subjected to a simplification program:

- Combined turn and bank indicator and artificial horizon:
  replacement by an electric turn and bank indicator
- Repeater compass:
  replacement by simple magnetic compass
- Round counter box:
  replacement by simple visual indicators
- Fuel warning light:
  deleted
- Clock:
  Often not installed
- Undercarriage position indicators
  Replacement by sight window and mechanical indicators

Equipment of the He 162 A:

No.	Equipment	Instrument Range	Requisition/Equipment Number
1	Takeoff-assist rocket jettison		
2	Rudder trim		
3	Undercarriage selector switch		8-111.429-24
4	Elevator trim		
5	Takeoff-assist rocket ignition		
6	Fuel cock lever		
7	Throttle lever with push-button		Fl 50911
8	Undercarriage lock disengage		
9	Undercarriage indicator, port		
10	Landing flap hand-pump		
11	Navigation equipment (from left):		
	AFN 2 homing indicator	Ln 27002	
	FK 38 master compass indicator	Fl 23233	
	Clock*	Fl 23885	
12	Flight instruments (from left):		
	Electric turn and bank indicator	Fl 22412	
	Airspeed indicator	100 – 900 km/h	Fl 22234
	Fine and coarse altimeter	0 – 16000 m	Fl 22326
	Vertical speed indicator	+30 / -30 m/s	Fl 22386
13	3 visual indicators for pitot tube and weapons as an alternative two Fl 32525 visual indicators for the two cannon were installed on the bottom right of the instrument panel	19-6824 B-1	
14	Canopy latch		
15	Revi 16 b gun sight		Fl 52955
16	Engine instruments (from top left):		
	Exhaust gas temperature gauge	300 - 1000°	Fl 20338
	Oil pressure gauge	0 – 10 kg/cm²	Fl 20504-10
	Fuel pressure gauge	0 – 160 kg/cm²	Fl 20516-1
	Fuel gauge	0 – 700 l	Fl 20723
	Differential pressure gauge (thrust)*	0 – 1 kg/cm²	Fl 20515
	Fuel warning light with red top*		Fl 32529
	Electric RPM indicator	2,000 – 15,000 rpm	Fl 20266
17	Oxygen system (from above):		
	Oxygen indicator		10-?
	Reversible high-altitude breathing apparatus		Fl 30403
18	Flare pistol		
19	Undercarriage indicator, starboard		
20	Controls for FuG 25 A (IFF)		Ln 28810
21	Receiver for FuG 24 (radio telephone)		Ln ?
22	Starter toggle switch		19-5832
23	Nozzle position selector switch (rotary switch)	19-5843	
24	9 circuit breakers of various strengths for battery, fuel pumps, weapons and gun sight, pitot tube heat, start and measuring system plus turn and bank indicator, adjustable nozzle, FuG 24, FuG 25 A and starter. Another circuit breaker was required for the use of takeoff-assist rockets.		19-5000
25	Ejection seat firing handle		
26	Rudder pedal adjustment		
27	Window to nosewheel bay		

* These devices were probably intended for installation in the He 162 and then were not installed or if at all in isolated cases only. They are therefore absent from the drawing and in some cases from the restored machine.

The lettering and operating instructions in the cockpit were either painted directly onto the surfaces or consisted of glued-on paper placards, some of which were created with a typewriter.

Two paper placards on the instrument panel provided important operating information and limiting speeds:

Attention!
Indicated airspeed 10% less than actual.
No pull-outs in excess of 4 g.
Negative acceleration for no longer than 3 sec., otherwise engine will flame out.

Limiting Speeds
Landing flaps – Takeoff Position Va: 500 km/h
Landing flaps – Landing Position Va: 300 km/h
Undercarriage down: Va: 350 km/h
Flight endurance 30 minutes

The drawing from the pilot's notes and the restored museum aircraft provide a good depiction of the layout of the He 162's cockpit. Together with historical photos, these assisted in the creation of the accompanying equipment list:

Heinkel He 219 *Uhu* (Eagle Owl)

Few aircraft had a more chequered development history than the He 219. Designed in 1940 as an advanced strategic reconnaissance aircraft, it was a twin-engined shoulder-wing monoplane with a two-seat pressurized cockpit and a tricycle undercarriage.

The He 219 was designed to be powered by the 2,000 H.P. DB 603 G, the 2,020 H.P. DB 614 or the 2,500 H.P. Jumo 222 compound engine.

By 1941 it was becoming apparent that the Ju 88 and Bf 110 night fighters were unable to meet the increasing demands being made of them. At that time General of Night Fighters Josef Kammhuber had been given authority to work directly with the aircraft industry to develop a new night fighter. He determined that the design with the greatest night fighter potential was the He 219. The conversion was accomplished with input from experienced night fighter pilots and by the beginning of 1943 the first aircraft was ready to fly.

Shortly before this, however, the RLM declared itself in favor of the more easily produced Ju 188. Comparative flight trials clearly demonstrated the Heinkel's superiority. To prevent further delays caused by the RLM, Kammhuber ordered the aircraft tested in combat. The results were impressive, however the RLM now insisted that it could not afford to allocate resources to specialized aircraft. As a result, by the end of the war production of the He 219 totaled just 298 machines.

The principal version was the He 219 A powered by two DB 603 E engines. Its flight characteristics were excellent, although the machine was slightly underpowered, and it was the first German aircraft to be equipped with ejection seats.

After the war a total of seven He 219s was sent to England and America for testing. One of these, WNr. 290202 (manufacturer's code GI+KQ, unit code G9+KQ) survives in the USA. It was captured by the Allies in Denmark, after which it was taken to the USA. The He 219 A-2 is now in storage at the National Air and Space Museum.

Allied test pilots considered the He 219's cockpit to be extremely advanced and well laid out. The pilot and radar operator sat back to back.

The instruments and control elements for the pilot were arranged in an instrument panel and two consoles on the left and right. The main instrument panel, which was made of wood, contained the most important flight, navigation and engine instruments.

The flight instruments were grouped in the classic international T-arrangement. The airspeed indicator, combined turn and bank indicator and artificial horizon and vertical speed indicator were placed in a

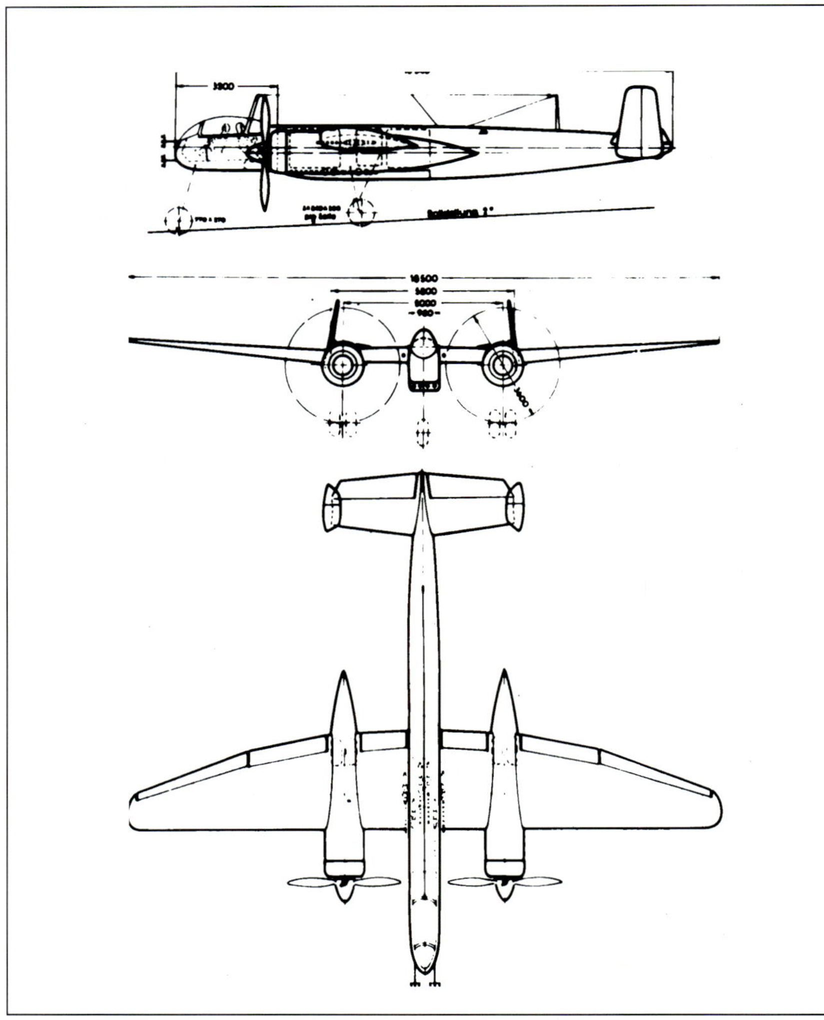

Three-view drawing of the He 219 from a series of instructional illustrations.

Left console with the trim buttons and throttle levers. At the top left are the controls for the American radio. (R.P. Lutz)

Cockpit of the He 219 A-2 stored at the National Air and Space Museum. The instrumentation is largely complete. (R.P. Lutz)

The right side of the pilot's instrument panel with temperature gauges. The clock (top) and back-up compass (center) are missing. Such decorative ITT were usually the first to go. (R.P. Lutz)

The right console with round counters and fuel gauges. Note the large red lever for firing the ejection seat, which was operated by compressed air. (R.P. Lutz)

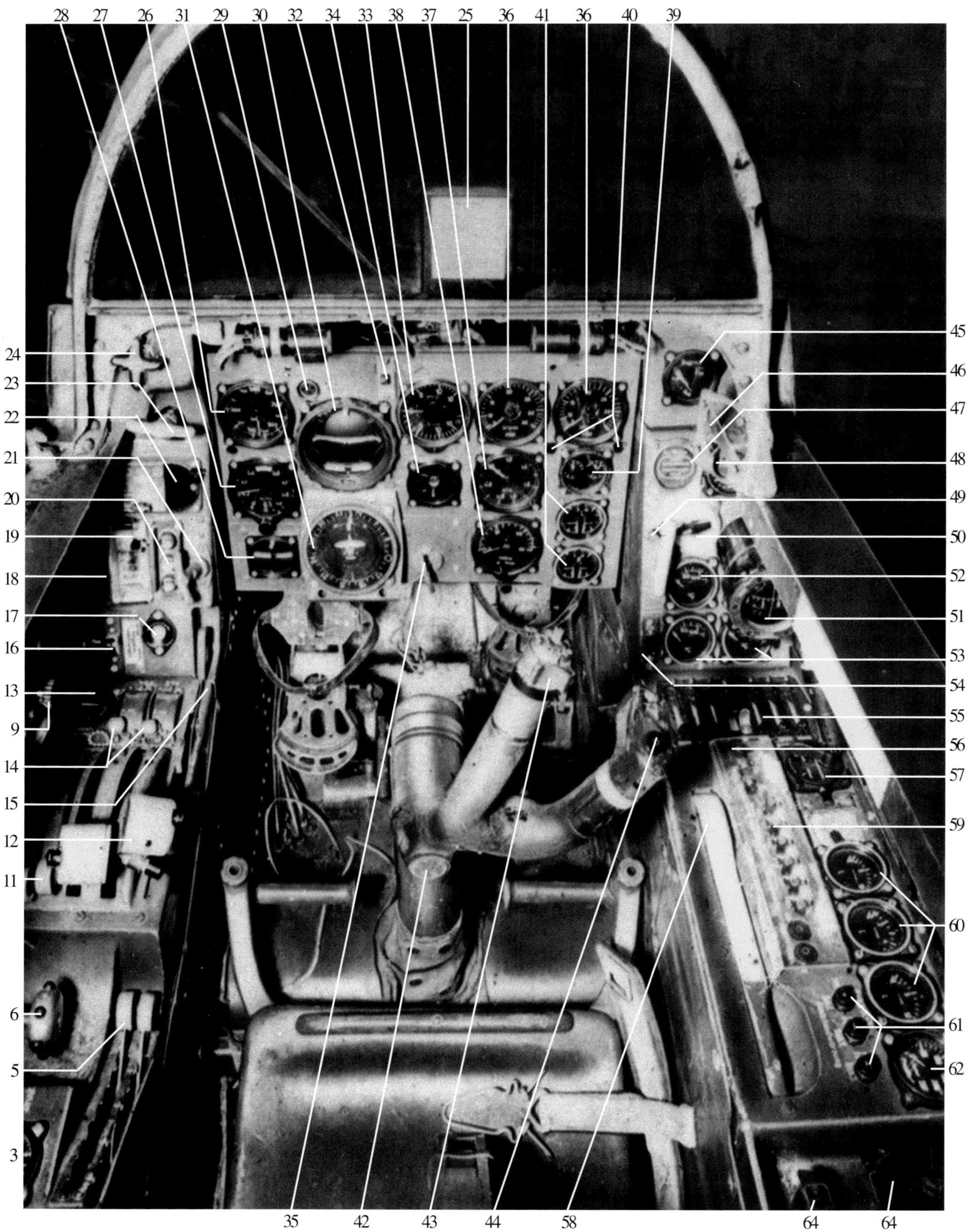

Pilot's position with instrument panel. Items 1, 2, 4, 7, 8, 10, 63, 65, 66, 67 and 68 are not visible in this photograph.

Equipment of the He 219 A:
Pilot's Port Console:

No.	Equipment	Instrument Range	Requisition/Equipment Number
1	Connection for heated flight suit		Fl 32403
2	Safety switch for self-destruct charge		
3	Double pressure gauge for compressed air	0 – 160 kg/cm²	Fl 20516-2
4	Push-button		19-5836 8
5	Cooling gills, emergency control		
6	Trim button		
7	FuG 17 control panel		
8	Intercom connector socket		
9	Cockpit heating control		
10	Operating data table and		HeN 16608
	Nav. Vordruck K5 deviation table		Fl 23905
11	RPM fine correction levers		
12	Throttle levers with thumb-switch for propeller pitch control		Fl 32337
13	Landing flap position indicator		Fl 22853
14	Ignition switches		Fl 21118
15	Rudder ground lock handle		
16	Automatic propeller pitch control lever		
17	Electrical system cutout switch		Fl 32315-2
18	Emergency flap-lowering lever		
19	Undercarriage switches		
20	DKS-C/2 landing flap switch		19-9206 A-1
21	Lever for lowering armored visor*		
22	Indicator lights (12) for undercarriage and landing flaps		Fl 32532
	or visual indicators (5) for undercarriage		19-6822 A-2
23	Main undercarriage emergency lowering lever		
24	Nosewheel emergency lowering handle (compressed air valve)		
*	This equipment not installed in all versions		

Pilot's Instrument Panel:

No.	Equipment	Instrument Range	Requisition/Equipment Number
25	Revi 16 B gun sight		Fl 52955
26	Airspeed indicator	100 – 900 km/h	Fl 22234
	or	100 – 1000 km/h	Fl 22241
27	Fine and coarse altimeter	0 – 13000 m	Fl 22322
28	Electric turn and bank indicator		Fl 22414-1
29	Pitot tube heat visual indicator		Fl 32530-7
30	Combined turn and bank indicator and artificial horizon		Fl 22411 or Fl 22415
31	Master compass indicator		Fl 23334 or Fl 23371
32	Autopilot emergency switch		Fl 32350
33	Vertical speed indicator	+15 / -15 m/s	Fl 22384
34	AFN 2 homing indicator		Ln 27002
35	Windscreen de-mist manual control		
36	2 RPM indicators	500 – 3,600 rpm	Fl 20269
37	Double pressure gauge	0.6 – 1.8 atm	Fl 20556
38	Indicator for FuG 101a radio altimeter	0 – 150 / 0 – 750 m	Ln 28330-1
39	Double propeller pitch indicator		127-1092 A
40	Propeller feathering indicator lights		Fl 32539-2
41	2 double indicators for fuel	0 – 3 kg/cm²	Fl 20572
	and oil	0 – 10 kg/cm²	
42	Control column		
43	Transmit button		
44	Cannon firing button		

row with the repeater compass beneath them. The engine instruments were arranged to the right of these.

The port console housed the controls and indicators for the undercarriage and landing flaps, trims and ignition switches and the engine controls.

The starboard console housed additional engine instruments, oxygen equipment for the crew, clock, magnetic compass, ammunition counters, electrical switches, fuel gauges and the firing handles for the ejection seats.

In addition to the controls for the radio and radar systems, the radar operator's position was also equipped with the most important navigation instruments.

The photographs presented here depict the He 219 A-2 (*Werknummer* 290202) stored in the USA. In anticipation of flight trials, American oxygen and radio systems were fitted. These systems are still present and will have to be replaced with German equipment when the aircraft is restored. As well, English labels were placed on the instruments for the American test pilots.

The radio operator's instruments. 69, 87 and 88 are not visible in this photograph.

Otherwise the interior of the museum aircraft is in very good condition, except for paint peeling off the main instrument panel. Except for the equipment mentioned above and various non-essential items such as the clock, magnetic compass and AFN 2 indicator, the equipment is largely complete and even the scopes for the FuG 220 *Lichtenstein* radar are still present.

Overall the machine gives a good impression of the instruments of a technically advanced German aircraft from the period 1944-45.

Pilot's Starboard Console (see photo on Page 202)

No.	Equipment	Instrument Range	Requisition/Equipment Number
45	Nosewheel position indicator (probably converted from Fl 23885 landing flap position indicator)		
46	Bo-UK 1 clock		Fl 23885
47	Oxygen flow meter		Fl 30489
48	Oxygen pressure gauge	0 – 250 kg/cm^2	Fl 30496
49	Canopy jettison handle		
50	Windscreen washer lever		
51	FK 38 magnetic compass		Fl 23233
52	2 coolant temperature gauges	0 - 130° C	Fl 20342
53	2 oil temperature gauges	0 - 130° C	Fl 20342
54	Selector switch		Fl 32350
55	SZK K 6 ammunition counters		Fl 47321
56	Switches for landing light, navigation lights and ultra-violet cockpit lights		
57	PSH-17 gyro control monitoring switch		127-180 B
58	Ejection seat firing handle		
59	Switches for autopilot, pitot tube heat and fuel pumps		
60	3 fuel gauges		Fl 20723
	Forward tank	0 – 1000 liters	
	Center tank	0 – 500 liters	
	Rear tank	0 – 1000 liters	
61	3 fuel warning lights		Fl 32350-2
62	Compressed air gauge for ejection seats	0 – 250 kg/cm^2	Fl 20519
63	Ultra-violet lighting dimmer switch		
64	Starter		Fl 21212
65	Ignition switch via external connector (assisted start)		
66	Fuel jettison lever		
67	SZK K 2 ammunition counter for oblique weapons		Fl 47317
68	Reversible high-altitude breathing system		Fl 30430

Instrumentation in Radar Operator's Position – Starboard Side:

No.	Equipment	Instrument Range	Requisition/Equipment Number
69	AFN 2 homing indicator		Ln 27002
70	Ammeter and voltmeter	-120 / +120 A/V	Fl 32501-3
71	Fine and coarse altimeter	0 – 13000 m	Fl 22322
72	Dimmer switch		Fl 32401
73	Ejection seat firing handle		
74	Morse key		
75	Airspeed indicator	100 – 900 km/h	Fl 22234
	or	100 – 1000 km/h	Fl 22241
76	Compressed air gauge for ejection seats	0 – 250 kg/cm^2	Fl 20519
77	RSS 6a DF loop control		Ln 28665
78	Headset connector socket		
79	Various switches and warning lights for the radio equipment		
80	Oxygen pressure gauge	0 – 250 kg/cm^2	Fl 30496
81	Oxygen flow meter		Fl 30489
82	Outside air temperature gauge	-60 / +40° C	Fl 20349
83	Oxygen system connector hose		
84	Heated flight suit connector socket	Fl 32403	
85	Reversible high-altitude breathing system		Fl 30430
86	Crank for retractable boarding ladder		
87	PTK/p2 DF repeater compass		Fl 23374
88	Radio and radar system controls		

As production went on there were, of course, variations from one version to another and also on account of the spare parts situation.

Ju 87 A photographed in flight.

Junkers Ju 87

Probably no other aircraft is as closely associated with the early years of the Second World War as the "Stuka", the two-seat Ju 87 with its characteristic gull wing. The aircraft and its howling sirens became a symbol of the German blitzkrieg.

The Ju 87 first saw combat in Spain in 1936-37 and subsequently served on every front in Europe and Africa during the Second World War. Its early successes were considerable, however as the enemy's defenses stiffened, the Stuka increasingly became an anachronism.

Although seen as largely ineffective by the British after the Battle of Britain in 1940, in 1941 the Stuka still managed to inflict heavy losses on the Royal Navy in the Mediterranean. The Ju 87 also served in large numbers in Russia until replaced by ground attack versions of the Fw 190. The Stukas were then relegated to training schools or were used in the anti-tank and night attack roles. A number of Ju 87s were employed as glider tugs or as flying test-beds, for example in the testing of ejection seats.

Aerodynamically, the Ju 87 was no beauty, but it was robust, had forgiving flight characteristics and, unlike almost all other dive bombers of the Second World War, was capable of diving vertically.

The most important variants were the Ju 87 A and B, the aerodynamically refined Ju 87 D, the long-range Ju 87 R derived from the B, and the Ju 87 G anti-tank aircraft armed with two 37-mm cannon. All versions were powered by versions of the Jumo 210 or 211 engine producing from 640 to 1,500 H.P. A small number of Stukas was exported.

Of the 5,709 machines which were built, all that remains are two more or less complete aircraft and seven wrecks.

Restored instrument panel of a Ju 87 B-1. The AFN 1 homing indicator on the right was planned, but probably never installed in service aircraft.

Instrument panel of the Ju 87 A. This photograph probably depicts an aircraft exported to Japan. Small white explanatory placards bearing Japanese text were placed near the instruments and controls. (via Wildmoser)

The instrument panel of the Ju 87 A from the left. The illustration is from a description of the offensive armament system. The capital letters indicate:
A: Master switch on the ASK-V bomb sequence selector panel
B: Visual indicator
C: Warning light
D: Safety
E: Emergency bomb release handle

The interior photographs presented here depict the Ju 87 G-2 (*Werknummer* 494085, manufacturer's code RI+JK) in the RAF Museum in London or were taken from aircraft handbooks.

The Ju 87 B-1 instrument panel illustrated on Page 205 was found in a junkyard in Pforzheim in 1980. It was laboriously restored over a period of years and was fitted with historically-accurate instruments.

Over the course of its development the Ju 87 was fitted with equipment and instruments typical of the late 1930s and 1940s. The instrument panel was made of metal and consisted of a fixed part, which was bolted to the fuselage frame in front of the pilot, and a panel containing the flight instruments on vibration-absorbing mounts in the center of the main panel. The instruments were attached with bolts and clinch nuts.

Historical photograph of a Ju 87 B-1 instrument panel. The clock and double boost gauge are missing. (via Wildmoser)

The Ju 87 B introduced a fuselage with revised aerodynamic shape. Seen here is a Staffel of Ju 87 B-2s.

Equipment of the Ju 87 A:

No.	Equipment	Instrument Range	Requisition/Equipment Number
1	Revi gun sight		
2	Supercharger control lever (low-high)		
3	Cockpit ventilation		
4	Ammeter/Voltmeter	+30/-30	Fl 32502-4
5	Dimmer switch		Fl 32401-?
6	Oscillation indicator	0 – 10	Fl 20930
7	Reserve fuel (visual indicator)		Fl 32525
8	Tank selector switch and fuel cock		
9	Central panel illumination		
10	Ignition switch		Fl 21118
11	Fire extinguisher valve control		
12	Electrical system cutout switch		Fl 32315-2
13	Turn and bank indicator sensitivity control		Fl 22405
14	Double pressure gauge for fuel and oil 0 – 0.5 / 0 – 10 kg/cm2		Fl 20512
15	Oil temperature gauge	0 - 160° C	Fl 20308 ?
16	Coolant temperature gauge	0 – 120° C	Fl 20308-4
17	Fine and coarse altimeter	0 – 10000 m	Fl 22320
18	Airspeed indicator	80 – 750 km/h	Fl 22231
19	FK 5 magnetic compass		Fl 23211
20	Turn and bank indicator (pneumatic)		Fl 22402
21	Bo-UK 1 clock (Junghans)		Fl 23885
22	Oxygen pressure gauge	0 – 250 kg/cm^2	Fl 30496
23	RPM indicator	600 – 3,600 rpm	Fl 20220
24	Boost pressure gauge	0.6 – 1.8 atm	Fl 20550
25	Fuel gauge selector switch for Tanks I and II		Fl 20754-2
26	Fuel gauge	0 – 220 l	Fl 20704
27	ASK-V bomb sequence selector panel		Fl ?
28	Bomb jettison handle		
29	Fuel gauge air pump		Fl 20740
30	Hand-pump actuator (emergency fuel shutoff valve)		
31	AP 8 starter injection pump		8-4505 A
32	Oil cooler flap control		

Some of the Fl numbers have been reconstructed, as there is no replacement parts list for the Ju 87 A

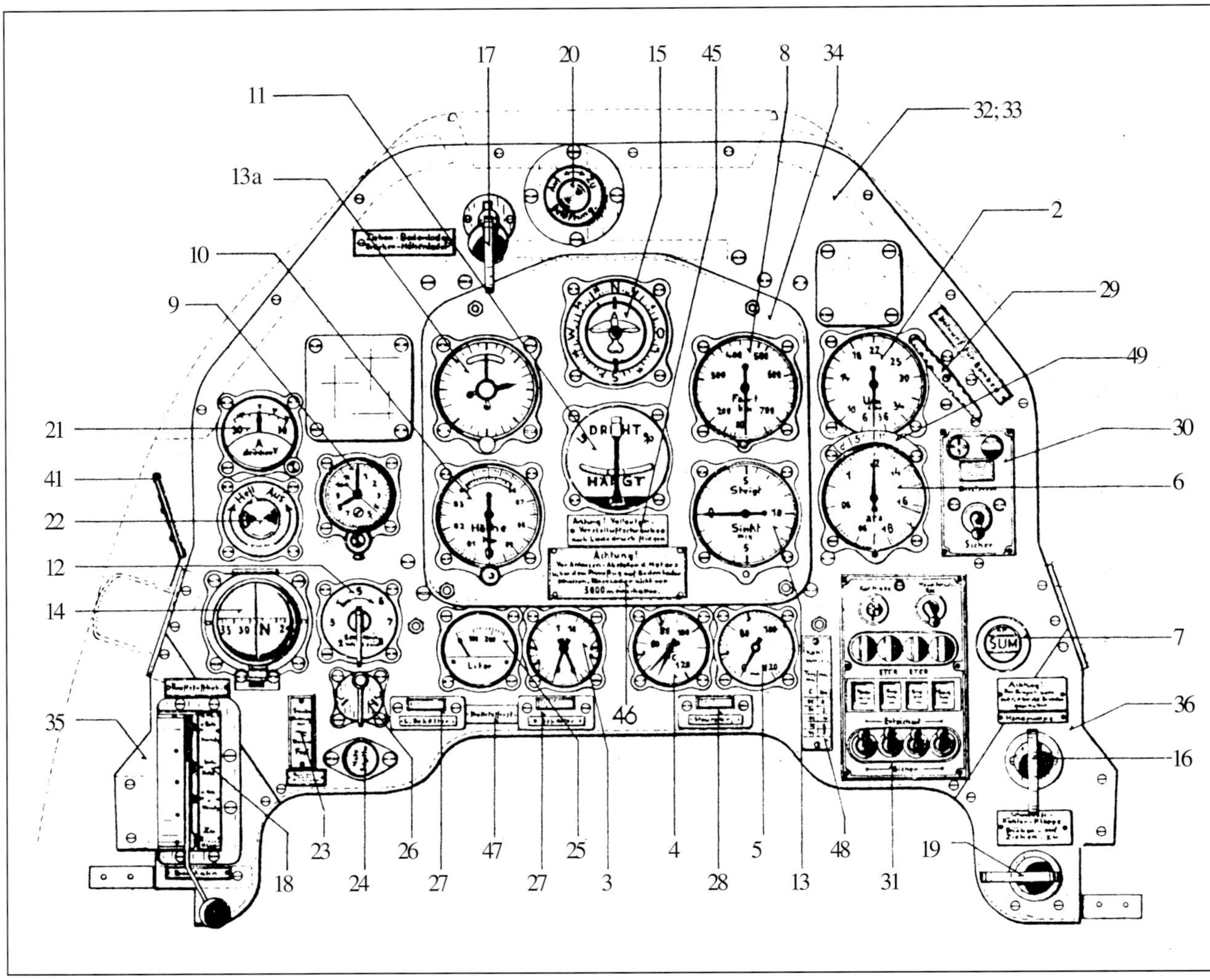

Equipment of the Ju 87 B-1

During the aircraft's service life, the instrumentation of the Ju 87 B-1 was revised, supplemented and in some cases rearranged. More modern electrical indicators were installed, especially for the fuel system. The control system for the air-dropped weapons was also expanded. The numbering of equipment is based on a drawing from the replacement parts list.

No.	Equipment	Instrument Range	Requisition/Equipment Number
1	Instrument panel, complete		87.490
2	RPM indicator	600 – 3,600 rpm	Fl 20222
	or	500 – 3,600 rpm	Fl 20222-3
3	Double pressure gauge for fuel and oil 0 – 2 / 0 – 10 kg/cm2		Fl 20512-2
4	Double oil temperature gauge	0 – 120° C	Fl 20330-4
5	Double coolant temperature gauge	0 – 120° C	Fl 20308-4
6	Boost pressure gauge	0.6 – 1.8 atm	Fl 20550
7	SUM AP 8 starter injection pump		8-4505 A
8	Airspeed indicator	80 – 750 km/h	Fl 22231
9	Bo-UK 1 clock		Fl 23885
10	Fine and coarse altimeter	0 – 10000 m	Fl 22320
11	Turn and bank indicator		Fl 22402
12	Turn and bank indicator sensitivity control		Fl 22405
13	Statoscope-vertical speed indicator	-10 / +10 m/s	Fl 22381-10
	or vertical speed indicator	-10 / +10 m/s	Fl 22382-10

14	FK 5 magnetic compass or FK 38		Fl 23211 Fl 23233
15	Master compass indicator		Fl 23334
16	Hand-pump (emergency fuel shutoff valve)		
17	Supercharger control lever (low-high)		
18	Fuel valve lever		
19	Oil cooler flap control lever		
20	Cockpit ventilation		
21	Ammeter/Voltmeter	-30 / +30 A/V	Fl 32502-2
22	Dimmer switch		Fl 32401-4
23	Ignition switch		Fl 21207 or Fl 21212
24	Electrical system cutout switch		Fl 32315-2
25	Fuel gauge		Fl 20723
26	Fuel gauge selector switch		Fl 32331
27	Fuel level visual indicator (left and right)		Fl 32525
28	Pitot tube heat visual indicator		Fl 32525-3
29	Emergency bomb release handle		
30	ASK-V bomb sequence selector panel		Fl ?
31	ASK-L bomb sequence selector panel		Fl 50962
32, 33	Instrument panel, rigid		87.940-0101
34	Instrument panel, vibration-proof		87.940-0102
35	Side panel, left		87.940-0104
36	Side panel, right		87.940-0103
41	Frame for operating data table		87.940-07
45	Placard: Attention! Fully-automatic Variable-pitch propeller Fly according to boost pressure		
46	Placard: Attention! Switch supercharger to low before starting – shutting down engine and before commencing dive. Do not set supercharger to high before 3000 m.		
47	Placard "Reserve Fuel"		
48	Placard for coolant temperatures at specified altitudes		
49	Placard for maximum endurances of boost pressure values		

Other items of equipment near the pilot's seat:

•	Ignition switch (on throttle lever)	Fl 21119
•	Revi C 12/D gun sight (in windscreen superstructure)	Fl 52095
•	ZSK 243 st bomb arming panel	

There were various changes in some Ju 87 B-1 aircraft:
- Radiator cooling flap switch (above RPM indicator)
- Installation of the large observer-repeater compass

The arrangement of the instruments and control elements was as follows:

- **Port side of the cockpit:** Throttle lever, trims and landing flap controls, ammunition counter for the fixed weapons.
- **Starboard side of the cockpit:** Main electrical panel, oxygen system.
- **Instrument panel:** **Left:** Ignition and starter switches, instruments and controls for the electrical and radio systems, magnetic compass and clock.
- **Center: (vibration-proof panel):** flight instruments.
- **Bottom:** fuel gauge and engine instruments.
- **Right:** engine instruments, levers and control box for the armament.

This configuration was retained in almost every version of the Ju 87. The equipment installed in the aircraft changed as more advanced devices became available and the aircraft's role changed. Equipment was modified or modernized during repairs to meet new requirements or as a result of the difficult spares situation. An example of this is provided by the restored instrument panel from the Ju 87 B-1 (Page 205). Shutter-type visual indicators were initially installed as fuel gauges. These were later replaced a panel with two sets of warning lights to indicate reserve and tanks full. Finally, this modification was reversed, and visual indicators were once again installed.

The standard instrumentation of the Junkers Ju 87 A to G is revealed in drawings from operating manuals, replacement parts lists and historical photographs. These can only serve as examples, however, as the equipment installed on the production line and front-line modifications changed with time.

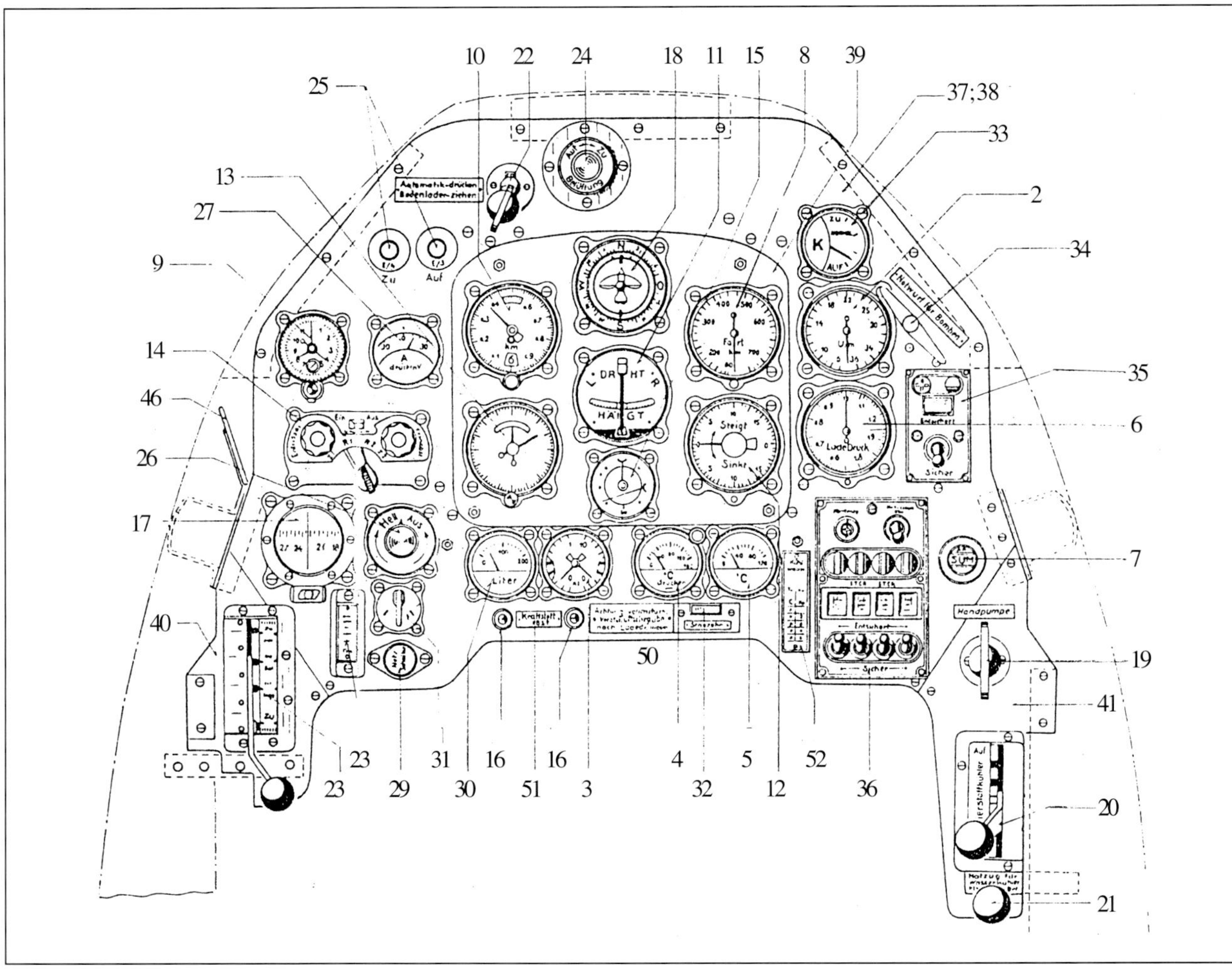

Drawing of the instrument panel of the Ju 87 B-2 from the replacement parts list. The instrument panels of the B-1 and B-2 differed only in detail.

Changes in the Ju 87 B-2 Series:

This list contains only that equipment which differed in position and type from that installed in the Ju 87 B-1. The numbers are based on the drawing in the corresponding replacement parts list.

No.	Equipment	Instrument Range	Requisition/Equipment Number
1	Instrument panel, complete		87.9066
4	Oil temperature gauge, switchable	0 – 160° C	Fl 20343
5	Coolant temperature gauge	0 – 120° C	Fl 20342-2
9	Bo UK 1 clock		Fl 23885
10	Fine and coarse altimeter	0 – 10000 m	Fl 22320
12	Vertical speed indicator	+15 / -15 m/s	Fl 22382
13	Contact altimeter	0 – 6000 m	Fl 22317
14	FBG 4 remote-control unit		Ln 26668
15	AFN 2 homing indicator		Ln 27002
16	Fuel warning lights (red) left and right		Fl 32529-1
17	FK 38 magnetic compass		Fl 23233
20	Oil cooler flap control lever		
21	Emergency radiator flap control		
25	Push-buttons for radiator flap operation		Fl 32334
26	Dimmer switch		Fl 32401-?
27	Ammeter/Voltmeter	-30 / +30	Fl 32502-4
33	Radiator flap position indicator		Fl 20853-1

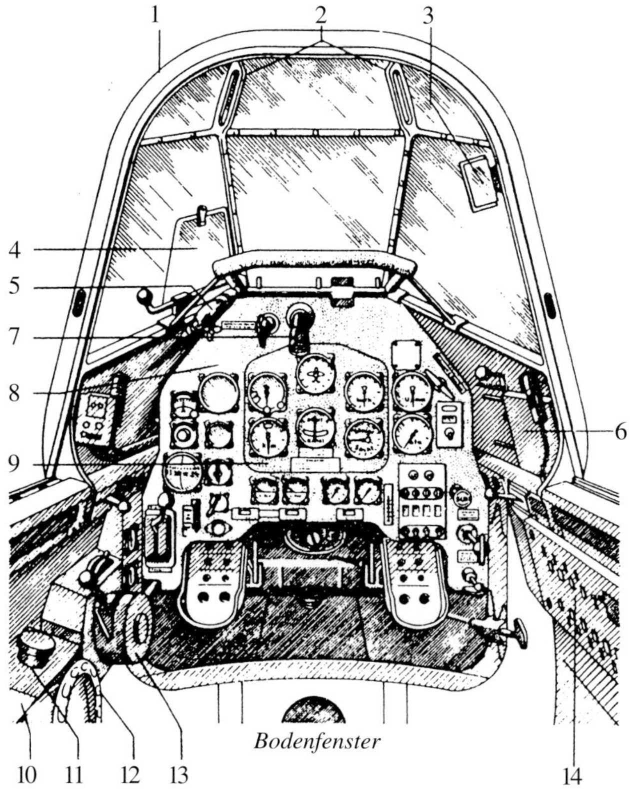

1 festes Führerraumdach
2 Haltegriffe
3 Rückblickspiegel
4 vordere Klappe
5 Leuchtpistoleneinbau
6 Leuchtpatronenkasten
7 Belüftungsdüse, verstellbar
8 festes Gerätebrett
9 elastisches Gerätebrett
10 Schaltkasten
11 Seitenrudertrimmung
12 Höhenrudertrimmung
13 Drosselhebelkasten
14 Schalttafel mit Selbstschalter

The cockpit of the Ju 87 B-1 with various control elements. (Hafner Archive)

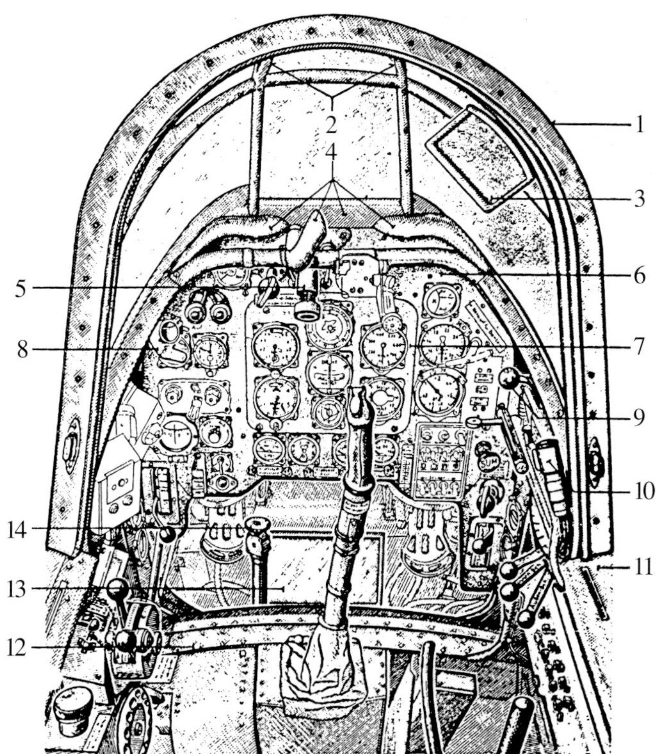

1 Festes Führerraumdach
2 Haltegriffe
3 Rückblickspiegel
4 Scheibenspülanlage
5 Verstellung der Scheibenspülanlage
6 Festes Gerätebrett
7 Elastisches Gerätebrett
8 Leuchtpistoien-Halterung
9 Leuchtpatronenkasten, abwerfbar
10 Führerraumbeleuchtung
11 Oberholm
12 Träger I
13 Bodenfenster mit Abdeckblende
14 Handrad für Bodenfenster

Pilot's position in the Ju 87 D-1. (Hafner Archive)

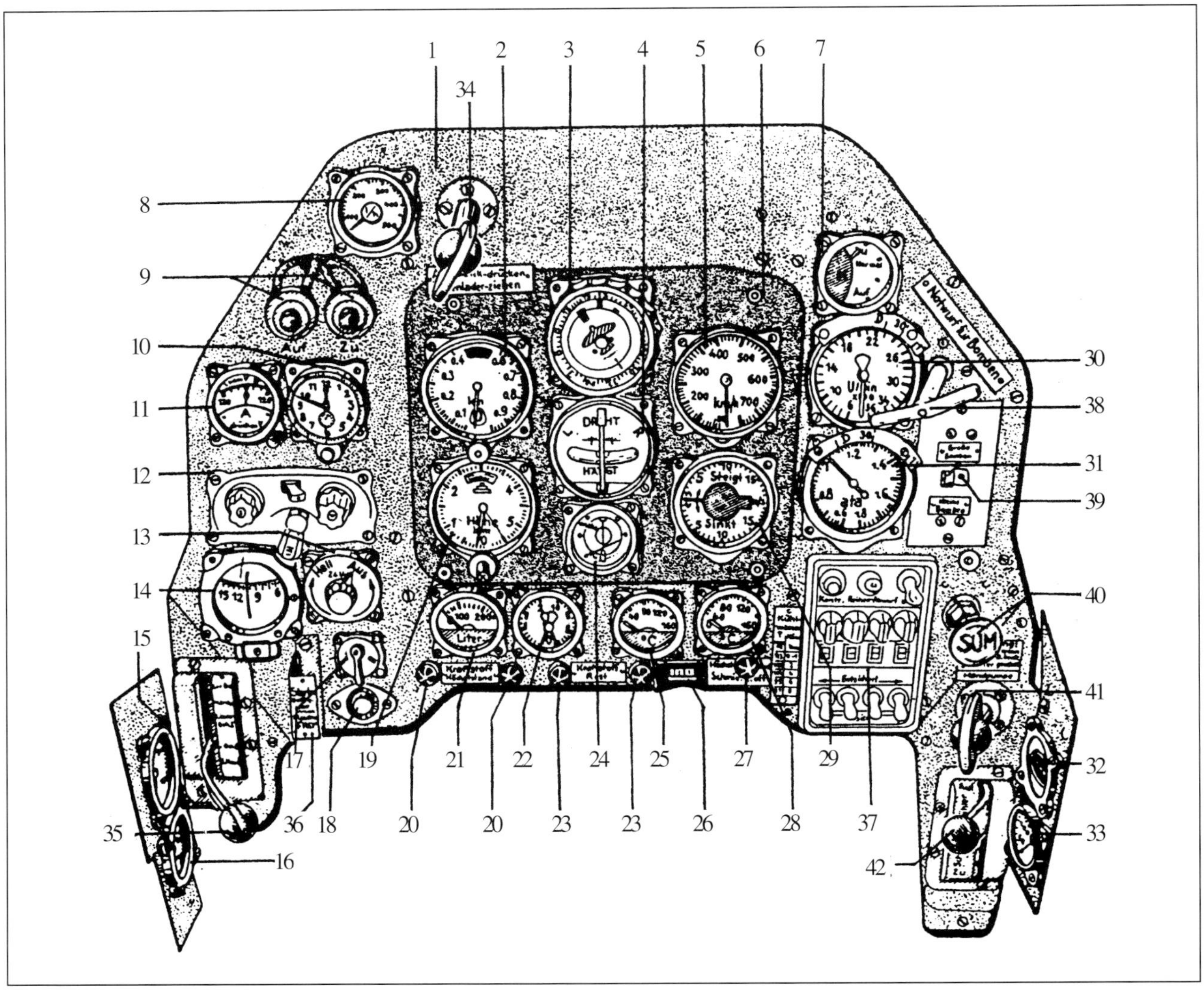

Taken from the pilot's notes, a diagram identifying the instrumentation of the Ju 87 D-1. (Hafner Archive)

Cockpit of an early Ju 87 D. (Griehl Collection)

Equipment of the Ju 87 D-1:

The equipment installed in early-production D-series aircraft was almost identical to that of the B-2. Later more modern equipment was installed and the flight instruments, in particular, were changed, primarily through the addition of a combined turn and bank indicator and artificial horizon. Other changes resulted from modified armament.

No.	Equipment	Instrument Range	Requisition/Equipment Number
1	Instrument panel, complete		
2	Fine and coarse altimeter	0 – 10000 m	Fl 22320
3	Master compass indicator		Fl 23334
4	Electric turn and bank indicator		Fl 22406
5	Airspeed indicator	80 – 750 km/h	Fl 22231
6	Vibration-proof instrument panel		
7	Position indicator for the radiator flaps		Fl 20853-1
8	Fuel consumption gauge (not in all aircraft)	0 – 500 l/h	Fl 20812
9	Push-buttons for radiator flap operation		Fl 32334
10	Bo UK 1 clock		Fl 23885
11	Ammeter/Voltmeter	-120 / +120	Fl 32502-5
12	FBG 4 remote-control device		Ln 26668
13	Dimmer switch		Fl 32401-?
14	FK 38 magnetic compass (not in all aircraft)		Fl 23233
15	Hydraulic pressure gauge for operation of landing flaps and dive brakes	0 – 120 kg/cm²	Fl 20516-2
16	Hydraulic pressure gauge for operation of tailplane trim, dive brakes and radiator flaps	0 – 120 kg/cm²	Fl 20516-2
17	Fuel gauge selector switch		Fl 32331
18	Electrical system cutout switch		Fl 32315-2
19	Contact altimeter	0 – 6000 m	Fl 22317
20	Full fuel tank indicator light (green)		Fl 32529
21	Fuel gauge	0 – 250 l	Fl 20723
22	Double pressure gauge for fuel and oil	0 – 2 / 0 – 10 kg/cm²	Fl 20512-2
23	Fuel warning light (red)		Fl 32529-1
24	AFN 2 homing indicator		Ln 27002
25	Oil temperature gauge, electric	0 – 130° C	Fl 20342
26	Pitot tube heat visual indicator		Fl 32525
27	Full oil tank indicator light (green)		Fl 32529
28	Electric coolant temperature gauge	0 – 130° C	Fl 20342
29	Vertical speed indicator	+15 / -15 m/s	Fl 22382/22384
30	RPM indicator	500 – 3,600 rpm	Fl 20222-3
31	Boost pressure gauge	0.6 – 1.8 atm	Fl 20555
32	Oxygen flow meter		Fl 30489
33	Oxygen pressure gauge	0 – 250 kg/cm²	Fl 30496
34	Selector handle for supercharger low-high		
35	Tank selector switch and fuel cock		
36	Starter		Fl 21212
37	ASK-R bomb sequence selector panel		Fl 50967
38	Emergency bomb release handle		
39	Selector switch for large and small bombs		
40	SUM AP 8 starter injection pump		8-4505 A
41	Hand-pump (emergency fuel shutoff valve)		
42	Oil cooler flap control lever		

Numbering is based on a drawing in the pilot's notes.
Additional equipment in area of pilot's seat:

	Equipment		Number
•	Revi C 12/D gun sight in windscreen superstructure		Fl 52095
•	Ignition switch (in throttle lever quadrant)		Fl 21118
•	BG 25 A IFF control panel (port side)		Ln 28810
•	SZK K 2 ammunition counter (port side)		Fl 47317
•	ZSK 244 A bomb arming panel (starboard side)		Fl 50869

The aircraft illustrated here was probably a prototype of the Ju 87 D. The aircraft has the forward canopy of a Ju 87D while retaining the instrument panel of a Ju 87 B-1. (Factory Photo)

A Ju 87 D-5 peels off into a dive. Note the improved aerodynamic shape compared to the Ju 87 B. (Griehl Collection)

Forward cockpit of the Ju 87 G in London. Several instruments are missing. The central panel on elastic mounts was rebuilt by the English during restoration and is not identical to the original. At the bottom right are the switches for the 37-mm cannon, in the position occupied by the Abwurfschaltkasten R bomb selector panel in bomber versions.

Bisherige Ausführung:

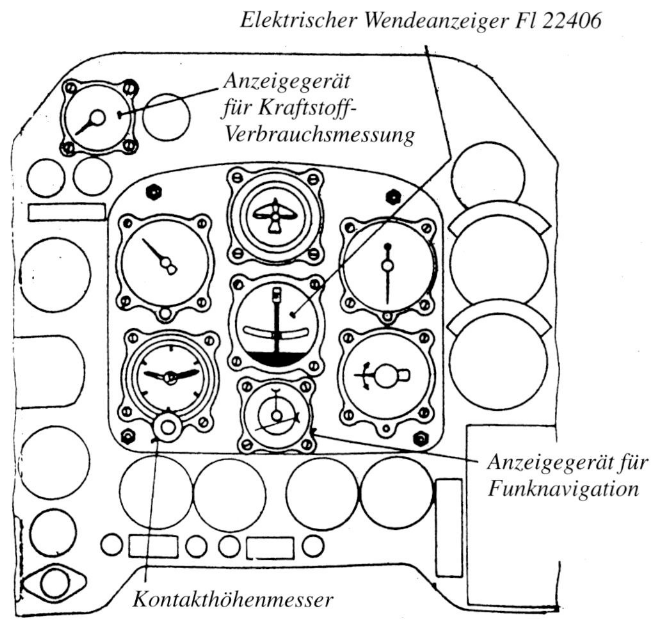

Neue Ausführung:

Einbau des pneumatischen Horizontes, Teil 2, und Versetzen des elektrischen Wendezeigers, Kontakthöhenmeser und Anzeigegerätes für Funknavigation in den Ju 87 D-1, D-3, G-1 Flugzeugen

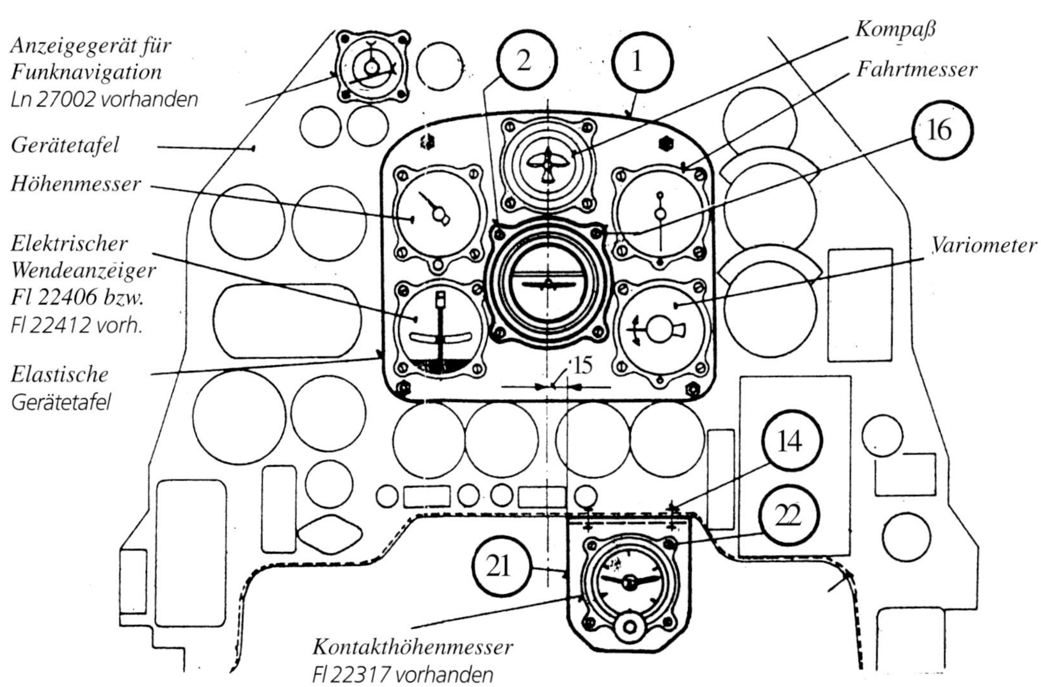

Extract from an RLM directive concerning modification of the Ju 87 for night missions. Changes include the installation of a pneumatic artificial horizon and relocation of the turn and bank indicator, contact altimeter and homing indicator.

Instrument panel of a Ju 87 D-5. Note the combined turn and bank indicator and artificial horizon and the bomb selector panel (ASK 87 ?) on the right with pre-selection option. (Griehl Collection)

Equipment of the Ju 87 G:

The Ju 87 G anti-tank aircraft was equipped much the same as the D-series, from which it was derived. The major difference was the installation of control boxes for the two 37-mm cannon carried beneath the aircraft's wings in place of the ASK-R. This equipment may be seen on the bottom right of the main instrument panel of the Ju 87 G-2 of the Royal Air Force Museum. Other equipment associated with the bombing role was also deleted.

There were variations in the equipment installed in various production versions of the Ju 87 D, for example the Ju 87 D-5:

4	Combined turn and bank indicator and artificial horizon (the turn and bank indicator was deleted and the AFN 2 homing indicator was moved)	Fl 22415
13	AFN 2 homing indicator (dimmer switch on instrument panel deleted)	Ln 27002
14	FK 38 deleted	
37	Bomb sequence selector panel (ASK 87 ?) for fuselage and wing bombs	
	SWA 10/X/I switchbox for the weapons system (on cockpit floor in front of instrument panel)	Fl 50959

Modifications for night operations:
For night ground-attack missions, D- and G-series were modified as follows as per a directive dated 9 August 1944:

- Revi C 12/D or 16 D replaced by Nachtrevi C 12/N or 16 D/N
- The high-altitude breathing apparatus and fuel consumption measuring system were deleted
- Installation of ultra-violet lighting for the instruments
- Installation of position lights and additional navigation lights

4	Artificial horizon (Sperry)		Fl 22427
8	AFN 2 homing indicator		Ln 27002
	Contact altimeter	0 – 6000 m	Fl 22317
	(Installed in the fixed instrument panel beneath the temperature gauges)		

Newly-delivered Ju 88 A, still wearing its factory code VK+CT.

Junkers Ju 88

The Junkers Ju 88 had its origins in a specification issued by the *Reichsluftfahrtministerium* in autumn 1935. It called for a bomber which could carry a payload of at least 500 kg for 1000 kilometers at a speed of 500 km/h. To meet these requirements, Junkers had to adopt some then innovative design features. The result was a twin-engined low-wing monoplane of stressed skin construction. The usual Junkers "double wing" was discarded in favor of split ailerons and landing flaps. The Jumo inline engines were equipped with annular radiators and the crew of four was grouped in the nose.

In 1937 the aircraft's role was changed to include dive-bombing, which resulted in significant changes to the design. Nevertheless, the Ju 88 exceeded the specified performance in some respects and in March 1939 was able to set two world payload-speed records.

From then on the Ju 88 was assigned a high priority and in 1939 the type entered large-scale production, for which the design was well-suited. The basic design proved extremely adaptable and more than sixty variants were developed by the end of the war. Of the six major series, the Ju 88 A was built in by far the greatest numbers.

The Ju 88 served well in a multitude of roles, including those of night fighter, dive-bomber, strategic fighter, low-level attack aircraft, trainer, transport, torpedo aircraft, anti-tank aircraft and guided missile (Mistel). The much-loved type underwent more than 3,000 changes and with 15,000 built, the Ju 88 represented one of the largest German aircraft procurement programs.

Close-up of the control column of a Ju 88 A-1. Visible behind it is the drift sight, either a Kuvi 1 or 2. (Eriksen via F. Selinger)

Cockpit of a Ju 88 A-1. (Aders Collection)

From the training manual, a drawing of the pilot's and bomb aimer's positions in the Ju 88 A-1. (Hafner Archive)

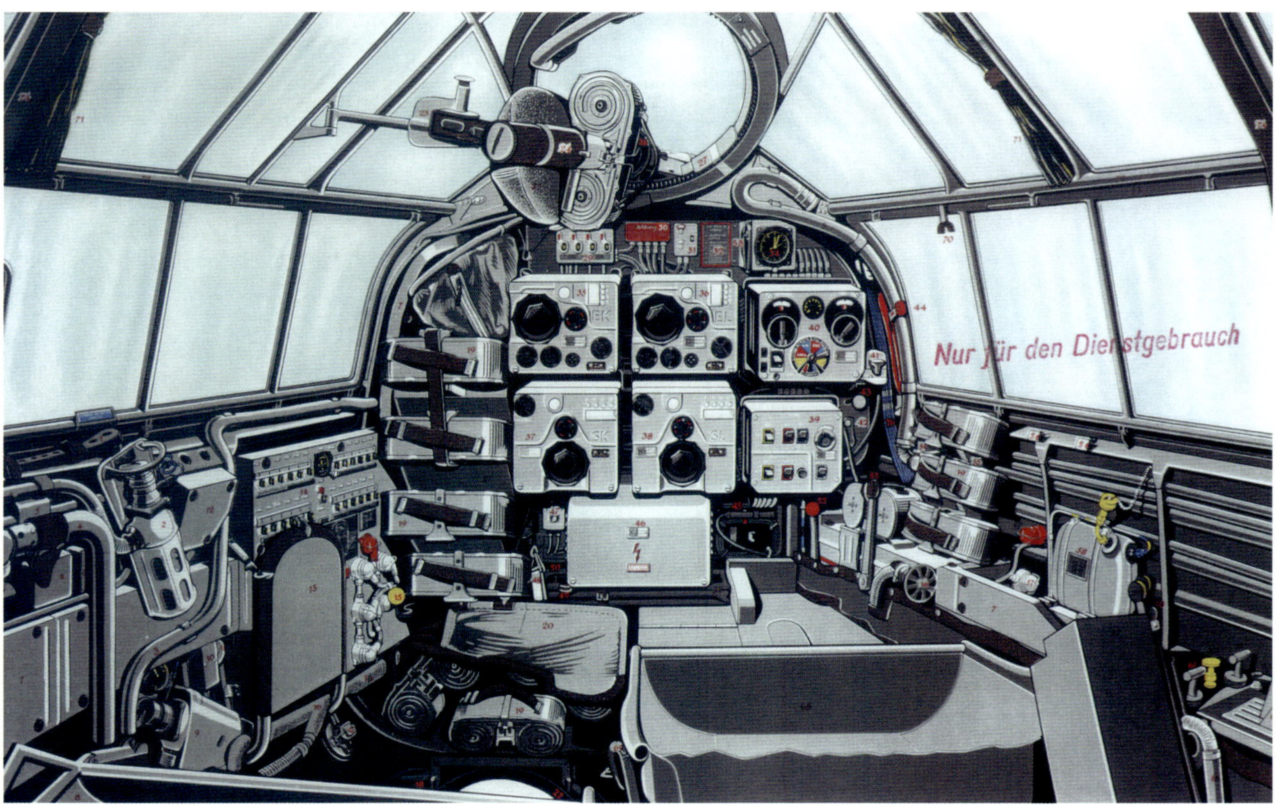

Radio operator's position in the Ju 88 A-1. (Hafner Archive)

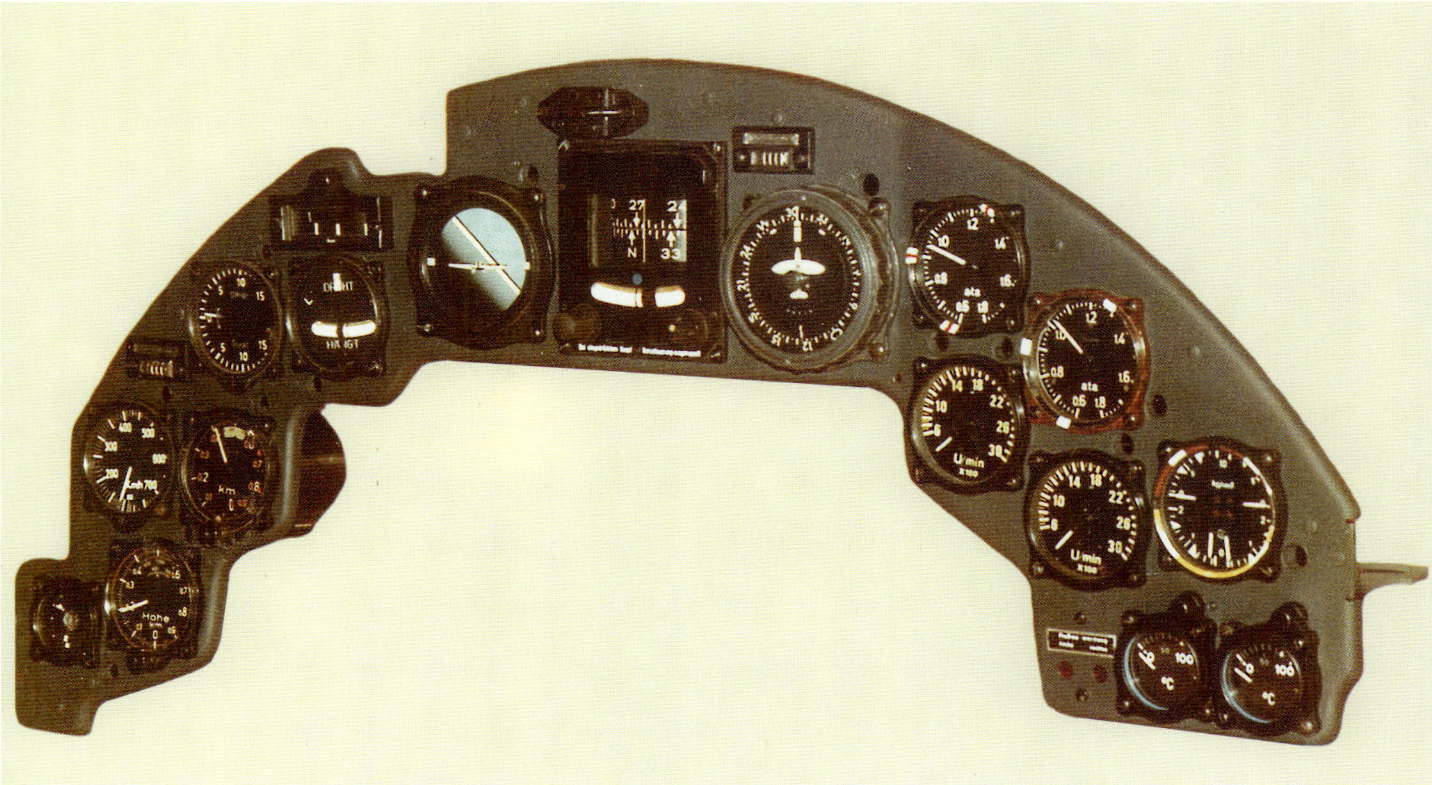

Restored instrument panel from a Ju 88 A-5 in Norway.

The type was also exported to Finland, Italy, Hungary and Romania. In France the Ju 88 flew until the end of the 1940s. From all the aircraft produced, only two have survived intact, along with the remnants of 20 others.

Some of the photographs presented here are of the following aircraft:

Ju 88 D-1/trop, WNr. 430650, in the USAF Museum in Dayton, Ohio

Ju 88 R-1, WNr. 360043, D5+EV, in the RAF Museum in London.

The equipment and instrumentation installed in the Ju 88 differed greatly from variant to variant, although the arrangement of the equipment stayed much the same.

The pilot sat in the usual position on the port side of the cockpit, with a large console on the port fuselage wall with the engine controls and trim wheels.

The instrument panel was arranged beneath the windscreen and was curved and relatively shallow, allowing the pilot an excellent view to the front through the glazed nose.

Historical color photograph taken inside a Ju 88 D-1 weather reconnaissance aircraft. This aircraft's instrumentation has been supplemented by an air pressure gauge and a fine altimeter (bottom right). (F. Selinger Collection)

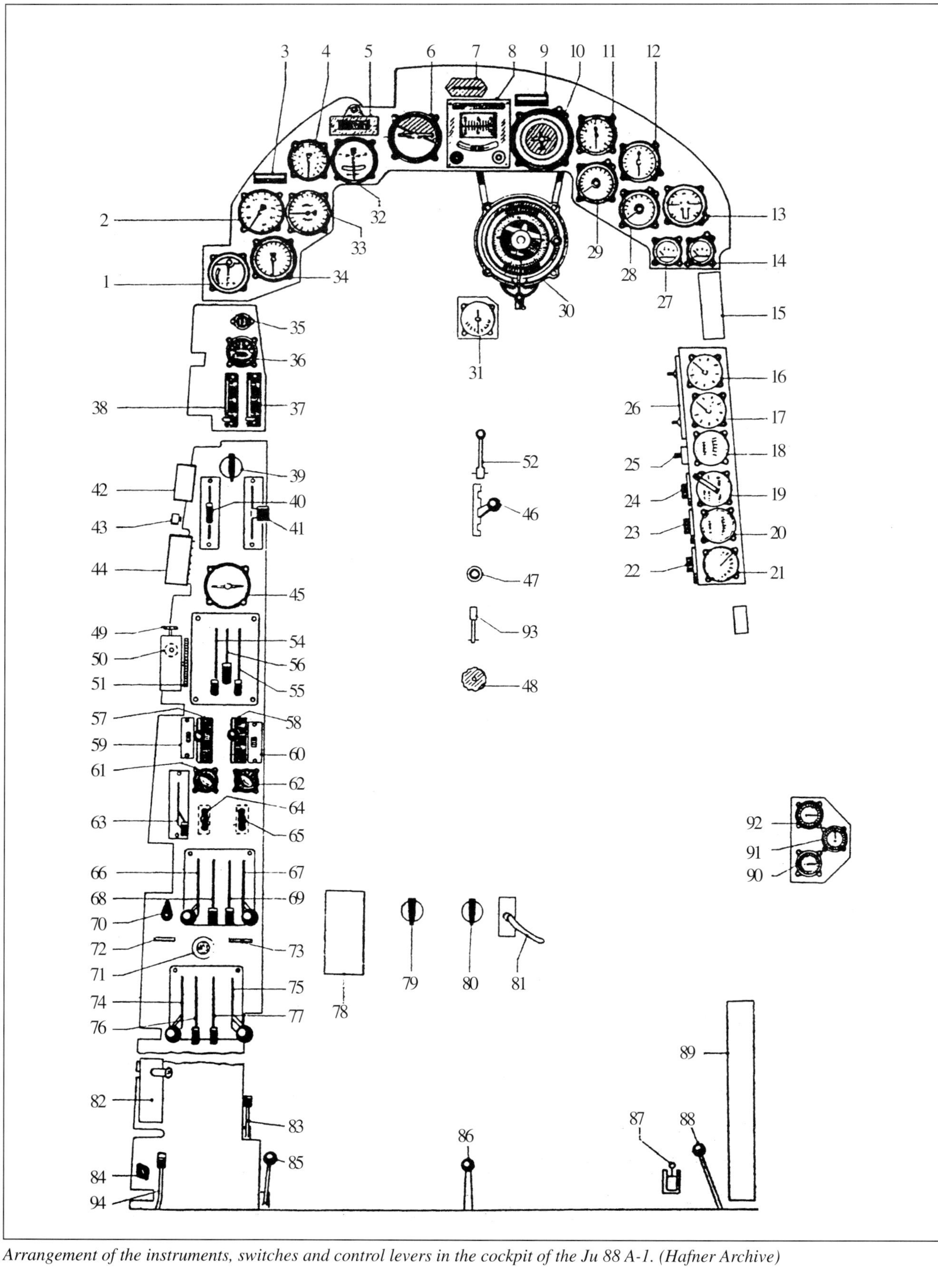

Arrangement of the instruments, switches and control levers in the cockpit of the Ju 88 A-1. (Hafner Archive)

The **Ju 88 A-1** powered by two 1,175 H.P. Jumo 211 B engines was the first production version. A Siemens K4ü autopilot and Patin compass system already formed part of the aircraft's standard equipment.

Equipment of the Ju 88 A-1:

No.	Equipment	Instrument Range	Requisition/Equipment Number
1	AFN 1 homing indicator		Ln 27000
2	Airspeed indicator	80 – 750 km/h	Fl 22231
3	Pitot tube heat visual indicator		Fl 32525-4
4	Fine and coarse altimeter	0 – 10000 m	Fl 22320
5	Lkz 3 course indicator		Fl 22562
6	Artificial horizon (Sperry)		Fl 22426
7	Slide tray for DBS 1 operating data		Fl 23501
8	Lku 4 gyro compass		Fl 22561
9	Autopilot visual indicator		Fl 32525-2
10	PfK/f3 master compass indicator		Fl 23338
11	Boost pressure gauge, port engine	0.6 – 1.8 atm	Fl 20555
12	Boost pressure gauge, starboard engine	0.6 – 1.8 atm	Fl 20555
13	Fuel/oil pressure gauge	2 x 0-2 / 2 x 0-10 kg/cm²	Fl 20514-2
14	Coolant temperature gauge, starboard	0 – 120° C	Fl 20242-2
15	RAB 14c bomb sequence selector		Fl 50933
16	Oxygen pressure gauge (pilot)	0 – 150 kg/cm²	Fl 20496
17	Oxygen pressure gauge (bomb aimer)	0 – 150 kg/cm²	Fl 20496
18	Fuel/oil gauge		Fl 20723
19	Fuel/oil gauge selector switch		Fl 32336-3
20	Fuel contents gauge	0 – 1200 / 0 – 420 l	Fl 20723
21	Outside air temperature gauge	-40 / +40° C	Fl 20342-1
22	Dimmer switch for engine instrument panel		Fl 32401-3
23	Dimmer switch for starboard instrument panel		Fl 32401-3
24	Dimmer switch for console and forward instrument panel		Fl 32401-3
25	Bomb selector switch		Fl 32327
26	ZSK 244 A bomb arming panel		Fl 50869
27	Coolant temperature gauge, port	0 – 120° C	Fl20342-2
28	Distant-reading RPM indicator, starboard engine	0 – 3,000 rpm	Fl 20384-3
29	Distant-reading RPM indicator, port engine	0 – 3,000 rpm	Fl 20384-3
30	Radio DF indicator with DF repeater compass PFA/R		Fl 23470
31	FK 38 standby compass		Fl 23233
32	Turn and bank indicator, electric		Fl 22406
33	Statoscope-vertical speed indicator	-10 / +10 m/s	Fl 22381-10
	later replaced by vertical speed indicator	-15 / +15 m/s	Fl 22382
34	Contact altimeter	0 – 6000 m	Fl 22317
35	Electrical system cutout switch		Fl 32315-2
36	Autopilot master switch		Fl 22559-1
37	Ignition switch, starboard engine		Fl 21119
38	Ignition switch, port engine		Fl 21119
39	Tailwheel locking switch		8-2768 E-3
40	Undercarriage control lever		
41	Landing flap and tailplane trim control lever		
42	Circuit breakers		
43	Back-trim button		
44	Fuel transfer control panel and mixture control switch		
45	Undercarriage and landing flaps position indicator		Fl 22854
46	Emergency bomb release lever		
47	Autopilot emergency disengage button		Fl 22557
48	Bomb-aimer's rudder trim button		
49	Aileron trim control		
50	Rudder trim control		
51	Elevator trim control		
52	Bomb arming lever		
53	Deleted		
54	Throttle lever, port engine		
55	Throttle lever, starboard engine		
56	Dive-brake control lever		
57	Propeller pitch control switch, port		9-9502

For space reasons other instruments were installed on the starboard side of the fuselage and in the engine nacelles. The radio equipment was installed on the rear wall of the cockpit.

This configuration was retained in versions with a "solid" nose. In aircraft with nose-mounted weapons, the guns and ammunition boxes projected into the cockpit beneath the instrument panel.

The Ju 88 G, the final night fighter variant, was equipped much more extensively and was scarcely comparable to the early versions. It is not possible to describe the instrumentation of every version of the Ju 88, therefore two bomber, one trainer, one reconnaissance, one *Zerstörer* and two night fighter versions will be depicted as examples.

During the course of large-scale production of the Ju 88 and other types, older aircraft were often updated and modified to the standards of newer variants. As well, many damaged aircraft were recovered and repaired, during which they were brought up to the latest technical standard. As a result, the instrument panels of Ju 88s often contain features of several variants, making it impossible to assign a precise designation.

The Bo-UK 1 clock (Fl 23885) was located in the control yoke. The Ju 88 A used a special lighting system for the instruments. Each instrument had its own light, which conveyed light to the face of the instrument by means of an illuminated frame.

No.	Item	Range	Part No.
58	Propeller pitch control switch, starboard		9-9502
59	Propeller pitch selector switch, port (manual/automatic)		
60	Propeller pitch selector switch, starboard (manual/automatic)		
61	Cooling gills control switch, port engine		FLE 6313-01
62	Cooling gills control switch, starboard engine		FLE 6313-01
63	Tail and propeller de-icing lever		
64	Ignition switch (starter), port engine		Fl 21212
65	Ignition switch (starter), starboard engine		Fl 21212
66	FB and FBH armature lever, port engine		
67	FB and FBH armature lever, starboard engine		
68	Supercharger control lever, port engine		
69	Supercharger control lever, starboard engine		
70	Engine priming control switch		
71	SUM AP 8 engine primer hand-pump		8-4505 A
72	Cockpit heating and ventilation control (port engine)		
73	Cockpit heating and ventilation control (starboard engine)		
74	Wing de-icing lever, port engine		
75	Wing de-icing lever, starboard engine		
76	Fuel hand-pump lever, port engine		
77	Fuel hand-pump lever, starboard engine		
78	Ignition battery box		
79	Emergency hydraulic switch for emergency operation of landing flaps and dive brakes		
80	Emergency hydraulic switch for emergency operation of undercarriage and undercarriage doors		
81	Hydraulic system hand-pump		
82	Starter fuel tank		
83	Lever for oil transfer, hand-pump		
84	Oil transfer system switch		
85	Emergency jettison lever for external tanks		
86	Lever for battery of fuel cocks, fuel jettison		
87	Impulse cross-valve control lever for fuel hand-pump, forward fuselage tank		
88	Fuel hand-pump lever, forward fuselage tank		
89	Electrical system circuit breaker panel with circuit breakers		
93	Emergency lever for three-button switch		
94	Life raft release lever		
Nacelle-mounted instruments:			
90	Oil temperature gauge	0 – 160° C	Fl 20308-3
91	Propeller pitch indicator		9-4548
92	Hydraulic pressure gauge	0 – 120 kg/cm²	Fl 20516-2

The improved **Ju 88 A-4** appeared in 1941. Powered by two 1,420 H.P. Jumo 211 J engines, it was produced in greater numbers than any other version of the Ju 88. The aircraft had extended wings, beneath which bomb racks were fitted. The **Ju 88 A-5** was an interim version between the A-1 and A-4. Powered by two Jumo 211 G engines, it was essentially the fuselage of the A-1 combined with the wings of the A-4.

At the time of its development, the Ju 88 was the fastest twin-engined bomber in service with the *Luftwaffe*, which made it a candidate for the reconnaissance and weather observation roles.

The **Ju 88 D** was based on the Ju 88 A-4 (D-1) or the A-5 (D-0, D-2) and differed little from the bomber versions. Additional fuel tanks and cameras were installed in the fuselage, resulting in some changes to the instrumentation.

The instrumentation of the subsequent Ju 88 G and P variants was in general derived from that of the examples given, but with additional equipment to meet their specialized roles.

Right side of the cockpit of the Ju 88 D-1 in the USA with control panel for the takeoff-assist rockets. (R.P. Lutz)

Cockpit of the Ju 88 D-1/trop in the USAF Museum. Some of the instruments have been replaced or supplemented by American equipment. Note the yellow-marked fuel consumption gauge at the top right. (R.P. Lutz)

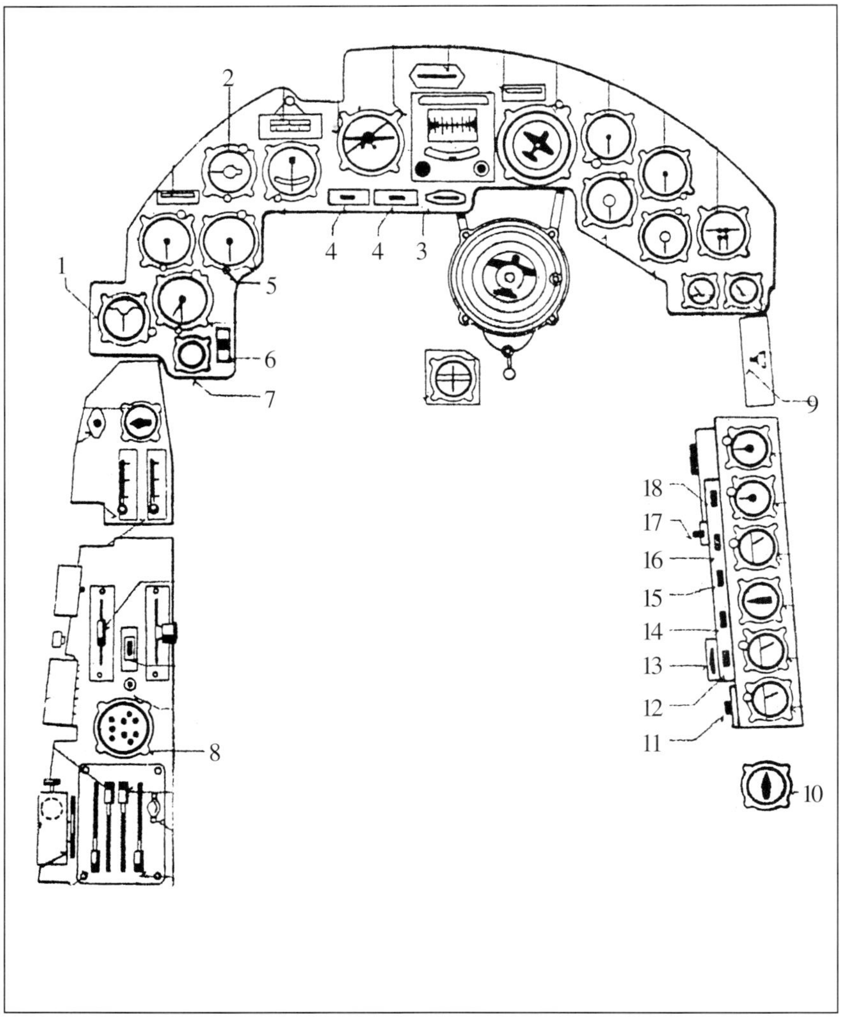

Instrumentation of the Ju 88 A-4. (Hafner Archive)

With the introduction of new radar and navigation aids, the equipment carried by the Ju 88 G night fighter, in particular, became ever more extensive. Further changes resulted from operational experience, crew requests, conversions and improvisations, resulting in instrument panels in which the instruments seem to have been placed at random and which bore little resemblance to those of the early Ju 88s.

The instrumentation of the **Ju 88 G-1** depicted on Page 228 was compiled based on historical photographs. Particularly interesting is the installation of a Siemens LGW-automatic navigator in this aircraft. This device, which was installed in some aircraft beginning in 1943, was a course calculator which determined distance flown and lateral deviation from a selected course.

The selected course or baseline was entered into a course selector along with the air temperature at altitude and the wind speed and direction. Two indicators showed the distance flown and the deviation from the selected track.

The most important changes in instrumentation of the Ju 88 A-4 compared to the Ju 88 A-1:

No.	Equipment	Instrument Range	Requisition/Equipment Number
1	Homing indicator later replaced by AFN 2		Ln 27002
2	Vertical speed indicator	-15 / +15 m/s	Fl 22382
3	Slide tray for DBS 1 compensation table		Fl 23501
4	External cargo carrier jettison switch		Fl 32349-2
5	Fine and coarse altimeter	0 – 10000 m	Fl 22320
6	Fuel consumption gauge selector switch		Fl 32345 ?
7	Fuel consumption gauge	0 – 600 l/h	9-2184 A-1
8	Undercarriage and landing flap position indicator (nine light system)		19-6818 A-1
9	Cruise/Homing selector switch		Fl ?
10	AKS-M4 control panel for takeoff-assist rockets		Fl 18330-4
11	Switch for single-engine flight		FL E 581506 D
12	Switch for auxiliary lights		Fl 32350
13	Propeller de-icing switch		Fl ?
14	Ultra-violet lighting switch		Fl 32350
15	Heated windscreen switch		Fl 32350
16	Engine lights switch		Fl 32350
17	Bomb selector switch		Fl 32327
18	Cockpit lighting switch		Fl 32350
	Propeller pitch indicators in engine nacelles deleted.		

Produced in 1944, the **Ju 88 A-16** was based on the A-4 and was the final training version of the Ju 88. It had an enlarged instrument panel housing two complete sets of flight instruments. The student occupied the left seat and the instructor the right.

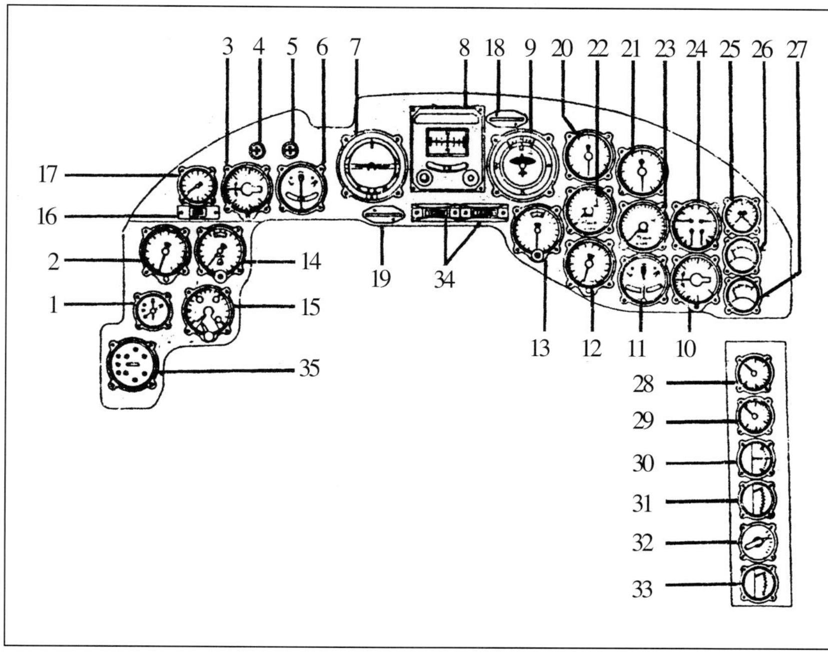

Ju 88 A-16 Instrumentation:

No.	Equipment	Instrument Range	Requisition/Equipment Number
1	AFN 2 homing indicator		Ln 27002
2	Student's airspeed indicator	80 – 750 km/h	Fl 22231
3	Student's vertical speed indicator	-15 / +15 m/s	Fl 22384
4	Pitot tube heat visual indicator		Fl 32530
5	Autopilot visual indicator		Fl 32530
6	Student's turn and bank indicator, electric		Fl 22406
7	Artificial horizon		Fl 22427
8	Lku 4 gyro compass		Fl 22561
9	PfK/f3 master compass indicator		Fl 23338
10	Instructor's vertical speed indicator	-15 / +15 m/s	Fl 22384
11	Instructor's turn and bank indicator, electric		Fl 22406
12	Instructor's airspeed indicator	80 – 750 km/h	Fl 22231
13	Contact altimeter	0 – 6000 m	Fl 22317
14	Fine and coarse altimeter	0 – 10000 m	Fl 22320
15	Radio altimeter (FuG 101a)	0 – 150/ 0 – 750 m	Ln 28330-1
16	Fuel consumption gauge selector switch		Fl 32345 ?
17	Fuel consumption gauge	0 – 600 l/h	9-2184 A-1
18	DBS 1 slide tray for operating data		Fl 23501
19	DBS 1 slide tray for deviation table		Fl 23501
20	Boost pressure gauge, port engine	0.6 – 1.8 atm	Fl 20555
21	Boost pressure gauge, starboard engine	0.6 – 1.8 atm	Fl 20555
22	Distant-reading RPM indicator, port engine	0 – 3,000 rpm	Fl 20384-3
23	Distant-reading RPM indicator, starboard engine	0 – 3,000 rpm	Fl 20384-3
24	Fuel/Oil pressure gauge	2 x 0-2 / 2 x 0-10 kg/cm²	Fl 20514-2
25	Hydraulic fluid double pressure gauge	2 x 0 – 160 kg/cm²	Fl 20512-6
26	Coolant temperature gauge, port	0 - 130° C	Fl 20342
27	Coolant temperature gauge, starboard	0 - 130° C	Fl 20342
28	Oxygen pressure gauge	0 – 250 kg/cm²	Fl 20496
29	Oxygen pressure gauge	0 – 250 kg/cm²	Fl 20496
30	Outside air temperature gauge	-60/+40° C	Fl 20349
31	Fuel/oil contents gauge		Fl 20723
32	Fuel/oil contents gauge selector switch		Fl 32336-3
33	Fuel gauge	0 – 1200 / 0 – 420 l	Fl 20723
34	External cargo carrier jettison		Fl 32349-2
35	Undercarriage and landing flap position indicators, nine lights		19-6818 A-1

Junkers Ju 88 R-1 in the RAF Museum. This night fighter was developed from the Ju 88 C-6.

The **Ju 88 C-6**, a *Zerstörer* with a heavy nose-mounted armament, entered service in 1942. It was based on the Ju 88 A-4 and also formed the basis for the radar-equipped **Ju 88 R-1** night fighter, which was powered by two BMW 801 radial engines.

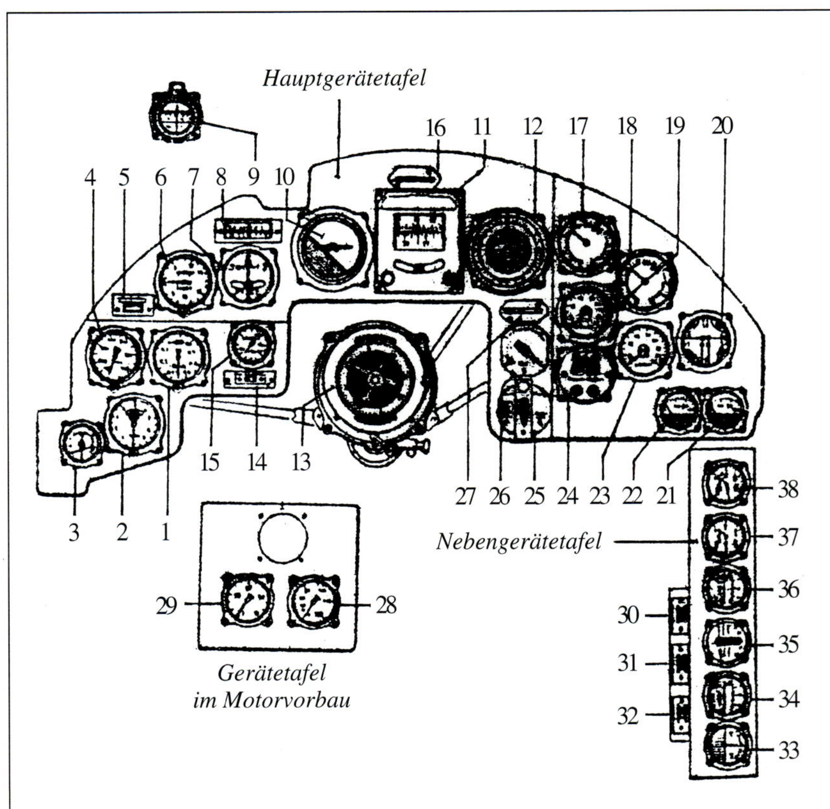

Instrumentation of a Ju 88 C-6.

Ju 88 C-6 Instrumentation:

No.	Equipment	Instrument Range	Requisition/Equipment Number
1	Fine and coarse altimeter	0 – 10000 m	Fl 22320
2	Coarse altimeter	0 – 10000 m	Fl 22316-10
3	AFN 2 homing indicator		Ln 27002
4	Airspeed indicator	80 – 750 km/h	Fl 22231
5	Pitot tube heat visual indicator		Fl 32525-4
6	Vertical speed indicator	-15 / +15 m/s	Fl 22384
7	Turn and bank indicator, electric		Fl 22406
8	Lkz 3 course indicator		Fl 22562
9	FK 38 standby compass		Fl 23233
10	Artificial horizon		Fl 22427
11	Gyro compass		Fl 22561
12	PfK/f3 master compass indicator		Fl 23338
13	Radio DF indicator with DF repeater compass PFA/R		Fl 23470
14	Fuel consumption gauge selector switch		Fl 32345 ?
15	Fuel consumption gauge	0 – 600 l/h	9-2184 A-1
16	DBS 1 slide tray with aircraft operating data		Fl 23501
17	Boost pressure gauge, port engine	0.6 – 1.8 atm	Fl 20555
18	Boost pressure gauge, starboard engine	0.6 – 1.8 atm	Fl 20555
19	Distant-reading RPM indicator, port engine	0 – 3,000 rpm	Fl 20384-3
20	Coolant/oil pressure gauge	2 x 0 – 2 / 2 x 0 – 10 kg/cm²	Fl 20514-2
21	Coolant temperature gauge, starboard	0 – 130° C	Fl 20342
22	Coolant temperature gauge, port	0 - 130° C	Fl 20342
23	Distant-reading RPM indicator, starboard engine	0 – 3,000 rpm	Fl 20384-3
24	ZVK-FF cannon round counter (MG FF)		
25	Autopilot switch		
26	Propeller de-ice switch		
27	DBS 1 slide tray with deviation table		Fl 23501
30	Gun sight glass heat switch		Fl 32350
31	Ultra-violet light switch		Fl 32350
32	Auxiliary light switch		Fl 32350
33	Outside air temperature gauge	-60 / +40° C	Fl 20349
34	Fuel contents gauge	0 – 1200 / 0 – 420 l	Fl 20723
35	Fuel/oil contents gauge selector switch		Fl 32336-3
36	Fuel/oil contents gauge		Fl 20723
37	Oxygen pressure gauge (observer)	0 – 250 kg/cm²	Fl 20496
38	Oxygen pressure gauge (pilot)	0 – 250 kg/cm²	Fl 20496
	Nacelle-mounted instruments:		
28	Oil temperature gauge	0 - 160° C	Fl 20308-3
29	Hydraulic system pressure gauge	0 – 120 kg/cm²	Fl 20516-2

Pilot's station of the Ju 88 R-1 in the RAF Museum. Visible at the bottom right are the ammunition boxes for some of the nose-mounted weapons. Some instruments are missing.

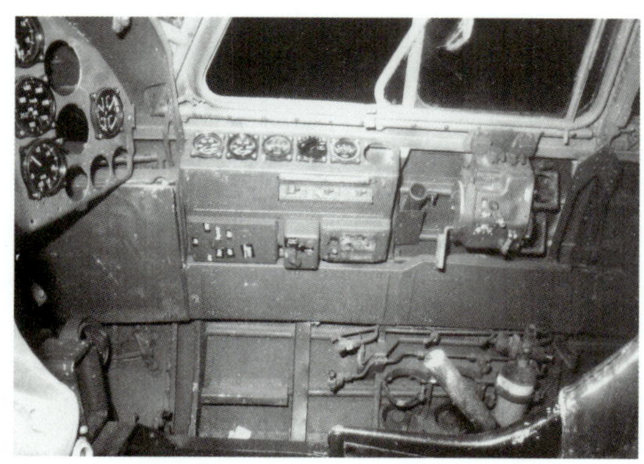

Right side of the cockpit of the Ju 88 R-1 with auxiliary instrument panel.

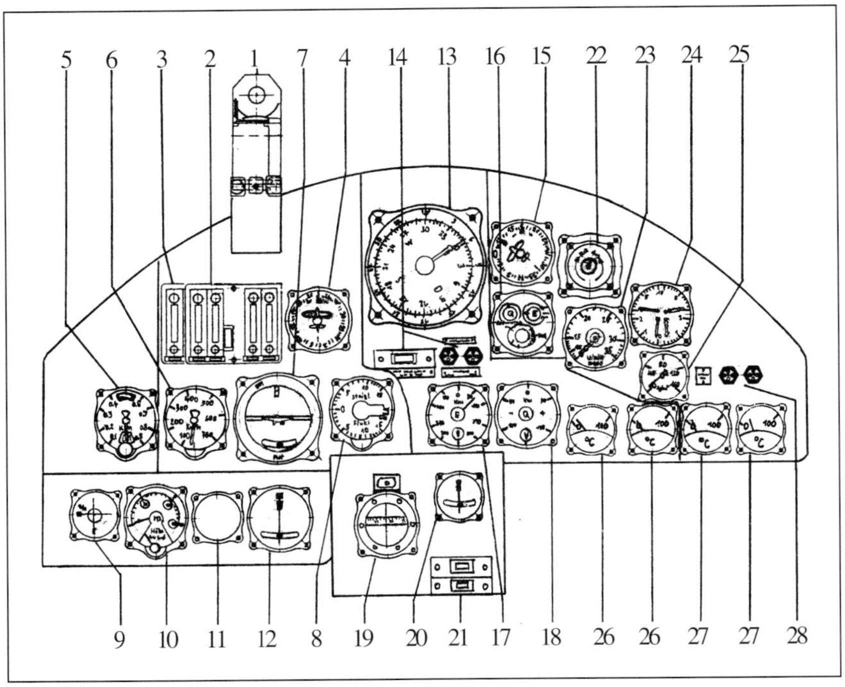

Instrumentation of a Ju 88 G-1 with automatic navigator:

No.	Equipment	Instrument Range	Requisition/Equipment Number
1	Revi 16 B gun sight		Fl 52955
2	ZSK K 4 ammunition counter		Fl 47319
3	SZ 500 ammunition counter		Fl 47312
4	PfK/f2 master compass indicator		Fl 23334
5	Fine and coarse altimeter	0 – 10000 m	Fl 22320
6	Airspeed indicator	80 – 750 km/h	Fl 22231
7	Combined turn and bank indicator and artificial horizon		Fl 22411
8	Vertical speed indicator	-15 / +15 m/s	Fl 22384
9	AFN 2 homing indicator		Ln 27002
10	FuG 101a radio altimeter	0 – 150 / 0 – 750 m	Ln 28330-1
11	Unidentified (outside air temperature gauge?)		Fl 20349 ?
12	Turn and bank indicator, electric		Fl 22412 ?
13	Patin KT/p2 DF repeater compass		Fl 23474
14	Selector switch, purpose not known		Fl 32345
	2 visual indicators, purpose not known		Fl 32530
15	PfK/f2 master compass indicator (course selector for navigation computer?)		Fl 23334
16	Automatic navigator control device		
17	Automatic navigator indicator for ranges of	0 – 500 km	
18	Automatic navigator deviation indicator left/right of baseline	0 – 150 km	
19	FK 38 magnetic compass		Fl 23233
20	Emergency turn and bank indicator		Fl 22413
21	2 selector switches		Fl 32345 ?
22	Cockpit lighting dimmer switch		Fl 32401
23	Double RPM indicator	2 x 500 – 3,600 rpm	Fl 20270
24	Fuel/oil pressure gauge	2 x 0 – 2 / 0 – 10 kg/cm²	Fl 20514-2
25	Hydraulic system pressure gauge	0 – 160 kg/cm²	Fl 20516-3
26	2 coolant temperature gauges	0 - 130° C	Fl 20342
27	2 oil temperature gauges	0 - 130° C	Fl 20342
28	2 visual indicators, purpose not known		Fl 32350

Missing from the instrument panel are the gyro compass and boost pressure gauges for the two BMW 801 D engines of the Ju 88 G-1. These instruments were probably located elsewhere in the cockpit.

Ju 388 L-1 in storage at the National Air and Space Museum. (P.F. Selinger)

Junkers Ju 388

At a relatively stage in the development of the Ju 88, Junkers began thinking about a successor. Then, in 1939, came the "Bomber B" program, a specification for a high-performance bomber to enter service in 1943. The Jumo 222, a 24-cylinder engine capable of producing 2,000 H.P., was in the test stage at that time and it became inextricably linked with the program.

Junkers developed the twin-engined Ju 288, which combined the new engine and a number of technical innovations. By 1942, however, it had become obvious that the new wonder bomber would never enter production, and the "Bomber B" program was subsequently abandoned.

With the *Luftwaffe* now seeking a high-altitude, high-performance bomber more than ever, Junkers concentrated on the Ju 188, which was a privately funded development of the Ju 88. It differed from its predecessor in having a roomy, spherically-glazed cabin and larger overall dimensions. The aircraft was also equipped with more powerful engines such as the BMW 801 and the Jumo 213.

Various projects derived from the Ju 188 were abandoned, until in autumn 1943 Junkers put forward the Ju 388, a high-altitude aircraft which would be capable of intercepting the British Mosquito. Three variants were projected, the Ju 388 J *Zerstörer* and night fighter, the Ju 388 K bomber and the Ju 388 L reconnaissance aircraft. Proposed power plants were the Jumo 213, Jumo 222 and, in particular, the 2,760 H.P. BMW 801 TJ with exhaust-driven turbosuperchargers and four-blade propellers.

Cockpit of the stored Ju 388 L-1. On the right is a radar scope and beneath it elements of a radio system installed by the Americans for test flights. (R.P. Lutz)

Close-up of the pilot's instrument panel housing the flight instruments. The stickers on the instruments were applied by the Americans. (R.P. Lutz)

Part of the right fuselage side wall with some of the engine instruments. (R.P. Lutz)

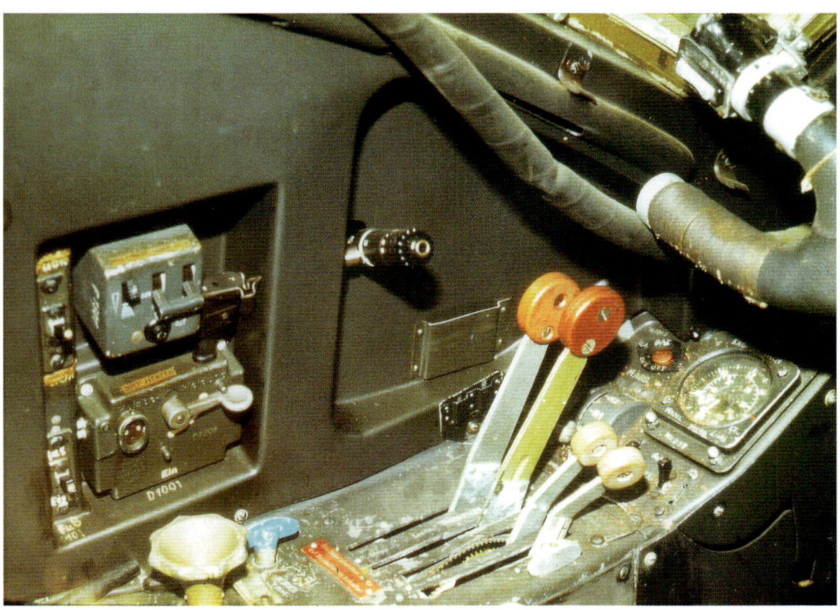

Close-up of the left console with throttle levers and control horn in the folded position. (R.P. Lutz)

In response to the high priority assigned to this aircraft, Junkers opted to use components from the airframe of the Ju 188 E. The design also included a pressurized cockpit, hot-air de-icing and a remote-controlled barbette in the tail.

Production of the Ju 388 began in autumn 1944 and only about 150 machines were delivered. From a technical standpoint, the Ju 388 was one of the best piston-engined aircraft of its day.

The only survivor is a Ju 388 L-1 (*Werknummer* 560049) which was found by the Americans in Merseburg in May 1945. In September 1945 the aircraft was test flown in the USA. Since then it has been in storage for the National Air and Space Museum. The interior photographs presented here depict this aircraft.

Like most German aircraft with a glazed fuselage nose, the Ju 388's crew were grouped in the forward fuselage. Depending on the version, the crew

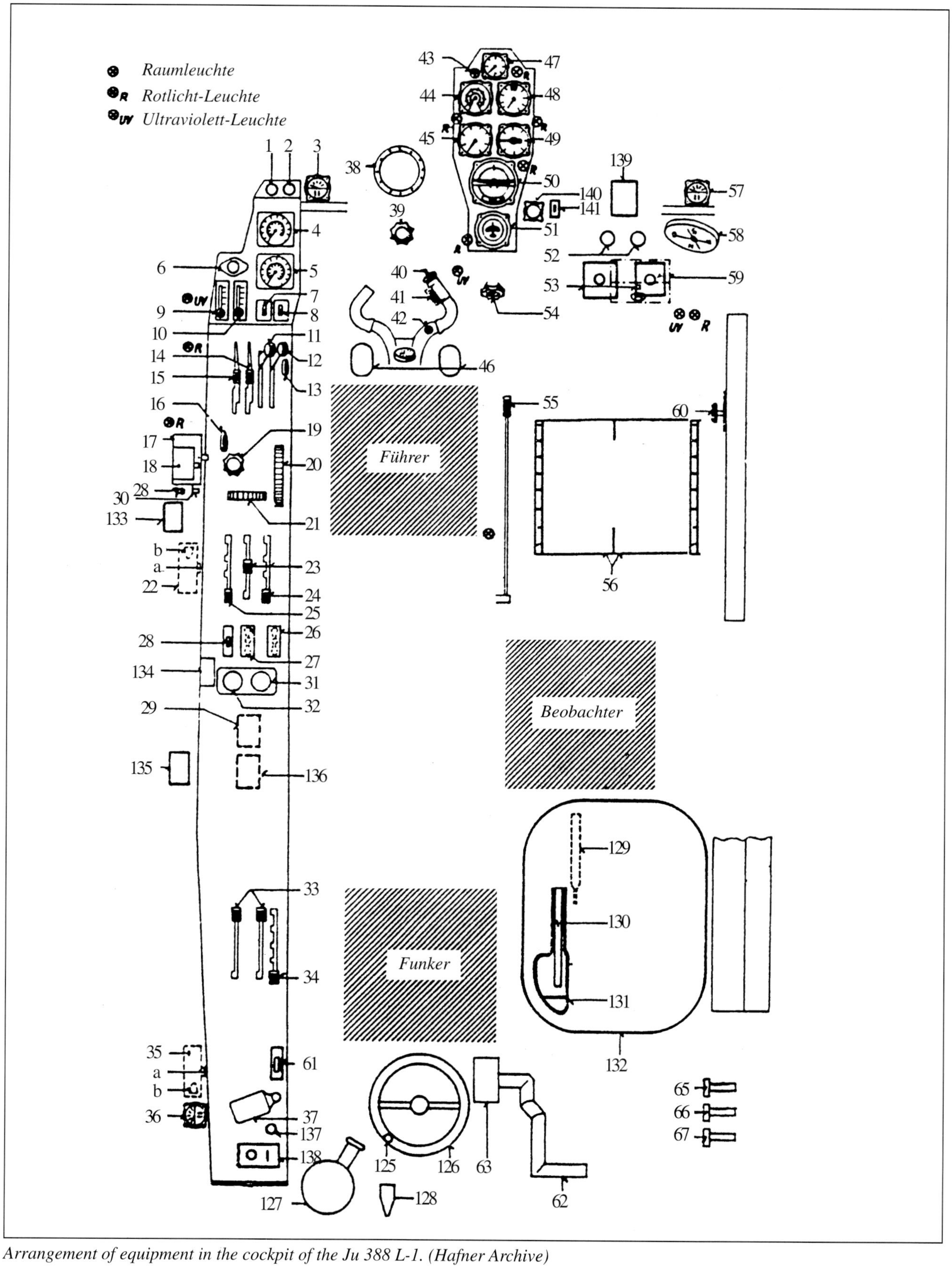

Arrangement of equipment in the cockpit of the Ju 388 L-1. (Hafner Archive)

consisted of three or four men. The basic layout of the cockpit was derived from the Ju 188.

On the left was a large console containing the engine controls, the most important engine instruments and the trim controls. In front was a narrow panel with the flight and navigation instruments. The right side wall accommodated the remaining engine instruments, the undercarriage and flap controls, the main electrical panel and, in the bomber version, the bomb sequence selector panel. The radio equipment was located against the rear wall of the cockpit.

The accompanying list of equipment for the **Ju 388 L-1** was compiled based on the operating notes for the Ju 388 J-1 and L-1 and photographs of the aircraft interior.

Equipment of the Ju 388 L-1:

No.	Equipment	Instrument Range	Requisition/Equipment Number
1	Visual indicator, mixture control port engine		Fl 32530
2	Visual indicator, mixture control starboard engine		Fl 32530
3	Pilot's oxygen indicator		
4	RPM indicator-boost pressure gauge for starboard engine		Fl 20569
5	As 4 for port engine		Fl 20569
6	Electrical system cutout switch		19-5836 A-1
7	Automatic propeller pitch control switch, port engine		
8	Automatic propeller pitch control switch, starboard engine		
9	Ignition switch, port engine		Fl 21118
10	Ignition switch, starboard engine		Fl 21118
11	Turbine control operating lever, port engine		
12	Turbine control operating lever, starboard engine		
13	Brake lever		
14	Throttle lever, starboard engine		
15	Throttle lever, port engine		
16	Ventilation control handle (left)		
17	Pilot's heated flight suit plug		Fl 32403
18	Pilot's intercom system controls		
19	Rudder trim wheel		
20	Elevator trim wheel		
21	Aileron trim wheel		
22	Pilot's high-altitude breathing apparatus		
23	Fuel jettison lever		
24	Operating lever for FB armature, starboard engine		
25	Operating lever for FB armature, port engine		
26	Ignition switch (starter), starboard engine		
27	Ignition switch (starter), port engine		
28	Transmit button selector switch		Fl 32346
29	Remote controls for radio set (R/T)		
30	Radio altimeter (FuG 101) switch		
31	Engine primer hand pump, starboard engine		
32	Engine primer hand pump, port engine		
33	Wing de-ice control levers, left and right		
34	Cockpit climate control vent control lever		
35	Radio operator's high-altitude breathing apparatus		
36	Radio operator's oxygen OR		
37	Morse key		
38	FK 42 back-up compass ?		Fl 23238
39	Box wrench for high-speed compensating valve (climate control)		
40	LRg turn control with autopilot coupling switch		
41	Trim setting switch		
42	Transmit button		
43	Pitot tube heat visual indicator		Fl 32530-6
44	FuG 101a indicator	0 – 150 / 0 – 750 m	Ln 28330-1
45	Airspeed indicator	100 – 900 km/h	Fl 22234
46	Mainwheel brakes foot pump		
47	AFN 2 homing indicator		Ln 27002
48	Fine and coarse altimeter	0 – 13000 m	Fl 22322
49	Vertical speed indicator	+15 / -15 m/s	Fl 22384
50	Combined turn and bank indicator and artificial horizon		Fl 22415-1
51	PFK/f2 master compass indicator		Fl 23334
52	Night photography system frame indicator		
53	Night photography system frame control		
54	Box wrench for high-speed compensating valve (climate control)		
55	Canopy jettison handle		
56	Floor window cover pane;		
57	Observer's oxygen indicator		
58	Patin KT-p2 DF repeater compass		Fl 23374
59	Daylight photography interval control		
60	Ventilation control handle, right		
61	Morse selector switch		
62	Hydraulic hand pump lever		

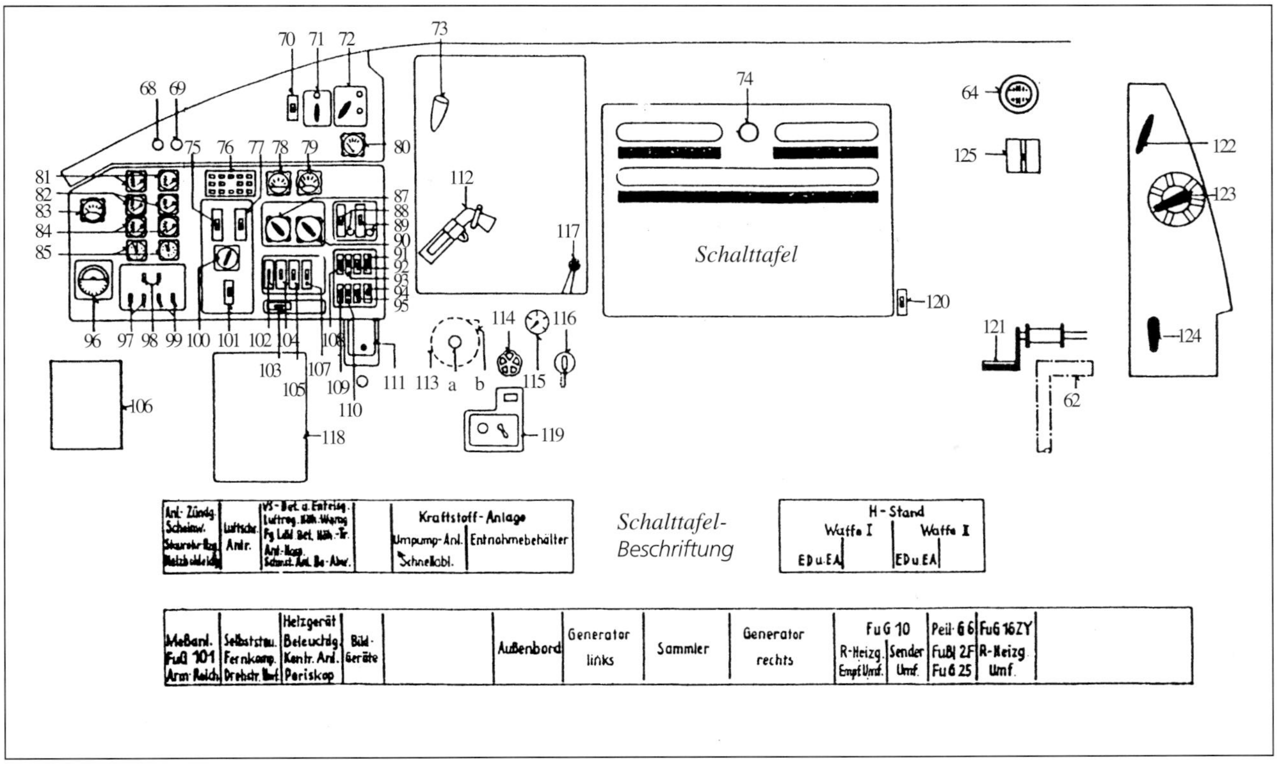

Arrangement of equipment on the right fuselage side wall of the Ju 388 L-1. (Hafner Archive)

63	Hydraulic hand pump		
64	Cockpit pressure warning horn		
65	Pilot's oxygen flow valve		Fl 30508
66	Observer's oxygen flow valve		Fl 30508
67	Radio operator's oxygen flow valve		Fl 30508
68	Warm air heating visual indicator, port wing		Fl 32530
69	Warm air heating visual indicator, starboard wing		Fl 32530
70	FuG 25 toggle switch		
71	DF loop control switch		
72	Intercom controls		
73	Flare pistol firing port		
74	Voltmeter		
75	Toggle switch for landing flap and tailplane trim controls		
76	Visual indicators for undercarriage and landing flaps		19-6822 A
78	Oil and fuel contents gauge	0 – 400 / 1200 l	Fl 20723
79	Fuel contents gauge	0 - ? l	Fl 20723
80	Hydraulic fluid pressure gauge	0 – 160 kg/cm²	Fl 20516-3
81	Oil inlet temperature gauge	0 - 130° C	Fl 20358
82	Oil pressure gauge	0 – 15 kg/cm²	Fl 20584
83	Outside air temperature gauge	-60 / +40° C	Fl 20349
84	Fuel pressure gauge	0 – 3 kg/cm²	Fl 20582
85	Propeller pitch indicator		Fl 20845
86	Deleted		
87	Fuel transfer and jettison switch		
88	Bomb door toggle switch and visual indicator		
89	Toggle switch and indicator lights for on-board heating (tailplane de-ice)		
90	Fuel gauge selector switch		
91	Pitot tube heat toggle switch		Fl 32350 ?
92	Ultra-violet lighting toggle switch		Fl 32350 ?

Instead of an oxygen indicator combined with the oxygen flow meter, early production aircraft were apparently equipped with a separate oxygen pressure gauge (Fl 30496) and oxygen flow meter (Fl 30489). The oxygen pressure gauge for the pilot and observer in the stored Ju 388 L is located at the top left of the panel on the starboard side of the aircraft. An oxygen flow meter is also installed there in place of the new oxygen indicator.

The stored Ju 388 has several other deviations in equipment. The propeller pitch indicator is missing and an additional switch (19-5843) is present beneath the outside air temperature gauge. As well a radar scope is present beside the forward instrument console.

93	Navigation lights toggle switch		Fl 32350 ?
94	Instrument lights toggle switch		Fl 32350 ?
95	Propeller de-ice toggle switch		Fl 32350 ?
96	Cockpit pressure gauge	0 – 15 km / 0 – 0.6 atm	Fl 22325
97	Toggle switch – oil cooler air control		
98	Propeller pitch control manual selector switch		
99	Toggle switch – cylinder cooling air control		
100	Gyro compass selector switch		
101	Autopilot master switch		Fl 32346
102	Toggle switch – 2nd reserve pump in port relief tank		Fl 32346
103	Fuel jettison toggle switch, auxiliary fuel tank in starboard wing		
104	Toggle switch – 2nd reserve pump in starboard relief tank		Fl 32346
105	Toggle switch – reserve pump in forward fuselage tank		Fl 32346
106	Unidentified		
107	Toggle switch – reserve pump in rear fuselage tank		Fl 32346
108	Landing light toggle switch		Fl 32350 ?
109	Auxiliary navigation lights toggle switch		Fl 32350 ?
110	Fuel transfer system toggle switch		Fl 32350 ?
111	Intercom controls		
112	Flare pistol		
113	Observer's high-altitude breathing apparatus		
114	Hand-wheel		
115	Pressure gauge	0 – 160 kg/cm^2	Fl 20516-3
116	Filler point		
117	Operating lever		
118	ZZG 1/24 delayed-action fuse control		
119	Observer's heated flight suit connector socket		Fl 32403
120	Cockpit lighting toggle switch		Fl 32350 ?
121	Hand crank for operation of sliding cover over camera window in bomb bay		
122	Life raft jettison handle		
123	Emergency hydraulic switch		
124	Operating lever for battery of fuel valves on Frame 9		
125	Canopy button		
126	FA 15 controls		
127	Periscope		
128	Periscope foot-switch		
129	Lever for opening entry hatch from outside		
130	Lever for opening entry hatch from inside		
131	Recessed handle for jettisoning entry hatch		
132	Entry hatch		
133	Connector socket, pilot		
134	Relay box for FuG 16 ZY		
135	Resistance box		
136	AD 17 connector socket		Ln 26991
137	Transmit button		
138	Controls for radio operator's intercom		
139	SKF 35 control panel (for night operations)		
140	Infrared lights dimmer switch		Fl 32402
141	Infrared lights switch		

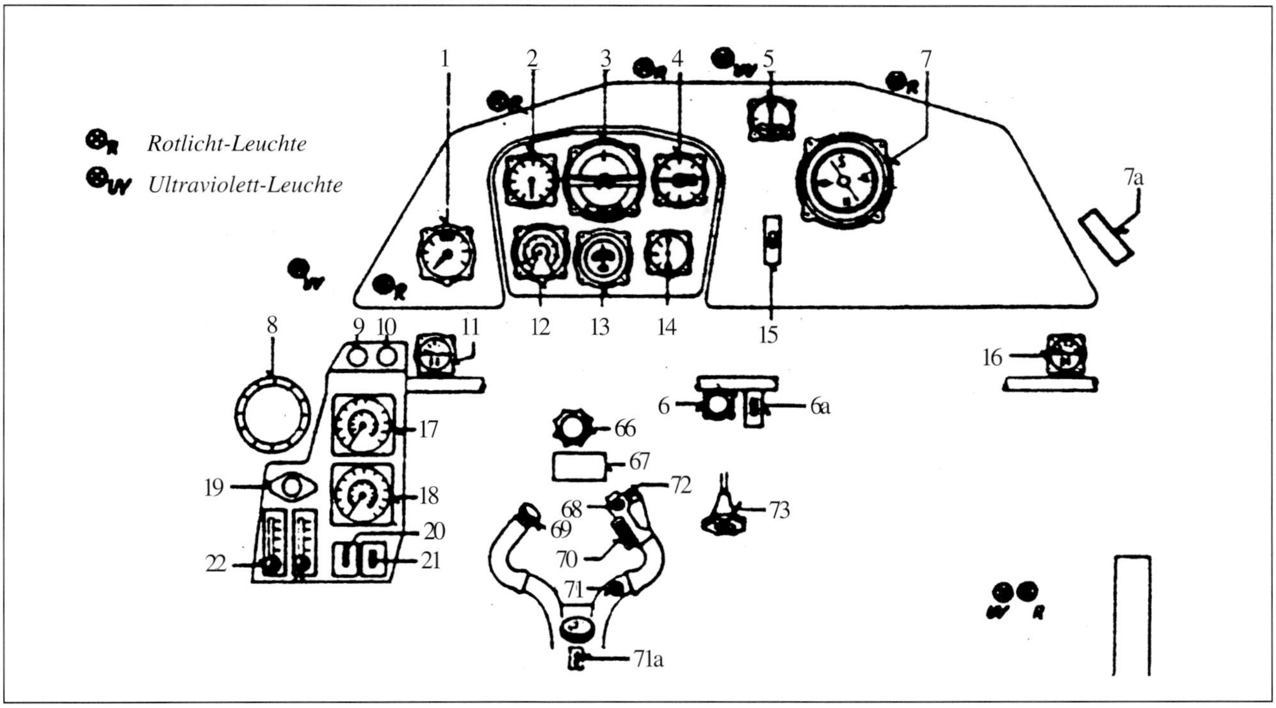

Instrumentation of the Ju 388 J-1. (Hafner Archive)

Forward instrument panel of the Ju 388 J-1:

No.	Equipment	Instrument Range	Requisition/Equipment Number
1	Fine and coarse altimeter	0 – 13000 m	Fl 22322
2	Airspeed indicator	100 – 900 km/h	Fl 22234
3	Combined turn and bank indicator and artificial horizon		Fl 22415-1
4	Vertical speed indicator	+15 / -15 m/s	Fl 22384
5	Supplementary turn and bank indicator		Fl 22412 ?
6	Infrared lights dimmer switch		Fl 32402
6a	Infrared lights switch		Fl 32350
7	Patin KT-p2 DF repeater compass		Fl 23374
7a	Gun sight stowed position		
8	FK 42 (?) back-up compass		Fl 23238
9	Mixture control visual indicator, port engine		Fl 32350
10	Mixture control visual indicator, starboard engine	Fl 32350	
11	Pilot's oxygen indicator		
12	FuG 101a indicator	0 – 150 / 0 – 750 m	Ln 28330-1
13	PFK/f2 master compass indicator		Fl 23334
14	AFN 2 homing indicator		Ln 27002
15	Safety switch		
16	Radio-radar operator's oxygen indicator		
17	RPM indicator/boost pressure gauge, starboard engine	500 – 3,600 rpm/ 0.6-1.8 atm	Fl 20569
18	RPM indicator/boost pressure gauge, port engine	500 – 3,600 rpm/ 0.6-1.8 atm	Fl 20569
19	Electrical system cutout switch		19-5836 A-1
20	Automatic pitch control switch, port engine		
21	Automatic pitch control switch, starboard engine		
22	Ignition switches, port and starboard engines		Fl 21118
66	Box wrench for high-speed compensating valve (climate control)		
67	Reflector gun sight		
68	Firing button		
69	LRg 12 B turn control		Fl 22536
70	Trim selector switch		
71	Transmit button		
71a	Control surface drive coupling switch		
72	Firing button		
73	Ventilation control, right		

The **Ju 388 J** had a solid nose and the flight instruments were contained in the standard blind flying panel. The remaining equipment was virtually identical to that of the other versions, with minor exceptions.

There were, no doubt, deviations in the described equipment or it is possible that some instruments may have been deleted due to equipment shortages.

An early Bf 109 B with Schwarz wooden propeller.

Messerschmitt Bf 109

Willy Messerschmitt made a name for himself in the early 1930s by designing a number of successful sporting and commercial aircraft. Then, in the summer of 1934, he was invited by the recently-founded State Ministry of Aviation (RLM) to participate in the development of a modern fighter aircraft. Messerschmitt agreed, although he felt his chances of success were slim. His competitors already had prototypes and he had no experience designing military aircraft.

The specification called for a monoplane with the smallest possible airframe and the most powerful available German engine. In the months that followed, the sleek Messerschmitt Bf 109 took form on the drawing boards. It was a cantilever monoplane of stressed-skin construction with an enclosed cockpit and retractable undercarriage. The small airframe resulted in a fairly high wing loading and the design incorporated high-lift devices—automatic leading edge slats and slotted ailerons.

The first prototype, powered by a Rolls Royce engine, took to the air for the first time in May 1935. The Bf 109 subsequently won the competition, in no small part because it had been designed with ease of production in mind. The *Luftwaffe*'s standard fighter had been born.

The Bf 109 was shown internationally for the first time in 1937 and soon afterwards a specially modified version captured the world speed record for land planes for Germany.

Seven major production variants were produced (B, C, D, E, F, G and K), with over 100 sub-variants, and the Messerschmitt Bf 109 was built in greater numbers than any other German aircraft.

The demand for improved performance resulted in the installation of ever more powerful engines. The spectrum ranged from the 680 H.P. Jumo 210 (Bf 109 B) through the 1,100 H.P. DB 601 (Bf 109 E) and the 1,475 H.P. DB 605 A (Bf 109 G) to the 1,800 H.P. DB 605 D in the Bf 109 K.

The airframe and undercarriage of the Bf 109 were strengthened several times to keep pace with weight increases. As the aircraft's external dimensions remained virtually unchanged, the addition of new equipment resulted in external fairings and covers, which ultimately resulted in the aircraft being nicknamed "*Beule*" (bump or bulge).

As the aircraft's weight increased and its aerodynamic form deteriorated, handling qualities suffered, a problem which was never completely solved. Another problem area was the type/s narrow-track undercarriage, which led to numerous accidents, especially in training.

By the end of the war in May 1945, almost 31,000 Messerschmitt Bf 109s had left the production lines. In addition, the type was built under license in the CSSR (550) and Spain (ca. 170). The type was flown by the air forces of Switzerland, Hun-

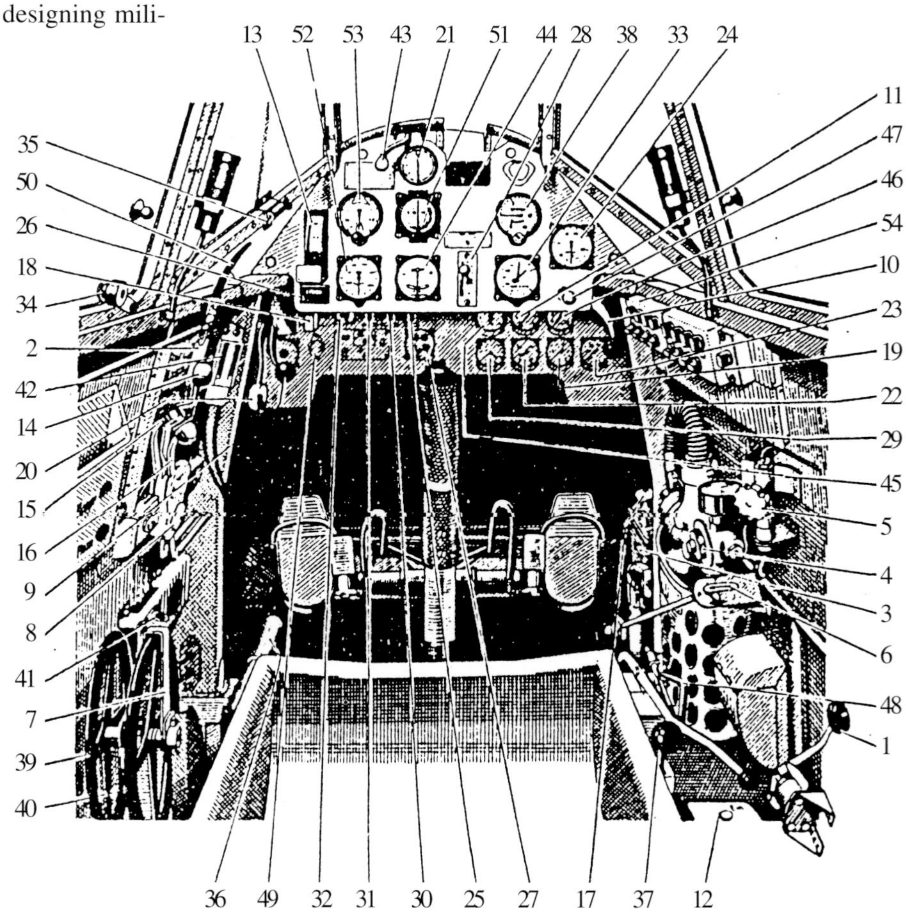

Cockpit of the Bf 109 B. (Hafner Archive)

Bf 109 B Equipment:

	Equipment	Instrument Range	Requisition/Equipment Number
1	Tailwheel locking lever		
2	Operating data table		
3	Tank associated with 17		
4	Breathing apparatus		Fl 30400-2
5	Remote-control valve		
6	Undercarriage switch		
7	Landing flaps control lever and tailplane trim wheel		
8	Wing-nut for throttle friction lock		
9	Fuel cock lever		
10	Lever for fuel hand-pump		
11	Fuel pressure gauge	0 – 0.5 kg/cm²	Fl 20505
	or differential pressure gauge	0 – 0.5 kg/cm²	D 1005
12	Remote controlled master switch		Fl 32314
13	Ignition switch		Fl 21119
14	Throttle lever		
15	High-altitude throttle lever		
16	Supercharger operating lever		
17	SUM APB 6 engine primer hand-pump	8-4506 A	
18	Ignition switch (starter)		Fl 21211
19	Oil pressure gauge	0 – 10 kg/cm²	Fl 20606
20	Radiator flap lever		
21	Clock (Junghans)		Fl 22600
22	Coolant temperature gauge	30 - 120° C	Fl 20314-4
23	Double oil temperature gauge	0 – 120° C	Fl 20330-4
24	RPM indicator	600 – 3,600 rpm	Fl 20220
25	Pitot tube heat switch		Fl 32316
26	Pitot tube heat visual indicator		Fl 32525-3
27	Undercarriage position indicator (four lights)		Fl 32526
28	Propeller pitch control switch*		9-9500-20
29	Mechanical propeller position indicator		9-9500-60
30	Navigation lights switch		Fl 32316
31	Instrument panel lighting switch		Fl 32316
32	Dimmer switch		Fl 32402
33	Boost pressure gauge	0.5 – 1.5 atm	Fl 20550
34	Cockpit canopy lever		
35	Sliding panel lock		
36	Seat adjustment lever		
37	Belt adjustment lever		
38	Statoscope-vertical speed indicator	–10 / +10 or –15 / +15 m/s	Fl 22381
39	Landing flap control wheel		
40	Tailplane trim wheel		
41	Tailplane trim visual indicator		
42	Undercarriage position visual indicator		
43	Cockpit ventilation hand-lever		
44	Turn-and-bank indicator, pneumatic		Fl 22402
45	Turn-and-bank indicator sensitivity control		Fl 22405
46	Fuel contents gauge	0 – 340 l	Fl 20704
47	Fuel gauge pump		Fl 20742-1
48	Undercarriage emergency lowering handle		
49	Electrical system cut-out switch		Fl 32315
50	Canopy jettison lever		
51	FK 5 magnetic compass		Fl 23211
52	Airspeed indicator	120 – 750 km/h	Fl 22231
53	Fine and coarse altimeter	0 – 10000 m	Fl 22320
54	Circuit breaker panel		Fl 32361-1
		and	Fl 32362

In addition there was the gun sight connector socket (Fl 32624) and the Revi (3 C or C/12) gun sight on the upper instrument panel. An oscillation indicator (Fl 26751) was installed to the left of 49.

*The position indicator and pitch control switch were absent on early Bf 109 B-1s with Schwarz wooden propellers.

gary, Yugoslavia, Croatia, Bulgaria, Romania, Italy, Finland and Slovakia.

Having been produced in such large numbers, and because of the type's ongoing popularity, more than 80 complete and partial aircraft have survived. Thirty of these are former Spanish air force machines.

The interior shots presented here include photographs of the following aircraft:

Bf 109 E-1 (E-3), WNr. 790 in the Deutsches Museum
Bf 109 E-3, WNr. 2422, J-355 in the aviation museum in Dubendorf, Switzerland
Bf 109 G-2/trop, WNr. 14753 "White 3" in the Laatzen Aviation Museum
Bf 109 G-6 WNr. 163284 in the Australian War Memorial, Canberra
Bf 109 G-6 (HA 1112, serial number 156) D-FMBB of the Messerschmitt Foundation
Bf 109 G-14/AS WNr. ??? 345 "White 13" privately owned
HA 1112 M-1L (C.4K-156), 471-28 in the Musée de l'Air, Paris

From the beginning the small airframe of the Bf 109 meant that space within the cockpit was minimal. The arrangement of controls and instruments around the pilot followed the standards of the day.

On the left were the trim wheels, engine primer hand-pump and the throttle lever. The instrument panel was located in the center, while on the right were the electrical panel with circuit breakers, oxygen system and, beginning with the F-series, the controls for the radio equipment.

Late Bf 109 E with FK 38 master compass. (Fernandez-Sommerau Collection)

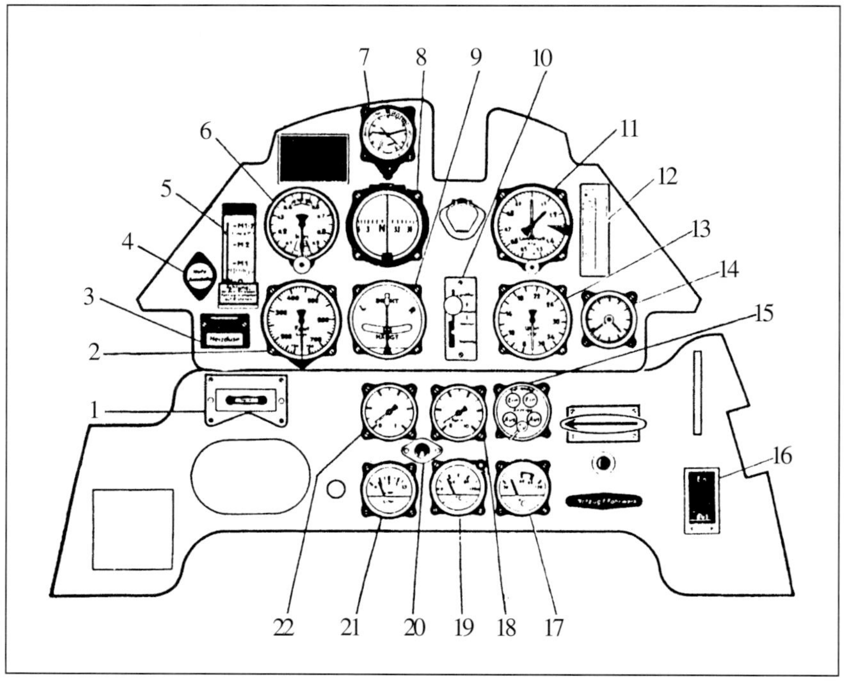

Bf 109 C and D Instrument Panel:

Equipment		Instrument Range	Requisition/Equipment Number
1	Starter switch		Fl 21211
2	Airspeed indicator	120 – 750 km/h	Fl 22231
3	Pitot tube heat visual indicator		Fl 32525-3
4	Electrical system cut-out switch		Fl 32315-2
5	Ignition switch		Fl 21119
6	Fine and coarse altimeter	0 – 10000 m	Fl 22230
7	Bo-UK 1 clock		Fl 23885
8	FK 5 magnetic compass		Fl 23211
9	Turn-and-bank indicator, pneumatic		Fl 22402
10	Propeller pitch control switch		9-9500-20
11	Boost pressure gauge	0.6 – 1.8 atm	Fl 20550
12	Deviation table		Fl 23906
13	RPM indicator	600 – 3,600 rpm	Fl 20220
14	Propeller pitch indicator, mechanical	9-9500-31	
15	Undercarriage position indicator (four lights)		Fl 32526
16	Undercarriage position indicator, mechanical		BFW
17	Coolant outlet temperature gauge	40 – 120° C	Fl 20342-2
18	Fuel – oil pressure gauge	0 – 2 /	Fl 20512-2
	Bf 109 D:	0 – 10 kg/cm²	
	Oil pressure gauge	0 – 10 kg/cm²	Fl 20625
604	Indicator (switchable) for oil inlet – outlet temperature	0 – 120° C	Fl 20343
20	Low fuel warning light (red)		Fl 32262-1
21	Fuel contents gauge	0 – 400 l ?	Fl 20723
22	Fuel differential pressure gauge (Bf 109 D only)	0 – 1 kg/cm²	Fl 20515

Instrument panel of a Bf 109 E with telescopic gun sight. (Griehl Collection)

Messerschmitt Bf 109 E-3 in the Deutsches Museum.

Cockpit of the Bf 109 in the Deutsches Museum. The aircraft came from Spain and was restored in 1960. Some placards bear Spanish text. The propeller pitch control switch on the instrument panel should not be there, as the thumb switch is present on the throttle lever.

Three variations of instrument panel were installed in the Bf 109 during the course of its development.

In versions up to and including the Bf 109 E, the instrument panel was in two parts, an upper part housing the flight and navigation instruments plus the most important engine instruments, and a lower part with the remaining engine instruments, the undercarriage indicators and the control boxes for the fixed weapons. Fighter-bomber versions of the Bf 109 E were also fitted with an auxiliary panel housing the bomb selector panel.

The Bf 109 F and G had a single instrument panel with a separate, vibration-damped center-section (blind-flying panel) for the four most important flight and navigation instruments. All of the engine instruments were grouped to the right of the blind-flying panel. The instrument panel support frame housed the round counters, reflector sight and clock. Beginning roughly with the Bf 109 G-4, the instrument panel and its support frame were made of birch plywood in an effort to conserve metals.

The instrument panel of the Bf 109 K was similar in configuration to that of the G, however the standard blind-flying panel (Fl 22000) was incorporated in the center of the instrument panel.

The HA 1109 and HA 1112, which were built under licence in Spain after 1945, were based on the Bf 109 G-2 and had similar instrument panels.

The **Bf 109 B** was the first version delivered to the Luftwaffe in numbers. Later it saw widespread use in fighter training schools. The **Bf 109 C and D** had comparable instrumentation, however there was some variation in the instruments installed. The vertical speed indicator was deleted and was not adopted as standard again until the appearance of the Bf 109 K.

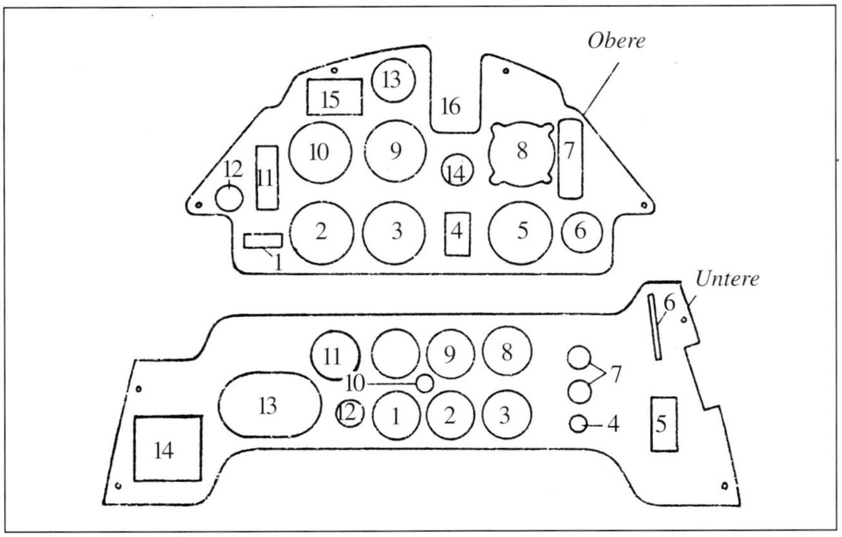

Bf 109 E Instrumentation – Upper Panel:

	Equipment	Instrument Range	Requisition/Equipment Number
1	Pitot tube heat visual indicator		Fl 32523-3
2	Airspeed indicator	80 750 km/h	Fl 22231
3	Turn-and-bank indicator, pneumatic		Fl 22402
4	Propeller pitch control switch (later replaced by Fl 32337 thumb-switch on throttle lever)		9-9500-20
5	RPM indicator	600 – 3,600 rpm	Fl 20222
	or	500 – 3,600 rpm	Fl 20222-3
6	Propeller pitch indicator, mechanical		Fl 18503-2
7	Deviation table		Fl 23906
8	Boost pressure gauge	0.6 – 1.8 atm	Fl 20550
9	FK 5 magnetic compass (later FK 38)		Fl 23211
10	Fine and coarse altimeter	0 – 10000 m	Fl 22230
11	SSH 45/8 Z ignition switch		Fl 21121-2
12	Electrical system cut-out switch	Fl 32315-2	
13	Bo-UK 1 clock		Fl 23885
14	Gun sight connector socket		Fl 32624
15	Landing flap data placard		
16	Revi C/12 C reflector gun sight		Fl 52161
	or Revi C/12 D (and others)		Fl 52095

Bf 109 E Instrumentation – Lower Panel:

	Equipment	Instrument Range	Requisition/Equipment Number
1	Fuel contents gauge	0 – 400 l	Fl 20723
2	Indicator (switchable) for oil inlet-outlet temperature	0 – 160° C	Fl 20343
3	Coolant outlet temperature gauge	0 – 120° C	Fl 20342-2
4	Undercarriage emergency lowering handle		
5	Undercarriage position indicator, mechanical		
6	Fuel hand-pump		
7	Undercarriage switch		
8	Undercarriage position indicator (four lights)		Fl 32526
9	Fuel – oil pressure gauge	0 – 2/0 –10 kg/cm²	Fl 20512-2
10	Low fuel warning light (red)		Fl 32262-1
11	Dimmer switch (not in all versions)		Fl 32401-2
12	Firing button		Fl 32302
13	SKK 224 control box for fixed weapons		Fl 47293
14	Radio system control panel		

Fighter-bombers had an auxiliary panel mounted beneath the main panel housing:

Equipment	Requisition/Equipment Number
• ZSK 244 A bomb arming panel	Fl 50869
• Remote controlled master switch for bombs (automatic switch)	Fl 32408-1
• 4 bomb indicator lights	Fl 32529

The instrumentation of the Bf 109 E was based largely on that of the Bf 109 C, although some instruments were replaced with more modern equipment. Fighter-bombers were fitted with an auxiliary panel beneath the main panel housing the bomb selector panel.

A placard contained the following information:

Maximum speed with flaps fully lowered 250 km/h		
Landing flap position		Neutral position
Takeoff	20°	0°
Landing	40°	

The equipment of the Bf 109 Es operated by the Swiss differed in several respects:

- Clock (Revue) and altimeter (Thommen) were of Swiss manufacture.
- The weapons mounted above the engine were also Swiss-made. Two cocking handles were installed in the upper instrument panel.
- The propeller pitch selector switch was replaced by a unit of Swiss design on the throttle lever.
- Controls for the Swiss signalling system (flares), a round counter for the wing cannon and a Morse key were installed in the lower instrument panel.
- The KG 12 control grip was replaced by a circular KG 11 unit.

The cockpit of a Swiss Bf 109 E-3 in the Fliegermuseum in Dübendorf. Apart from some Swiss modifications, the aircraft gives a good impression of a Bf 109 E from the period 1939-40. (Wildmoser)

The Bf 109 F and early versions of the Bf 109 G differed only in detail. Here is the Bf 109 G-2 on display in the Laatzen Aviation Museum. (Lill via L.M. Laatzen)

The instrumentation of the **Bf 109 F** was completely redesigned and included a blind-flying panel installed on rubber mounts to reduce vibration. This series also introduced the Patin distant-reading compass as standard equipment, this replacing the magnetic compass. As well, the electrical system's circuit breaker box on the starboard side of the cockpit was redesigned and enlarged.

The instrument panel of the **Bf 109 G-1 to G-4** was largely unchanged from that of the Bf 109 F. The only change to the blind flying panel was the introduction of a Fl 22410-1 or Fl 22411 combined turn-and-bank indicator and artificial horizon. This resulted in a repositioning of the compass indicator, airspeed indicator and altimeter.

Instrument Panel of the Bf 109 F-1 to F-4:

	Equipment	Instrument Range	Requisition/Equipment Number
a	Bo-UK 1 clock		Fl 23885
b	SZK K 3 ammunition counter or SKK 224		Fl 47318
c	Instrument panel bearer		
d	Fine and coarse altimeter	0 – 10000 m	Fl 22320
e	Airspeed indicator	80 – 750 km/h	Fl 22231
f	Turn-and-bank indicator, electric		Fl 22406
g	PFK/f2 master compass indicator		Fl 22234
h	Revi C/12 C gun sight		Fl 52161
i	Boost pressure gauge	0.6 – 1.8 atm	Fl 20555
j	Gun sight connector socket		Fl 32624
k	Direct-reading RPM indicator	500 – 3,500 rpm	Fl 20222-3
l	Propeller pitch indicator		9-9548 B
m	Low fuel warning light (red)		Fl 32262-1
n	Indicator (switchable) for coolant and oil inlet temperature	0 – 160° C	Fl 20343
o	Fuel contents gauge	0 – 400 l	Fl 20723
p	Fuel / oil pressure gauge	0 – 2 / 0 – 10 kg/cm²	Fl 20512-2
q	Flare pistol		
r	Ignition switch		Fl 21121-2
s	Electrical system cut-out switch		Fl 32315-2
t	Ignition switch (starter)		Fl 21211
u	Undercarriage position indicator (four lights)		Fl 32526
v	Undercarriage switch		
w	Pull-handle for sparkplug cleaning		
x	Auxiliary bombing control panel with		
	ZSK 244 A bomb fusing panel		Fl 50869
	Remote controlled master switch		Fl 32408-1
	4 warning lights		Fl 32529
y	Undercarriage emergency lowering handle		

The two circular openings on the left and right of the instrument panel were necessary for changing the barrels of the two MG 17s above the engine.

Cockpit of the Bf 109 G-2 in Laatzen. During restoration much effort was expended to ensure historical accuracy.

The best-known Bf 109 G-6 is the tradition aircraft of the Messerschmitt Foundation, actually a conversion of a Spanish Hispano HA 1112. Here it seen during an engine run-up at an old timers meet in Hahnweide in 1997.

During production the switchable temperature gauge was replaced by the simpler Fl 20342 temperature gauge (0 - 130° C). Switching was then accomplished by means of a push-button beside the instrument or a Fl 32350 toggle switch, which was installed to the right of the starboard opening for changing the barrels of the MG 17s.

The introduction of the **Bf 109 G-6** resulted in significant changes in instrumentation, although the shape of the instrument panel remained largely unchanged. The installation of two MG 131s above the engine resulted in the deletion of the two openings in the instrument panel for changing the barrels of the MG 17s. The space thus made available was used to house additional equipment. Also deleted were the Revi socket and the pull-handle for the spark plug cleaning system.

The instrument panel of the **Bf 109 G-10** and **G-14** remained largely unchanged except for equipment installed as a result of special requests from pilots and specialized variants. The only major addition was the installation of a 19-5843 frequency selector above or beside the double pressure gauge at the bottom right of the instrument panel. In aircraft equipped with methanol-water injection, the toggle switch for the FuG 16 at the top right of the instrument panel was replaced by a Fl 32350 toggle switch for the MW 50 system.

The instrumentation of all Bf 109 G-6 to G-14 aircraft was similar in most respects. Here the cockpit of the restored Bf 109 G-14/AS, aircraft serial number ...345, White 13. Some equipment is still missing.

Comparison view of the cockpit of the Bf 109 G-6 tradition aircraft FM+BB. An effort was made during restoration to accurately depict the instrumentation of a Bf 109 G-6. The small panel beneath the main instrument panel houses a vertical speed indicator, VOR indicator and radio controls. The cockpit interior should in fact be Black-Gray 66, not Gray 02.

Close-up of the cockpit of a late Bf 109 G-6, serial number 163824, in the Australian War Memorial. The oxygen system and control panels for the FuG 25 and FuG 16 are clearly visible. The frequency selector seen to the left of the circuit breaker panel was standard equipment in late G-series aircraft. (K.A. Merrick)

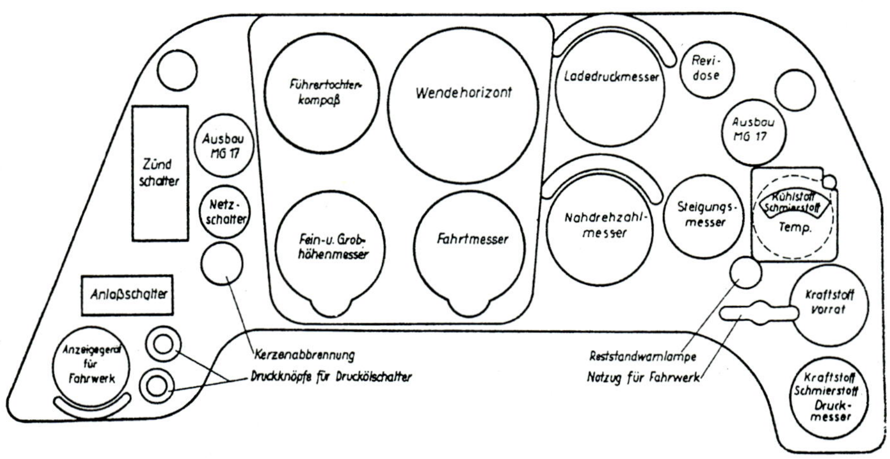

Instrumentation of the Bf 109 G-1. (Hafner Archive)

Explanation of the differences in instrumentation of Bf 109 G-6 and subsequent versions from earlier G-series aircraft. (Bokelmann)

Cockpit pressure gauge (a) in the Bf 109 G-1, G-3 and G-5. (Hafner Archive)

The Bf 109 G-12 was a two-seat training aircraft and had a simplified second instrument panel in the rear cockpit, as in the Arado Ar 96.

In the G-1, G-3 and G-5 high-altitude versions, a Fl 22325 cockpit pressure gauge was installed above the circuit breaker box.

The instrument panel of the **Bf 109 K** underwent significant changes because of the integration of the standard blind flying panel into the instrument panel. The series also introduced a new circuit breaker box and a redesigned oxygen control panel on the starboard side of the cockpit.

Bf 109 G-5 and G-6 Instrument Panel:
(changes from Bf 109 G-1 to G-4):

1	Indicator lights (white) for wing weapons cocked		Fl 32529
2	Revi C/12 D increasingly replaced by Revi 16 b		Fl 52955
3	Cockpit pressure warning light (red) (G-5 only)		Fl 32529-1
4	Ignition switch		Fl 21118
5	Temperature gauge selector switch		Fl 32345-2
6	Fine and coarse altimeter	0 – 13000 m	Fl 22322
7	Airspeed indicator	100 – 900 km/h	Fl 22234
8	Combined turn-and-bank indicator and artificial horizon		Fl 22410-1 or Fl 22411 or Fl 22415
9	AFN 2 homing indicator		Ln 27002
10	FuG 16 selector switch for radio-telegraphy (FT) or homing (ZF) (Fl 32350 switch was also used)		Fl 32336-3
11	Coolant and oil temperature gauge	0 – 130° C	Fl 20342
12	Windscreen cleaner (gasoline) valve		8-4592 A-2

The G-5 was the last variant of the Bf 109 with a pressurized cockpit.

Bf 109 G-10, D-FDME, Black 2, in the markings of a Bf 109 K-4. (Schmidtdesign)

Souvenir taken by an American soldier. This instrument panel came from one of the many incomplete Bf 109 Ks found at the end of the war. Some instruments, such as the combined turn and bank indicator and artificial horizon and the repeater compass, were never installed. The markings on the instrument panel were stamped on. At the top left, a pressure gauge for the MW 50 system was installed in place of the clock. (Bokelmann)

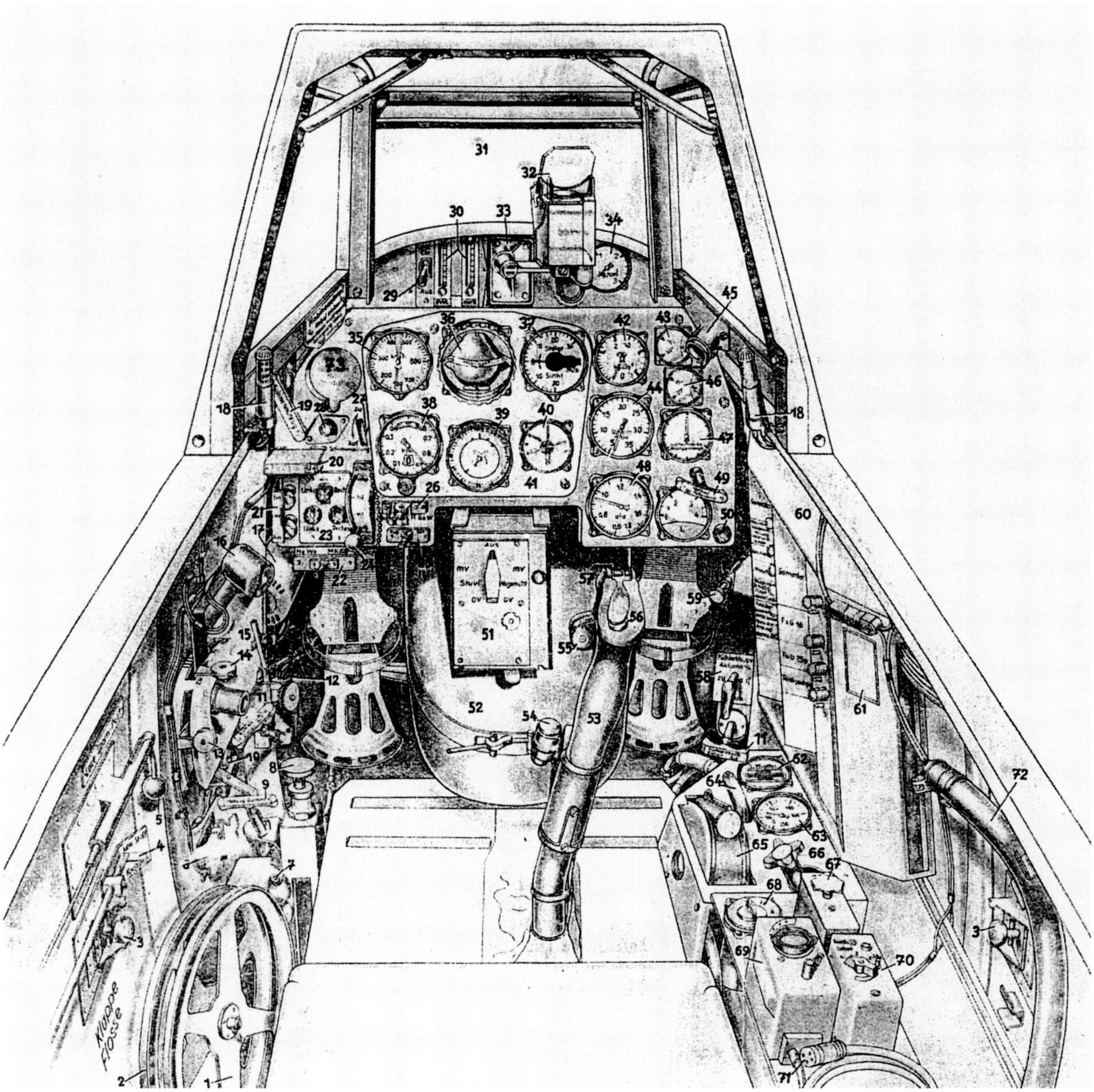

Equipment of the Bf 109 K-2 and K-4:

	Equipment	Instrument Range	Requisition/Equipment
1	Tailplane trim wheel		
2	Landing flap control wheel		
3	Cockpit ventilation lever		
4	Fuel selector handle		
5	Tailwheel locking lever		
6	Connector socket for heated gloves		
7	Tailplane trim indicator		
8	Engine primer hand-pump		
9	Emergency release for bombs or external fuel tank		
10	Automatic propeller pitch control selector switch		
11	Radiator shutoff switch*		
12	Momentary limit switch		
13	Quick-stop lever		
14	Fuel cock lever		
15	Cold start handle		
16	Throttle lever with thumb-switch for propeller pitch control		Fl 32337

No.	Item	Range	Part no.
17	Transformer for the electric combined artificial horizon and turn-and-bank indicator		
18	Ultra-violet lights		
19	Canopy emergency jettison lever		
20	Ignition switch (starter)		Fl 21211
21	Undercarriage push-buttons		
22	Selector switch for rockets or MK 108 **		Fl 32346
23	Undercarriage position indicators:		
	Undercarriage indicator system (four lights)		Fl 32526
	or two visual indicators		18-6820 A
	or 1 green warning light and 2 red warning lights		Fl 32529
24	Ignition switch		Fl 21118
25	Toggle switch for MW 50 system		Fl 32346-3 or Fl 32350
26	Toggle switch for rocket tube jettison **		Fl 32345 ?
27	Windscreen cleaner lever		
28	Electrical system cut-out switch		19-5836 A
29	Safety switch on ammunition counter panel		
30	SZK K 3 ammunition counter panel or SZK K 2		Fl 47318 or Fl 47317
31	Armored windscreen		
32	Revi 16 B gun sight		Fl 52955
33	Gun sight mount		
34	MW 50 system pressure gauge	0 – 3 kg/cm²	Fl 20504-3
35	Airspeed indicator, pressure-tight	100 – 1000 km/h	Fl 22234
	or pressure-free	100 – 900 km/h	Fl 22234
36	Combined turn-and-bank indicator and artificial horizon		Fl 22410
37	Vertical speed indicator, pressure-tight	-15 / +15 m/s	Fl 22384
	or pressure-free	-20 / +50 m/s	Fl 22383
	or	-30 / +30 m/s	Fl 22386
38	Fine and coarse altimeter	0 – 13000 m	Fl 22322
	planned	0 – 16000 m	Fl 22326
39	PFK/f2 master compass indicator		Fl 23334
40	AFN 2 homing indicator		Ln 27002
41	Blind-flying panel		Fl 22000
42	Fuel-oil pressure gauge	0 – 2 / 0 – 10 kg/cm²	Fl 20512-2
43	Coolant temperature gauge	0 – 160° C	Fl 20358
44	RPM indicator	400 – 3,600 rpm	Fl 20227
46	Oil temperature gauge	0 – 160° C	Fl 20358
47	Mechanical propeller pitch indicator		Fl 18503-2
48	Boost pressure gauge	0.6 – 1.8 atm	Fl 20555
49	Undercarriage emergency lowering handle		
50	Low fuel warning light (red)		Fl 32259-1
	Tank full indicator light (green) planned		Fl 32529
51	Auxiliary panel with ZSK 244 A bomb arming panel		Fl 50869
52	MK 108 cannon cover		
53	KG 13 A control stick grip		Fl 47915
54	Cocking button for MK 108		
55	B2 button for releasing external stores		
56	B1 button for firing the MK 108 and underwing cannon		
57	A button for firing MG 131s		
58	Radiator flap control		
59	Fuel jettison handle		
60	Circuit breaker panel		
61	Deviation table		
62	Oxygen flow meter		Fl 30489
63	Oxygen pressure gauge	0 – 250 kg/cm²	Fl 30496
64	Auxiliary fuel tank system sight glass		
65	High-altitude breathing apparatus		Fl 30403-1
66	Oxygen shut-off valve		Fl 30508
67	Remote control for FuG 16 ZY		Ln 27188
68	Frequency selector for FuG 16 ZY		19-5843
69	Headset connector socket		
70	BG 25a control box for FuG 25a		Ln 28810
71	Headset jack		
72	Oxygen hose		
73	Bo-UK 1 clock (planned)		Fl 23885

(the MW 50 pressure gauge was also installed in some machines)

* only in early production aircraft

** deleted in course of rationalization program

Some pilots remember a vertical speed indicator installed in later versions of the Bf 109 G, for example the G-14. This instrument may have been installed after delivery or perhaps the K-4 instrument panel was installed in a few G-series aircraft.

Viewed historically, the Spanish-built **Hispano HA 1109 and HA 1112** were the final versions of the Bf 109. They were based on the Bf 109 G-2 and had a similar metal instrument panel, though with a larger blind flying panel. In the beginning most of the instruments were license-built versions of Askania equipment, however these were later replaced by Spanish or converted English instruments.

Other equipment in the cockpit was similar to that of the Bf 109 G with the exception of the radio. Versions powered by the Rolls Royce Merlin 500/45 were fitted with instruments designed for that power plant. As a rule a magnetic compass was installed in the HA 1112. Relatively late in their service lives some aircraft were fitted with an additional radio compass.

This handbook illustration is one of the few known photographs of the cockpit of a Bf 109 K. (Soppa Collection)

Spanish Hispano HA 1112 M.1L in the Musée de l'Air in Paris. This aircraft differed from the Bf 109 G-6 mainly in the installation of a Rolls Royce engine.

This view of the cockpit of the HA 1112 M.1L in Paris reveals its close relationship to the Bf 109 G.

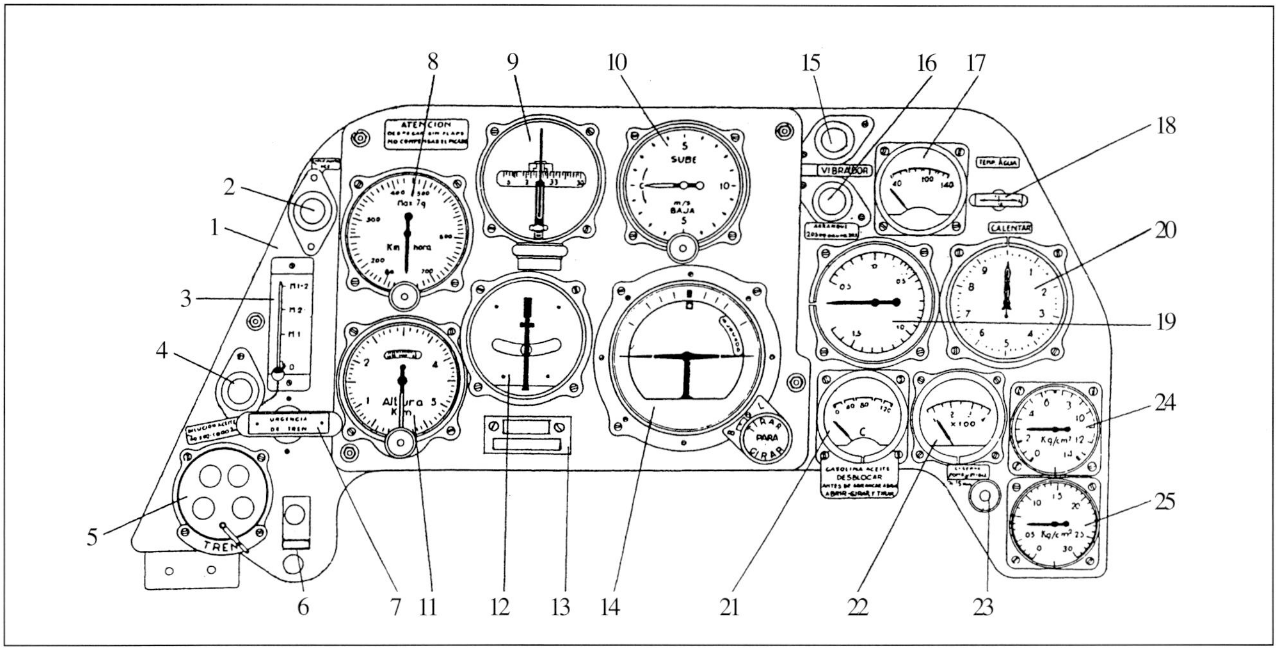

Hispano HA 1112 M.1L Instrumentation:

	Equipment	Instrument Range	Requisition/Equipment Number
1	Instrument panel		
2	Electrical system cut-out switch		
3	Ignition switch		Bosch
4	Push-button for thinning oil		
5	Undercarriage position indicator (four lights)		Siemens
6	Undercarriage controls		
7	Undercarriage emergency lowering handle		
8	Airspeed indicator	80 – 750 km/h	Marconi
9	A 200 magnetic compass		Marconi
10	Statoscope-vertical speed indicator	-10 / +10 m/s	Marconi
11	Altimeter	0 – 6000 m	Marconi
	or	0 – 10000 m	
12	Turn-and-bank indicator, pneumatic		Marconi
13	Pitot tube heat visual indicator (not in all aircraft)		Siemens
14	Artificial horizon		Marconi
15	Push-button for power boost		
16	Starter push-button		
17	Coolant temperature gauge	40 – 140° C	Smiths
18	Heating handle		
19	Boost pressure gauge	-0.5 - +1.7 atm	Smiths
20	RPM indicator	0 – 5,000 rpm	Smiths
21	Oil temperature gauge	0 – 120° C	Smiths
22	Fuel gauge	100 – 400 l	Bressel
23	Fuel warning light (red) 15 min. fuel remaining		Gerhardt
24	Oil pressure gauge	0 – 14 kg/cm^2	Smiths
25	Fuel pressure gauge	0 – 3 kg/cm^2	Smiths

Messerschmitt Bf 110

This twin-engined aircraft with a crew of two had its origins in a specification issued by the *Reichsluftfahrtministerium* for a heavy fighter, or *Zerstörer*, which would have the range to escort bombers to their targets while possessing the maneuverability of a single-engine fighter. Of course these conflicting requirements could not be completely met and the resulting design compromise which gave rise to much controversy.

The first production variants were the Bf 110 A and B, which appeared in 1936. They were powered by two 680 H.P. Jumo 210 D or 730 H.P. Jumo 210 G engines, respectively, as the DB 601 was not yet available. These variants both proved to be underpowered and were soon relegated to the training role.

The first major production version was the Bf 110 C *Zerstörer* powered by two 1,175 H.P. DB 601 A engines. This was followed by the Bf 110 D long-range *Zerstörer*, some of which were equipped with the *Dackelbauch* auxiliary fuel tank. The Bf 110 was not a success as an escort fighter, and when this became apparent the type was successfully adapted for a number of other roles.

The Bf 110 E, which was powered by two 1,275 H.P. DB 601 N engines was operated mainly as a fighter-bomber and reconnaissance aircraft, while the slightly revised Bf 110 F was also operated as a *Zerstörer* and night-fighter.

The version built in the greatest numbers was the three-seat Bf 110 G. Powered by two 1,475 H.P. DB 605 B engines and equipped with radar, this version enjoyed great success as a night-fighter. In 1942, following the failure of its planned successor, the Me 210, production of the Bf 110 was resumed. The aircraft remained in production until the end of the war, by which time approximately 6,000 examples were completed.

Rare photograph of a Bf 110 B in service with a training unit. This version is easily identified by the large radiator fairings of its Jumo 210 engines.

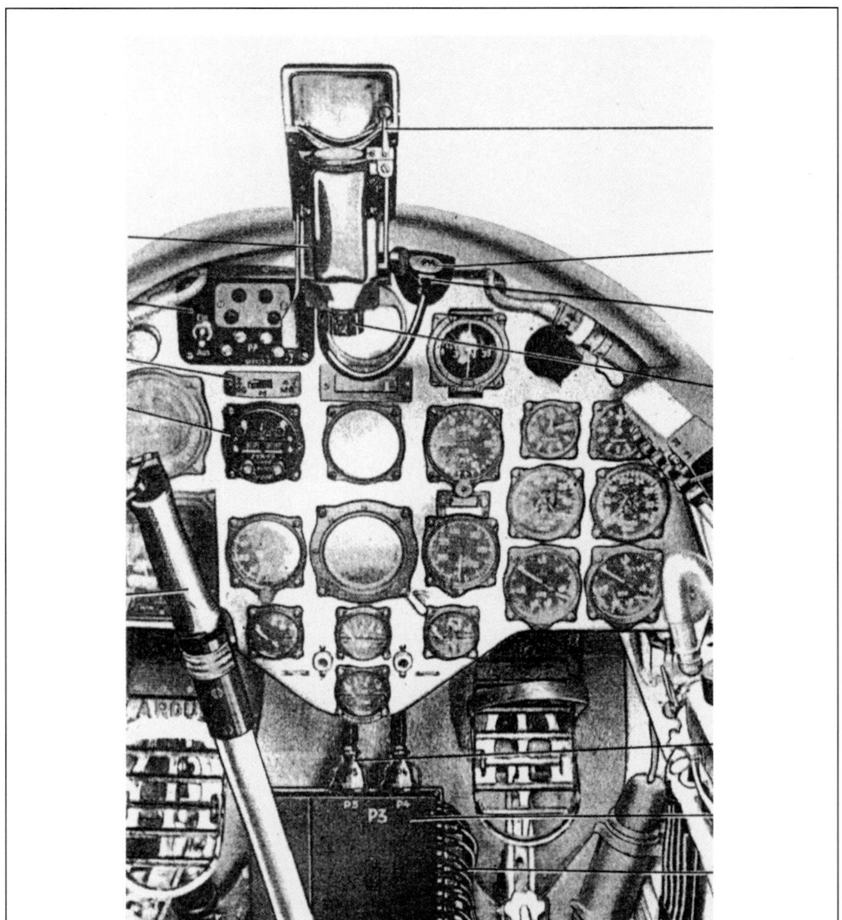

The only known photograph of a Bf 110 B instrument panel is from an armament manual. (Hafner Archive)

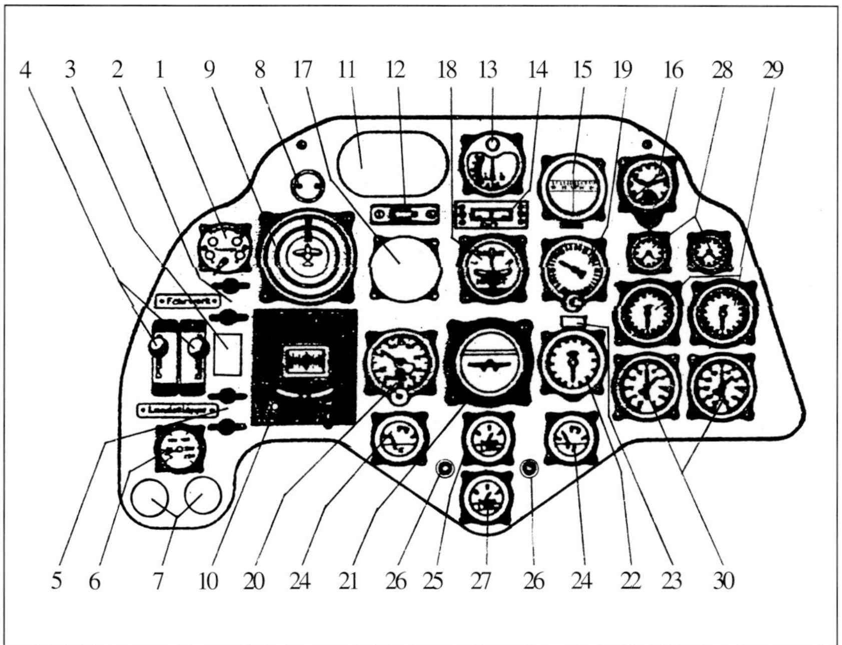

Instrument panel of a Bf 110 C. This photograph was also taken from an armament handbook. (B. Lange Archive)

Instrument panel of the Bf 110 B:

	Equipment	Instrument Range	Requisition/Equipment Number
1	Undercarriage position indicator		Fl 32526
2	Undercarriage control handle		
3	Undercarriage and landing flap operation placard		
4	Propeller pitch control switch	9-9502 B ?	
5	Landing flap control handle		
6	Compressed air pressure gauge	0 – 250 kg/cm²	Fl 20519
7	Compressed air valve for emergency operation of undercarriage and landing flaps		
8	Autopilot emergency disengage button		Fl 22557
9	PfK/f3 master compass indicator		Fl 23338
10	Lku 4 gyro compass		Fl 22561
11	SKK 404/2 switch- and control box for MG 17s		Fl 47292
12	Selector switch 2 MG/4 MG		Fl 32317-1
13	AFN 1 homing indicator		Ln 27000
14	Lkz 3 course indicator		Fl 22562
15	FK 5 magnetic compass		Fl 23211
16	Bo-UK 1 clock		Fl 23885
17	ZVK-FF cannon round counter		
18	Turn-and-bank indicator		Fl 22402
19	Statoscope-vertical speed indicator	-15 / +15 m/s	Fl 22381-15
20	Fine and coarse altimeter	0 – 10000 m	Fl 22320
21	Lgab 8 artificial horizon		Fl 22426
22	Airspeed indicator	80 – 750 km/h	Fl 22231
23	Pitot tube heat visual indicator		Fl 32525-3
24	2 coolant temperature gauges	0 – 120° C	Fl 20342-2
25	Fuel contents gauge (forward tank)	0 – 380 l	Fl 20723
26	2 low fuel warning lights (red) left and right		Fl 32262-1
27	Fuel contents gauge (rear tank)	0 – 270 l	Fl 20723
28	2 propeller pitch indicators, electric		Fl 18505-1
29	2 RPM indicators, electric	600 – 3,600 rpm	Fl 20286 ?
30	2 boost pressure gauges	0.6 – 1.8 atm	Fl 20550

Only two Bf 110s have survived intact. Bf 110 G-4/R6, formerly D5+RL of I./NJG 3, is on display in the RAF Museum in London. Some of the photographs presented here depict this aircraft. The second, a Bf 110 F-2 (LN+NR of 13.(Z)/JG 5) was restored for the German Technical Museum in Berlin. In addition to these, the more or less complete remains of 12 aircraft also exist.

The Bf 110's cockpit was very well laid out. The pilot and radio operator occupied separate compartments and had adequate working space. The three-seat Bf 110 G night-fighters had a third crewman, a gunner, resulting in a rather cramped cockpit.

Bf 110 C in service with a training unit.

The pilot was provided with a well-organized instrument panel with the usual controls such as throttle levers, trim wheels and ignition switches. On the right was a console with the pilot's oxygen system, lighting switches, the starting switches for the engines, fuel tank switches and the engine start primer pumps.

In the front of the radio operator's compartment was the radio equipment and a small instrument panel. On the cockpit walls were the main electrical panel and additional controls for the radio equipment. In training versions of the Bf 110 the instructor occupied the rear cockpit, in which a duplicate pilot's instrument panel was fitted. For space reasons some of the engine instruments were installed in the engine nacelles. The fuselage profile of the Bf 110 was very slender, resulting in a relatively small main instrument panel.

This configuration remained virtually unchanged in all versions of the Bf 110. Equipment was modernized to meet changing requirements or was updated during repairs. The Bf 110 was built in numerous variants, and the instrumentations described here are only examples.

Handbooks, replacement part lists and photographs make it possible to reconstruct the instrumentation of the Bf 110 B, C, D, E, F and G and describe their differences, as well as several equipment variations.

Powered by two Jumo engines, the **Bf 110 B** had no requirement for large underwing radiators and the switch for the radiator flaps present in later models was not required. Production of the Bf 110 B totaled just 55 machines.

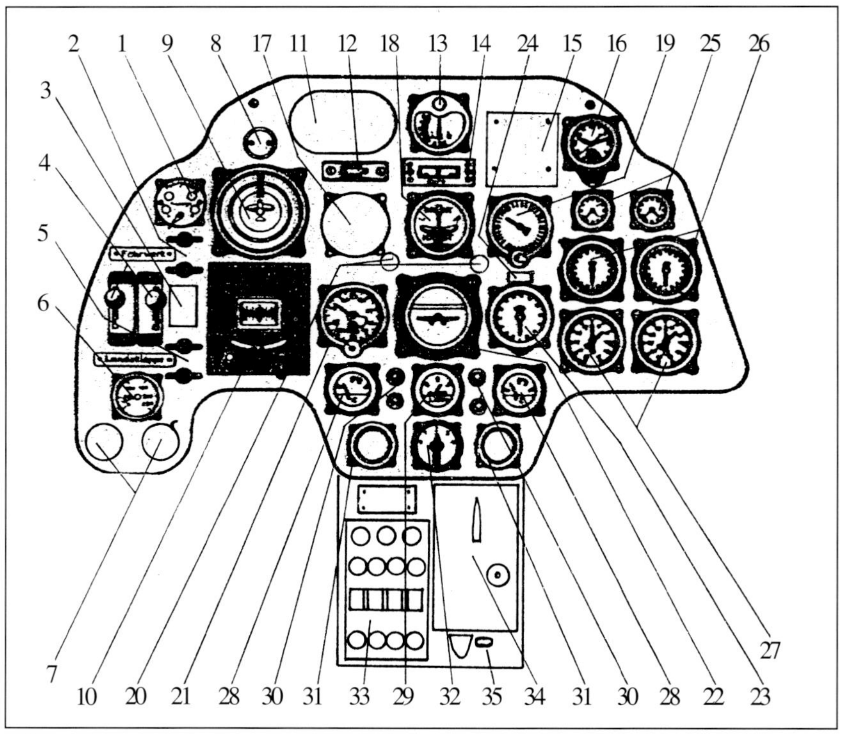

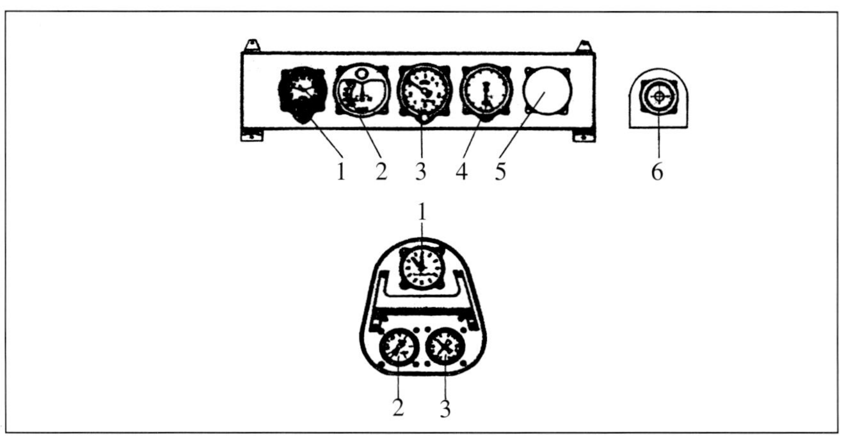

Observer's instrument panel in the Bf 110 C to F as well as some G-2s (above) and the instruments housed in the engine nacelles (below).

Bf 110 C instrument Panel:

	Equipment	Instrument Range	Requisition/Equipment Number
1	Undercarriage position indicator		Fl 32526
2	Undercarriage control handle		
3	Undercarriage and landing flap operation placard		
4	Propeller pitch control switch		9-9502 B ?
5	Landing flap control handle		
6	Compressed air pressure gauge	0 – 250 kg/cm^2	Fl 20519
7	Compressed air valve for emergency operation of undercarriage and landing flaps		
8	Autopilot emergency disengage button		Fl 22557
9	PfK/f3 master compass indicator		Fl 23338
10	Lku 4 gyro compass		Fl 22561
11	SKK 404/2 switch- and control box for MG 17s		Fl 47292
12	Selector switch 2 MG/4 MG		Fl 32317-1
13	AFN 1 homing indicator		Ln 27000
14	Lkz 3 course indicator		Fl 22562
15	Beginning with the Bf 110 C, the magnetic compass was as a rule attached to the starboard cockpit wall. In some cases the AFN 1 was installed in its place and Position 13 was covered with a blanking cover.		
16	Bo-UK 1 clock On some machines the clock was mounted on the frame in front of the instrument panel to the left or right of the gun sight, as later became standard.		Fl 23885
17	ZVK-FF cannon round counter		
18	Turn-and-bank indicator		Fl 22402
19	Statoscope-vertical speed indicator	-10 / +10 m/s	Fl 22381-10 or Fl 22381-15
20	2 fuel transfer indicator lights (white) (not in all aircraft)		Fl 32262-4
21	Fine and coarse altimeter	0 – 10000 m	Fl 22320
22	Lgab 8 artificial horizon		Fl 22426
23	Airspeed indicator	80 – 750 km/h	Fl 22231
24	Pitot tube heat visual indicator		Fl 32525-3
25	2 propeller pitch indicators, electric		Fl 18505-1
26	2 RPM indicators, electric	600 – 3,600 rpm	Fl 20286 ?
27	2 boost pressure gauges	0.6 – 1.8 atm	Fl 20555
28	2 coolant temperature gauges	0 – 120° C	Fl 20342-2
29	Fuel contents gauge	0 – 380 / 0 – 270 l	Fl 20723
30	4 low fuel warning lights (red) left/right, fore/aft		Fl 32262-1
31	2 radiator flap control switches (FI E 630 201)		9-9007 A
32	Fuel contents gauge selector switch 0 – 4		Fl 32336-1
33	ASK/R bomb sequence selector panel		Fl 50967
34	ZSK 244 A bomb arming panel		Fl 50869
35	Automatic switch (bombs)		Fl 32408-1

Observer's Panel in the Bf 110 C to F:

	Equipment	Instrument Range	Requisition/Equipment Number
1	Bo-UK 1 clock		Fl 23885
2	AFN 1 homing indicator (replaced by AFN 2, Ln 27002, in Bf 110 F)		Ln 27000
3	Coarse altimeter	0 – 10000 m	Fl 22316-10
4	Airspeed indicator	80 – 750 km/h	Fl 22231
5	ZVK-FF cannon round counter (deleted in aircraft without MG FF)		
6	In a number of Bf 110 Gs an AFN 2 was installed in a small console. In some Bf 110 G-4 night-fighters the observer's equipment was installed to the left of the FuG 16.		

Radio operator's instrument panel in a Bf 110 C. Note the Morse key on the right. Visible at the bottom are elements of the FuG 10 and the large Patin DF repeater compass. (Trenkle Collection)

The **Bf 110 C**, which was built in much larger numbers and which also served as a fighter-bomber, was powered by DB 601 engines, resulting in some changed in instrumentation.

A placard on the instrument panel (3) contained limiting speed information:

Attention
Do not lower undercarriage
at speeds in excess
of 400 km/h.

Attention
Landing flaps
must be completely retracted
at speeds in excess of 250 km/h

Some early Bf 110 Cs were equipped with a Patin distant-reading compass system instead of the Siemens autopilot. In such cases the gyro compass, course indicator and autopilot emergency disengage button were not installed. Instead, a Fl 23300 course selector was installed in place of the gyro compass for the distant-reading compass. Course deviations, which were usually read from the course indicator, were taken from the repeater compass.

The Bf 110 C through F versions had an observer's instrument panel for the radio operator in the rear cockpit.

Three engine instruments were installed in each engine nacelle to save space in the cockpit.

The **Bf 110 D** was a long-range *Zerstörer* and reconnaissance aircraft. Some were equipped with a fixed long-range fuel tank beneath the fuselage (Dackelbauch). This drag-producing fixture soon proved impractical and was deleted.

The instrument panel of the Bf 110 D differed from that of the C in a number of respects and these changes are listed in the accompanying table. Some changes resulted from the use of a Patin distant-reading compass system.

The replacement part lists do not always state whether the equipment listed was installed in corresponding positions in the aircraft. It is possible, for example, that the magnetic compass was installed on the starboard side of the cockpit as early as the Bf 110 C.

The instrumentation of the Bf 110 G was based on that of the Bf 110 F, with the addition of some more modern equipment and updates installed to meet changing operational requirements. There were numerous variants and towards the end of the war some equipment was deleted in the course of "rationalization".

An example of a late variant is provided by the Bf 110 G-4/R6 in possession of the RAF Museum. The aircraft has an instrument panel made of plywood, while the earlier variants of the Bf 110 were fitted with an instrument panel made of 3-mm Duraluminum.

The many illustrations in the Bf 110 G handbooks suggest that was an especially large number of variations in equipment.

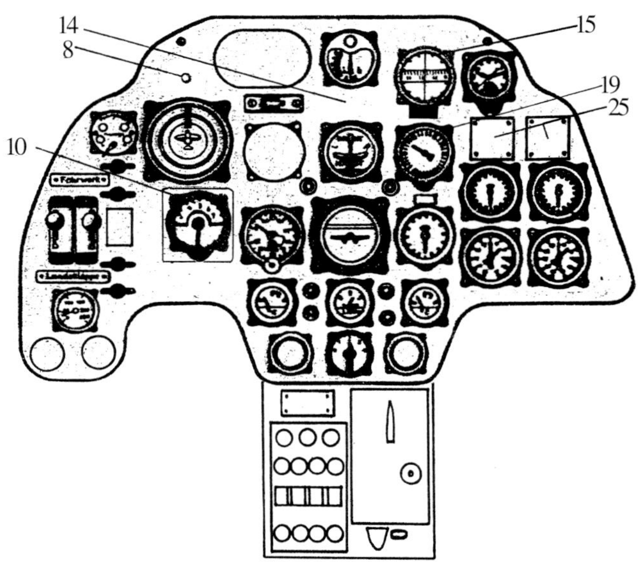

Bf 110 D

Instruments installed in the engine nacelles:

	Equipment	Instrument Range	Requisition/Equipment Number
1	Propeller pitch indicator, mechanical		9-9548
2	Oil inlet and outlet temperature gauge	0 – 120° C	Fl 20330
3	Fuel/oil pressure gauge (for oil inlet) (see drawing Page 254)	0 – 2 / 0 – 10 kg/cm²	Fl 20512-2

Instrument panel of a Bf 110 E. (Trenkle Collection)

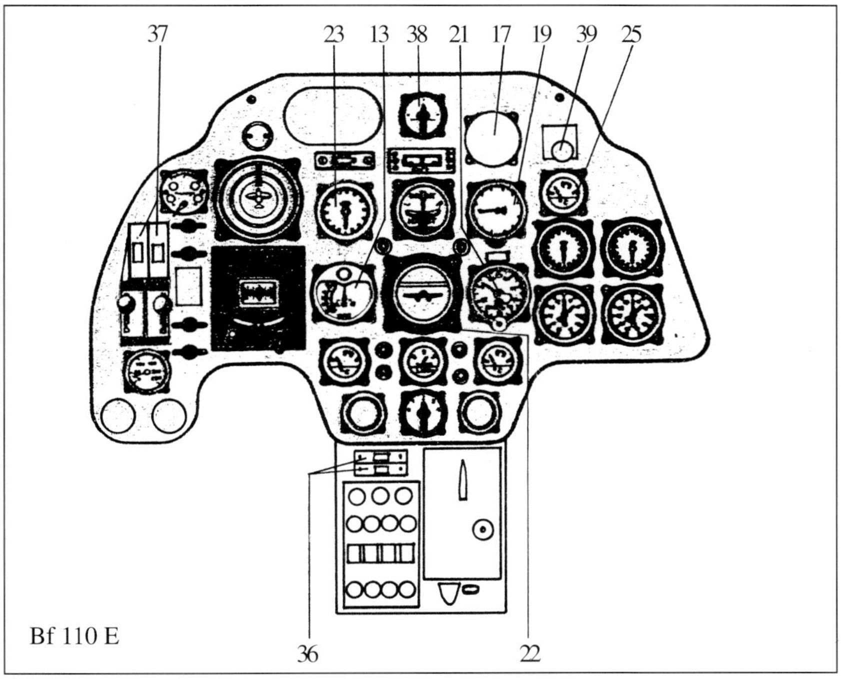

A late-production Bf 110 E with the larger radiator fairings of the Bf 110 F.

Bf 110 D pilot's instrument panel: (Changes compared to Bf 110 C)

	Equipment	Instrument Range	Requisition/Equipment Number
8	Autopilot emergency disengage button deleted		
10	Directional gyro for Patin distant-reading compass		Fl 23300
14	Course indicator deleted		
15	FK 5 magnetic compass		Fl 23211
	or FK 38		Fl 23233
19	Vertical speed indicator	-15 / +15 m/s	Fl 22382
25	Propeller pitch indicator in the instrument panel deleted		

Bf 110 E pilot's instrument panel: (Changes compared to Bf 110 C)

	Equipment	Instrument Range	Requisition/Equipment Number
13	AFN 1 homing indicator		Ln 27000
17	ZVK-FF cannon round counter (MG FF)		
19	Vertical speed indicator	-15 / +15 m/s	Fl 22382
	or		Fl 22384
21	Fine and coarse altimeter	0 – 10000 m	Fl 22320
22	Artificial horizon with Lgab 19-L locking ring		Fl 22427
23	Airspeed indicator	80 – 750 km/h	Fl 22231
25	Outside air temperature gauge	-40 / +40° C	Fl 20342-1
36	2 selector switches for wing/fuselage bombs		Fl 32346-3
37	2 selector switches for propeller pitch control (automatic/manual)		Fl 32327
38	LSch 4ü autopilot master switch		Fl 22559-1

The following placard was applied beneath the airspeed indicator:

Maximum diving speed 700 km/h

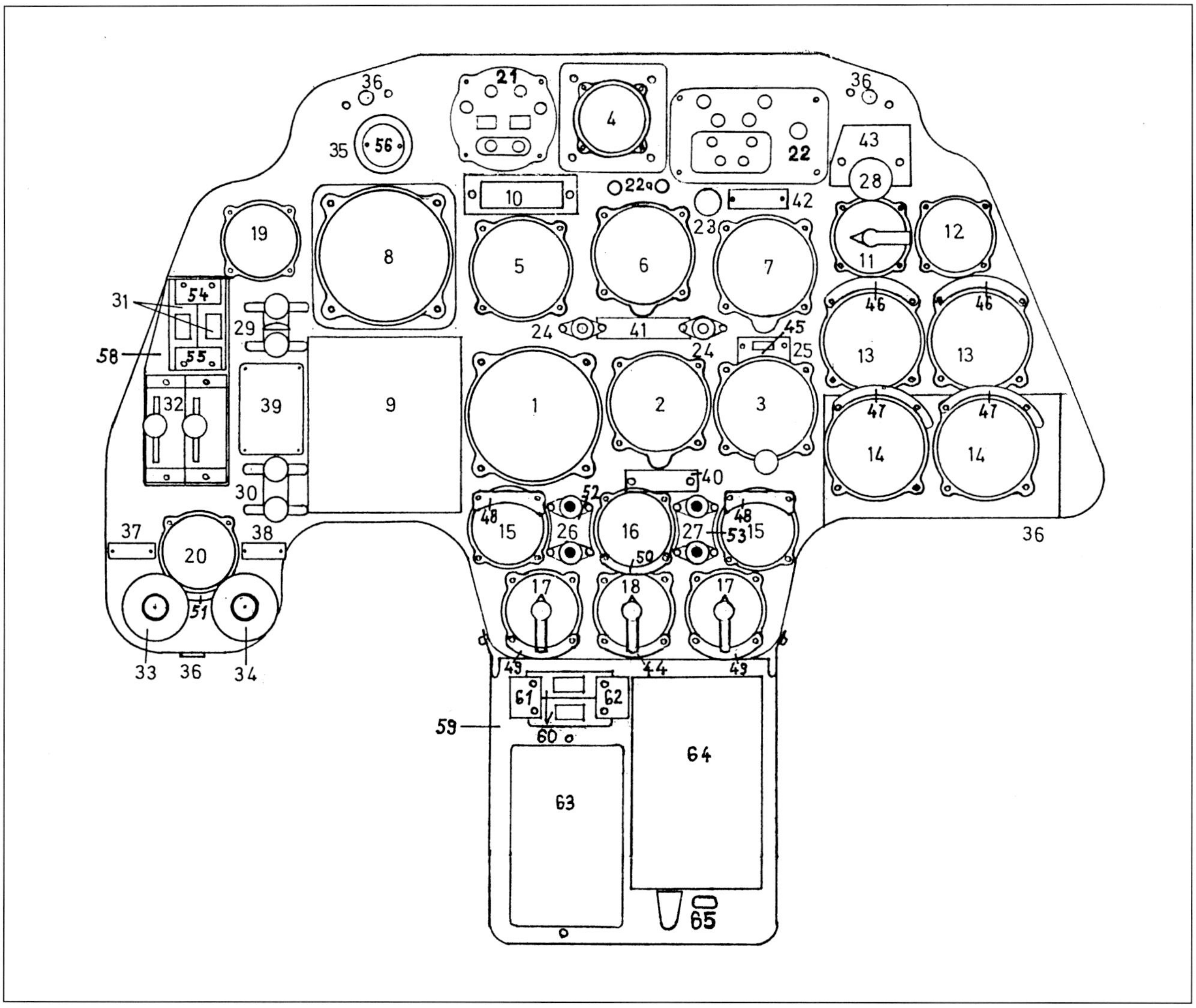

The arrangement of the instruments in the main panel was revised once again in the Bf 110 F.

Messerschmitt 110 F pilot's instrument panel:

	Equipment	Instrument Range	Requisition/Equipment Number
1	Artificial horizon with Lgab 19-1 locking ring		Fl 22427
2	Airspeed indicator	80 – 750 km/h	Fl 22231
3	Coarse altimeter	0 – 10000 m	Fl 22316-10
	or fine and coarse altimeter	0 – 10000 m	Fl 22320
4	AFN 2 homing indicator		Ln 27002
5	Turn-and-bank indicator, electric		Fl 22406
6	Vertical speed indicator	-15 / +15 m/s	Fl 22384
7	Fine altimeter	0 – 1000 m	Fl 22316-1
8	PFK/f3 master compass indicator		Fl 23338
9	Lku 4 gyro compass		Fl 22561
10	Lkz 3 course indicator		Fl 22562
11	Lschü 4 autopilot switch		Fl 22559-1
12	Outside air temperature gauge	-40 / +40° C	Fl 20342-1

13	2 RPM indicators	500 – 3,600 rpm	Fl 20286-3
14	2 boost pressure gauges	0.6 – 1.8 atm	Fl 20555
15	2 coolant temperature gauges	0 – 120° C	Fl 20342-2
16	Coolant contents gauge	0 – 380 / 0 – 270 l	Fl 20723
17	2 radiator flap control switches		Fl E 630 201
18	Fuel gauge selector switch		Fl 32336-1
19	Undercarriage position indicator		Fl 32526
20	Compressed air pressure gauge	0-250 kg/cm^2	Fl 20519
21	ZVK-FF control box and round counter for MG FF (in some cases replaced with AFN 2)		
22	SKK 404-2 control box for MG 17s		Fl 47392
22a	2 indicator lights for gun cocking check (white)		Fl 32529
23	Armor glass heating visual indicator		Fl 32530
24	Fuel tank selection warning lights (white)		Fl 32262-4
25	Pitot tube heat visual indicator		Fl 32525-3
26	2 fuel warning lights (red) for port fuel tank		Fl 32262-1
27	2 fuel warning lights (red) for starboard fuel tank		Fl 32262-1
28	Cockpit heat handle		
29	Undercarriage control handle		
30	Landing flap control handle		
31	2 propeller pitch selector switches (AUTOMATIC/MANUAL)		Fl 32327
32	2 propeller pitch control switches		9-9502 B
33	Compressed air valve handle for emergency undercarriage lowering		
34	Compressed air valve handle for emergency flap lowering		
35	Autopilot emergency release button		Fl 22557
36	Instrument panel attachment points		
37	"Undercarriage" placard		
38	"Landing Flaps" placard		
39	Placard with operating instructions for undercarriage and landing flaps		
40	Placard with maximum diving speeds		
41	Placard "Fuel Tank Selection Warning – LEFT-RIGHT		
42	Placard "Armored Windscreen Heating"		
43	Placard with heating control instructions		
44	Placard "Selector"		
45	Legend "Pitot Heat"		
46	Placard with continuous, climb and takeoff power ratings (rpm)		
47	Placard with continuous, climb and takeoff power ratings (boost pressure)		
48	Placard with temperature limits		
49	Placard "Coolant Selector Switch"		
50	Placard "Fuel Contents Gauge"		
51	Placard "Compressed Air"		
52	Placard for fuel warning lights, port tank		
53	Placard for fuel warning lights, starboard tank		
54	Placard "Automatic Pitch Control"		
55	Placard "Manual Pitch Control"		
56	Placard "Autopilot – Pull – Emergency Release"		
57	Deleted		
58	Port console		
59	Auxiliary instrument panel		
60	2 selector switches for underwing/fuselage bombs		Fl 32346-3
61	Placard "Wing"		
62	Placard "Fuselage"		
63	ASK-R bomb selector panel		Fl 50967
64	ZSK 244 A bomb fusing panel		Fl 50869
65	Automatic bomb release switch		Fl 32408-1

Some placards were deleted during the course of repairs, for example 49, 50 or 51

Instrument panel of a Bf 110 F. (Hafner Archive)

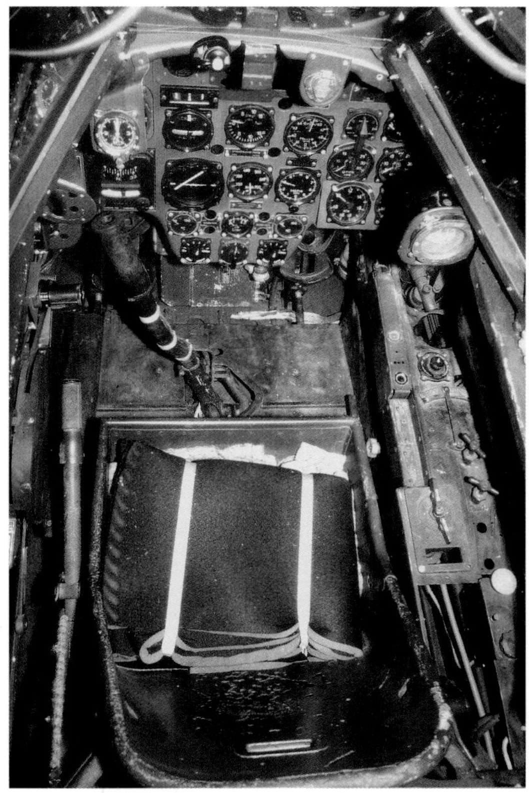

Cockpit of the Bf 110 F-2 in the German Technical Museum shortly before the completion of restoration.

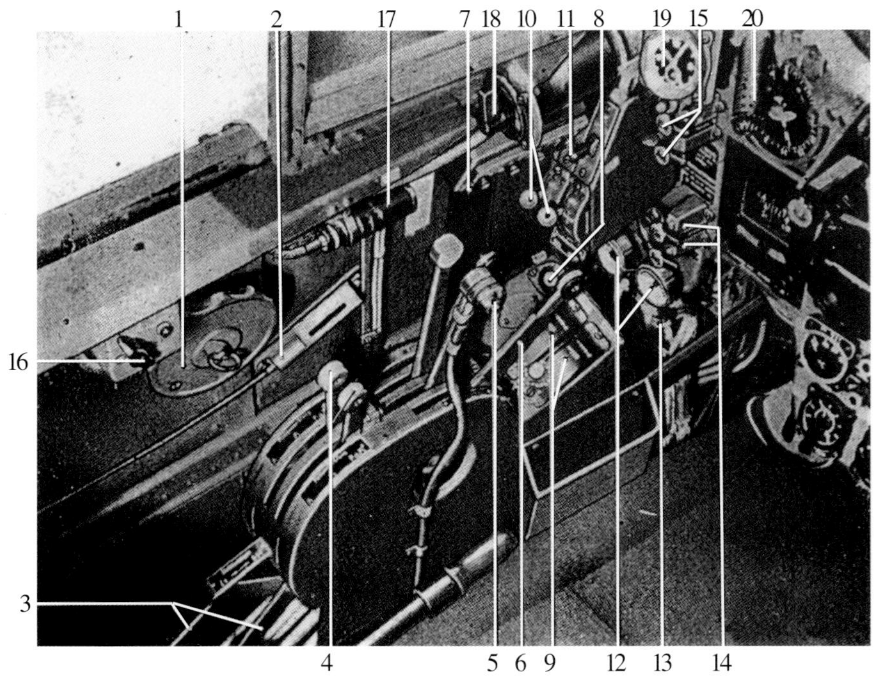

Other instruments and controls were housed in consoles on the left and right sides of the cockpit.

Equipment on the Left Side of the Cockpit (Bf 110 F):

	Equipment	Instrument Range	Requisition/Equipment Number
1	Elevator trim tab control wheel		
2	Landing flap position indicator		
3	Oil cooler flap control lever		
4	Fuel cock lever		
5	Signal lamp control button		Fl 32302
6	Fuel hand-pump lever		
7	Auxiliary switchbox with circuit breakers		Fl 32408
8	Electrical system cut-out switch		Fl 32315-2
9	Ignition switches		Fl 21121-2
10	Propeller pitch control switches		9-9502 B
11	Automatic pitch control switch		Fl 32327
12	Undercarriage and landing flap emergency lowering switches		
13	Compressed air pressure gauge	0 – 150 kg/cm^2	Fl 20519
14	Landing flap switch		
15	Undercarriage switch		
16	FuG 25a control panel (moved to right windscreen frame in Bf 110 G)		Ln 28810
17	Cockpit lighting		Fl 32353-2
18	Autopilot course selector (integrated into control stick in Bf 110 G)		Fl 22573
19	Bo-UK 1 clock		Fl 23885
20	Ultra-violet lighting		Fl 32269-1/2

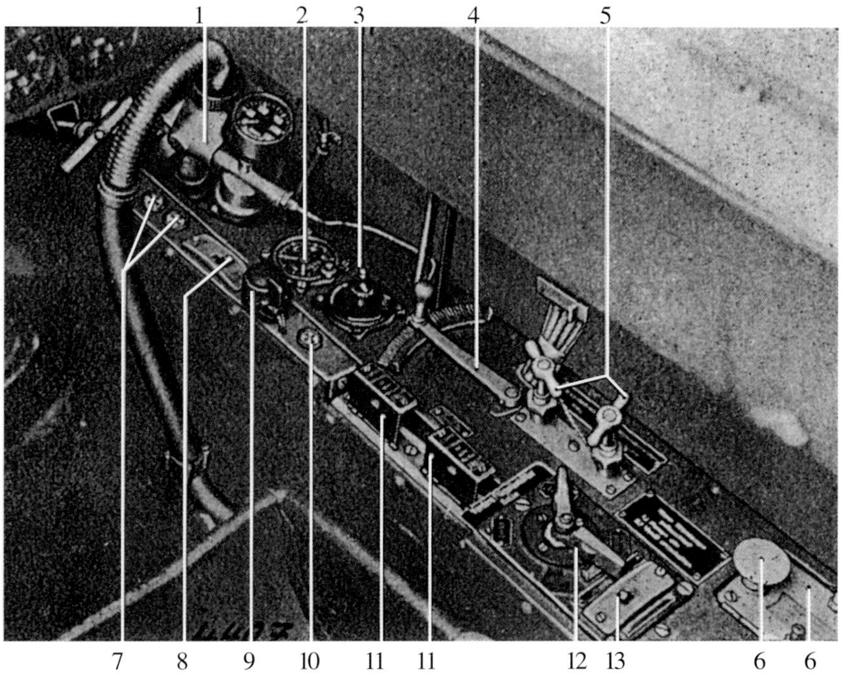

Equipment on the right side of the cockpit (Bf 110 F):

	Equipment	Instrument Range	Requisition/Equipment Number
1	Oxygen equipment		Fl 30402
	in Bf 110 G replaced by		Fl 30403-1
	Oxygen flow meter		Fl 30489
	Oxygen pressure gauge	0 – 250 kg/cm²	Fl 30496
2	Contact altimeter	0 – 6000 m	Fl 22317
	In the Bf 110 C to E variants a suction regulator for the negative-pressure instruments was installed here		
3	Cockpit lighting dimmer switch		Fl 32401-2
1	Rudder trim tab control lever		
2	Sparkplug cleaning lever (deleted in Bf 110 G)		
3	APB 6 starter injection pump with tank		8-4506 A
4	Visual indicators, purpose unknown		8-4511 A-1
5	Toggle switch, purpose unknown		Fl 32530
6	Switch for additional identification lights ?		Fl 32317
7	Additional identification lights visual indicator		Fl 32322
8	Starter handles		Fl 21212
9	Double indicator switch for fuel system		
10	Fuel tank pump selector switch		Fl 32317-1

The side consoles and panels differed little among the various versions of the Bf 110.

Restored instrument panel of a Bf 110 G-2. Apart from the round counters and toggle switches in the center, instrumentation is identical to that of the Bf 110 F. (Schneider)

Left side of the pilot's cockpit of the Bf 110 G-4/R6. The aircraft has some additional equipment compared to the Bf 110 F.

18	Undercarriage emergency lowering pressure gauge	0 – 250 kg/cm²	Fl 20519
19	Two coupling release handle		
20	Skid and tailwheel switch		
21	Undercarriage emergency lowering valve		
22	Compressed air pressure gauge	0 – 160 kg/cm2	Fl 20516-3
23	Fuel jettison handle		
24	Cockpit unlocking lever		
25	Cockpit jettison handle		
26	Armored windscreen		
27	Cockpit ventilation		
28	FK 38 magnetic compass (behind armored windscreen in production aircraft)		Fl 23233
29	Revi 16 B reflector gun sight		Fl 52955
30	Gun sight and compass support		
31	Deviation table		Fl 23906
32	Frequency selector switch (in production aircraft 19-5843 rotary switch on right side of instrument panel)		Fl 32350 ?
33	FuG 25a control panel		Ln 28810
34	Headset connector socket		
35	SZK K 2 ammunition counter (in production aircraft also just a Fl 32350 toggle switch for arming weapons)		Fl 47317
36	Central instrument panel		
37	Port instrument panel		
38	Undercarriage position indicator (four lights) (in production aircraft two 19-6819 visual indicators)		Fl 32526
39	Electrical system cutout switch		18-5836 A-1
40	Bo-UK 1 clock (deleted from production aircraft)		Fl 23885
41	Thrust indicators:		
	Turbine pressure gauge	0 – 6 kg/cm²	Fl 20521 ?
	Combustion chamber pressure gauge	0 – 25 kg/cm²	Fl 20521 ?
42	Temperature gauge (in Position 52 in production aircraft)	300 – 1000° C	Fl 20338
43	Airspeed indicator	100 – 1000 km/h	Fl 22241 or Fl 22245
44	Combined turn and bank indicator and artificial horizon (Fl 22412 electric turn and bank indicator in production aircraft)		Fl 22411
45	Vertical speed indicator	-150 / +150 m/s	Fl 22385
	or	-25 / +150 m/s	Fl 22385
46	Pitot tube heat visual indicator (deleted from production aircraft)		Fl 32530
47	FuG 16 frequency control knob		
48	Vibration-proof instrument panel (standard blind-flying panel) Fl 22000		
49	Fire warning light (in Position 41 in production aircraft)		Fl 32262-1
50	Fine and coarse altimeter	0 – 13000 m	Fl 22322
51	RPM indicator	0 – 12,500 (= 100%)	Fl 20265
52	Fuel consumption gauge (production aircraft in Position 42 or deleted)	0 – 21 x 100 kg	Fl 20815
53	KG 12 E control grip		
54	MK 108 arming button		
55	Oxygen flow meter		Fl 30489
56	Starboard instrument panel		
57	High-altitude breathing apparatus remote valve		Fl 30508
58	Oxygen pressure gauge	0 – 250 kg/cm²	Fl 30496
59	Console with 8 circuit breakers		19-5000
60	Canopy emergency jettison pushrod		
61	Oxygen hose		
62	Helmet headset connector		
63	High-altitude breathing apparatus		Fl 30403

This instrumentation is an example only. Further deviations may have occurred during production or as a result of the changing spares situation.

Both aircraft give a good impression of an operational Me 163 B and both display numerous deviations and simplifications compared to the cockpit illustration in the pilot's notes.

The cockpit of the Me 163 seems quite roomy and well laid-out compared to that of the Bf 109. Equipment was restricted to what was absolutely necessary, as a result of which the cockpit does not appear cluttered.

Two fuel tanks (T-Stoff) flank the pilot's seat. The corrosive nature of the fuel made leaks a constant hazard and pilots always wore a protective suit during flight.

The instruments and control elements are arranged according to the standards of the day. On the left are the engine, trim and landing flap controls. A standard blind-flying panel was mounted in the center of the instrument panel, but with instruments suitable for a rocket-powered aircraft. The flight instruments were grouped in the center and the engine instruments on the right. On the right side of the cockpit were the circuit breakers associated with the electrical system and the pilot's oxygen system.

The Me 262 A-1a in Chino, USA, (R.P. Lutz)

Messerschmitt Me 262 *Sturmvogel*

The Me 262 was the world's first turbojet-powered aircraft to enter production and the first operational jet fighter. In 1939 the RLM received data from BMW and Junkers on the first turbojet engines, after which the *Technische Amt* tasked Messerschmitt with the development of a twin-engined jet fighter aircraft. The first prototype was completed in 1941, however development of the new jet engines was proceeding slowly due to technical difficulties. As a result, the aircraft made its first flight powered by a Jumo 210 piston engine.

In 1942 the prototype made its first flight powered by Jumo turbojets. Both engines failed shortly after takeoff, however the piston engine had been retained as a safety feature and this saved the project. The problems associated with the first jet engines were to overshadow the Me 262 throughout its life, preventing it from achieving its full potential. The engines had an operating life of only a few hours and the number of technical defects was shockingly high.

The Me 262's design incorporated a number of features which would become standard in later jet fighter designs:

Stressed-skin construction with flush riveting resulting in a very smooth external surface, thin swept wings with automatic leading edge slats and two Jumo 004 axial-flow turbojets each producing 900 kg of thrust.

Production began in 1944, but it suffered as a result of air attacks, shortages of materials, a disrupted transportation system, decentralization of production facilities and a shortage of skilled labor. In spite of these difficulties, however, production continued until the end of the war, in some cases in well-camouflaged outdoor facilities in forests and through the use of forced labor. Approximately 1,400 machines were completed, but of these only about 300 actually saw service. While these few machines could not alter the course of the war, they did give their pilots a feeling of superiority once more.

The most-produced variant was the single-seat Me 262 A, some of which were equipped with air-to-air rockets. Messerschmitt also built a small number of Me 262 B-1a two-seat trainers and Me 262 B-1a/U1 night fighters plus various prototypes. Eight Me 262s survive worldwide.

Some of the photographs here depict the following museum aircraft:

Me 262 A-1b, WNr. 500071, "White 3" in the Deutsches Museum in Munich.
Me 262 A-1/U3, "White 9" in the Planes of Fame Museum in Chino, California.
Me 262 B-1a/U1, WNr. 110305, "Red 8" in the National War Museum in Johannesburg.

Cockpit of the Me 262 A-1b in the Deutsches Museum. The aircraft is equipped with racks for R4M rockets.

The cockpit of the Me 262 A-1a in Chino has been painstakingly restored. The aircraft was originally an Me 262 A-1/U3 interim reconnaissance version with cameras in the fuselage nose. The large repeater compass suggests that the Patin fighter autopilot was installed. Instrumentation has been reduced to the absolute minimum. (Bokelman)

Instrument panel of an Me 262 A-1 with full equipment and pressurized cockpit. (Hafner Archive)

Left side of the cockpit of the Me 262 in Chino, showing the throttle levers. (Bokelman)

Equipment of the Me 262 A-1 and A-2:

No.	Equipment	Instrument Range	Requisition/Equipment Number
1	Instrument panel		
2	Blind-flying panel		Fl 22000
3	Airspeed indicator	100 – 1000 km/h	Fl 22245
4	Combined turn and bank indicator and artificial horizon		Fl 22411-1 or Fl 22410 or Fl 22415
5	Vertical speed indicator	-20 / +50 m/s	Fl 22383
	or	-30 / +30 m/s	Fl 22386
6	Fine and coarse altimeter	0 – 10000 m	Fl 22320
7	PfK/f2 master compass indicator		Fl 23334
	or PKT/f8 (small version)	127-659a	
	or PFK/f3 (large version) in aircraft with Patin autopilot		Fl 23338
8	AFN 2 homing indicator	Ln 27002	
9	Pitot tube heat visual indicator*	Fl 32530-6	
10	Bo-UK 1 clock*	Fl 23885	
11	Cockpit pressure gauge*	0 – 15 km / 0 – 0.6 atm	Fl 22325
12	SZK K 2 ammunition counter		Fl 47317
13	2 electric RPM indicators	2,000 – 15,000 rpm	Fl 20266
	or	2,000 – 12,000 rpm	Fl 20266
14	2 differential pressure gauges*	0 – 1 kg/cm²	Fl 20515
15	2 gas temperature gauges	300 – 1,000° C	Fl 20338
16	2 injection pressure gauges	0 – 60 kg/cm²	Fl 20516-1
	or	0 – 160 kg/cm²	Fl 20516-3
17	2 oil pressure gauges*	0 – 10 kg/cm²	Fl 20504-10
18	Fuel contents gauge (forward tank)	0 – 940 l	Fl 20723
19	Fuel contents gauge (rear tank)	0 – 940 l	Fl 20723
20	2 low fuel warning lights (red)*		Fl 32529-1
21	Cockpit pressure warning light (red)*		Fl 32529-1
22	4 "Armed" visual indicators (MK 108)*		EG 271-3
23	Revi 16 B gun sight (above 13)		Fl 52955

Unlike other jet aircraft which appeared shortly before the end of the war, the Me 262 was not subjected to the rationalization process with reduced, simplified equipment. Nevertheless, wood was used extensively in instrument panels, consoles and cover panels.

The Me 262 had a roomy, well laid-out cockpit which was praised by Allied test pilots who flew the aircraft. Seated relatively high in the cockpit, the pilot had an outstanding all-round view through the three-piece canopy. In front of the pilot was a large instrument panel which included the standard blind flying panel. On his left and right were two consoles housing various controls, all of which were within easy reach.

With some minor variations, instrumentation remained virtually unchanged in all variants of the **Me 262 A**. The equipment installed in the rear cockpit of the two-seat trainer was virtually identical to that of the front cockpit. The rear cockpit of the night fighter variant housed additional radio and radar equipment.

In some cases simplified instrumentation was installed in production aircraft, and instruments and equipment which were deleted are annotated with an asterisk. Most Me 262s were not fitted with a pressurized cockpit and the associated instruments were not installed.

The fighter-bomber version was fitted with an auxiliary panel beneath the main instrument panel housing a ZSK 244 A bomb-fusing panel (Fl 50969) and two visual indicators (Fl 32530) for the bombs.

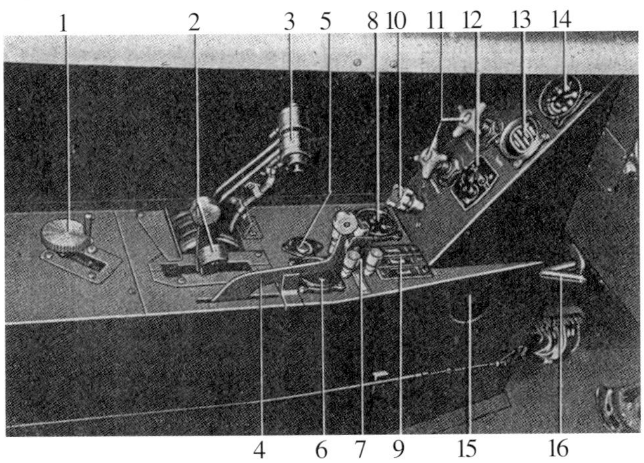

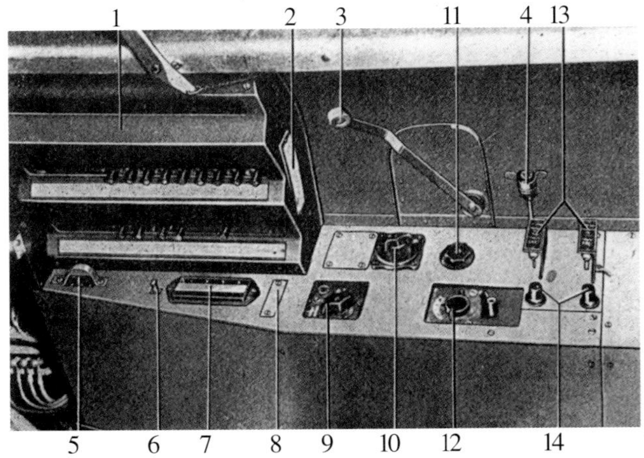

In fighters equipped with R4M rockets, the auxiliary panel housed a SWA X B switchbox (Fl 50958) and two toggle switches (Fl 32350) to arm the rockets and select firing method.

The Me 262 B-1a/U1 night fighter, which was produced in small numbers, was a conversion of the B-1a two-seat trainer. The number of engine instruments available to the pilot was reduced. These were replaced with additional flight instruments required for night operations.

The radar-radio operator occupied the rear cockpit. In front of him was a FuG 16 radio set and beneath it a small instrument panel housing important flight and navigation instruments plus the radar scope. The side consoles housed other controls for the radio and radar systems.

Port Console:

No.	Equipment	Instrument Range	Requisition/Equipment Number
1	Rudder trim wheel		
2	Fuel cock switch lever		
3	Throttle levers with starter push-buttons		
4	Tailplane setting lever		
5	Electrical system cut-out switch		19-5836 A-1
	or		Fl 32315-2
6	Tailplane position indicator		
7	Undercarriage and landing flap switches		
8	Compressed air pressure gauge	0 – 160 kg/cm²	Fl 20516-3
	or	0 – 250 kg/cm²	Fl 20519
9	Undercarriage position visual indicator	19-6819	
10	Oxygen valve		Fl 30508
11	Emergency valves for undercarriage (top) and landing flap (bottom)		
12	Takeoff-assist rockets switch		Fl 18330-7
13	Oxygen flow meter		Fl 30489
14	High-altitude breathing apparatus		Fl 30403
15	Nosewheel brake lever		

Starboard Console:

No.	Equipment	Instrument Range	Requisition/Equipment Number
1	Main electrical panel with circuit breakers		
2	Deviation table		Fl 23906
3	Bomb jettison lever		
4	Headset connector		
5	Heated gloves connector plug ?		
6	Signal flare ammunition selector switch		
7	Befa 4 push-button box for flare ammunition		Ln 24515
8	FuG 25a self-destruct switch		
9	BG 25a control panel for FuG 25		Ln 28810
10	Radio frequency selector switch (FuG 16)		19-5843
11	FuG 16 remote control		Ln 27188
12	Headset connector plug		
13	2 ignition switches (starter)		
14	2 RPM indicator selector switches		

Forward cockpit of the Me 262 B-1a/U1 in South Africa. After its capture by the Allies, all of this aircraft's instruments were replaced with British equipment. (National War Museum)

Me 262 B-1a/U1 in Johannesburg. This is the only surviving Me 262 night fighter. (National War Museum)

Equipment of the Me 262 B-1a/U1
Pilot's instrument panel:

(Changes compared to Me 262 A)

No.	Equipment	Instrument Range	Requisition/Equipment Number
4	Combined turn and bank indicator and artificial horizon		Fl 22415
5	Vertical speed indicator (revised housing shape)		Fl 22386
7	KT/f3 master compass indicator (Patin autopilot)		127-118 A
14	Differential pressure gauge deleted		
	Replaced by emergency turn and bank indicator		Fl 22413
17	Oil pressure gauge deleted		
	Ammeter installed in its place	0 – 120 A	Fl 32509-3
18	Fuel contents gauge (forward tank)		0 – 610 l Fl 20723
	Landing flap position indicator (right, next to SZK K 2)	0 - 60°	Fl 22851
	Double boost pressure gauge (in auxiliary panel)	2 x 0.6 – 1.8 atm	Fl 20556
•	It is likely that the following were also installed (bottom left)		
	FuG 101a radio altimeter	0 – 150 / 0 – 750 m	Ln 28330-1
	Outside air temperature gauge	-60 / +40° C	Fl 20349

(numbering based on illustration at top of Page 273)

Observer's instrument panel:

No.	Equipment	Instrument Range	Requisition/Equipment Number
*	Airspeed indicator	100 – 1000 km/h	Fl 22245
*	Fine and coarse altimeter	0 – 10000 m	Fl 22320
*	Vertical speed indicator (revised housing shape)	-30 / +30 m/s	Fl 22386
*	PKT/f8 master compass indicator (small version)		127-659a
*	Radar scope		
*	Radar controls		
*	Spk.f.1 transmit button	Ln 26663	

Radar operator's position in the Me 262 B-1a/U1. The FuG 16 radio is missing, however the radar scope is still in place. (National War Museum)

Developments After 1945

After the Second World War the Allies imposed a total ban on aircraft construction in Germany and thus brought developments in the field of instruments to an end as well. Not until 1951 were the restrictions relaxed to allow glider flying and then in 1955 permission was granted to build powered aircraft.

Until that time some German aviation technicians and engineers had been able to continue their research or develop new aircraft abroad. As aviation became increasingly globalized, more international standards were accepted in aircraft construction and equipment, and as a result uniquely German developments disappeared.

Some German standards from before 1945 were accepted elsewhere and in some cases developed further. Nations which operated German-designed aircraft well into the 1950s, such as the CSSR and France, adopted some German standards.

For decades after the war elements of German instrumentation such as the combined turn-and-bank indicator and artificial horizon, oxygen indicator, some switches and fittings and the color marking system were to be found in Russian aircraft.

After the lifting of the ban on aircraft construction in Germany instruments left over from wartime production were used, especially in gliders. Automatic switches were Fl numbers were even used in the Do 27. New developments followed, however these were often based on foreign products. Each company again had its own standards, for centralized controls as exerted by the Ministry of Aviation prior to 1945 no longer existed. Aircraft manufacturers, many of which are now multi-national companies, adopt standards which offer the greatest export possibilities and national standards have become redundant.

Bölkow Bo 209 VR Monsun, photographed at the Berneck airfield in 1980.

Bölkow Bo 209 Monsun

This two-seat, low-wing monoplane is considered one of the best postwar German sporting aircraft. In 1965 Hermann Mylius, head of Bölkow's light aircraft design section, proposed a successor to the Bölkow Bo 208 Junior. The new aircraft was to have a comfortable cabin with two seats side by side, more luggage space and a more powerful engine. Other features were a retractable nosewheel and folding wings to allow the aircraft to be towed behind an automobile.

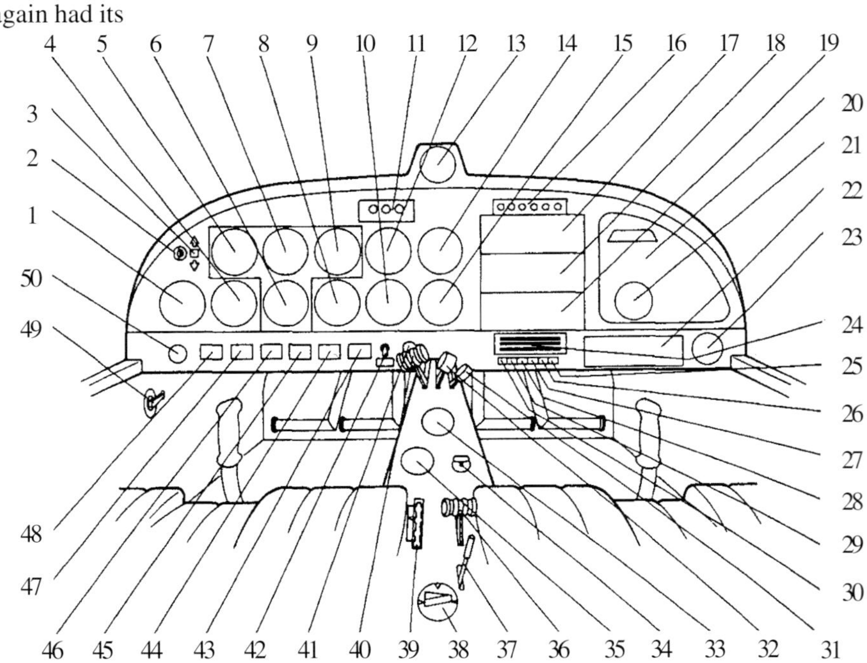

Complete blind flying instrumentation of the Bo 209 from a company brochure.

Equipment of the Monsun Based on the Brochure of 1970

1	ADF indicator
2	Undercarriage switch
3	Undercarriage position indicator
4	Turn-and-bank indicator
5	Airspeed indicator
6	Gyro compass
7	Artificial horizon
8	Vertical speed indicator
9	Altimeter
10	VOR indicator II
11	Marker beacon receiver
12	VOR indicator I
13	Compass
14	RPM indicator
15	Fuel and boost pressure gauges
16	Radio and navigation equipment switches
17	NAV/COMM I
18	NAV/COMM II
19	ADF
20	Glove box
21	Clock
22	Circuit breakers
23	Suction indicator
24	Climate controls
25	Landing light switch
26	Navigation lights switch
27	Rotating beacon switch
28	Pitot tube heat switch
29	Gyro master switch
30	Auxiliary fuel pump switch
31	Altitude corrector
32	Propeller pitch control
33	Exhaust temperature indicator
34	Landing flap switch
35	Landing flap position indicator
36	Brake lever
37	Parking brake lever
38	Tank selector switch
39	Elevator trim with indicator
40	Throttle lever
41	Carburettor pre-heat
42	Master switch with indicator lamp
43	Tank indicator right
44	Tank indicator left
45	Ammeter
46	Oil pressure gauge
47	Oil temperature gauge
48	Cylinder head temperature gauge
49	Undercarriage emergency lowering lever
50	Ignition and starter switches

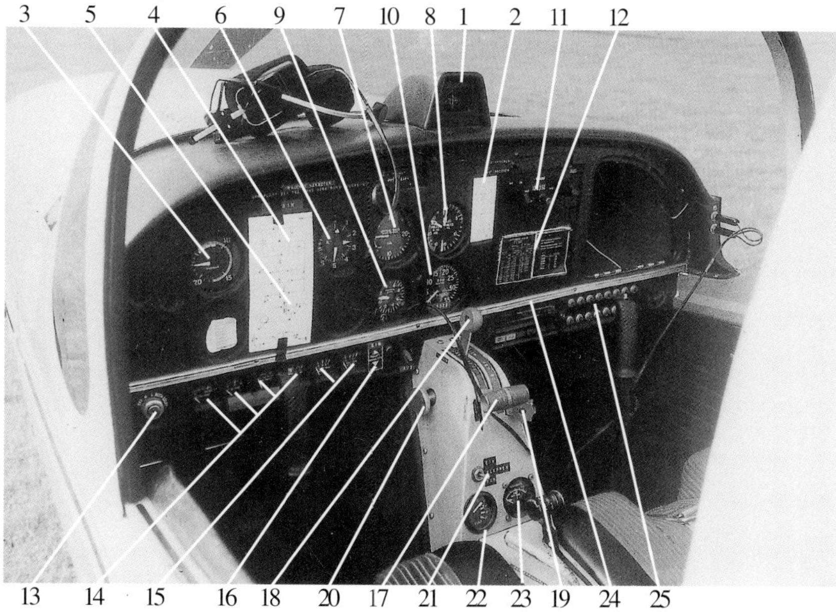

The cockpit of D-EAIN. The instruments are well laid out and there is room for expansion. A placard advises that daytime VFR flights are only permitted when no icing conditions are present.

Equipment of Bo 209 D-EAIN in 1980:

No.	Equipment	Instrument Range
1	Magnetic compass	
2	Deviation table	
3	Airspeed indicator	0 – 250 mph
4	Artificial horizon (covered by glued-on aerobatics program)	
5	Gyro compass (covered)	
6	Altimeter	0 – 20,000 ft
7	Vertical speed indicator	-2,000 / +2,000 ft/min
8	Fuel/oil pressure gauge	0 – 15 / 0 – 40 psi
9	Accelerometer	- 5 / + 10 g
10	RPM indicator with operating hours counter	0 – 3,500 rpm
11	Radio equipment	
12	Operating data placard	
13	Ignition switch	
14	Engine instruments (from left): Cylinder head temperature gauge Oil temperature and pressure gauge Ammeter	
15	Fuel contents gauges left and right	
16	Master switch	
17	Throttle lever	
18	Propeller pitch control lever	
19	Altitude corrector	
20	Throttle and mixture levers locking screw	
21	Landing flaps switch	
22	Landing flaps position indicator	
23	Exhaust gas temperature gauge (EGT)	
24	Climate control system, including switches for lighting, pitot tube heat, etc.	
25	Circuit breakers	

Design work was completed in late 1965, however the company's management hesitated to approve the project. Bölkow employees Mylius, Heynen and Krauss subsequently set up their own company in Ottobrunn and built the aircraft themselves as the MHK-101. The prototype made its first flight on 22 December 1967.

The aircraft attracted much interest at the Hanover Airshow in 1968 and Bölkow was convinced to produce the Bo 209 as the successor to the Junior. The aircraft was powered by Lycoming horizontally-opposed engines of 150-160 H.P. and had dual controls. There was also an aerobatic version, the Bo 209 VR, with a 160-H.P. fuel-injected engine.

Production was halted in 1972 after 100 aircraft had been built, even though orders had been placed for 275. Proposals to continue production privately or abroad did not reach fruition. The economy was in large part responsible for ending the career of a promising aircraft. approximately fifty Monsuns are still registered worldwide. The ITN of the Bo 209 was conventional for its day. The instrument panel with its black front and instruments, mainly American, installed from the rear resembled those of many foreign products from Cessna or Morane.

There was nothing to be seen of German instruments or standards. The decision to adopt this style of instrumentation was of course influenced by export considerations and the increasing internationalization of aviation.

Instrumentation, like equipment and color schemes, usually depended on the wishes of the customer. There was a simple basic layout plus various additions. The company brochure depicts a fully-equipped panel with blind flying instruments. It includes the T-arrangement of airspeed indicator, artificial horizon, vertical speed indicator and gyro compass.

Used here as an example is the Do 209 VR D-EAIN, an aerobatic version with simplified instrumentation and dual controls, which corresponded to the basic equipment listed in the brochure.

The engine controls are in the center where they could be easily reached from either seat. The instruments are located on the left of the panel, with the radio and circuit breakers plus a map case on the right.

Several years after these photos were taken, D-EAIN was lost in a crash.

Do 27 A-4, D-EEPN, is prepared for a flight in Laupheim.

Dornier Do 27

The Do 27 was the first German aircraft to enter large-scale production after the resumption of aviation activities in 1955. Approximately 570 were built between 1956 and 1977, including 50 built under license in Spain. The basis of the design was the Do 25, which Dornier engineers had developed in Spain in 1953-54. With the exception of the engine, the Do 25 had all the design features of the later Do 27.

The Do 27 was a cantilever shoulder-wing monoplane with a spacious cockpit and large glazed areas. Leading edge slots and an appropriate wing profile guaranteed excellent short takeoff and landing characteristics. The principal versions were the Do 27 A and B for the German Air Force, which was the largest customer for the type and which operated it until 1980 as an observation, liaison, training and air ambulance aircraft.

The aircraft's equipment was as varied as its roles and it was built with single and dual controls. The most common power plants were Lycoming horizontally-opposed engines producing from 274 to 340 H.P.

The Do 27 was also widely used by civilian operators. The H to Q versions were intended for civilian use. They were equipped with from four to eight seats and could be fitted with a conventional wheeled undercarriage, floats or skis. Civilian Do 27s, including former *Luftwaffe* aircraft, served in a wide variety of roles

Instrument panel of a Portugese Do 27 in the aviation museum in Alvercal, Portugal. The basic instrumentation is similar to that of German versions. The additional radio equipment takes up a great deal of space. The clock on the right is missing. The electrical panel no longer made use of former Luftwaffe equipment. (P.F. Selinger)

The instrument panel of Do 27, D-EEPN. Note the many placards containing information for the pilot.

and some remain in service. The type was exported to 17 nations. Portugal was the second largest operator after the German Air Force, receiving 149 aircraft, many of them former German military machines.

The cockpit of the Do 27 is very roomy with good visibility through the extensive glazed areas. Instrumentation largely depended on the wishes of the operator. Equipment of *Luftwaffe* aircraft varied according to role. The Do 27 A observation aircraft had a single set of controls and instruments, while the Do 27 B trainer had dual controls and a double set of instruments. Calibration of instruments followed NATO standards, mainly in American measurements.

The arrangement of the instruments and controls followed the classic layout for aircraft with side-by-side seats. The flight and navigation instruments were placed on the left in front of the pilot. In the center, within reach of both seats, were the engine instruments and controls. On the right side were the radio equipment, electrical switches and circuit breakers, and, in training aircraft, a second set of flight instruments.

Export aircraft were in some cases equipped rather differently. Portuguese aircraft, for example,

No.	Equipment	Instrument Range	Manufacturer/Remarks
1	Magnetic compass		Ludolph
2	Vertical speed indicator	-2500 / +2500 ft/min	Ludolph
3	Turn-and-bank indicator		
4	Radio compass		
5	Airspeed indicator	20 – 210 kts	
6	Artificial horizon		
7	Remote-reading compass indicator		
8	Altimeter	0 – 30,000 ft	
9	Radio compass controls		
10	Operating instructions placard		
11	Switches for ADF, homing and landing light		
12	Clock		Sinn
13	Boost pressure gauge	0.3 – 2.1 atm	
14	Fire warning light (red)		
15	Booster pump indicator light (yellow)		
16	Cylinder head temperature gauge	0 – 300 or 0 – 350° C	
17	Fuel pressure gauge	0 – 21 lbs	
18	RPM indicator	0 – 10,000 rpm	
19	Oil temperature and pressure gauge	0 – 14 kg/cm2 / 0 – 120° C	
20	Fuel contents gauge	2 x 0 – 100 l (each 116 l total)	
21	Voltmeter		Bosch
22	SH/ZH 2/1 ignition switch		
23	Starter button		
24	Emergency fuel shutoff handle		
25	Radiator flap control handle		
26	Throttle quadrant with throttle lever, fuel cock and mixture control		
27	Landing flap control lever		
28	Radio equipment		
29	Cockpit heat and ventilation controls		
30	Master switch		
31	Two circuit breakers for ignition switch and booster pump 19-5000		
32	Flight hours counter		
33	Main electrical panel with circuit breakers		some 19-5000

had more extensive radio equipment for operations in remote areas of the colonies. The example chosen to represent the instrumentation of the Do 27 is a Do 27 A-4, serial number 395, D-EEPN of the Laupheim Sport Flying Group. The aircraft has dual controls and double instrumentation and was originally a *Bundeswehr* aircraft (56+87).

The following placard appears in the cockpit:

Forbidden Are: Aerobatics – Spins – Instrument Flight Takeoff in Icing Conditions Low-Level Stalls

Some of the equipment in the aircraft is from wartime *Luftwaffe* stocks. For example, most of the circuit breakers are Type 19-5000. The ignition switch was built after 1945, however it is similar to the Fl 21118. The vertical speed indicator by Ludolph is an converted baffle plate variometer by Horn.

Klemm Kl 107 (Bölkow)

The Kl 107 was both the end of light aircraft development by Klemm prior to 1939 and the beginning of German aircraft construction after the lifting of the ban by the Allied powers in 1955.

Although the Second World War had the effect of halting German light aircraft development for fifteen years, it was apparent that few American production aircraft of 1955 could match the performances of pre-war German machines—an indication of the leading position held by the German light aircraft industry in those years.

In 1938 Klemm introduced the Kl 107, an aircraft of semi-monocoque plywood construction powered by a 105-H.P. Hirth HM 500 engine. As a result of the outbreak of war, only a handful of aircraft were built by 1940.

In 1955 the combined team of Bölkow and Klemm reworked the design of the Kl 107. The type was equipped with a Continental C 95 engine and an unbraced undercarriage.

The prototype Kl 107 A first flew in 1955 and later entered production as the Kl 107 B with a 150-H.P. Lycoming engine. It remained in production by Bölkow until 1961, the final version being the three-seat Kl 107 C with faired undercarriage. This was followed by the Kl 107 D or Bölkow 207, a four-seater. Many of these aircraft are still flying.

Approximately five Kl 107 Bs and twelve Kl 107 Cs from the 55 produced after 1955 have survived and continue to be flown.

Klemm Kl 107 C, D-ECIH, photograph in St. Johann, Austria.

The cockpit of Kl 107 B, D-EKAT. Note the black finish of the instrument panel. In addition to a turn and bank indicator the aircraft is equipped with an artificial horizon. Barely visible above it is the magnetic compass. The radio equipment is positioned on the right.

The instrument panel of Klemm Kl 107 C, D-ECIH. Numerous printed or engraved placards are present to assist the pilot. Most of the instruments are installed from the rear. Visible on the left is the yellow throttle lever grip. The second throttle lever is in the center console.

The Kl 107 C was offered with the following equipment:

No.	Equipment	Instrument Range	Manufacturer/Remarks
1	2 ventilation nozzles		
2	Fine and coarse altimeter	0 – 10000 m	Fl 22320
3	Airspeed indicator (a heated pitot tube could be installed if desired)	0 – 350 km/h	Fl 22228
4	Electric turn-and-bank indicator (*)		
5	FK 38 magnetic compass		Fl 23233
6	Vertical speed indicator (*)	+10 / -10 m/s	Fl 22382-10
7	Deviation table		
8	Oil temperature gauge	0 – 120° C	
9	Boost indicator lamp		
10	Double pressure gauge for fuel and oil	0 – 1 / 0 – 10 kg/cm²	Fl 20512-1
11	RPM indicator with flying hours counter	500 – 3,500 rpm	VDO
12	Fuel contents gauge for Tank 1 (65 l)		
13	Fuel contents gauge for Tank 2 (65 l)		
14	Bo-UK 1 clock with stop mechanism (*)		Fl 23885
15	Cylinder head temperature gauge 0 – 300° C		
16	Fuel cock with tank selector switch		
17	landing light switch		
18	Pitot tube heat switch		
19	Navigation lights switch		
20	Radio switch		
21	VHF radio (*)		
22	Switch for turn-and-bank indicator		
23	Electrical system master switch		
24	Ignition switch		
25	Starter push-button		
26	Throttle lever		
27	Fuel hand pump		
28	Tank selector switch: Tank 2: 65 l (aerobatics) Tank 1: 65 l (hand pump) Fuel cock OFF		
29	Cockpit heating control		
30	Parking brake handle		
31	Placard with operating data		
32	Starter injection pump		
33	Carburettor pre-heat control		
34	Altitude corrector control		
35	Throttle lever locking screw		
36	Landing flap control lever		

The cockpit and the pale gray instrument panel were equipped with lighting. As well the aircraft was equipped with seat belts, a fire extinguisher (*) and a first-aid kit (*).
The items marked with an (*) were optional equipment on the Kl 107 B.

The instrument panel of **Kl 107 C, D-ECIH**, reflects this standard equipment. Over time a number of newer instruments and additional equipment were added:

No.	Equipment	Instrument Range	Manufacturer/Remarks
2	Three-pointer altimeter	0 – 35,000 ft	Kollsman
4	Electric turn-and-bank indicator	2 min turn	
5	Magnetic compass		Airpath
6	Vertical speed indicator	+4,000 / -4,000 ft/min	
37	Negative pressure gauge for the vacuum pump		
38	Artificial horizon		
39	Gyro compass		Sperry
40	Rotating beacon switch		
41	Intercom switch		
42	Voltmeter for electrical system		

The photographs presented here depict Kl 107 B, D-EKAT, which no longer exists, and Kl 107 C, serial number 128, D-ECIH, which belongs to the Böblingen Sport Flying Group.

The cockpit and the equipment of the Klemm 107 are typical for a German aircraft from the time of the rebirth of sport flying in Germany after 1945.

The instrument panel is dominated by round instruments, some of them from the former *Luftwaffe*. Others are foreign-built, mainly American, or are modified automobile instruments.

The arrangement of the instruments on the three-part instrument panel is similar to that of the Bücker Bestmann with flight instruments on the left, and engine instruments and controls in the center. Flight instruments could also be installed on the right side if desired. The aircraft has dual controls.

The cockpit is finished in typical prewar style, while painting was to Bölkow standards or as desired by the customer.

A comparison of the equipment in an aircraft built in 1958 with that of one from 1939 reveals that little changed in the construction of the instrument panel.

During their flying careers, which in some cases spanned decades, the Kl 107s were subjected to numerous repairs, in the course of which older instruments were replaced with newer types. As a result, it is likely that each Kl 107 has its own individual suite of instruments and cockpit finish.

Equipment of a **Kl 107 from 1939**:

Equipment	Instrument Range	Manufacturer/Remarks
• SUM AP 8 starter injection pump		8-4505 A
• Airspeed indicator	50 – 350 km/h	Fl 22228
• FK 38 magnetic compass		Fl 23233
• Turn and bank indicator		
• Vertical speed indicator	+10 / -10 m/s	Fl 22382-10
• Fine and coarse altimeter	0 – 10000 m	Fl 22320
• Double pressure gauge for fuel and oil	0 – 1/0–10 kg/cm²	Fl 20512-1
• Pitch indicator (?)		
• Fuel contents gauge		
• RPM indicator	600 – 3,600 rpm	Fl 20222-3
• Bo-UK 1 clock		Fl 23885
• Ignition switch		Fl 21118

Gliders

As a sport, gliding had its beginnings in the 1920s, when it provided idealists, aviation enthusiasts and former military pilots with an opportunity to fly in difficult economic times. Most early gliders were one of a kind machines and the emphasis was on flying rather than equipment. Flights were usually of short duration and therefore no instruments were required.

As designs improved, performance increased and flights became of longer duration, the need for flight instruments grew. At first operators turned to equipment used in the First World War as a cheap alternative. Those who could afford to bought foreign equipment, from France for example, as the German aviation industry was still restricted by the terms of the Treaty of Versailles and new developments were slow in coming. As well, French manufacturers such as Badin were leaders in the field of instrument design.

Photographs from the period reveal that most early gliders were equipped with First World War instruments, such as a cup anemometer for an airspeed indicator. Occasionally a fine altimeter was included as an aid in locating thermals.

The most important instrument in glider flying is in fact the vertical speed indicator, as rate of climb or descent can reveal the presence of thermals. In keeping with this, the vertical speed indicator is usually located in the center of the instrument panel. An airspeed indicator is also important for monitoring aircraft speed and avoiding stalls.

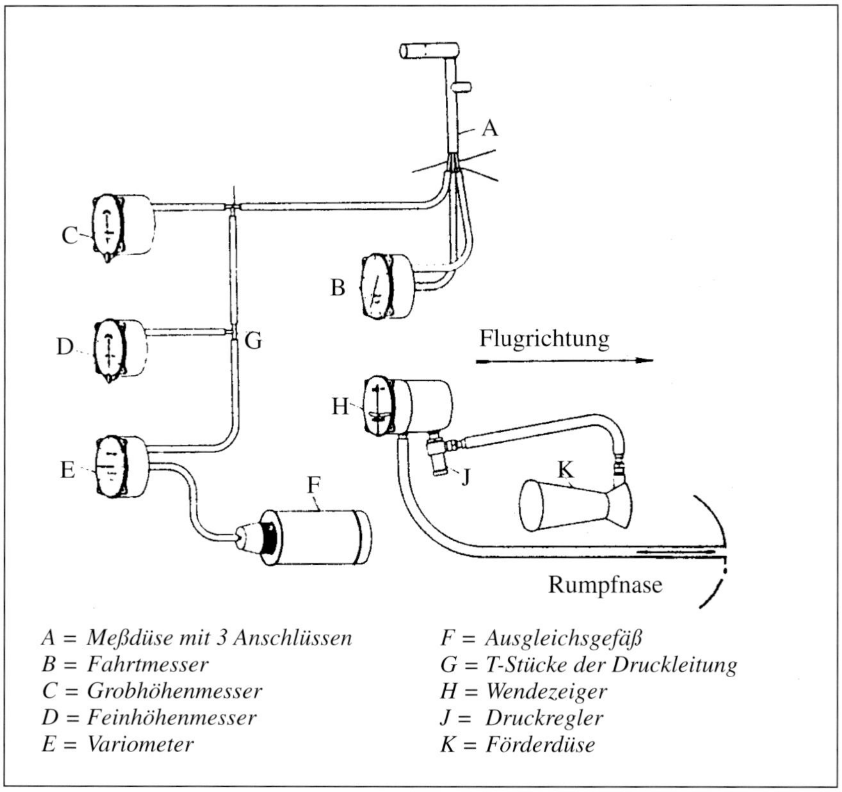

Schematic drawing of instrument installation in a glider.

Not until 1932 did the vertical speed indicator become standard equipment in glider flying, even though such instruments had been used in ballooning from very early on. Pilots engaged in competitive glider flying came to value the vertical speed indicator, however as many were trying to make a living from gliding, they kept their experiences secret from their contemporaries. Wolf Hirth was the first to reveal the significance of the vertical speed indicator to a circle of airmen with his publications.

As instruments were still very expensive in the 1920s and early 1930s, at first their use was limited to a few experts and those few who could afford them. For safety, many high-performance pilots had two vertical speed indicators installed in their aircraft.

It is worth noting that Ernst Philipp built his own vertical speed indicator using mainly materials from his own home: wood for the housing, a toothbrush handle as a bearer, a dry blade of grass for a needle, a dandelion seed for cushioning, and a condom for a membrane.

Beginning in 1932 the recommended instrumentation for a glider consisted of turn-and-bank indicator, compass, vertical speed indicator, airspeed indicator and altimeter. As flight endurance increased, pilots frequently flew for periods in cloud and in the long run a pilot's senses and experience could not replace instruments.

In 1937-38 an Mü 17 used for record-setting flights was equipped with a radio, although the weight of the equipment made it necessary to increase the glider's wingspan. In a few cases an artificial horizon was also installed with a hand pump to power the instrument in case of icing.

These were instruments for the top pilots, however. Most glider pilots were content with a vertical speed indicator, airspeed indicator, altimeter and perhaps a compass.

For gliders engaged in competitions and record attempts, another device of importance is the recording altimeter, which documents the altitudes flown. Another tool is the camera, used to document turning points when flying triangular courses.

This instrumentation remained unchanged until the introduction of the first electronic equipment in the 1970s. Today light-

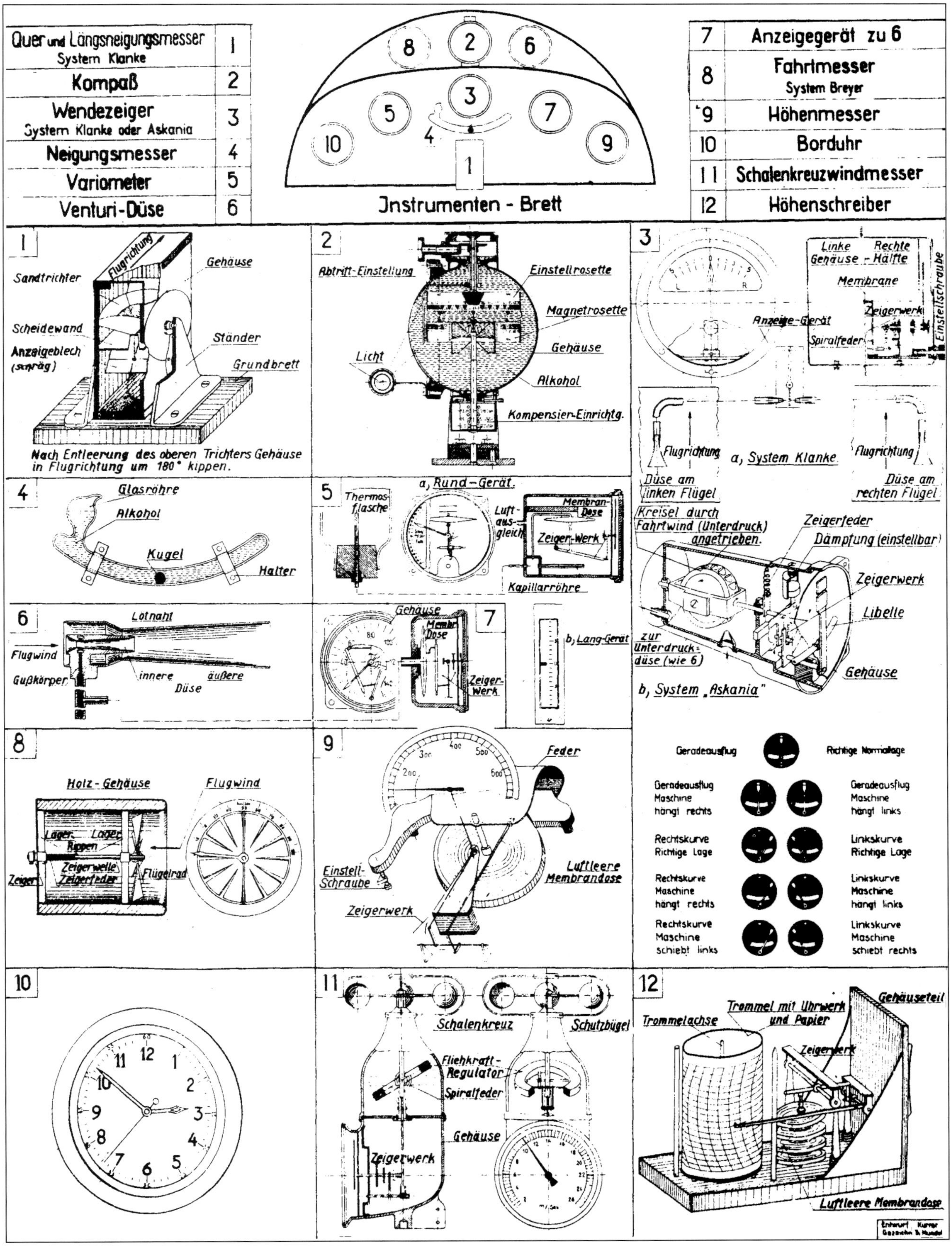

Glider instruments from the 1930s from glider construction manuals.

The Mü 13 d, D-6293, on the Wasserkuppe prior to going on display in the Glider Museum. (Burlan)

weight radios, computers and GPS systems have become standard equipment in gliders.

Until the 1970s most gliders were made of wood with fabric covering and had to be protected inside and outside against the effects of weather. Most early types were painted with a clear protective finish. Later the State Ministry of Aviation (RLM) specified color RLM 05 *Elfenbein* (ivory) for gliders. Beginning in July 1944 this bright color was replaced by a camouflage finish of *Braunviolett* 81 (brown-violet) and *Hellgrün* 82 (light green).

Homebuilt gliders and machines built after 1951 were usually painted to meet the desires of the purchaser. Often the outside and inside were painted the same color. Instrument panels, too, were often painted in the same color as the exterior or in various shades of gray and in some cases black. Today the emphasis is on smoothness of finish for increased performance rather than protection from the elements.

Akaflieg München Mü 13

The Mü 13 was a single-seat development of the Milan and was the only aircraft of the Munich school to be produced in quantity before 1945. Many of its design features would become standard in postwar gliders: cantilever trapezoidal wing, fabric-covered steel tube fuselage and a cockpit integral with the overall design.

Two prototypes of the Mü 13, *Merlin* and *Atalante*, were built in 1935-36. Their designs differed in a number of details. The Mü 13 became known quickly after winning at the 17th Rhön Gliding Competition, where it set a new endurance record of 13 hours and 40 minutes.

The Schwarzwald-Flugzeugbau Jehle in Donaueschingen subsequently obtained a license to produce the glider. The Mü 13 d production version was based on a slightly modified *Atalante* and 150 were built.

The Mü 13 was one of the most popular German gliders and it reappeared when gliding was once again permitted in Germany in 1951. Some were built by Scheibe from components from Mü 13 E production. A total of ten Mü 13 d gliders have survived worldwide. One is D-6293 in the gliding museum on the Wasserkuppe. While still flying, for many years it had an unusual redesigned nose, however the aircraft was restored to its original configuration before it was placed on display. The photographs presented here depict this aircraft.

As the Mü13 was used both as a training aircraft and as a performance aircraft in competitions, instrumentation varied. D-6293 in the gliding museum has simple instrumentation typical of a training machine and similar to that of the Grunau Baby.

Photographs from the CSSR depicting the instrumentation of an Mü 13 d (OK-8078) in 1960 make it possible to reconstruct the instrumentation of a professional's aircraft.

The instrument panel has various openings and some German instruments, and by comparing it with those of other gliders of the same period it is possible to determine, though not with 100% certainty, its original equipment.

Instead of an artificial horizon, the Czech machine has three electric toggle switches whose purpose is unknown. Perhaps an electric turn-and-bank indicator and radio were installed.

Instrumentation of the Mü 13 d in the Gliding Museum:

No.	Equipment	Instrument Range	Manufacturer/Remarks
1	Turn-and-bank indicator (Askania)		Fl 22402
2	Fine and coarse altimeter	0 – 10000 m	Winter
3	Vertical speed indicator	+5 / -5 m/s	
4	Airspeed indicator	30 – 200 km/h	Winter
	With the exception of the turn-and-bank indicator, the instruments were post-1945 equipment with similar instrument ranges. Compromises often have to be made during restorations when original instruments cannot be found.		

Professional Instrumentation of an Mü 13 d:

No.	Equipment	Instrument Range	Manufacturer/Remarks
1	Vertical speed indicator (Askania or Horn)		+5 / -5 m/s Fl 22379
2	Artificial horizon (Askania Lgab 8)		Fl 22426
3	Fine and coarse altimeter (Askania)	0 – 10000 m	Fl 22319
	or Fuess		Fl 22320
4	Airspeed indicator (Bruhn Velocat)	20 – 150 km/h	Fl ?
5	Turn-and-bank indicator for gliders (Askania Lg 18r)		Fl 22402-2
6	Magnetic compass (Askania Lke 6)		Fl 23226
	or (Ludolph FK 38)		Fl 23233
7	Clock (Kienzle 8-Day)		Fl 23886-1
	or (Askania Lu 1K)		

Cockpit of *Mü 13 d, D-6293. The windscreen is faired into the leading edge of the wing.*

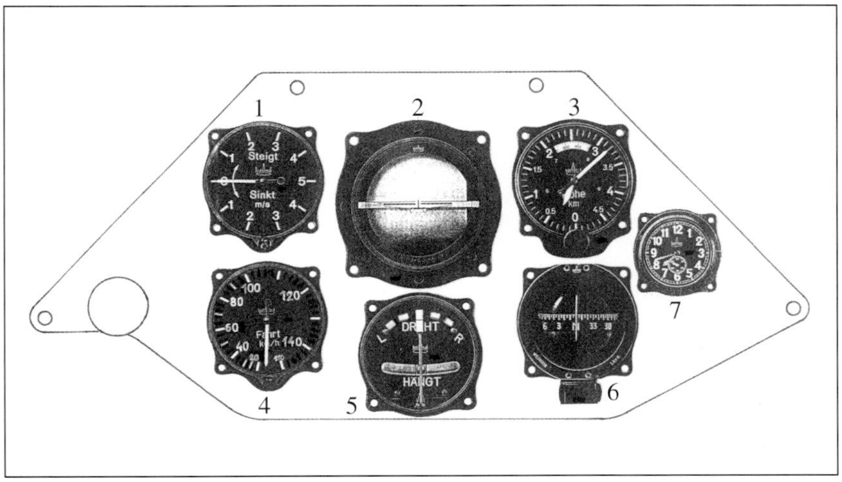

Reconstruction of the instrumentation installed in an Mü 13 d for professional pilots. (not to scale)

DFS Olympia *Meise* (Titmouse)

Following the decision to introduce gliding as a sport in the 1940 Olympic Games, in 1938 the International Olympic Committee wrote a competition for a standard Olympic glider to be used by all competing nations. All submissions were required to adhere to the following conditions:

- wingspan of 15 meters
- gross weight of 160 kg
- plywood, pine and steel as standard building materials
- wings with dive brakes
- cockpit to accommodate a pilot 1.80 meters tall with back parachute
- skid for takeoff and landing

Thus the standard class in gliding was established in 1938. The selection competition took place in Secce, Italy in February 1939. The technical committee and six internationally-known glider pilots were to evaluate five competing designs from Italy, Poland and Germany.

The winner was the Meise, designed by Hans Jacobs of the DFS. It was a simple shoulder-wing design which was simple to build and easy to maintain. The design incorporated experience gained with the *Reiher* and *Weihe*, and the *Meise* was essentially a smaller version of the Weihe.

The 1940 Olympic Games fell victim to the Second World War, however the nickname Olympia remained with the *Meise* and its international future was assured in spite of political intrigues.

Even before 1945 gliding clubs around the world built the type in large numbers and after the Second World War it made a major contribution to the resurgence of gliding in Europe.

As the Nord 2000 in France, Eon Olympia in England or Zlin ZG 25 Sohaj in the CSSR, the *Meise* was to be found on many airfields. As well, many examples were built by amateurs in the Federal Republic of Germany and Spain. All told, approximately 1,000 *Meisen* were built.

Almost all of the *Meisen* which survive in Germany today were built after the resumption of gliding in 1951. While most *Meisen* in West Germany were amateur-built, the majority of those in East Germany were produced by VEB in Lomatzsch.

A small number of *Meisen* continue to fly, while others are on display in museums. Approximately 60 Meisen, not including built-built aircraft, survive today.

The instrumentation of the *Meise* is graphically illustrated in a replacement parts list produced by Schmetz in 1943. Schmetz produced the glider for training purposes during the war.

With standard equipment of compass, turn-and-bank indicator and clock, the *Meise* was well-suited for long-range and performance flights and could be flown in less than perfect weather. Most *Meisen* built in West Germany after 1945 were constructed by amateurs. While they were built from original plans, there were many modifications by the builders. This is reflected in the equipment installed in the aircraft and their finishes.

Meise D-1420 during a visit to Italy. (Dr. Ziller)

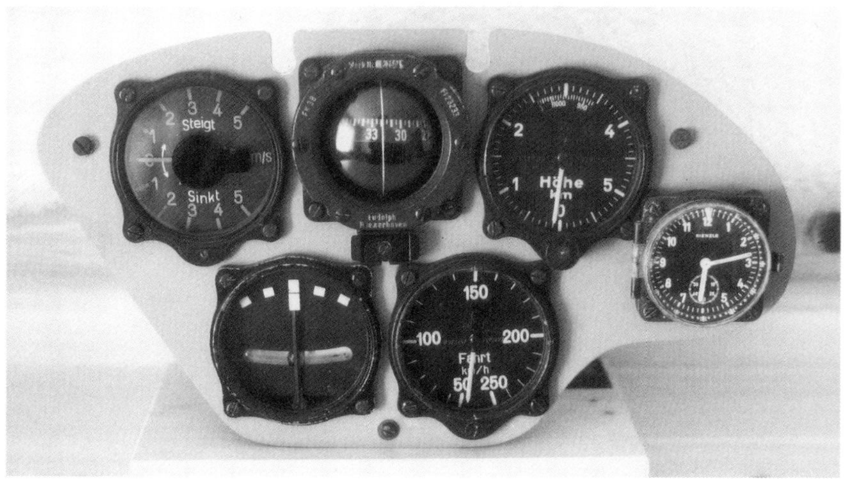

Replica of the Meise instrument panel.

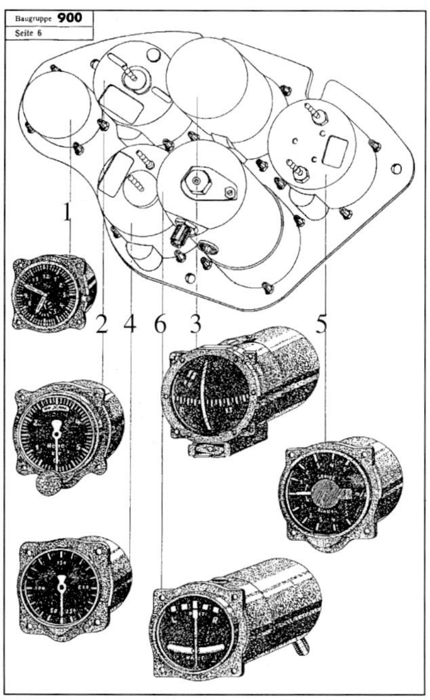

Drawing of the Meise's instrument panel from the replacement parts list dated 1943.

Instrument panel of Meise D-1420. Varnished plywood was used. Almost all of the instruments were installed from the back.

Instrumentation of the Meise Based on the Replacement Parts List:

No.	Equipment	Instrument Range	Manufacturer/Remarks
(see drawing on Page 286)			
1	Clock		Fl 23886-1
2	Altimeter	0 – 6000 m	Fl 22316-6
3	FK 38 magnetic compass		Fl 23233
4	Airspeed indicator	50 – 250 km/h	Fl 22215
5	Vertical sped indicator (Horn)	+5 / -5 m/s	
6	Turn-and-bank indicator for gliders (Askania Lg 18r)		Fl 22402-2

Other items of equipment included:

	Item		Manufacturer/Remarks
•	Lreg 9A suction regulator (on turn-and-bank indicator)		
•	Compensator for vertical speed indicator		Fl 22360
•	Ldü 35 feed jet for the turn-and-bank indicator gyroscope		
•	Calibrated nozzle for the airspeed indicator		Fl 22287

There was also a release lever for the tow coupling and a canopy locking handle.
The Meise's instrument panel was of aluminum sheet and the instruments were held in place by bolts and lock-nuts.

Equipment of Meise D-1420:

Equipment	Instrument Range	Manufacturer/Remarks
• Clock		
• Vertical speed indicator (Horn)	+5 / -5 m/s	
• FK 16 magnetic compass (Ludolph)		post-1945
• Radio (Winter)		post-1945
• Airspeed indicator (Winter)	40 – 250 km/h	post-1945
• Altimeter	0 – 3000 m	post-1945
• Placard with pre-takeoff and pre-landing checks		
• Data table		

DFS Meise	
Allowable speeds	
Winch takeoff	up to 80 km/h
Towed takeoff	up to 100 km/h
Turbulent conditions	up to 100 km/h
Calm conditions	up to 175 km/h

Trim Plan	
Load in seat	91 to 100 kg
Shortfall in occupant weight to be made up with ballast	

Equipment of Meise D-4679:

Equipment	Instrument Range	Manufacturer/Remarks
• Vertical speed indicator (Horn)	+5 / -5 m/s	
• FK 16 magnetic compass (Ludolph)		post-1945
• Airspeed indicator (Winter)	50 – 250 km/h	post-1945
• Vertical speed indicator (capillary device)	-6 / +6 m/s	
• Turn-and-bank indicator		Fl 22412
• Fine and coarse altimeter	0 – 10000 m	Fl 22320

Cockpit of Meise, D-4679, in the Glider Museum on the Wasserkuppe. Some of the instruments date to before 1945. Note the linear capillary variometer, bottom center.

As a rule, instrumentation was similar to that of prewar *Meisen* but frequently differed in detail. Early aircraft relied on surplus *Luftwaffe* instruments, while later machines were equipped with a mixture of old and new German equipment and foreign instruments. There were many variations, however most later aircraft had some sort of miniature radio.

Two examples are the *Meisen* in the Gliding Museum on the Wasserkuppe (D-4679) and the aircraft of Jörg Ziller (D-1420). Both are amateur-built machines from the 1950s.

FVA 10b Rheinland

The first academic flying groups (*Akafliegs*) formed in the universities soon after the end of the First World War. Many like-minded and capable scientists found an ideal forum where they could conduct experiments under ideal conditions relating to scientific problems in the field of aviation. One of the most active of these groups was the *Flugwissenschaftliche Vereinigung Aachen* (FVA), which was created shortly after the end of the First World War. In the beginning its members brought little but their enthusiasm, for materials were very expensive and the occupying authorities extremely mistrustful. It was under these adverse conditions that the group in Aachen built its first glider, the *Schwarze Teufel* (Black Devil). It was the first cantilever monoplane in the history of gliders.

The Black Devil rewarded the faith of its designers by flying successfully at the first Rhön competition, setting a world record and simultaneously initiating the use of the elastic cord takeoff.

FVA 10b Rheinland in flight over England. (M. Beach)

Compared to the first designs, the FVA 10a of 1936 was a highly modern glider which was characterized by its elegant aerodynamic shape. The cockpit was almost totally integrated into the fuselage contours and the slim wing had a slight gull shape. The FVA 10g flew in the Alpine Gliding Meet for Akafliegs in August 1936 and gave an impressive performance, although it did not succeed in crossing the Alps. This feat was not achieved until one year later, when Hanna Reitsch accomplished it in a Junior Sperber.

In May 1937 designer Felix Kracht test-flew his redesigned and considerably improved FVA 10b *Rheinland*. Soon afterwards he participated in the FFG Alpine Flight Research Meet, where he finally succeeded in crossing the Alps. The Rheinland won first prize for technical merit at the 1937 Rhön competition, its retractable undercarriage, in particular, attracting much attention.

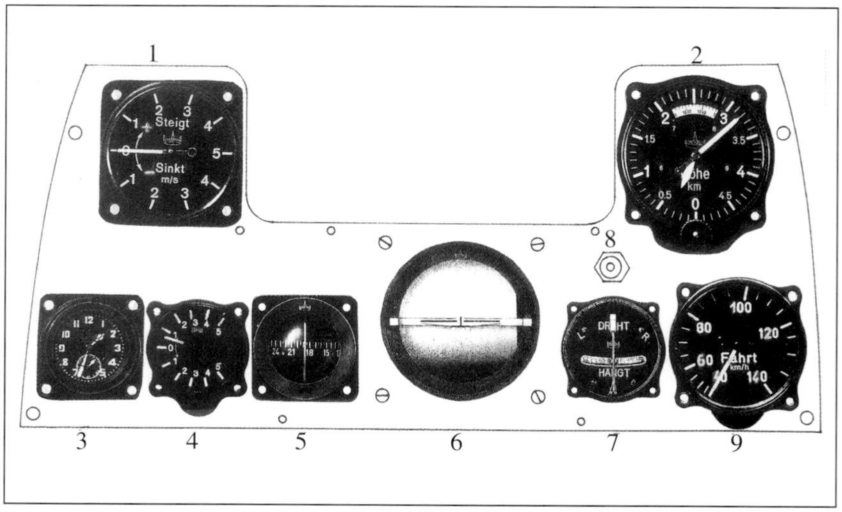

Instrumentation of the Rheinland based on an historical photograph (not to scale).

Altogether just 29 examples of the FVA 10b were built, of which two survive. The *Rheinland* illustrated here was built in 1939 and until 1959 was used as a trainer by the RAF at RAF Geilenkirchen. It was subsequently shipped to England, where it was fully restored and returned to active flying as BGA 1711.

The FVA 10b was restored again in 1985-86, during which it was painted in an authentic RLM 05 Ivory finish and given the markings D-12-354. In late 1994 the gliding museum on the Wasserkuppe obtained the aircraft for its collection.

A high-performance glider designed mainly for research purposes, the Rheinland was usually equipped with more than the standard instrumentation of vertical speed indicator, airspeed indicator and altimeter. The instrument panel was attached to the hood by struts. The aircraft's instrumentation is illustrated in an accompanying drawing based on an historical photograph.

Typical equipment installed in an FVA 10b:

No.	Equipment	Instrument Range	Manufacturer/Remarks
1	Vertical speed indicator (Askania)	+5 / -5 m/s	
2	Fine and coarse altimeter	0 – 10000 m	Fl 22319
3	Clock (Askania or Kienzle)		
4	V5 or V7 vertical speed indicator (Horn)		+5 / -5 m/s
5	Lke 1/s magnetic compass (Askania)		
6	Artificial horizon (Sperry)		Fl 22426
7	Electric turn-and-bank indicator		Fl 22413
8	Switch for turn-and-bank indicator		
9	Airspeed indicator	40 – 140 km/h	Fl 22216

Instrumentation of the FVA 10b in the Gliding Museum:

Equipment		Instrument Range	Manufacturer/Remarks
1	Magnetic compass		
2	Airspeed indicator	10 – 140 kts	
3	Vertical speed indicator (Winter)	+5 / -5 m/s	
4	MK 19 fine and coarse altimeter	0 – 60,000 ft	

The Rheinland in the gliding museum has an equipment console designed by its last British owner with much simpler instrumentation than the FVA 10 delivered in 1939. The cockpit is painted in the standard RAF Interior Green used in the 1940s.

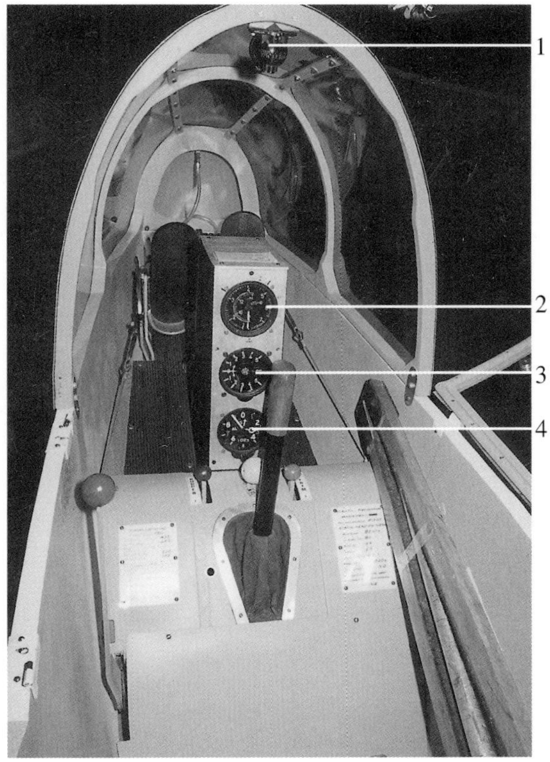

The cockpit of the Rheinland in the Glider Museum. The long wooden part on the right is a locking mechanism for the rudder.

Grunau Baby

From 1930 gliding spread all over the world and this period also saw the beginning of high-performance gliding. The international badge of achievement, the Silver C, was also brought into being at this time.

What was lacking, however, was a standard type of cheap, light glider which could be used for training purposes but also as a high-performance machine. In an effort to meet this need, in 1930031 Edmund Schneider designed his Grunau Baby. Six Baby Is took part in the Rhön competition in 1932 and soon drawings were made available for private construction.

In autumn 1932 Emil Rolle, under Schneider's supervision, designed the rather larger Baby II. With its six-sided fuselage, the single seat high-wing monoplane was very simple to build, making it possible for gliding groups to construct the glider themselves.

The Baby proved an outstanding performer and, as a result of the positive experiences with the type, in 1933 it was redesigned.

Baby IIb, D-1203, during a flying day at Malmsheim.

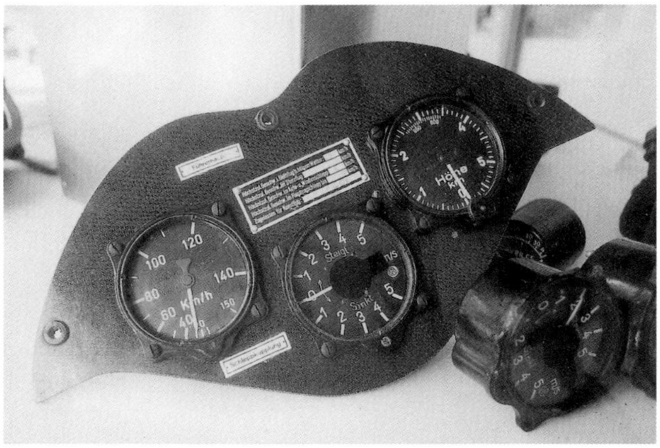

Original instrument panel made of synthetic material (Pertinax) from a Baby IIb produced by the aviation industry. The two small placards contain instructions for jettisoning the canopy (top) and releasing the tow coupling. The photograph was taken in the former air museum in Augsburg.

Instrument panel from an amateur-built Baby IIb dating from about 1951 and now in the Glider Museum on the Wasserkuppe. A rarity is the Friebe fluid variometer. Instruments operating on the same principle appeared at the end of the First World War.

The wing was extended to further improve the Baby's handling characteristics. The resulting Baby IIb became the most popular and widely-built training glider of the 1930s and 1940s.

In the same year the Baby set a new world record of 36 hours and 36 minutes and by 1934-35 it had become the most widely used glider in the world. Although it had been developed solely for training purposes, the Baby was capable of flights of up to 200 km.

More than 5,000 Babys were built by various manufacturers and gliding groups in and outside Germany, making it the most numerous glider in history.

When gliding was allowed to resume in Germany after the Second World War, the Grunau Baby once again became the basic equipment of gliding groups in the east and west. Beginning in 1950, private groups and manufacturers began overhauling or building various versions of the Baby.

The improved Baby III, which had been conceived by Edmund Schneider during the war, was built in small numbers from 1951. Compared to its predecessors, it had a revised fuselage with enclosed cockpit. The wing and tail surfaces were also modified. The most obvious difference, however, was the semi-recessed wheel housed in the landing skid. The final variant, which appeared in 1955, was the two-seat Grunau Baby V with steel-tube fuselage. Beginning in 1939, a small series of about 25 Motorbabys, powered by an 18-H.P. Kroeber M 4 engine, was built. It was the first truly usable motorized glider to be built anywhere.

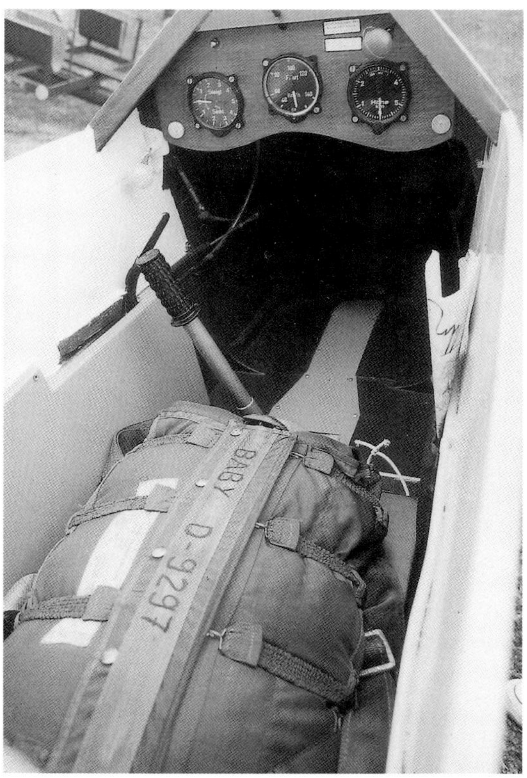

Cockpit of Baby III, D-9297. Apart from some minor changes in shape, the instrument panel is little changed. Vertical speed indicator, airspeed indicator and altimeter remain the only instruments.

Because of the Baby's simple construction and its intended role—mainly for visual flight near an airfield—the cockpits of most production Baby IIb gliders were equipped with only the most essential instruments:

Instrument	Range	Make
• Airspeed indicator	20 – 150 km/h	(Bruhn)
• Vertical speed indicator	-5 / +5 m/s	(Askania V7)
• Altimeter	0 – 6000 m	(Fuess Fl 22316-6)

A placard in the cockpit listed maximum allowable speeds:

Maximum allowable speed in gliding flight in turbulence	90 km/h
Maximum allowable diving speed	200 km/h
Maximum allowable speed in auto or winch takeoff	80 km/h
Maximum allowable speed in towed takeoff	90 km/h
Allowable for aerobatics	none

There was also a lever for releasing the tow coupling and for unlocking the cockpit hood or canopy.

The newly-built Musterle in flight. (P. Selinger)

A few Babys remain on the civil register and continue to be flown. Approximately 230 Baby IIb, 80 Baby III, one Baby V and one Motorbaby have survived.

The Baby's instrument panel was usually made of aircraft plywood, although some were made of the synthetic material Pertinax.

In addition to the standard equipment of Babys produced by the aviation industry, there were many variations in privately built and owned machines. The most common add-ons were the compass and turn-and-bank indicator. Radios were not installed until after 1945, when smaller and lighter sets reached the market.

Following the resumption of gliding in Germany in 1951, most Babys were equipped with former *Luftwaffe* instruments, however as time went on these were replaced by new or foreign equipment.

Hirth Musterle

On August 25, 1909 five students aged 15 to 16 years founded the Darmstadt Air Sport Association. In 1911 the group discovered the Wasserkuppe for gliding. After the First World War this tradition was continued by former military pilots who founded the Darmstadt Academic Flying Group. Success was not long in coming, and in 1924 the group was victorious in the Rhön competition, establishing for itself in a leading place in German glider design.

This *Akaflieg* developed many well-known aircraft types such as the *Konsul*, which is considered to be the father of all gliders. One of the group's later designs was the H II PL *Lore*, designed by Paul Laubenthal. He based the design of the *Lore* on experience

Wolf Hirth displays the cockpit hood housing the instrument panel. Note the venturi tube affixed to the outside of the hood. (Heyn Collection)

with the *Darmstadt I*. The *Lore* in turn inspired Wolf Hirth's *Musterle*, which was his pet name for his wife. The Musterle was manufactured by the Segelflugzeugbau Kassel and the selling price was 8,500 *Reichsmark*, a small fortune in those days, enough to purchase a small house.

In autumn 1930 Wolf Hirth took his Musterle to the American National Gliding Competition in Elmira, New York. There he flew with a vertical speed indicator for the first time and on 4 October 1930 he succeeded in his first clear-air thermal flight. Other successes by the Musterle included:

- 1929 two first prizes in the Rhön competition
- 1930 four first prizes in Elmira
- 1931 a flight over New York and a bad weather flight over the Rhön
- 1932 first prize in the distance competition at the Rhön competition

Beginning in 1931 the Musterle was fitted with a plywood hood over the cockpit with four windows to protect the pilot from the elements. Hirth installed a radio in the hope that he would be able to determine his approximate position in relation to known radio stations. His experiments met with little success, however.

The aircraft's registration was D-Musterle and at times it also bore the name of its sponsor, Wanderer. The Musterle came to a sad end in Stuttgart in 1939 when it was destroyed in a hangar fire.

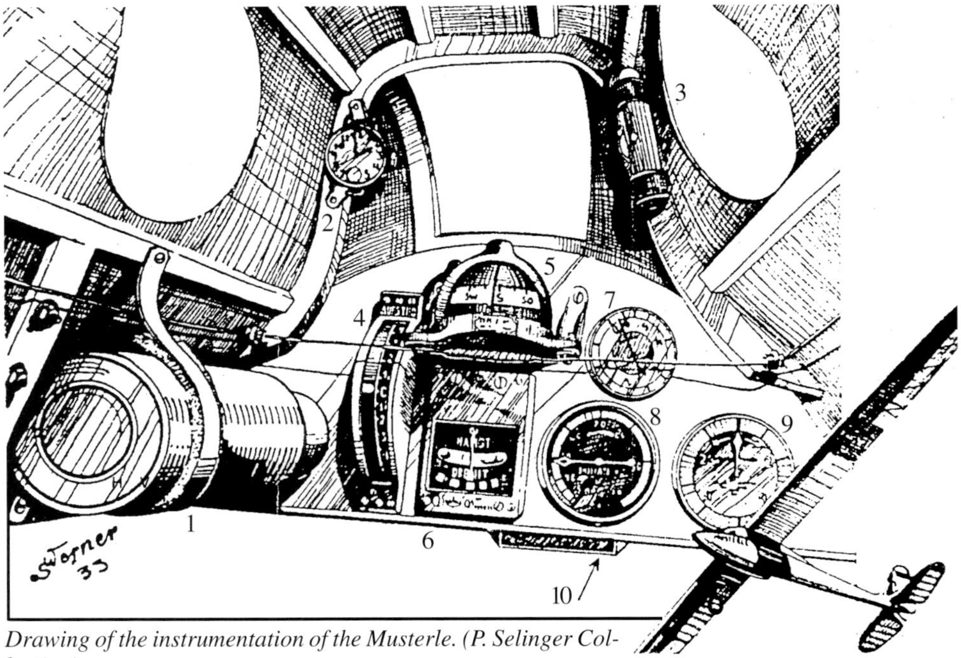

Drawing of the instrumentation of the Musterle. (P. Selinger Collection)

Instrumentation of the *Musterle*:

No.	Equipment	Instrument Range	Manufacturer/Remarks
1	Compensator for the vertical speed indicator		
2	Clock		
3	Flashlight		
4	Vertical speed indicator (Askania)	+5 / -5 m/s	
5	Magnetic compass (Plath)		
6	Turn-and-bank indicator (Askania)		
7	Altimeter (Lufft ?)	0 – 6000 m	
8	Airspeed indicator (Badin)	20 – 120 km/h	
9	Vertical speed indicator (Badin)	+5 / -5 m/s	
10	Radio		

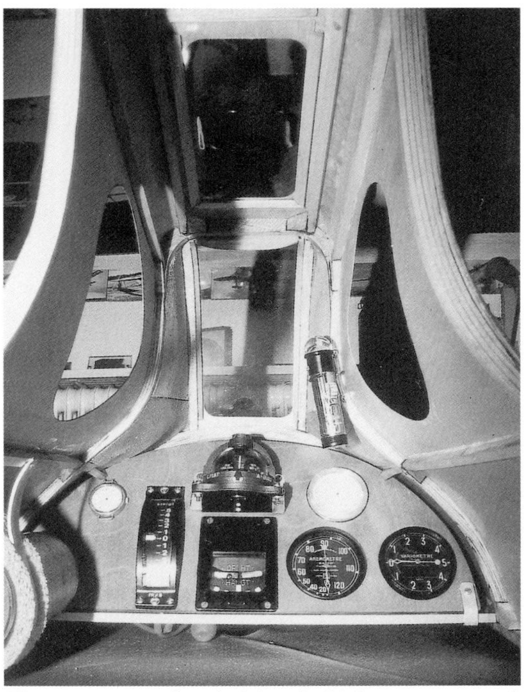
The reconstructed cockpit hood with instrument panel. (P. Selinger)

In 1992 the glider specialist Klaus Heyn, who had already built copies of the *Rhönadler* and the Schulz *Besenstiel*, began work on a reconstruction of the *Musterle*. Some years earlier he had reproduced a rudder from this aircraft. As few drawings had survived many parts had to be redesigned at much cost. Siegfried Lorenz provided plans for the seat from the H II PL. After many hundreds of hours of work, in September 1999 the aircraft made its first flight in Aalen-Elchingen. Klaus Heyn undertook a number of modifications to suit the glider for modern flight operations. The aircraft was flown with an open cockpit for better visibility and the reproduction of the hood-mounted instrument panel was replaced by one with modern round instruments. The prototype *Musterle* had originally flown with an open cockpit too.

Wolf Hirth had provided the Musterle with instrumentation suitable for a high-performance glider, which far surpassed what was standard for a glider in the late 1920s. Flying the Musterle, Hirth became convinced of the value of a vertical speed indicator for detecting the presence of thermals.

The Rhönadler in the Glider Museum. Visible on the fuselage nose is the nozzle for the airspeed indicator.

In the early days of gliding in the 1920s, most gliders were not equipped with instruments. Those who could afford them installed surplus instruments from the First World War, foreign equipment or home-made devices. A fine altimeter was sometimes used to aid in the search for thermal fields.

Although the vertical speed indicator had been recognized as an important indicator since the days of ballooning, it was not until 1932 that such instruments became standard equipment in gliders. Alexander Lippisch had already pointed out the importance of the vertical speed indicator in gliding in 1928, however the competition pilots of the day kept their findings to themselves to prevent a rival from gaining an advantage.

Wolf Hirth saw things differently, however, and published articles in aviation magazines describing his experiences with the vertical speed indicator in the *Musterle*.

A drawing taken from a contemporary aviation magazine depicts the instrumentation and equipment installed in the *Musterle* (Page 292).

The installation of two vertical speed indicators is almost universal in modern-day gliders. At the end of the 1920s the French company Badin was the leader in the building of vertical speed indicators and other aircraft instruments. Wolf Hirth selected instruments made by this manufacturer.

Klaus Heyn's reconstruction is based on the historical documents. Deviations for modern flight operations included the registration D-8365, the Federal German flag on the tail, spoilers on the wing upper surfaces and a tow coupling. In his day Hirth used the elastic cord method exclusively, which would also be possible with the reproduction. Instruments are modern round devices and consist of: magnetic compass, altimeter, airspeed indicator, vertical speed indicator, acoustic variometer and a radio. Klaus Heyn flies with a parachute. Wolf Hirth flew without one and therefore had more room in the small cockpit.

For display purposes, the copy of the original instrument panel has been installed in the reconstructed Musterle. Instruments are historical items of similar equipment.

Instrumentation of the *Rhönadler* in the Glider Museum:

Equipment	Instrument Range	Manufacturer/Remarks
• Bank indicator (spirit level)		
• Vertical speed indicator	+5 / -5 m/s	Badin
• Airspeed indicator	20 – 150 km/h	
• Altimeter	0 – 4500 m	
• Clock		

Rhönadler (Rhön Eagle)

Hans Jacobs, today considered the most successful German designer of gliders, began working with Alexander Lippisch in the technical department of the Rhön-Rossitten Association on the Wasserkuppe in 1927.

To supplement his earnings, Jacobs began working part time for Alexander Schleicher's recently-established glider company. His first design was the *Rhönadler*, a single-seat high-performance glider with a shoulder-mounted cantilever wing and enclosed cockpit.

The first aircraft took part in the Rhön competition in 1932 and the results led Jacobs to redesign the *Rhönadler*. The glider's wingspan was reduced, while the fuselage cross-section and tail surfaces were enlarged and the wing profile changed.

By 1937 the *Rhönadler*, 65of which were built by Schleicher, had become the most popular high-performance glider in Germany. Production of the *Rhönadler* ended in 1940. While a number of aircraft survived the war, the only remaining authentic *Rhönadler*

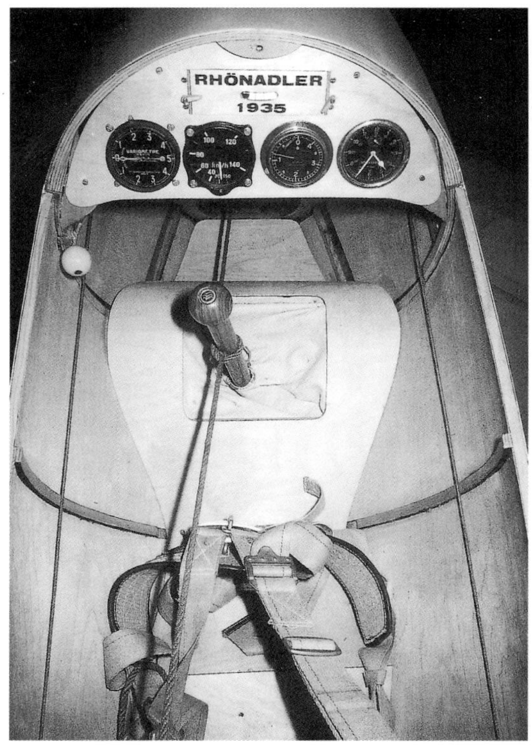

The simple and purposefully laid out cockpit of the Rhönadler with the instrument panel. The control cables are uncovered.

A beautiful Rhönsperber still flying in England. Registered BGA.260, the aircraft has the tail surfaces of a Rhönbussard. (P. Selinger)

is probably the one in a private collection in Waterford, Pennsylvania in the USA. In 1987 the glider expert Klaus Heyn built a flying replica of a *Rhönadler* from the year 1935. Bearing the registration D-Günter Grohenhoff, the glider is on display in the gliding museum on the Wasserkuppe.

The *Rhönadler* is a typical high-performance glider of the early 1930s whose relatively sparse instrumentation depended on the wishes of its pilot or owner. The example in the glider museum is typical of an aircraft with very specialized equipment. It is very likely that a magnetic compass would also have been included. The vertical speed indicator is a French instrument built by the Badin company. The altimeter is an old instrument from the time of the First World War or early 1920s as it reads counter-clockwise. Only the airspeed indicator has a housing conforming to the large standard introduced in 1932.

It was originally intended that the *Rhönadler* replica should be flown and it was planned to install a radio in the space above the four instruments covered by a wooden plate housing a spirit level.

Rhönsperber (Rhön Sparrow Hawk)

During the 1934 Rhön competition the weather was such that for the first time the glider pilots were able to take advantage of thermal updrafts for their endurance flights. As no glider existed which could fully exploit these updraft conditions, designer Hans Jacobs began thinking of ways to improve his *Rhönbussard*. To improve the type's flight characteristics he replaced the shoulder wing with a gull wing of increased span mounted mid-fuselage. Jacobs also designed a fully-enclosed cockpit offering the pilot improved comfort and good visibility, which was important on extended flights in bad weather. The cockpit design also included a seat which could be adjusted in flight, adjustable rudder pedals with covered control cables and an easily viewed instrument panel.

One innovation was spoilers on the upper surfaces of the wings, something which is a feature of every modern glider.

The *Rhönsperber* soon achieved its first successes and went on to become the best-known German high-performance glider in the years 1935 to 1938. The *Rhönsperber*, of which about 100 were built by Schweyer in Ludwigshafen, inspired later gliders such as the *Kranich* and *Habicht*. Only five *Rhönsperber* have survived to the present day.

Cockpit of Rhönsperber D-Pineta. The instruments are, from top left: altimeter, compass, clock, airspeed indicator, turn and bank indicator and vertical speed indicator. Visible are the calibrated nozzle for the airspeed indicator on the left and the feed nozzle on the right.

Instrumentation of *Rhönsperber* D-Pineta:

	Equipment	Instrument Range	Manufacturer/Remarks
1	Lh 19r altimeter	0 – 3000 m	Fl 22312
2	Lke 6 "Kleiner Emil" magnetic compass		Fl 23226
3	Lu 3r clock		
4	Lr 16r-250 airspeed indicator	50 – 250 km/h	
5	Lg 18r turn-and-bank indicator for gliders		Fl 22402-2
6	Lv 7r-5 vertical speed indicator	+5 / -5 m/s	Fl 22379

Other items of equipment included:

- Lreg 9a suction regulator on the turn-and-bank indicator
- Compensator for the vertical speed indicator
- Ldü 41 feed nozzle for the turn-and-bank indicator gyroscope
- Ldü 17 calibrated nozzle for the airspeed indicator and vertical speed indicator

As well there were release levers for the tow coupling, the spoilers and the canopy release.

The instrumentation of the ***Rhönsperber*** in the gliding museum consists of equipment built before and after 1945. It is impossible to say which of these instruments were used when the aircraft was being flown and which are mere stopgaps installed during restoration.

	Equipment	Instrument Range	Manufacturer/Remarks
1	Lv 7r-10 vertical speed indicator (Askania)	+10 / -10 m/s	
2	FK 38 magnetic compass (Ludolph)	Fl 23233	
3	Vertical speed indicator (Horn)	+5 / -5 m/s	
4	Fine and coarse altimeter (Winter)	0 – 10000 m	post-1945
5	Turn-and-bank indicator (Askania)	Fl 22402	
6	Airspeed indicator (Winter)	30 – 140 km/h	post-1945

The feed and calibrated nozzles were apparently built into the fixed portion of the fuselage as the attachment tubes hanging down in the photo show. It would have made more sense to also install these in the canopy.

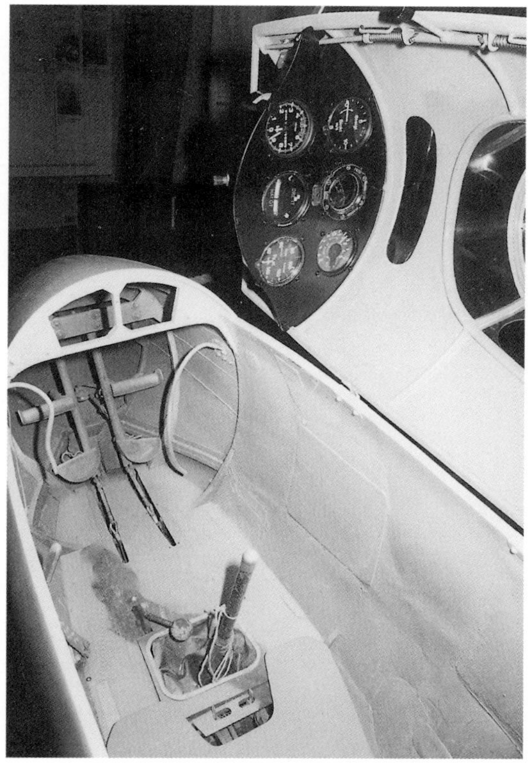

The cockpit of the Rhönsperber in the Glider Museum. Note the rudder pedal control cables emerging from beneath the floor. There is small window in the hood in front of the instrument panel for the purpose of illuminating the instruments.

Some of the photographs presented here depict the *Rhönsperber* in the glider museum on the Wasserkuppe. The aircraft is finished as a pre-war machine in RLM 05 and carried the registration D-Rhönsperber. Some years earlier it was registered D-6262.

The *Rhönsperber* is known to have been equipped with two types of instrument panel. A photograph in the catalogue of the instrument manufacturer Askania from 1938 depicts the *Rhönsperber* with the registration D-Pineta. This aircraft has an instrument panel mounted rigidly in the nose of the aircraft.

The aircraft in the Wasserkuppe museum has an instrument panel incorporated into the folding hood. This version made it easier to service the instruments as they could be accessed without removing them from the panel.

The types of instrument installed in the two versions were probably similar, varying according to the wishes of the pilots. The Askania brochure provides a fine illustration of the instrumentation of a *Rhönsperber* in the years prior to 1939 which, in its composition, was similar to that of a DFS Meise.

Schempp-Hirth Gö 3 *Minimoa*

The *Minimoa*, designed by Wolf Hirth and Reinhold Seeger in early 1935, is surely among the most beautiful gliders ever built. Their basic idea was to create a glider which could be manufactured in quantity but which possessed a performance and handling qualities matching the most expensive models. The design was based on the Moazagotl, named for a type of lenticular cloud common in the Giant Mountains. The glider had a cantilever wing, which was shortened by three meters, hence the name *Mini-Moazagotl*, or *Minimoa* for short.

A characteristic of the glider was its gull wing with trailing ailerons, which made the Minimoa resemble a seagull in the air.

The Schempp-Hirth Sportflugzeugbau founded in 1935 constructed a total of 110 examples of the *Minimoa* from 1936 to 1939, making it the first mass-produced high-performance glider.

Among the type's accomplishments were a world record climb to 6687 meters above the Wasserkuppe in 1938 and a German dis-

Minimoa D-8064. The swept gull wing gives the aircraft a beautiful appearance in flight. (P. Selinger)

tance record of 523 kilometers in 1939. Other records were set in France, England, South Africa and the USA.

About ten *Minimoas* have survived, of which four are still registered.

As a high-performance glider, the *Minimoa* was instrumented to meet the needs of the purchaser, however as a rule they were more extensively equipped than most gliders. Standard equipment consisted of vertical speed indicator, airspeed indicator and altimeter. An example is provided by an historical photograph depicting a *Minimoa* flown in the CSSR after 1945. This makes it possible to reconstruct the instrumentation of an aircraft flown by an expert pilot. There were generally no standards after 1945 and the remaining Minimoas were equipped as their owners saw fit. In some cases aircraft were fitted with the mushroom-shaped instrument panel now standard in most gliders.

Examples of two such aircraft are D-1163 from Münster, which once flew in Japan, and HB-282, which is on display in the glider museum on the Wasserkuppe. Both machines have some modern equipment such as acoustic variometers and radios.

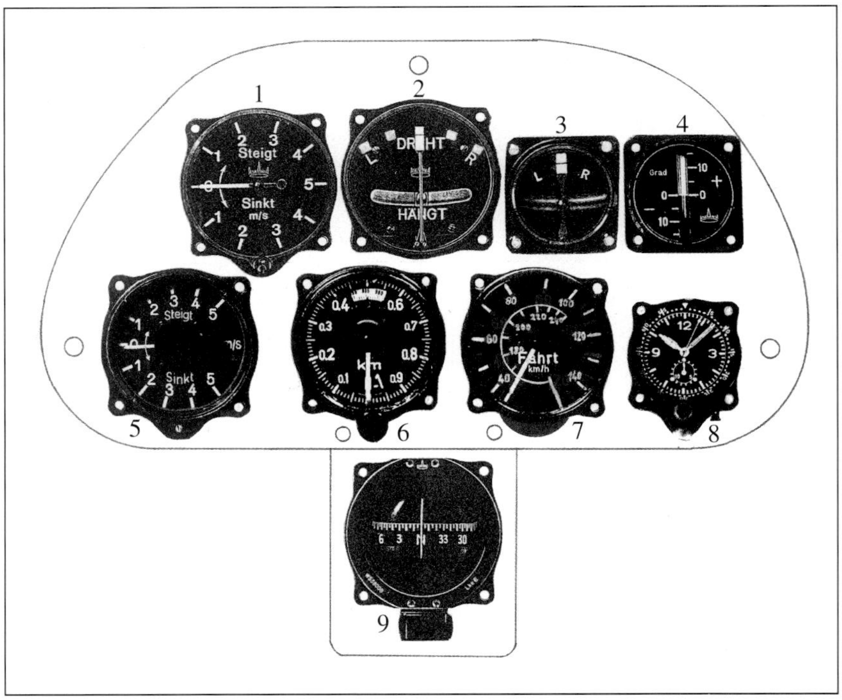

Reconstructed instrumentation of a Minimoa.

Instrumentation of a *Minimoa* Equipped for Endurance Flights:

No.	Equipment	Instrument Range	Manufacturer/Remarks
1	Lv 7r vertical speed indicator (Askania) +5 / -5 m/s		Fl 22379
2	Lg 18r glider turn-and-bank indicator (Askania)		Fl 22402-2
3	Lge 1k electric turn-and-bank indicator (Askania)		
4	La 1K pitch indicator (Askania)		
5	V 7 vertical speed indicator (Horn)	+5 / -5 m/s	
6	Fine and coarse altimeter (Fuess)	0 – 10000 m	Fl 22320
7	Airspeed indicator	40 – 240 km/h	
8	Bo UK 1 clock (Junghans)		Fl 23885
9	Lke 6 "Kleiner Emil" magnetic compass (Askania)		Fl 23226

Cockpit of *Minimoa* HB-282 in the Glider Museum.

Instrumentation of *Minimoa* D-1163. (P. Selinger)

Instrumentation of *Minimoa* HB-282:

No.	Equipment	Instrument Range	Manufacturer/Remarks
1	Clock		
2	Pitch indicator	+15 / -15°	
3	Magnetic compass		Ludolph
4	Unidentified		
5	Vertical speed indicator	+5 / -5 m/s	Haenni
6	Airspeed indicator	30 – 200 km/h	
7	Turn-and-bank indicator		Haenni ?
8	Vertical speed indicator	+30 / -30 m/s	Horn Fl 22386
9	Altimeter	0 – 10000 m	Thommen

Most instruments were Swiss-built.

Instrumentation of *Minimoa* D-1163:

No.	Equipment	Instrument Range	Manufacturer/Remarks
1	Acoustic variometer		
2	Airspeed indicator	50 – 250 km/h	Winter
3	Digital clock ?		
4	Lv 7r vertical speed indicator	+5 / -5 m/s	Askania
5	Radio		
6	Fine and coarse altimeter	0 – 5000 m	
7	FK 16 magnetic compass		Ludolph
8	Bank indicator		Winter
9	Tow coupling release lever		
10	Spoiler lever		
11	Wheel brake lever		

Sources and Acknowledgments

Books

Aders, Gebhard "Geschichte der Deutschen Nachtjagd 1917-1945", Stuttgart 1978

Aero Detail 1 "Messerschmitt Bf 109 E", Tokyo 1989

Aero Detail 2 "Focke Wulf Fw 190 D", Tokyo 1990

Aero Detail 5 "Messerschmitt Bf 109 G", Tokyo 1992

Aero Detail 6 "Focke Wulf Fw 190 A/F", Tokyo 1993

Aero Detail 9 "Messerschmitt Me 262 A", Tokyo 1993

Aero Detail 10 "Messerschmitt Me 163 & Heinkel He 162", Tokyo 1994

Aero Detail 11 "Junkers Ju 87 D/G STUKA", Tokyo 1994

Aero Detail 16 "Arado Ar 234 BLITZ", Tokyo 1996

Aero Detail 18 "Heinkel He 111", Tokyo 1997

Aero Detail 20 "Junkers Ju 88", Tokyo 1998

Aero Detail 21 "Messerschmitt Bf 110", Tokyo 1998

Aichner, P. "Luftwaffe Flugzeug-Ausrüstungsgegenstände" Band FA/01, Brixen 1997

AMF Dübendorf "Normalisierung der Fokker D VII", Dezember 1925

Bennewitz, Kurt "Flugzeuginstrumente", Berlin 1922

Brinkmann, G./v. Gersdorff, K./Schwipps, W. "Sport- und Reiseflugzeuge – Leitlinien einer vielfältigen Entwicklung", Bonn 1995

Brown, Eric "Berühmte Flugzeuge der Luftwaffe 1939-1945", Stuttgart 1999

Bürkle, Helmut "Abriss der Instrumentenkunde", Berlin 1940

Bürkle, Helmut "Instrumentenkunde", Berlin 1942

Cohausz, Peter "Cockpit Profile", Heft 1-5, Illertissen 1997-99

Cohausz, Peter "Deutsche Flugzeuge bis 1945", Oberhaching 1998

Coombs, L.F.E. "The Aircraft Cockpit", Wellingborough, GB, 1990

DeBaud, G.C. "Pilot's and Mechanics' Aircraft Instrument Manual", New York 1942

Erblich, Heinz "Fliegerschule", Berlin 1918

Hermann, D. "Focke Wulf Ta 152 – Der Weg zum Höhenjäger" Oberhaching 1998

Hitchcock, T. H. "Taifun", monogram close-up 5, Boylston 1979

Hitchcock, T. H. "Blohm & Voss Bv 155", monogram close-up 20, Sturbridge 1990

Hoch, Georg "Die Messerschmitt Me 109 in der Schweizer Flugwaffe", Payerne 1999

Horten, R./Selinger, P.F. "Nurflügel", Graz 1987

Immler, W. "Flugzeug-Kompasswesen und Flugsteuerkunde", Berlin 1918

Jane's "Aircraft of the World 1919"

Kay, Antony L. "Buzz Bomb", monogram close-up 4, Boylston 1977

Klinker, Bruno "Elektrische Flugzeugausrüstung", Berlin 1938

König, Erwin "Die Bücker-Flugzeuge", Martinsried 1987

Kracheel, Kurt "Flugführungssysteme – Blindfluginstrumente, Autopiloten, Flugsteuerungen", Bonn 1993

Kranzhoff, Jörg A. "Arado", Oberhaching 1995

Krzyzan, M./Steinle, H. "Die Halberstadt Cl.IV D-IBAO", Herford 1992

Krzyzan, M./Steinle, H. "Die Jeannin Stahltaube A.180/14", Herford 1989

Lang, Gerhard "Dornier Do 27", Flugzeug Profile 2, Illertissen o.J.

Lange, Bruno "Das Buch Der Deutschen Luftfahrttechnik", Mainz 1970

Lange, Bruno "Tante Ju – Alles über die Ju 52", Mainz 1976

Lange, Bruno "Typenhandbuch der deutschen Luftfahrttechnik", Koblenz 1986

Löwe, Karl F. "Flugzeugortung", Berlin 1934

Lommel, Horst " Der erste bemannte Raketenstart der Welt", Stuttgart 1998

Merkle "Einführung in die Gerätekunde", Braunschweig um 1939

Merrick, Kenneth A. "German Aircraft Interiors 1935 – 1945", Sturbridge 1996

Mikesh, R. C. "Albatros D.Va – German Fighter of World War I", Washington 1989

Moser, Sepp "Flieg weiter, Ju 52", Zürich 1992

Myhra, David "Horten 229", monogram close-up 12, Sturbridge 1990

Nauroth, H./Held, W. "Messerschmitt Bf 110 – Zerstörer an allen Fronten 1939-1945", Stuttgart 1978
Nijboer, Donald "Cockpit", Shrews-bury 1998
Nissen, Jens "Museumsstücke im Detail – Messerschmitt Me 163", Zweibrücken 2000
Nowarra, Heinz J. "Die Deutsche Luftrüstung 1933-1945", Koblenz 1993
NSFK "Gerätekunde", Berlin 1939
Paniagua Magán, P.M. "Monografico Aero H.A. 1112 – M11 Buchon", Madrid o.J.
Pletschacher, Peter "Lufthansa Junkers Ju 52", Planegg 1989
Prien, J./ Rodeike, P. "Messerschmitt Bf 109 F, G, & K Series", Atglen 1995
Radinger, W. / Schick, W. "Messerschmitt Me 109", Oberhaching 1997
Rehder, Kurt "Flugzeug-Instrumente", 1. und 4. Auflage, Berlin 1933 und 1938
Rempp, Roland "Der Nachtjäger Heinkel He 219", Oberhaching 1999
RLM "Flugzeug-Ausrüstungsgeräte", Berlin 1944
RLM "Lehrblätter für die technische Ausbildung in der Luftwaffe – Gerätekunde", Berlin 1938
RLM "Lehrbuch über Luftnavigation und Blindflug", Berlin 1938
Robinson, Anthony "In the Cockpit", Secaucus, N.J., USA 1991
Rodeike, Peter "Focke Wulf Jagdflugzeug Fw 190 A, Fw 190 Dora, Ta 152", Hamburg 1998
Roos, J.M. "Vliegtuiginstrumenten", Amsterdam 1941
Sarkowski, Heinz "Berühmte Bordfunkgeräte", Grafenau 1983
Schlie, Alfred "Handbuch für den Luftfahrt-Unterricht", Duisburg 1936
Schneider, Helmut "Flugzeug-Typenbuch", Ausgabe A, Leipzig 1939/40
Simons, Martin "The Worlds Vintage Sailplanes 1908-45", Melbourne 1986
Smith, J.R./Creek, E.J. "Arado 234 Blitz", Sturbridge 1992
Smith, J.R./Creek, E.J. "FW 190 D", monogram close-up 10, Boylston 1986
Smith, J.R./Creek, E.J. "Jet Planes Of The Third Reich", Boylston 1982
Smith, J.R./Creek, E.J./ Hitchcock, T.H. "Dornier 335 Arrow", Sturbridge 1997
Sönnichsen, Theo E. "Die Luftfahrt-Navigation", Berlin 1940
Thebis, R. / Römmler, G. "Instrumenten-Kunde des Fliegers" Berlin 1919
Trenkle, Fritz "Bordfunkgeräte – Vom Funkensender zum Bordradar", Koblenz 1986
von Langsdorff, W. "Fortschritte der Luftfahrt", Frankfurt 1926, 1927/28, 1929/30
Vogelsang, C. Walther "Vergaser und Zündapparate für Flugmotoren", Berlin 1917
Weal, J.A. / Barker, R. "Das große Buch der Militärflugzeuge Weltkrieg II", Stuttgart 1984
Wenke, Helmuth "Die Flugzeuggeräte, I. Teil – Triebwerk- u. Flugwerk-Überwachungsgeräte", Berlin 1943
Wenke, Helmuth "Die Flugzeuggeräte, III. Teil – Geräte-Musterblätter", Berlin 1943
Widfelt, Bo "The Luftwaffe in Sweden 1939-1945", Boylston 1983
Zacharias, H./Otto, E. "Gerätewartung", Berlin 1939

Magazines

Aeroplane Monthly
Flugzeug
Jet & Prop
Klassik Uhren
Luftfahrt International
SCALE
World War One Aero

Aircraft Brochures

Arado Ar 66, ohne Jahr
Arado Ar 79, 1938
Bölkow Bo 209, September 1970
Dornier Do 24, o.J.
Erla 5, o.J.
Junkers F 13, August 1924

Aircraft Replacement Parts Lists (Extracts)

Bü 131 D, Ersatzteilliste, 1939
Bü 131, Einbauten, Ausrüstung & Wiege-Protokoll, Dornier/Altenrhein 1937
Bü 133 C, Ersatzteilliste, 1938
Bü 181 B-1, Ersatzteilliste, Oktober 1942
CASA 1.131 E, Serie 2000, Ersatzteilliste, 1979
DFS 230, Ersatzteilliste, September 1941
Do 335 A-1, Allgemeine Geräteliste, Februar 1944
Fw 44 D-G und J, Ersatzteilliste, 1938
Fw 190 A, Ersatzteilliste, Juni 1944
Fw 190 D, Ersatzteilliste, Oktober 1944
He 219 A-7, Ersatzteilliste, Oktober 1944
Ju 87 B-1, Ersatzteilliste, September 1940
Ju 88 A-1, Ersatzteilliste, September 1939
KL 25 D, Ersatzteilliste 1936
KL 35 B und D, Ersatzteilliste, Juli 1940
Nord 1000 (Bf 108 D), Matériels et Organes d'Équipement, um 1946
Bf 109 B, Ersatzleilliste, 1938
Bf 109 E-7, Ausrüstungs- und Geräteverzeichnis
Bf 109 F, Ersatzteilliste, Januar 1942
Bf 109 G, Ersatzteilliste, 1942
Bf 109 G, Ersatzteilliste, Januar 1944
Bf 109 K, Ersatzteilliste, 1944
HA 1112 M.1L, Ersatzteilliste
Bf 110 D, Ersatzteilliste
Bf 110 E, Ersatzteilliste
Bf 110 F, Ersatzteilliste
Me 262 A, Ersatzteilliste, Oktober 1944
DFS 108-70 Olympia, Ersatzteilliste, Juni 1943

Aircraft Handbooks and Technical Descriptions

Ar 96 B-1, Flugzeug-Handbuch Teil 9 A Allgemeine Ausrüstung, September 1941
Do 335 A-1, Flugzeug-Handbuch Teil 2 Fahrwerk, 1944
Fi 156, Flugzeug-Handbuch, 1940
Fw 190 A-1, Flugzeug-Handbuch Teil 9 A Allgemeine Ausrüstung, 1943
Fw 190 A-2, A-3, A-4, Flugzeug-Handbuch Teil 9 A Allgemeine Ausrüstung, 1943
Fw 190 A-5, A-6 Flugzeug-Handbuch, 1943/44
Fw 190 A-7 bis A-9 Flugzeug-Handbuch, 1943/44
Ta 152 H-0 und H-1, Vorläufiges Flugzeug-Handbuch, Januar 1945 Höhenjagdflugzeug Ta 152 H, Vorläufige Baubeschreibung Nr. 271, Januar 1944
He 111 E/F, Flugzeug-Handbuch, 1. – 8. Teilheft, 1940
He 111 J, Flugzeug-Handbuch, 9. Teilheft, IX. Anlagen, 1940
He 111 H, P und D, Beschreibung, 1939
He 219 A-0, Handbuch, März 1944
Ju 52/3m, Baubeschreibung, 1938
Ju 52/3m g5e, Flugzeug-Handbuch, Teil 9 A Allgemeine Ausrüstung, 1941
Ju 52/3m g14e, Description d'Ensemble, um 1946
Ju 87 D-1, D-3, D-5, G-1, G-2, Änderungsanweisung Nr. 2056, Juni 1944
Ju 87 D-1 trop, Flugzeug-Handbuch, Teil 9 A Allgemeine Ausrüstung
Ju 87 G-2, Flugzeug-Handbuch Teil 12 A Schußwaffenanlage, Oktober 1943
Ju 88 A-16, Flugzeug-Handbuch Teil 9 A Allgemeine Ausrüstung, August 1944
Ju 88 C-6, Flugzeug-Handbuch Teil 9 A Allgemeine Ausrüstung, 1942
KL 107 B, Baubeschreibung, Juli 1958
Bf 109 B, Handbuch, 1937
Bf 109 C, Handbuch
Bf 109 F-1 bis F-4, Flugzeug-Handbuch Teil 9 A Allgemeine Ausrüstung, 1941
Bf 109 G-1, Flugzeug-Handbuch Teil 9 A Allgemeine Ausrüstung, September 1942
Bf 109 G-1, Flugzeug-Handbuch Teil 9 B Elektrisches Bordnetz, September 1942
Bf 109 G-1, Flugzeug-Handbuch Teil 9 G Pneumatische Anlage, September 1942
Bf 109 G-5, Flugzeug-Handbuch Teil 8 D Sonderwaffenanlage, Juli 1944
Bf 109 K-4, Flugzeug-Handbuch Teil 9 A Allgemeine Ausrüstung, Dezember 1944
HA 1112, Flugzeug-Handbuch
Bf 110 E, Flugzeug-Handbuch Teil 9B Elektrisches Bordnetz
Bf 110 F, Flugzeug-Handbuch Teil 9 A Allgemeine Ausrüstung, Oktober 1942
Bf 110 F, Flugzeug-Handbuch Teil 9B Elektrisches Bordnetz, Oktober 1942
Bf 110 G-2, Flugzeug-Handbuch Teil 8A Schußwaffenanlage, April 1943
Bf 110 G-2, Flugzeug-Handbuch Teil 8A Beiheft 1: 2 MK 108, January 1944
Bf 110 G-3, Flugzeug-Handbuch Teil 9 A Allgemeine Ausrüstung, Juni 1943
Me 262 A-1/A-2, Flugzeug-Handbuch Teil 9 A Allgemeine Ausrüstung, 1944
Bauvorschriften für Segelflugzeuge

Aircraft Operating Manuals (Pilot's Notes)

Ar 96 B-3, Bedienungsvorschrift-Fl, Juni 1941
Ar 234 B-2, Bedienungs-Karte für den Flugzeugführer, Oktober 1944
Ar 234 B-2, Bedienungsvorschrift mit Rüstanweisung, 1944
Do 24 T-3, Notice Provisoire d'Utilisation, Octobre 1945
Fw 190 A-1, A-2, A-3, Bedienungsvorschrift-Fl, 1942
Ta 152 H-0, Bedienungskarte für den Flugzeugführer, Januar 1945
He 111 H-16, Bedienungsvorschrift-Fl, März 1943
He 111 H-20, Bedienungsvorschrift-Fl, 1944
He 162 A, Bedienungsvorschrift, 1945
Ju W 34, Betriebsanweisung, 1939
Ju 87 B, Bedienungsvorschrift Abwurfwaffe, 1938
Ju 87 B-1, Kurz-Betriebsanweisung, Januar 1939
Ju 87 B-1, Betriebsanweisung, April 1939
Ju 87 B-2, Betriebsanleitung 1940
Ju 88 A-1, Kurz-Betriebsanleitung, 1940
Ju 88 A-4, Bedienungsvorschrift-Fl, 1942
Ju 88 A-4, Exerzier-Karte, November 1942
Ju 88 D-5 und D-5 trop, Bedienungsvorschrift-Fl, Juni 1942
Ju 388 J-1, L-1, Bedienungsvorschrift-Fl, Dezember 1944
KL 107, Bedienungsvorschrift, um 1959
Bf 108 B, Kurzbetriebs- und Rüstanleitung, März 1939
Bf 108 D-1, Bedienungsvorschrift-Fl, Februar 1943
Bf 109 D, Kurz-Betriebsanleitung, 1940
Bf 109 E, Kurz-Betriebsanleitung, 1938
Bf 109 G-2, G-4, G-6, Bedienungsvorschrift-Fl, Juni 1943
Bf 110, Bedienungs- und Beladevorschrift für die Abwurfwaffe, Juli 1940
Bf 110 B, Bedienungsvorschrift für die Schußwaffe, 1940
Bf 110 C, Kurz-Betriebsanleitung, Februar 1940
Bf 110 G, Bedienungsvorschrift-Fl, April 1943
Bf 110 G-4, Bedienungsvorschrift Schußwaffe, 1943
Me 163 B, Bedienungsvorschrift-Fl, September 1944
Me 262 A-1/A-2, Bedienungsvorschrift-Fl, August 1944
Me 262 A-1/A-2, Bedienungskarte, 1944

Equipment and Systems Descriptions and Handbooks

Askania "Askania Bordgeräte", Berlin 1937/38

Askania "Luftfahrtinstrumente", Berlin 1936

Askania, diverse Druckschriften und Prospekte 1935-1937

Bosch "Bosch Luftfahrtgeräte", Stuttgart 1941

Fliegertechnische Schule 5, Schulungsunterlagen 1941

Friebe "Flüssigkeits-Variometer" o. J.

Haenni "Messinstrumente für Industrie und Flugzeug", Jegensdorf/ CH 1943

Hartmann & Braun "Elektrische Temperaturmessung in Flugzeugen", Einbau- und Gebrauchs-Vorschriften der Muster AA1,AG1,TG1,ZG1 und ZG2, Frankfurt 1937

Hartmann & Braun "Elektrische Vorratsmessung in Flugzeugen", Einbau- und Gebrauchs-Vorschriften Baumuster VG 2, Frankfurt 1937

Horn "Elektrische Umdrehungsfernzeiger für Flugzeuge", Leipzig 1927

L.Dv.242 "Entwurf einer Beschreibung, Einbau und Wartungsvorschrift für die Druckmesser: Eckardt RA 57/711, RA 57/111 und Maximall UA 3/57, UA 4/57, D 1101, D 1302, D 2202, D 1112 und das Rohrbruchventil: Maximall MRV.", Berlin 1935

L.Dv.541 "Entwurf einer Beschreibung und Bedienungsvorschrift des Schaltkastens ASK-V IX.", Berlin 1940

Luftfahrtgerätewerk Hakenfelde "Elektrischer Höhenmesser FuNG 101", Berlin 1942

Patin "Vorläufige Kurzbeschreibung der Jäger-Kurssteuerung KS 12 b-1", 1944

Peravia "Instruments de Bord et Appareils pour l'Aeronautique", Bern/CH 1945

Siemens "Werbe- und Beschreibungsmaterial über Luftfahrt-Bordgeräte, Berlin 1939

Siemens Kurssteuerung K 4 i für Ju 52, Berlin1939

Other

Kataloge des Auktionshauses Kuncze, Geisenhausen 1991 bis 2000

Acknowledgements

This book would not have been as complete, especially in regard to photographs, without the kind assistance of many people.
The author would first like to thank his wife Birgitta and his daughters Amelie and Clarissa for their patience and understanding in giving up their free time to assist my efforts.
The author also wishes to thank the publisher Peter Pletschacher and the staff of Aviatik Verlag for their interest and willingness to publish this book.
For searching deep in archives or for extra photographic work, the author would like to express his sincere gratitude to:

Philippe Couderchon (France)
Manfred Griehl
Harald Hartwig
Udo Hafner
Richard P. Lutz (USA)
Kenneth A. Merrick (Australia)
Franz Selinger
Peter F. Selinger
Konrad Soppa
Horst Rienecker
Christiaan Vanhee (Belgium)
Hans-Günther Wildmoser

For other assistance the author wishes to thank:

Dirk Bende
Andreas Braatz
Rudi Burian
Deutsches Technikmuseum, Dr. Holger Steinle
Dornier Archive
Joachim Fege
Marco-Fernandez-Sommerau (Belgium)
Fliegermuseum Dubendorf (Switzerland)
Roger Gämperle (Switzerland)
Thomas Göritz
Thomas Hampel
Klaus Heyn
Interessengemeinschaft Ju 53 e.V.
Albert Kleikamp
Theo Lederer
Horst Lommel
Luftfahrt Museum Laatzen
Lufthansa
R.D. Meyers (USA)
Militaire Luchtvaart Museum (Holland)
Imre Mitter (Hungary)
National War Museum, Johannesburg
Helmut Schmidt
Jens Schneider

Index of Described Instrumentations